Americans are eating their vegetables—and loving them! Now all the great produce of America's farmlands is given star treatment in 666 irresistible recipes collected here by the food editors of Farm Journal Magazine.

AMERICA'S BEST
VEGETABLE RECIPES
Edited by Nell B. Nichols

AMERICA'S BEST VEGETABLE RECIPES

Edited by Nell B. Nichols
__Farm Journal__ Field Food Editor

Selected and tested by the
Food Editors of __Farm Journal__

BALLANTINE BOOKS • NEW YORK

Library of Congress Catalog Card Number: 74-89068

ISBN 0-345-30345-8

This edition published by arrangement with DOUBLEDAY & COMPANY. INC.

Printed in Canada

First Ballantine Books Edition: June 1982

Contents

INTRODUCTION

Vegetables Your Family Will Like

HAVE YOU ever gathered tomatoes, warm from the sun and about to drop from the vine in plump goodness? Have you husked sweet corn on the way from the field to the house so you could hurry it into the big kettle of boiling water with no delay? Popped a few peas from the pod into your mouth to savor their sweetness? Enjoyed the lovely sharp tang of hot vinegar and bacon drippings trickling over tender leaves of the year's first wilted lettuce? If you have, you need no "sell" on this cookbook; you already have a high regard for garden-fresh vegetable flavors.

But, every woman is interested in selling her family on vegetables—in preparing dishes they'll like. And when guests rave about your vegetable dishes, you'll feel especially rewarded. So often monotony is taken for granted, when vegetables are merely considered "necessary." In AMERICA'S BEST VEGETABLE RECIPES, we give them star treatment!

No one denies that garden-fresh vegetables are wonderful—slender young carrots pulled from the earth when 5 inches long, and green or wax beans so crisp they snap between the fingers picking them. But if you can't have a garden plot, you still can do right by vegetables; most of today's supermarket produce counters offer fabulous vegetable selections. Our country is so big and has so many climatic and soil variations that almost all of the world's vegetables grow within its borders. Excellent transportation facilities hurry them to markets. We are so fortunate!

Even though your husband and children think they prefer desserts to vegetables, you can do a lot to change their attitudes if you give vegetables special attention. It takes imagination and a little planning ahead, but the tasty results are worth it—*and* the contribution you can make to the health of your family. In this cookbook, we'll help you take vegetables from garden, markets, freezers, and canned or dried from cupboard shelves, and convert them into dishes not only they will praise, but also your guests.

This cookbook will inspire you and show you how to make many new and different vegetable treats. We are especially proud of the recipes in it. They're favorites of farm and ranch women in many states, members of the FARM JOURNAL Family Test Group, of our own FARM JOURNAL Test Kitchens and of homemaker-home economists—good cooks with families of their own to feed. Many of them are home gardeners, too, and know quality.

We believe AMERICA'S BEST VEGETABLE RECIPES comes off the presses at an ideal time, especially if you can have a garden. Seed catalogues this year are showing wonderful new varieties to plant. Read this cookbook before you order—you'll be sure to find mouth-watering recipes for which you'll want to plant the "makings." Try some that are new to your family, and surprise them this summer.

Spend an hour some afternoon looking at an old cookbook. You'll see how good we have it today. When you find the vegetable chapter among the yellow pages, it will be brief. The season for them was short. Today, with fresh vegetables available the year around, homemakers want new and exciting ways to fix and serve them. This is our contribution to your family's pleasure.

Chapter 1 introduces all our important vegetables in the hope that you'll make new friends among them. Have you cooked globe artichokes? When did you last fix kohlrabi about the size of a pullet's egg, with its tender green leaves? And have you enjoyed salsify (oyster plant) within the past year? One woman told of her family's move from California back to the Iowa farm: "We wanted the children to grow up in the country with farm chores to do. And I wanted to grow salsify. I could never forget how good it tasted when we brought it from the garden and Mother cooked it. That was a part of autumn as much as the red leaves on the maples."

The first chapter also tells how to select fresh vegetables for quality, how to store them at home and how to cook them to develop their finest flavors. The cardinal rule, as this cookbook points out, is to cook vegetables only until they are tender-crisp—that is, until they test tender, but still retain a little crispness. So cooked, they hold their shape, their best flavor and above all, they aren't flabby or mushy. We're convinced that cooked texture is a big factor in whether or not people enjoy vegetables.

And color—think how dull meals would be without the yellow, green and red vegetables with white potatoes. Protect their brightness when cooking them. Fortunately, the yellow color is sturdy. You can't easily destroy it when you cook carrots, sweet potatoes, corn and rutabagas. But green vegetables turn a dull, unappetizing olive color when overcooked. Ruby-red beets and red cabbage take on violet or blue tinges unless you add a little vinegar or lemon juice, which our recipes do. Hard water creates a problem with white vegetables; it yellows such favorites as potatoes, cauliflower, turnips and onions. You can prevent the change of color by adding a teaspoon of white vinegar or lemon juice to the water in which you cook white vegetables.

The first—and largest—chapter in this cookbook deals with garden-fresh (or market-fresh) vegetables. The next two chapters, 2 and 3, present recipes and suggestions for frozen and canned vegetables. These foods, which make the calendar stand still, chronicle a fascinating story of scientific agriculture and its achievements. The development of varieties with superior flavors that man can gather with mechanical harvesters has much to do with our plentiful, inexpensive, year-round supply and quality. Without painstaking research by both universities and growers, we would not enjoy the fine quality in frozen and canned vegetables that we sometimes take for granted today.

Another chapter deals with long-time country-favorites, dried vegetables, which you keep on hand in the cupboard and which have a flavor all their own. From them you make such treats as beans baked in earthen pots, and split pea soup that purrs thickly as it simmers, waiting for the family to come in for supper on a cold day.

No matter how much we tried to corral vegetables in the different classifications, they jumped fences on us. So in Chapter 5 we include recipes for combinations of two or more vegetables in dishes that taste and look unusually good. Mixing vegetables frequently gives added eye and flavor appeal.

You'll also find all of the fresh, frozen, canned and dried vegetables popping up in the chapters on salads, soups and main dishes. Vegetables fit into all parts of the meal—even dessert; once you cook fresh pumpkins and squash by our directions, chances are you'll turn them into spicy sweet pies. But we have a good Index, and we urge you to use it. Read it for ideas, in fact.

We have a chapter on seasoning and saucing vegetables which includes special dressings for gorgeous salads; and there's a separate chapter of excellent vegetable salads, some with their own special dressing. Others feature main dishes, soups, appetizers and relishes. Up-to-date directions for freezing and canning vegetables round out the cookbook.

Many women tell us in candor that they know they don't use much imagination in cooking vegetables. We think that with the little special push of a new cookbook, many women will welcome the chance to be more creative with even the humblest vegetables.

You'll find in AMERICA'S BEST VEGETABLE RECIPES, for instance, many suggestions for shake-on seasonings and quick sauces, some of them made with canned soups and dry mixes. We cover herbs, which do so much for subtle flavor improvement. You're very familiar with one of them, parsley, but do you take time to chop it or snip it fine with scissors and sprinkle it over vegetables to add color and a bit of flavor? Grow it near the house—or in a window in the winter—handy to cut and bring to the kitchen. A Wisconsin farm woman says: "Not until I planted a border of parsley around my pansy bed did I realize how decorative it is in the yard—and on vegetable dishes."

Give dill, perhaps the most universally preferred herb in country homes, an opportunity to perform its magic in seasoning. It brings out the glories of vegetable dishes, such as hot and cold soups, salads, green vegetables, potatoes and sliced cucumbers in sour cream. Be adventuresome and sprinkle a bit of tarragon on cauliflower, chopped chives on broccoli and sweet basil on thick, juicy tomato slices. This cookbook offers many more such suggestions. Your family will enjoy guessing which herb you used— they'll be experts when they eat out in famous restaurants later in life.

When winter comes, use the dried herbs (we list them and the vegetables they best flavor) or those from your own garden—stored in the freezer. Chapter 11 tells how to freeze them to preserve the fresh taste.

Some vegetables have a special affinity for meats— carrots, onions and potatoes for beef, for example. Green beans and peas get along famously with lamb. But in vegetable-meat combinations, as in stews, most women think first of the meat; the vegetables are an afterthought. How natural this is! Americans are a meat-eating people. So regardless of which gets the credit for superb flavors, meat or vegetables, you'll want to bring out your new stew pot when you read the chapter on main dishes.

Just about everybody who objectively analyzes American cookery agrees that our finest culinary talents do not extend to vegetables. The simmering soups and gorgeous salads score high, but cooked vegetables in general often fall short of appetite appeal and pleasing flavors. No doubt this contributes somewhat to the unpopularity of vegetable dishes with some people. We designed this cookbook to help you change that situation! Some of the most unusual —and the tastiest—recipes for vegetables in our cookbook are the adaptations of international (foreign) vegetable dish specialties. You'll find a good selection of them sprinkled all through the book, in appropriate chapters. Don't let names like Ratatouille, Eggplant Parmigiana or Pot-au-feu intimidate you. Be adventurous, and try them!

Those of you who belong to homemakers' clubs or have children in 4-H Club activities frequently hear references to the importance of vegetables in well-rounded, balanced meals. But persuading your family to eat vegetables because they are "good for you" fails in many homes. Reminds you of the truth of Grandpa's homey saying: "You can lead a horse to water but you can't make him drink." Certainly, fixing and serving vegetables that look and taste good accomplishes more than using the good-for-you approach. And that's where this cookbook can assist you.

Of course, *your* knowledge that vegetables are valuable, healthful foods will reinforce your ambition to win your family over to them. You have ample proof of their importance to back you up in your silent crusade. Of the three most grievous deficiences in our meals, as revealed by a recent nationwide survey conducted by the U. S. Department of Agriculture, vegetables contain sizable amounts of two of them—vitamins A and C. And you can reduce the shortage of the third diet lack, calcium, by teaming vegetables with cheese and milk. Many of our recipes do this; adding the dairy products also results in superior flavors as well as good nutrition.

At the end of the book, just before the Index, we print a chart which tells you which vegetables supply important amounts of the vitamins, iron and calcium your family needs every day. Concentrate on these vitamin-rich vegetables to serve your family healthy meals. Use the psychological approach. Instead of asking your husband and children to eat broccoli because it is good for them, tempt them by combining it with some food that is a favorite. One of our readers shares her recipe for Fresh Broccoli with Orange Sauce in this book; she says the orange sauce taught her children how good broccoli can taste. They had acquired a fondness for the orange flavor in their breakfast drink. A Colorado mother, who despaired that her children ever would learn to eat zucchini, invented a dish combining zucchini with corn, which her children liked very much. You'll find her recipe for Zucchini-Corn Bake in Chapter 5. Her children ate the zucchini to get the corn and so learned to accept zucchini fixed other ways.

Serve vegetables attractively—this helps with appetite appeal. If you arrange two vegetables on a large platter—sweet potatoes and peas—you make both of them look better. Select vegetables with different shapes and colors. Think of the contrasts in color, shape and taste of kohlrabi, carrots and summer squash; tomatoes and green beans or okra; long green broccoli stalks and diced beets or parslied new potatoes.

As you turn the pages in this cookbook and read the recipes, we predict that your armchair tour will kindle excitement for trying many of the fascinating vegetable dishes. We believe your new adventure with vegetables will bring you much satisfaction and many compliments from family and friends.

CHAPTER ONE

Garden-Fresh Vegetables

HOME-GROWN TOMATOES, red-ripe and juicy, green beans so crisp they snap with the slightest bend, and juice-squirting ears of sweet corn picked and hurried to the house just in time to husk and cook for dinner—these are some of the joys that make the work of home gardening pay off.

But six months later when it's snowing and you're in the supermarket, you can still look at a vegetable wonderland, thanks to wheels, wings and refrigeration. Spread before you are all the reds, yellows and greens of fresh produce from many climates—visible proof of improvements made by developing new varieties and better methods of handling them from field to market. Spring, summer, fall or winter, vegetables can reach the kitchen in splendid condition. What happens then is up to you.

Is your family enthusiastic about vegetables? This is an important question, for Americans eat too few vegetables. If you want your husband and children to relish their vitamins, adopt a new sales pitch.

Refrain from mentioning that vegetables are good-for-you foods. This approach, tried for years, seems to have failed in many homes. Concentrate instead on making vegetable dishes so tempting and tasty that everyone will enjoy them. A good way to start is to team a vegetable with some well-liked flavor foods, such as bacon, ham, cheese, ketchup, ground beef. We have a special collection of such recipes in this chapter to help you get enthusiastic converts to vegetables. They are favorites of other farm and ranch families across the country, so they've successfully passed the test.

Preceding the recipes for each of the forty-one different vegetables we present, you'll find suggestions on how to recognize top quality, how to handle each in the kitchen before cooking, and then how to cook them to perfection in the basic way.

For most of the vegetables, we suggest the number

1

of days you can successfully hold them in your kitchen or refrigerator before cooking. But a few of them we advise you to "use quickly." By that, we mean use them as soon as you conveniently can, to enjoy them at their best. For example, fresh peas will not be unusable after two or three days' storage, but they lose some sweetness each day you hold them. So if you come home from the market with both peas and carrots in your shopping bag, refrigerate the carrots (they're good keepers) and serve those peas for supper tonight!

We give the approximate amount (in pounds) of vegetables it takes to make 4 servings. This will be a shopping guide, for even if you are a great gardener, there are seasons when you'll be buying some of your produce. Notice that we recommend, unless otherwise specified, that you cook vegetables in ½ or 1″ boiling salted water. *Allow ½ tsp. salt to each cup water used in cooking.*

Artichokes, Globe French or Italian

Globe artichokes are large, unopened flower buds of a thistle grown in California. Growers call the leaf-like parts, which make the bud, leaves or scales. While you find this vegetable in the market the year round, it's most plentiful in April and May.

Select plump, compact, heavy (in relation to size) buds with thick, green, tightly closed leaves. The brown spots sometimes observed on the surface indicate frost touched the bed. They do not affect eating quality—nor does the size of the bud.

Allow 1 artichoke per person (unless it's very large; then split lengthwise in half after cooking).

Store artichokes in the refrigerator. They hold in good condition for several days.

When ready to cook, wash, cut 1″ off bud top—use a sharp knife and cut straight across. Then cut about 1″ off stem at base, but leave a stub. Pull off loose leaves around the bottom and clip thorny tips from leaves with kitchen shears.

Cook artichokes in one of two ways: By the Eastern method you stand the artichokes upright in a deep saucepan, the right size to keep them from tipping to one side. Add 1 tblsp. salad oil, a small garlic clove and a thick lemon slice for each artichoke. Pour on 1″ boiling salted

2

water (add a little more water during cooking if necessary). Cover and boil 35 to 40 minutes if artichokes are large, 20 to 25 minutes if small, or until you can easily pull the leaves from the base and can easily pierce the stem with a fork. Lift from saucepan with two spoons and drain upside down.

With the Western method you drop artichokes into a kettle containing a large amount of boiling salted water with 1 tblsp. salad oil added for each artichoke. Add 1 or 2 garlic cloves and 1 lemon, sliced. (Some women weigh down artichokes with a plate to keep them from floating.) Cover and boil 20 to 45 minutes or until you can pull leaves easily from the base and pierce stem with a fork. Drain upside down.

Serve artichokes placed upright on individual salad plates (so waste leaves will not clutter dinner plates). Pour melted butter or margarine, plain or with a little lemon juice added, into little bowls to serve with hot artichokes. Chilled artichokes may be served for an appetizer or salad, along with lettuce cups holding mayonnaise or a favorite dip.

To eat artichokes, pull off leaves one by one and dip the base, or light-colored end, in the melted butter, mayonnaise or dip. Eat only the tender base of leaf by drawing it between the teeth, discarding the remainder. Continue eating leaves until you reach the fuzzy center or "choke." Remove it with knife and fork; discard. This exposes the heart or choicest part. Cut it in bite-sized pieces and, with fork, dip it into the melted butter or other accompaniment, and eat.

STUFFED ARTICHOKES ITALIAN

You don't have to go to Rome to eat marvelous stuffed artichokes—fix them in your kitchen this way

6 medium artichokes	1 tblsp. chopped parsley
2 c. crumbs from day-old bread	1 (7 oz.) can solid white tuna, drained
½ tsp. salt	1 c. water
⅛ tsp. pepper	½ tsp. salt
1 tblsp. salad oil	1 clove garlic
½ tsp. orégano leaves	½ bay leaf
¼ tsp. minced garlic	1½ tblsp. salad oil

Wash artichokes, cut off 1″ slice across tops and cut end from stem, leaving a stub. Remove a few of the lower leaves, which are tough. Snip tips from leaves with scissors. Slightly spread artichokes open and soak in cold, salted water 5 minutes. Drain upside down.

Place bread crumbs in bowl with ½ tsp. salt, pepper, 1 tblsp. salad oil, orégano, minced garlic and parsley. Toss to blend well; add tuna, broken in large pieces, and toss again.

Fill artichokes with bread-tuna mixture, putting it between leaves and in center (put most of this stuffing in center of artichoke). Each artichoke holds about ½ c. stuffing.

Pour water into 4-qt. saucepan with lid. Add ½ tsp. salt, garlic clove, bay leaf and 1½ tblsp. salad oil. Put artichokes in saucepan, squeezing them in so they will stand upright during cooking (a tight fit is desirable). Let come to a boil, cover and simmer 35 to 40 minutes, or until tender. To test for tenderness, pull out a leaf. It should come off from stem easily. Watch liquid in pan, adding a little more water if needed.

Serve 1 artichoke to each person in a bowl or other dish. Pour a little of the liquid from saucepan over each, first discarding bay leaf and garlic clove. Makes 6 servings.

NOTE: To eat artichoke, pull out the leaves, one at a time. Some of the stuffing adheres to each leaf. Eat stuffing from center, then remove the "choke" and eat the tender, flavorful heart.

VARIATION

Ham-Stuffed Artichokes: Substitute 1 c. chopped cooked ham for tuna.

SAUCED ARTICHOKES

The vegetable makes its own sauce

1 onion, chopped	6 tblsp. olive or salad oil
2 cloves garlic, minced	6 artichokes, trimmed
1 carrot, chopped	½ c. vinegar
2 tblsp. minced parsley	½ c. water
½ tsp. rosemary leaves	1 tsp. salt

4

In a large kettle, cook onion, garlic, carrot, parsley and rosemary in salad oil until onion is soft.

Wash and cut 1″ off artichoke tops and about 1″ of stem at base, leaving a stub. Wash and pull off loose leaves from around the base and clip thorny tips from leaves.

Add artichokes, vinegar, water and salt to kettle. Cover and cook until artichokes are tender, about 40 minutes. Serve each in a bowl with sauce from the pan; this sauce is used for dipping. Makes 6 servings.

Artichokes, Jerusalem

Jerusalem artichokes are roots or tubers that look something like knobby potatoes or ginger root; they are the same light brown color. People in Pennsylvania Dutch country and the southeastern states highly esteem this vegetable. It is available from late summer through winter.

Select roots or tubers that are firm and free from blemishes and mold.

Allow 1½ lbs. for 4 servings.

Hold the raw artichokes in a cool place or in the refrigerator crisper. They will keep several days.

To cook, scrub the vegetable with a brush and wash well; peel thinly and leave whole, dice or slice. Cook, covered, in 1″ boiling salted water until tender, 20 to 30 minutes. Drain, season with salt, pepper and butter or margarine. You can add flavor with a few squeezes of lemon juice, and color with a sprinkling of chopped parsley.

(To improve flavor, some women suggest cooking them in milk diluted with water, to cover, until tender. Many women prefer to cook the roots unpeeled in an effort to keep them whiter looking; the flesh, especially after peeling, has a tendency to turn oyster-gray when cooked.)

Asparagus

Green asparagus spears, pushing their tips above the earth, signal spring and promise good eating. They grow so fast, you have to be quick to cut and cook them while the delicate flavors are at their delicious peak—that is, while tips are still tightly closed.

Asparagus is available in markets from mid-February through June, with the greatest abundance from April through June.

Select spears that are round, smooth (without up and down ridges), deep green and brittle, and tender almost as far down as the green extends. The tips are tightly closed in top quality asparagus.

Allow 2 to 2½ lbs. for 4 servings.

Cut and bring asparagus from your garden to the kitchen as near mealtime as possible. But if it must wait, wrap the cut ends in wet paper towels, put in plastic bag and place in the coldest part of the refrigerator. Use quickly, within a day or two at the most.

When ready to cook, take each spear in both hands and bend gently. Brittle spears break, separating the tender upper ends from the tougher lower ends. Discard tougher ends. Cut scales from a few spears to see if sand, grit or mud lodges beneath them. If it does, cut off all the scales. Wash asparagus in cool water, brushing gently with a soft brush. Leave spears whole or cut them on the bias: Lay 2 spears at a time on cutting board, cut off tips and then cut remaining spears on the long diagonal, making slices that are about 1½″ long but only ¼″ thick.

Cook whole spears flat in one layer, or in two layers if cooking a large amount, in an electric or other heavy skillet. Sprinkle with ¾ tsp. salt and pour on boiling water to depth of 1″. Cover and cook 8 minutes; test lower part of spears with kitchen fork. If they are not tender-crisp, cover and cook 5 minutes more or until they are, adding more boiling water if necessary. Lift spears with two forks to a warm serving dish and season with salt, pepper and butter or margarine.

Another way of cooking asparagus spears is to tie the spears together and stand them upright in a deep container (some women use a coffee pot for this). Add enough boiling salted water to cover the lower half of stalks. Cook uncovered for about 10 minutes. Then cover the container and steam the tips until they are tender. If you don't have a container deep enough, stand asparagus spears in the bottom of a double boiler; turn the top half of the boiler over and use it as a cover.

To cook asparagus slices, follow directions in recipe for American-Chinese Asparagus (see Index).

Open-Face Asparagus-Egg Sandwiches

Spring is a many-sided thing. To an Iowa farmer's wife there are two never-fail signs that the welcome season is in full swing—stately asparagus stalks that snap crisply, and cheerful jonquils nodding.

"Asparagus sandwiches are a frequent supper selection at our house," she says. "When I go to the garden to cut the asparagus, I usually gather jonquils for a table bouquet.

"We have plenty of eggs so I often pair them with asparagus. My family—and this includes the boys, who are ardent hamburger fans—really like my Open-Face Asparagus-Egg Sandwiches," she adds. "Since I usually have homemade chicken broth in the freezer or a can of it in the cupboard, I make the sauce with equal parts of broth and milk. This flavor trick really makes a difference in the way the sandwiches taste," she emphasizes. Try the following recipe and see if you don't agree.

OPEN-FACE ASPARAGUS-EGG SANDWICHES

Hearty supper dish with flavor of spring

¼ c. butter or margarine	⅛ tsp. pepper
¼ c. flour	4 c. cooked asparagus, cut
1 c. milk	in 1½″ pieces (2 lbs.)
1 c. chicken broth	6 hamburger buns, split and
6 hard-cooked eggs, sliced	toasted
1 tblsp. instant minced	9 slices bacon, chopped,
onion	fried crisp and drained
1 tsp. salt	

Melt butter in saucepan; blend in flour. Add milk and broth; cook, stirring constantly, until mixture is thick and bubbly. Add eggs, onion, salt, pepper and asparagus. Heat thoroughly.

Serve on toasted bun halves. Sprinkle bacon over top. Makes 6 servings.

PIE-PAN ASPARAGUS

Chicken broth and two cheeses highlight
the delicate asparagus taste

¼ c. butter or margarine
¼ c. flour
¾ c. chicken broth
¾ c. milk
½ c. grated Cheddar cheese
¼ c. grated Parmesan
   cheese

½ tsp. salt
⅛ tsp. pepper
2 lbs. hot, freshly cooked
   medium asparagus spears
   (about 32 to 36)
2 tblsp. grated Parmesan
   cheese

Melt butter in saucepan; blend in flour. Add chicken broth and milk and cook, stirring constantly, until mixture is thick and bubbly. Add Cheddar cheese, ¼ c. Parmesan cheese, salt and pepper; stir until cheeses melt.

Place asparagus in 10″ pie pan. Pour sauce over. Sprinkle with 2 tblsp. Parmesan cheese. Broil until bubbly. Makes 6 servings.

COUNTRY ASPARAGUS PIE

Bake pie shell and cook eggs ahead
to assemble pie fast at mealtime

Baked 9″ pie shell
4 c. asparagus, cut in 1″
   pieces (about 2 lbs.)
3 tblsp. butter or margarine
3 tblsp. flour
1 c. milk

1 chicken bouillon cube
1 tsp. instant minced onion
¾ tsp. salt
4 hard-cooked eggs
⅛ tsp. pepper
½ c. grated Cheddar cheese

Cook asparagus in boiling salted water until tender. Drain thoroughly (in sieve).

Melt butter; blend in flour. Add milk and cook, stirring constantly, until mixture bubbles and is thickened. Add bouillon cube, onion, salt and pepper. Stir until bouillon cube is dissolved.

Remove from heat and add asparagus. Chop 3 eggs and add to creamed mixture.

Turn into baked pie shell. Sprinkle with grated cheese.

Bake in moderate oven (350°) until cheese melts, about 7 minutes. Remove from oven. Cut remaining egg in 6 wedges; arrange on center of pie with points of one end together, petal-fashion. Serve at once. Makes 6 servings.

American-Chinese Asparagus

Most of the countries around the world have influenced American vegetable cooking. Women living in our states that border the Pacific Ocean adopt many tricks from kitchens in the Far East. American-Chinese Asparagus is a classic example. Let it bring spring to your table when the delicate green spears appear in the garden or on the market.

American-Chinese Asparagus meets all the requirements of a superb vegetable dish. From the Chinese we borrow the custom of cutting spears diagonally and cooking them until tender, yet a little crisp. We season the vegetable simply, with salt, pepper and butter. You may add another Chinese specialty, monosodium glutamate, to bring out the fresh asparagus flavor.

AMERICAN-CHINESE ASPARAGUS

Taste-testers voted this the very best asparagus dish they ever sampled

2 lbs. asparagus	½ tsp. salt
⅓ c. butter or margarine	⅛ tsp. pepper
⅓ c. water	

Break off each asparagus stalk as far down as it snaps easily. Cut off scales with a knife. Scrub with soft brush to remove all sand. Lay 1 or 2 stalks together on a cutting board; cut diagonally, making bias slices about 1″ long and ¼″ inch thick. You will have about 4 c. asparagus.

Heat butter and water to boiling in heavy skillet with tight-fitting lid. Add asparagus and seasonings. Cover and cook over high heat 5 minutes, shaking skillet occasionally. Check with fork to see if asparagus is tender-crisp. If not, cook 1 or 2 minutes longer, adding 1 tblsp. water, if necessary. Water should be evaporated at end of cooking. Makes 6 servings.

Highly esteemed in Europe, fresh asparagus spears are usually served as a separate course.

Beans

Fava or Horse Beans: Fava beans are similar to lima beans, but they are larger. You see more of them in California, especially in Italian markets, but their acceptance is widening. Commonly called horse beans, they are most plentiful during the spring and summer months.

Select green pods that are thick and have a glossy sheen and are well filled with large beans.

Allow 3 lbs. for 4 servings.

Keep raw fava beans in the refrigerator crisper, but use quickly.

When you are ready to cook the beans, wash the pods and shell the beans. A good way to hasten the shelling is to cut off the outer edge of the pods with scissors and slip out the beans. Cook them in salted water to cover in a covered saucepan. (Frequently, women add a peeled garlic clove or a little chopped onion, bacon or ham to fava beans when cooking them.) Boil gently 20 to 25 minutes. Drain and add butter and, if needed, salt. A sprinkling of lemon juice contributes to good flavor.

Green Lima Beans: Green limas are a favored vegetable throughout the country, although many home gardeners no longer grow them because their season in any one garden is short and they are not easy to shell. They are available in markets from July through November.

The signs of top quality are the same as for fava beans: pods green, crisp and full of beans.

Allow 2 to 3 lbs. for 4 servings (4 to 6 c.).

Store them in the refrigerator crisper and use quickly.

When ready to cook, wash, snap pods open and push out limas. If the pods do not snap open easily, cut in a thin strip with a knife from the inner edge of the pod.

Cook green limas, covered, in 1″ boiling salted water 20 to 25 minutes. Drain and season with salt, pepper and butter or margarine.

Green Beans: Green beans, with their tender, edible pods, are one of the most popular vegetables in farm and ranch homes. They are also called string beans, although that name today is inaccurate thanks to selective growing which has produced beans without the fibrous string along the closing of the pod. Snap beans, another name for both green and wax beans, describes the young, crisp beans that snap when broken.

Green beans grow in practically all home gardens, either on vines that require support (pole beans), or on low bushes (bush beans). Most of the beans grown in vast commercial fields are bush beans. While summer is the peak of availability, green beans are on the market throughout the year.

Select clean, crisp pods that snap when bent and have a bright appearance, free of blemishes.

Allow 1 to 1½ lbs. green beans for 4 servings. Store beans in refrigerator crisper, but use quickly.

When ready to cook, wash beans and cut off both ends. Remove strings, if any. Snap or cut crosswise into 1 to 2″ pieces or in thin diagonal slices. If you want French-style beans, slit them lengthwise into thin strips.

Cook beans, covered, in 1″ boiling salted water until tender-crisp. This takes about 15 to 25 minutes for beans cut into 1 to 2″ pieces, 10 to 15 minutes for beans cut diagonally or for French-cut beans. For tender beans that retain some crispness, Western Vegetable Growers Association recommends cooking the 1″ pieces uncovered in ½″ boiling salted water, 15 to 20 minutes. Drain and season with salt, pepper and butter or margarine.

Wax Beans: Some home and commercial gardeners grow wax or yellow beans, but they are not so universally used as green beans. Wax beans are in greatest supply in summer.

Select slender, crisp yellow pods that snap.

Store the beans in the refrigerator crisper, but use quickly.

Prepare for cooking and cook like green beans.

Gourmet Snap Beans

You can use either slender green or yellow beans in this vegetable dish, which is a good escort for meat and poultry.

11

We base the recipe on well-established techniques of French kitchens, where vegetables so frequently are cooked with care and to perfection.

Since you can cook the vegetable ahead for quick and easy reheating and seasoning at mealtime, Gourmet Snap Beans are a wise choice for company meals. One of our home economists who tested the recipe was so impressed with how attractive and flavorful the beans were that she served them at a company roast beef dinner. She reported that the women asked her how she fixed the beans and the men ate them with enthusiasm. No hostess could ask for more.

GOURMET SNAP BEANS

This is an elegant, simple vegetable dish—
fix it for company

2 lbs. fresh green beans	2 tblsp. minced fresh
1 tblsp. salt	parsley
2 qts. boiling water	½ tsp. salt
3 tblsp. butter	⅛ tsp. pepper
2 tsp. lemon juice	

Snap or cut off ends of beans. Just before cooking, wash quickly under warm water. Add beans and 1 tblsp. salt to boiling water. Bring quickly to a boil and cook, uncovered, until tender-crisp, about 10 to 15 minutes, the exact time depending on age of beans. (French women test for doneness by eating one of the beans.)

Drain beans into colander. To serve them right away, melt butter in large skillet. Add drained beans and stir and heat until hot. Remove from heat, add lemon juice, parsley, ½ tsp. salt and pepper; toss to distribute. Serve at once. Makes 8 servings.

NOTE: You can cook the beans early in the day if you like. Drain cooked beans and put them immediately into a kettle of very cold water to cool quickly (this stops the cooking and helps them stay green and tender-crisp). Drain cooled beans, cover and refrigerate. Reheat and season just before serving.

SNAP BEANS WITH CHEESE

Try this for variety when beans are plentiful—
use young, slender beans

4 c. green beans, cut in 1"
  pieces (1 lb.)
½ c. chopped onion (1
  small)
2 slices bacon, diced

¼ c. milk
½ c. grated process
  American cheese
½ tsp. salt
⅛ tsp. pepper

Cook beans with onion and bacon in boiling salted water until tender. Drain, reserving liquid. Add ¼ c. bean liquid, milk, cheese, salt and pepper to beans. Stir until cheese melts. Makes 6 servings.

GREEN BEANS WITH ALMONDS
AND MUSHROOMS

Here's an easy-to-fix company dish
that gets an enthusiastic reception

6 c. cut green beans (1½
  lbs.)
3 tblsp. butter or margarine
¼ c. coarsely chopped
  toasted almonds

1 (4 oz.) can mushroom
  slices, drained
¾ tsp. salt
⅛ to ¼ tsp. savory leaves
1 tsp. lemon juice

Cook green beans in boiling salted water until tender; drain.

Melt butter and add almonds and drained mushrooms. Cook until mushrooms are heated. Add to beans along with remaining ingredients. Toss. Serve immediately. Makes 8 servings.

BEST-EVER GREEN BEANS

These beans deserve the adjective

4 c. cut green beans (1 lb.)
¼ c. finely chopped onion
3 tblsp. butter
2 tblsp. flour
2 tblsp. sugar
2 tblsp. minced parsley

¾ c. milk
2 tblsp. vinegar
1 c. dairy sour cream
4 slices bacon, diced,
  cooked and drained

13

Cook beans in boiling salted water until tender; drain.

Cook onion in butter until soft and transparent. Blend in flour, sugar, parsley and milk. Cook over low heat, stirring constantly, until mixture is smooth and comes to a boil. Stir in vinegar.

Add cooked beans and sour cream. Place over low heat, stirring occasionally, until of serving temperature; do not boil. Serve at once, topped with bacon. Makes 6 servings.

SAVORY GREEN BEANS

Simple hot vegetable companion for poultry
and meats—a gourmet choice

1 lb. green beans	1 tsp. basil leaves
2 tblsp. salad oil	½ tsp. sugar
1 clove garlic	⅛ tsp. pepper
1 tblsp. chopped onion	¼ c. boiling water
1½ tsp. salt	

Wash beans; remove tips, then cut in halves crosswise.

Heat oil in skillet. Cut garlic clove in half and add to oil along with onion; cook until soft. Remove garlic.

Add beans and remaining ingredients. Cover and cook over medium heat until tender-crisp, about 25 minutes. Add 1 tblsp. additional water if necessary. Makes 4 servings.

SWEET-SOUR GREEN BEANS

Take this dish to a picnic and you'll win praise.
It's on the sweet side

3 lbs. green beans	⅔ c. water
3 onions, thinly sliced and separated into rings	3 tblsp. salad oil
1⅓ c. vinegar	1½ tsp. salt
1⅔ c. sugar	½ tsp. pepper

Cut off tips of beans; leave whole. Cook in boiling salted water until tender. Drain.

Combine beans and onion rings in a large bowl. Stir together remaining ingredients. Pour over beans. Refrigerate at least 24 hours, stirring occasionally. Makes about 3½ qts. (14 c.).

CHINESE GREEN BEANS

An Oregon woman captured wonderful flavors of the Far East in this dish—it intrigues and impresses guests

3 c. green beans, cut
    diagonally in 1" slices
1 c. celery, cut diagonally
    in ¼" slices
1 (2½ oz.) can sliced
    mushrooms, drained

3 tblsp. salad oil
1 tblsp. cornstarch
1 tblsp. soy sauce
1 beef bouillon cube

Cook beans in boiling salted water until tender-crisp. Do not overcook. Drain, reserving liquid.

Meanwhile, cook celery and mushrooms in oil in skillet until celery is tender-crisp. Blend cornstarch with soy sauce, bean liquid, and bouillon cube. Add to celery mixture along with beans. Cook, stirring constantly until mixture comes to a boil and bouillon cube is thoroughly dissolved. Makes 6 servings.

SUPER GREEN BEANS

Children like beans creamed this way

8 c. fresh green beans (2
    lbs.)
¼ c. butter or bacon
    drippings
1 tsp. salt

½ tsp. basil leaves
½ c. boiling water
½ c. light cream or dairy
    half-and-half
⅛ tsp. pepper

Select tender green beans that snap easily. Wash, trim off ends and remove any strings. Place in bundles on cutting board and cut in 1" pieces.

Heat butter in electric skillet or heavy saucepan with tight-fitting lid; add beans, salt, basil and boiling water. Cover; cook on high heat until steam is produced, then turn as low as possible and cook 25 to 30 minutes, shaking pan occasionally and watching at the last to be sure beans do not burn (they should be barely tender).

Add cream and pepper; serve at once. Makes about 8 servings.

WEST COAST GREEN BEANS

Credit the seasonings for giving this dish its special taste

4 c. fresh green beans (1 lb.)	¼ c. snipped parsley
¼ c. butter or margarine	¼ tsp. rosemary leaves
¾ c. minced onion	¼ tsp. basil leaves
¼ c. minced celery	¾ tsp. salt
1 clove garlic, minced	

Wash beans and remove ends. Cut crosswise in thin, slanted slices. Cook, covered, in ½" boiling salted water about 15 minutes, or until tender-crisp; drain.

Meanwhile, melt butter in saucepan; add onion, celery and garlic; cook 5 minutes. Add remaining ingredients; cover and simmer 10 minutes. Add to beans and toss well. Makes 4 servings.

NOTE: This is an easy recipe to double.

GREEN BEANS WITH SOUR CREAM

This dish has a wonderful blend of flavors— do try it soon

5 c. fresh green beans (1¼ lbs.), or 2 (10 oz.) pkgs. frozen green beans	1 tsp. toasted sesame seeds, or ½ tsp. caraway seeds
3 to 4 tblsp. dairy sour cream	1 tblsp. grated Parmesan or Romano cheese

Cook beans in boiling salted water until tender-crisp; drain. Add sour cream and sesame seeds; stir to blend. Sprinkle with cheese and serve. Or chill and serve on bed of lettuce or curly kale. Makes 6 servings.

GREEN BEANS WITH GARLIC DRESSING

Garlic dressing and orégano plus bacon
are the flavor boosters

4 c. fresh green beans (1 lb.)	½ c. garlic French dressing
1 tsp. salt	2 tblsp. minced green onion
2 slices bacon	¼ tsp. orégano leaves

Cook beans, either whole or cut in 1" lengths, in ½ c. water with 1 tsp. salt added, for 10 minutes, or until just tender-crisp.

Cut bacon in ½" lengths and fry crisp; add bacon bits, without fat, to beans. Pour the salad dressing over, add onion and orégano; heat through and serve. Makes 4 servings.

NOTE: You can substitute 1 (1 lb.) can green beans for the fresh vegetable. Heat beans using liquid in can, drain and use like cooked fresh beans.

WAX BEANS PLUS

Mild cheese heightens delicate yellow bean taste
and dill enhances it

4 c. wax beans, cut in 1" pieces	¾ tsp. dill seeds
1 (3 oz.) pkg. cream cheese, softened	½ tsp. salt
	⅛ tsp. pepper
1 tblsp. milk	2 tblsp. chopped parsley

Cook beans in boiling salted water until just tender; drain.

Stir together cream cheese, milk, dill seeds, salt and pepper. Add to drained hot beans and toss until cheese is hot. Sprinkle with chopped parsley. Makes 4 servings.

Beets

Beets brighten meals with their rich, red color. They are available the year round, with June and July the peak season.

Select young beets, small or medium in size, and firm. Fresh beet tops, another sign of quality, are cooked as greens by some people.

Allow 2 lbs., without tops, for 4 servings.

Keep beets in a cool place, in the refrigerator crisper if space permits. Cut off the tops 2" above the beet crown, but do not remove roots. Place in plastic bag, close and refrigerate. They will hold several days.

When ready to cook, wash beets thoroughly, scrubbing with a brush. Do not trim the root. Do not remove the 2" stems remaining above beet crown.

Cover with salted water and cook, covered, until tender (about ½ to 1 hour for young beets). Older beets need to cook longer (1 to 2 hours). When tender, drain and hold under running cold water. Rub off skins and cut off tops and roots. Dice or slice and reheat with butter or margarine, adding a little lemon juice or vinegar to retain or revive the bright red color. Season with salt and pepper.

HOT SPICED BEETS

A spicy accompaniment for ham or pork—
perfect with an oven meal

4 c. sliced cooked beets	½ tsp. salt
2 tblsp. butter or margarine	¼ tsp. paprika
1 tblsp. flour	¼ tsp. ground cinnamon
2 tblsp. dark brown sugar	⅛ tsp. ground nutmeg
3 tblsp. vinegar	⅛ tsp. ground cloves
¼ c. boiling water	

Place beets in a greased 1½-qt. casserole. Melt butter; blend in flour and sugar. Add vinegar and boiling water, and cook, stirring constantly, until bubbly. Add remaining ingredients. Pour over beets.

Cover and bake in moderate oven (350°) 25 minutes. Makes 6 servings.

COUNTRY-SPECIAL BEETS

*Sour cream and green onions turn plain beets
into a true treat—rose-colored sauce
surrounds vegetables*

½ c. dairy sour cream
2 tblsp. vinegar
1 tblsp. minced green onion
1 tblsp. sugar

1 tsp. salt
⅛ tsp. pepper
4 c. sliced cooked beets

Stir together sour cream, vinegar, onion, sugar, salt and pepper. Pour over beets in saucepan. Heat slowly, stirring occasionally. Do not boil. Makes 6 servings.

NOTE: Instead of fresh beets, cooked, you can use 2 (1 lb.) cans beets.

Broccoli

This member of the cabbage family is a near relative of cauliflower. It is abundant throughout the year, but it grows better in cool weather, which means it is still available from Northern gardens in November. (New hybrids often do well in July and August.)

Select broccoli with a firm, compact cluster of small closed flower buds (none should be opened enough to show the bright yellow flower). Bud clusters should be dark or sage green or green with a purplish cast. Stems should not be thick or tough.

Allow 2 lbs. for 4 servings.

Store in closed plastic bag in the refrigerator crisper. Broccoli so stored keeps 4 to 5 days.

When ready to cook, wash and trim off stem ends. Make lengthwise slashes in stalks through stem up to buds; this hastens the cooking. Put in saucepan containing 1″ boiling salted water, cover, and cook rapidly until just tender, 10 to 15 minutes. Drain, season with salt, pepper and melted butter or margarine. (Or remove flowerets, cut stems in ¼″ diagonal slices and place them in 1″ boiling salted water. Cover and cook 5 minutes. Add flowerets, cover and cook another 5 minutes or until just tender.)

BROCCOLI AND MACARONI

Substantial, cheese-topped dish

½ lb. broccoli
2 tbslp. tomato sauce,
   ketchup or chili sauce
1 tblsp. olive or salad oil
1 tsp. salt
⅛ tsp. pepper

⅛ tsp. garlic salt
½ lb. macaroni, cooked
   and drained
¼ c. grated Parmesan
   cheese

Cook broccoli in boiling salted water until tender. Cut in pieces.

Mix tomato sauce, oil and seasonings. Add broccoli and simmer in sauce 10 minutes, stirring occasionally. Pour over macaroni. Sprinkle with cheese. Makes 5 to 6 servings.

SEATTLE GOURMET BROCCOLI

This successful recipe promotes broccoli
to the gourmet class

3 lbs. fresh broccoli, or 3
   (10 oz.) pkgs. frozen
   chopped broccoli
¼ c. butter or margarine
¼ c. flour
1½ tblsp. chicken-seasoned
   stock base
½ tsp. salt

2 c. milk
6 tblsp. butter
⅔ c. hot water
⅔ (8 oz.) pkg. herb-
   seasoned stuffing mix
⅔ c. coarsely chopped
   walnuts, or slivered
   almonds

Cook fresh broccoli in boiling salted water until tender-crisp; drain and chop coarsely. (Cook frozen broccoli as directed on package, then drain.)

Make white sauce by blending ¼ c. butter, flour, chicken stock base and salt; add milk and cook until thickened.

Meanwhile, melt 6 tblsp. butter in hot water; pour over stuffing mix. Add nuts and toss together.

Turn broccoli into greased 2-qt. casserole. Pour the white sauce over, and top with stuffing; press down slightly. Bake in hot oven (400°) 20 to 25 minutes. Makes 8 to 10 servings.

Fresh Broccoli with Orange Sauce

The mother who shares this recipe with you has great respect for the orange sauce. She says it taught her four children how good broccoli can be.

FRESH BROCCOLI WITH ORANGE SAUCE

They'll ask for second helpings

1½ lbs. fresh broccoli, or 2 (10 oz.) pkgs. frozen broccoli	2 tblsp. flour
	1 c. fresh orange juice
	⅛ tsp. salt
2 tblsp. butter or margarine	Paprika

Wash broccoli; cook in a little salted water until tender-crisp. (Cook frozen broccoli as directed on package, then drain.)

Meanwhile, melt butter in small saucepan; blend in flour and cook a few minutes. Add orange juice and salt; cook and stir until thick and smooth.

Drain broccoli and serve with orange sauce. Top with a sprinkle of paprika. Makes 4 to 5 servings.

Brussels Sprouts

Brussels sprouts are another close relative to cabbage. The sprouts develop as large buds, or little cabbage heads, on tall stems where each main leaf is attached. Although they are available from August through March, the peak season in the market extends from October through December.

Select sprouts with a fresh, bright green color and tight-fitting outer leaves, firm body and without blemishes.

Allow 1¼ lbs. for 4 servings.

Before storing, remove any loose or discolored leaves. Put in plastic bag, close and place in refrigerator crisper. The vegetable will hold a couple of days.

When ready to cook, wash well and cut a slice off the

stem ends. Then cut an "x" into stem ends to encourage fast cooking.

Cook, uncovered, in 1″ boiling salted water until tender, 10 to 20 minutes. Drain and season with salt, pepper and butter or margarine. Brussels sprouts lose their bright color and fresh flavor rapidly after cooking; serve them promptly.

SAN MATEO BRUSSELS SPROUTS

Scatter sliced pimiento-stuffed olives
over dish of sprouts for colorful trim

2 qts. Brussels sprouts (two 10 oz. tubs)	¼ c. minced fresh parsley
2 tblsp. butter	½ tsp. salt
¼ c. lemon juice	⅛ tsp. pepper
1 c. dairy sour cream	Sliced pimiento-stuffed olives (optional)

Wash sprouts. Trim stem ends and cut an "x" in stem to hasten cooking. Remove any loose or yellow leaves. Let stand a few minutes in cool, salted water.

Heat butter in skillet over medium heat. Drain sprouts; add to hot butter. Cover and steam about 10 minutes. Shake skillet occasionally. Check with fork to see if they are tender-crisp.

Add lemon juice and steam 2 minutes more. Add remaining ingredients, except olives. Heat, but do not boil. Serve topped with sliced olives, if desired. Makes 6 servings.

BRUSSELS SPROUTS WITH LEMON

Lemon brings out a garden-fresh taste

1½ qts. Brussels sprouts	Pepper
¾ c. butter	Lemon slices
Salt	

Trim sprouts, removing any imperfect leaves. Pour boiling salted water (1 tsp. salt to 1 qt. water) over them to cover; let stand 5 minutes; drain.

Melt butter in heavy skillet; add sprouts. Cover tightly and cook over very low heat just until they are tender, 10 to 20 minutes. Test for tenderness with a kitchen fork.

Add salt and pepper to taste. Serve garnished with thin lemon slices. Makes 4 to 5 servings.

BRUSSELS SPROUTS CASSEROLE

Cheese, almonds, water chestnuts and the taste of mushrooms turn these sprouts into a hostess-guest favorite

2 qts. Brussels sprouts (two 10 oz. cartons), or 2 (10 oz.) pkgs. frozen	¼ c. milk
	1 c. grated sharp process cheese
1 (5 oz.) can water chestnuts, sliced	½ tsp. salt
	⅛ tsp. pepper
1 can condensed cream of mushroom soup	½ c. slivered toasted almonds

Cook Brussels sprouts in boiling salted water until tender; drain. Place in 1½-qt. casserole; top with water chestnuts.

Meanwhile, combine soup and milk. Add cheese, salt and pepper, and cook, stirring, until cheese melts. Pour over Brussels sprouts. Sprinkle with almonds.

Bake in moderate oven (350°) until bubbling, 20 to 25 minutes. Makes 8 servings.

Cabbage

Green Cabbage: Green cabbage is a great country favorite. Fortunately, it has a long garden season and is available in markets throughout the year. It commonly is called new cabbage during the garden season. In some Northern states growers plant a late crop for use in August and September and to hold in storage for winter use. Cabbage reaching the market from storage often is called old cabbage.

Select firm or hard heads of cabbage, heavy for their size, with crisp-looking medium green outer leaves. Some of the early-crop cabbage is only fairly firm, but it is satisfactory if used quickly—spring cabbage is not a good keeper. Cabbage out of storage is trimmed of its outer leaves and lacks green color; it is satisfactory if not wilted or discolored.

Allow 1½ lbs. for 4 servings.

Store cabbage in closed plastic bag in the refrigerator crisper. It holds a week or longer.

When ready to cook, wash and discard any wilted leaves. Cut in wedges or wide shreds. Remove core, leaving just enough at bottom to hold wedges in shape.

Cook, covered, in a small amount of boiling salted water until tender-crisp, 5 minutes for shredded cabbage, 10 to 15 minutes for wedges. Drain and season with salt, pepper and butter or margarine. Cabbage is best when quick-cooked for a short period—also retains more vitamins.

Red Cabbage: Red cabbage, favored for salads, also is excellent cooked and served as a hot vegetable. It is available throughout the year.

Select heads that are heavy for their size with fresh-looking leaves.

Allow 1 to 1½ lbs. for 4 servings.

Store the cabbage head in closed plastic bag in the refrigerator crisper. It holds at least a week.

When ready to cook, wash and discard any wilted leaves. Cut in wide shreds or wedges.

Cook, uncovered, in a small quantity of boiling salted water with 2 tblsp. vinegar or lemon juice added to keep or restore the red color. Cook about 25 minutes. Drain and season with salt, pepper and butter or margarine.

Savoy Cabbage: This beautiful cabbage with crinkly green leaves has the same qualities as green cabbage. Store, prepare and cook it in the same ways.

CARAWAY-BUTTERED CABBAGE

Be sure to shred cabbage coarsely—
use a sharp knife. A dull knife bruises cabbage
and wastes vitamin C

¼ c. butter	2 tblsp. water
1 tsp. caraway seeds, crushed	6 c. coarsely shredded cabbage
1 tsp. salt	

Melt butter in saucepan. Add remaining ingredients. Steam until cabbage is tender, about 10 minutes. Stir to combine. Makes 4 servings.

FIVE-MINUTE CABBAGE

Makes its own sauce as it cooks

1¼ c. milk	2 tblsp. butter
8 c. finely shredded cabbage	1 tsp. salt
2 tblsp. flour	⅛ tsp. pepper
¼ c. milk	

Heat 1¼ c. milk in heavy skillet over medium heat. Add cabbage; cover and simmer 2 minutes.

Meanwhile, blend together flour and ¼ c. milk. Add to cabbage along with butter, salt and pepper. Stir until mixture comes to a boil and is thickened.

Cover and continue cooking over low heat 2 minutes. Stir. Serve in sauce dishes. Makes 6 servings.

CHOW MEIN CABBAGE

All taste-testers, including men and children, liked this quick dish

3 c. shredded cabbage	1 c. chopped onion (1
1 c. bias-cut celery	medium)
⅔ c. chopped green pepper	2 tblsp. butter
	½ tsp. salt

Combine vegetables.

Melt butter in skillet; add vegetables and salt. Cook 5 minutes, stirring constantly. Cover and cook until vegetables are tender-crisp, 3 to 5 minutes. Serve immediately, passing soy sauce. Makes 6 servings.

NOTE: Shred cabbage fine with knife for best results.

TART SCALLOPED CABBAGE

Here's a tasty casserole, quick to fix

6 c. shredded cabbage	¾ c. mayonnaise or salad
1/3 c. boiling water	dressing
3 eggs, slightly beaten	1½ c. coarsely crushed
½ tsp. salt	potato chips
6 tblsp. vinegar	

Parboil cabbage 2 to 3 minutes in boiling water with a little salt added; do not drain.

Combine eggs, salt, vinegar and mayonnaise. Add cabbage and any liquid that clings to it.

Pour into greased 1½-qt. casserole. Sprinkle potato chips over top.

Bake in moderate oven (350°) 25 minutes. Makes 6 servings.

CHEESE-SCALLOPED CABBAGE

You'll get no family complaints on cabbage
fixed this easy way

2 qts. shredded cabbage	1 tsp. instant minced onion
1 (1¼ oz.) pkg. cheese	1 tsp. green bell pepper
sauce mix	flakes
Milk	

Cook cabbage in boiling salted water 5 minutes. Drain.

Meanwhile, prepare cheese sauce mix with milk as directed on package, adding onion and green pepper before heating.

Combine cabbage and cheese sauce. Heat and serve. Or, place cabbage in greased 1½-qt. casserole. Top with ½ c. bread crumbs tossed with 2 tblsp. melted butter. Bake in moderate oven (350°) until bubbly, 20 to 25 minutes. Makes 6 servings.

COUNTRY SWEET-SOUR CABBAGE

Brown sugar and apples elevate this cabbage dish
above the commonplace

2 apples, cored and peeled	½ c. water
1 onion	½ c. brown sugar
1½ tblsp. shortening	½ c. vinegar
½ medium head cabbage,	Salt and pepper to taste
shredded	1 tblsp. butter

26

Chop apples and onion fine; cook in skillet in shortening about 10 minutes. Add cabbage and water, a little at a time; cook 10 to 15 minutes. When cabbage is tender, add sugar and vinegar. Before serving, add salt, pepper and butter. Makes 4 servings.

PENNSYLVANIA DUTCH CABBAGE

Just the dish to add variety to cold-weather meals—it's sweet-sour

8 c. shredded cabbage	½ c. water
4 slices bacon, chopped	⅓ c. vinegar
1 small onion, minced	½ tsp. salt
2 tblsp. brown sugar	⅛ tsp. pepper
2 tblsp. flour	

Cook cabbage in boiling salted water until tender, 5 to 7 minutes. Drain.

Meanwhile, cook bacon until crisp. Remove from skillet. Add onion to bacon drippings and cook until soft. Blend in brown sugar and flour. Add water and vinegar and cook, stirring constantly, until thickened. Add salt and pepper.

Add sauce and bacon to drained cabbage; heat thoroughly. Makes 6 servings.

CABBAGE AU GRATIN

An easygoing casserole with cheese and cream of celery soup seasoning

1 medium head cabbage, shredded (2 qts.)	1 c. grated process American cheese
1 can condensed cream of celery soup	½ tsp. salt
¼ c. milk	⅛ tsp. pepper
	½ c. bread crumbs
	2 tblsp. melted butter

Cook cabbage in boiling salted water until tender, 5 to 7 minutes. Drain.

Meanwhile, combine soup, milk, cheese, salt and pepper in saucepan. Heat, stirring, until cheese melts. Combine with cabbage. Place in greased 1½-qt. casserole.

Toss bread crumbs with butter until coated. Sprinkle on top of cabbage. Bake in moderate oven (350°) until thoroughly heated, about 15 minutes. Makes 6 servings.

RED CABBAGE AND PINEAPPLE

Different, distinctive and delicious fruit-vegetable
combination that adds cheerful color
and interest to meals

6 c. shredded red cabbage	1 tblsp. cornstarch
1 tblsp. lemon juice	½ tsp. salt
½ c. boiling water	1 (9 oz.) can pineapple
1 tblsp. butter	tidbits
2 tblsp. brown sugar	2 tblsp. vinegar

Place cabbage, lemon juice and boiling water in skillet. Cover and cook, stirring once or twice, until cabbage is tender, 10 to 12 minutes. Stir in butter.

Meanwhile, blend together brown sugar, cornstarch and salt. Drain juice from pineapple and blend into cornstarch mixture along with vinegar. Add cornstarch mixture and pineapple bits to cabbage. Cook, stirring, until mixture thickens and bubbles. Serve hot. Makes 6 servings.

Carrots

Carrots are the golden touch in many meals, adding brightness as well as flavor. They are harvested 12 months of the year.

Select firm, clean, smooth, well-shaped carrots with a good orange color and fresh green tops. Avoid carrots with green sunburned spots which have to be peeled away.

Allow 1 to 1½ lbs. for 4 servings.

Rinse roots in cold water, place in plastic bag and store in refrigerator crisper. If kept moist, they hold a week or two.

When ready to cook, cut off tops if carrots are not packaged. Scrape or peel with vegetable peeler to remove thin skin. Leave whole, cut in slices or strips or dice.

Cook, covered, in 1″ boiling salted water with ½ tsp. sugar added. Boil 20 minutes for whole carrots, 10 to 20 minutes for cut ones. Drain, season with salt, pepper and butter or margarine.

OREGON CARROT CASSEROLE

*Candied ginger provides the gourmet touch
and enhances carrot flavors*

20 medium carrots
½ tsp. salt (optional)
⅛ tsp. pepper
1 tblsp. finely chopped
  candied ginger
¼ c. butter or margarine

¼ c. undiluted evaporated
  milk
½ c. coarsely chopped
  walnuts or filberts
2 to 3 tblsp. corn flake
  crumbs

Peel and cook carrots, covered, in a small amount of boiling salted water until tender. Drain and mash well (you should have 1 qt.). Taste and add more salt if needed.

Add pepper, ginger, 2 tblsp. butter and evaporated milk to carrots. Beat well with electric mixer. Turn into a 1½-qt. casserole greased with remaining 2 tblsp. butter; sprinkle with nuts, then with crumbs.

Bake in moderate oven (370°) 20 to 30 minutes. Makes 6 servings.

CARROT PATTIES

*For company, serve these with ham and eggs
or with syrup or honey*

1½ c. grated raw carrots
3 tblsp. grated onion
3 c. bread crumbs
¾ tsp. baking powder
2 eggs, beaten

¼ c. milk
½ tsp. salt
⅛ tsp. pepper
3 tblsp. butter or bacon fat

Combine all ingredients, except butter. Mix well and form into patties similar to potato cakes, about 3″ in diameter (there should be 12).

Heat butter in a skillet; brown patties lightly on both sides. Makes 6 servings.

HARVARD CARROTS

Smart winter choice—carrots have tangy taste
and sunny appearance

½ c. sugar
1½ tblsp. cornstarch
¼ c. vinegar
¼ c. water

¼ tsp. salt
⅛ tsp. pepper
4 c. cooked sliced carrots
2 tblsp. butter

Combine sugar and cornstarch in saucepan. Blend in vinegar and water. Cook over medium heat until thick and bubbling, stirring constantly. Add salt, pepper and carrots. Heat until carrots are hot. Stir in butter. Makes 6 servings.

POLKA DOT CARROTS

Olive-green rings with bright red centers
decorate and flavor carrots

6 medium carrots
¼ c. butter
1 tblsp. minced onion
½ tsp. salt

½ tsp. sugar
⅛ tsp. pepper
½ c. sliced pimiento-stuffed
green olives

Peel carrots and cut in ¼" slices. Cook in boiling salted water until tender; drain.

Meanwhile, melt butter. Add onion and cook until onion is soft. Add to carrots along with remaining ingredients. Heat thoroughly and serve. Makes 6 servings.

COMPANY CARROTS

The name is correct—cheese and other
seasonings make them unusual

5 c. sliced carrots
1 c. dairy sour cream
1 (3 oz.) pkg. cream cheese
(softened)
3 tblsp. minced green
pepper

2 tblsp. minced green onion
½ tsp. salt
½ tsp. grated lemon peel
⅛ tsp. pepper

Cook carrots in boiling salted water until tender. Drain. Combine with remaining ingredients, stirring to blend. Heat thoroughly. Makes 6 servings.

SCALLOPED CARROTS

Your guests will take second helpings
of these well-seasoned carrots

4 c. sliced peeled carrots	⅛ tsp. pepper
1 medium onion, chopped	½ c. grated Cheddar cheese
3 tblsp. butter	3 c. herb-flavored bread
1 can condensed cream of	stuffing
celery soup	⅓ c. melted butter
½ tsp. salt	

Cook carrots in boiling salted water. Drain.

Meanwhile, cook onion in 3 tblsp. butter until soft. Stir in soup, salt, pepper, cheese and carrots. Place in greased 2-qt. casserole.

Toss bread stuffing mix with ⅓ c. melted butter. Spoon over carrots.

Bake in moderate oven (350°) until thoroughly heated, about 20 minutes. Makes 6 servings.

Golden Carrots Supreme

A French woman, visiting in Wisconsin, insists that the best way to treat carrots is to pull them while tender and young, peel, slice and cook in a little chicken broth instead of water, until the orange circles are just tender. They absorb the broth. Then season with salt, pepper and butter.

GOLDEN CARROTS SUPREME

You'll win new friends to carrots
if you use this simple French recipe

¼ c. butter or margarine	5 c. diagonally sliced (¼″)
¾ c. chicken broth	carrots
2 tsp. salt	2 tsp. lemon juice
⅛ tsp. pepper	¼ c. chopped parsley
2 tsp. sugar	

31

Add butter to boiling chicken broth. Stir in salt, pepper, sugar and carrots. Simmer, covered, until carrots are tender-crisp, about 10 minutes.

Stir in lemon juice and parsley. Makes 6 servings.

WALNUT CARROTS

Walnuts add crunchy note and flavor
to bright carrots, expertly seasoned

5 c. (3″) carrot sticks (32 young carrots)
1½ c. water
½ tsp. salt
½ c. melted butter or margarine
2 tsp. honey

1 tsp. salt
¼ tsp. coarse grind pepper
2 tblsp. lemon juice
¼ tsp. grated lemon peel
½ c. coarsely broken walnuts

Cook carrots in water with ½ tsp. salt added, until just tender. Drain thoroughly.

Meanwhile, heat remaining ingredients, except the walnuts. Pour this topping over the hot carrots. Toss in the walnuts. Makes 8 servings.

DANISH SUGAR-BROWNED CARROTS

An easy way to give carrots a special touch—
the buttery glaze is delicious

16 small carrots
¼ c. butter or margarine

6 tblsp. sugar
1 tsp. salt

Cook peeled carrots in boiling water until tender-crisp. Drain well.

Melt butter in large skillet or saucepan; stir in sugar and cook, stirring constantly, until mixture is a light caramel color.

Add carrots; continue cooking, shaking the skillet or saucepan to brown carrots evenly. Sprinkle with salt during cooking. Makes 8 servings.

CARROTS HAWAIIAN

Good team: pineapple and carrots

1 (8 oz.) can pineapple	**1 tsp. tapioca**
tidbits	**½ tsp. salt**
4 c. cooked sliced carrots	**⅛ tsp. pepper**
2 tblsp. brown sugar	**2 tblsp. butter**

Drain pineapple, reserving liquid.

Combine carrots and pineapple bits in 1½-qt. casserole.

Blend together sugar, tapioca, salt and pepper. Stir in pineapple juice. Pour over carrots; dot with butter.

Cover and bake in moderate oven (350°) 30 minutes. Makes 6 servings.

Always cut off carrot tops before storing carrots. If you leave them on, the tops absorb moisture from the carrots, causing them to shrivel.

Cauliflower

The edible part of cauliflower is called the curd; the heavy, green, outer leaves are called jacket leaves. Cauliflower usually appears in markets without the jacket leaves. The most abundant season for this vegetable is from September through January.

Select creamy white, compact, solid and clean curds. A slight granular or "ricey" look will not affect eating quality if the surface is compact. Pay no attention to small green leaflets extending through the curd. Green jacket leaves indicate freshness.

Allow 1 large head for 4 servings.

If you do not buy cauliflower in a cellophane covering, wrap the head in plastic bag, close and store in the refrigerator crisper. Use within 2 days.

When ready to cook, wash well and cut off jacket leaves and core. Leave head whole or separate into flowerets. If jacket leaves are available, lay them in the bottom of the saucepan, with the flowerets or head on top.

Cook, covered, in 1″ boiling salted water until tender-crisp, 8 to 10 minutes for flowerets, 20 to 30 minutes for whole heads. Drain, discard leaves and season with salt, pepper and butter or margarine.

CAULIFLOWER CASSEROLE

*Cauliflower and eggs complement each other
in this lunch or supper dish*

1 medium cauliflower	1 tsp. parsley flakes
3 tblsp. butter	(optional)
3 tblsp. flour	3 hard-cooked eggs, thinly
1½ c. milk	sliced
1 tsp. salt	½ c. cracker crumbs
⅛ tsp. pepper	2 tblsp. melted butter

Separate cauliflower into flowerets. Cook in boiling salted water until tender. Drain.

Meanwhile, melt 3 tblsp. butter in saucepan. Stir in flour; add milk and cook, stirring constantly, until mixture bubbles and is thickened. Remove from heat and stir in salt, pepper and parsley.

Combine cauliflower, eggs and sauce. Spoon into 1½-qt. casserole. Toss crumbs with butter. Sprinkle over top.

Bake in moderate oven (350°) 25 minutes. Makes 4 to 6 servings.

CAULIFLOWER WITH SHRIMP SAUCE

*Shrimp sauce and toasted almonds
enhance this hostess special*

1 head cauliflower	½ tsp. salt
1 can frozen condensed	⅛ tsp. pepper
cream of shrimp soup,	¼ c. slivered, toasted
thawed	almonds
½ c. dairy sour cream	

Separate cauliflower into flowerets. Cook in boiling salted water until tender; drain.

Meanwhile, blend together soup, sour cream, salt and pepper in saucepan. Heat, but do not boil.

Place cauliflower in serving bowl. Top with shrimp sauce, then toasted almonds. Makes 4 to 6 servings.

PARMESAN CAULIFLOWER

Browned butter and cheese season delightfully;
keep hot in covered dish

1 large head cauliflower
¼ c. butter or margarine
3 tblsp. dry bread crumbs,
   toasted

2 tblsp. grated Parmesan
   cheese
Paprika

Separate cauliflower into flowerets. Cook in small amount of boiling salted water until tender, about 10 minutes. Drain.

In heavy skillet, over medium heat, brown butter until delicate brown (watch that it does not burn). Coat cooked cauliflower with butter; toss with bread crumbs. Sprinkle cheese over top. Garnish with paprika. Makes 4 to 6 servings.

Celeriac

The common name for this vegetable is celery root. The root looks something like a turnip. Celery root is available from October through April.

Select firm, crisp roots that are clean.

Allow 1¼ lbs. for 4 servings.

Hold in cold, moist place or refrigerator crisper. It keeps for a week or longer.

When ready to cook, wash and scrub with a brush. Remove all traces of black dirt and cut off bits of leaves and root fibers. Do not peel.

Cook, covered, in boiling salted water 40 to 60 minutes. Drain, plunge into cold water, peel and slice or dice. Season with butter or margarine, salt and pepper and reheat.

MASHED CELERY ROOTS

The mild celery flavor pleases. Made ahead,
shaped in patties and browned in butter,
it's simply delicious

2 large celery roots	½ tsp. salt
1 large potato	¼ tsp. pepper
¼ to ½ c. chicken broth	Paprika
2 tblsp. butter	

Cut celery roots in fourths and peel. Cook in boiling salted water until partially tender. Add potato, peeled and cut in fourths. Continue cooking until vegetables are tender; drain.

Mash vegetables thoroughly. Add enough chicken broth to make a soft consistency (as for mashed potatoes). Then add butter, salt and pepper and whip (color will look gray-white). Sprinkle with paprika and serve hot. Makes 6 servings.

Celery

This low-in-calories vegetable contributes crunchiness and flavor to many meals. It is available throughout the year.

To follow recipes in this and other cookbooks, you should know the names of celery parts. Correctly, a *stalk* of celery is the same as a *bunch,* and it is made up of *branches* or *ribs.*

Select bunches of celery with leaves that have a fresh appearance. Avoid celery with a wilted look or flabby upper branches or leaf stems. (You can partially freshen celery by placing butt end of bunch in cold water.)

Allow 1 medium bunch for 4 servings.

Rinse in cold water before storing. Then wrap in plastic bag, close and store in the refrigerator crisper. If kept moist, it will hold 1 to 2 weeks.

When ready to cook, separate the branches, wash and scrub grooves with a brush. Trim off root and blemishes.

Cook, covered, in 1″ boiling salted water or beef or chicken broth until tender, 15 to 20 minutes. Drain, season with salt, pepper and butter or margarine.

SWEET-SOUR CELERY

Excellent pork go-with from Utah

3 c. sliced celery	⅛ tsp. pepper
1 egg, beaten	2 tblsp. vinegar
2 tblsp. flour	1 c. water
2 tblsp. sugar	¼ c. dairy sour cream
¾ tsp. salt	

Cook celery in boiling salted water until tender; drain.

Meanwhile, blend together egg, flour, sugar, salt and pepper in saucepan. Blend in vinegar and water. Cook over medium heat, stirring constantly, until mixture comes to a boil. Remove from heat and add sour cream. Add to drained celery. Makes 6 servings.

CELERY AND WATER CHESTNUT CASSEROLE

Cut celery branches on the bias for this elegant pork or chicken escort

2 chicken bouillon cubes	2 tblsp. cold water
1¾ c. boiling water	2 (5 oz.) cans water
1 bunch celery, bias cut in	chestnuts, drained and
¾″ pieces	sliced
½ tsp. salt	½ c. sliced almonds
Dash pepper	⅓ c. fine dry bread crumbs
½ tsp. crushed basil leaves	2 tblsp. melted butter or
2 tblsp. cornstarch	margarine

Dissolve bouillon cubes in boiling water.

Combine celery with bouillon and seasonings, cover and cook until celery is tender-crisp, about 10 minutes.

Blend cornstarch with cold water; gradually stir into celery mixture. Cook and stir until thickened. Add water chestnuts and almonds. Turn into 2-qt. casserole.

Toss crumbs with melted butter; sprinkle over top of celery.

Bake, uncovered, in moderate oven (350°) about 25 minutes. Makes 5 to 6 servings.

Corn on the Cob

A native of the Americas, corn is high in popularity. Farm women call it the king of vegetables. While available to some extent throughout the year, the peak season extends from May to September.

Select ears with fresh green husks. The cobs should be filled with kernels. The kernels of fresh corn spurt a thin milky juice when punctured with a thumbnail. If the milk is thick or the skin of the kernel is tough or rubbery, the corn is too old.

Allow 2 ears corn for each serving. Two ears yield about 1 c. fresh kernels.

Farm families like to gather corn as near mealtime as possible. If the ears must be held, put them, unhusked, in refrigerator. Use quickly.

When ready to cook, husk the corn and remove silk.

Cover ears with boiling unsalted water, cover and cook 3 to 5 minutes. Or cover ears with cold water and cook, covered, just until the water reaches a boil. Lift out of water with tongs, drain and serve at once. Pass butter or margarine, salt and pepper.

SWISS CORN BAKE

Scalloped corn seasoned with cheese—
sure to win your family's approval

3 c. fresh corn, cut from cob	⅛ tsp. pepper
1 (5⅓ oz.) can evaporated milk (⅔ c.)	1 c. shredded Swiss cheese
	½ c. cracker crumbs
1 egg, beaten	1 tblsp. melted butter or
2 tblsp. chopped onion	margarine
½ tsp. salt	

Cook corn in boiling salted water 2 to 3 minutes. Drain and combine with milk, egg, onion, salt, pepper and Swiss cheese. Place in greased 10 × 6 × 1½″ casserole.

Toss cracker crumbs with butter. Sprinkle over corn mixture. Bake in moderate oven (350°) 30 to 35 minutes. Let set a few minutes before serving. Makes 5 to 6 servings.

CORN "OYSTERS"

When your family has had its fill of roasting ears,
make up a batch of Corn "Oysters"—so named
because a spoonful of the corn mixture
puffs up like an oyster on the hot griddle

6 ears select corn
(fresh-picked or
frozen-thawed)
3 egg yolks, well beaten
¼ c. flour

½ tsp. baking powder
¾ tsp. salt
¼ tsp. pepper
3 egg whites, stiffly beaten

Cut corn off cob about two-thirds the depth of the kernel. Scrape cob to remove the remaining corn, but not any of the cob. Add egg yolks; blend.

Sift together flour, baking powder, salt and pepper. Stir into corn-egg mixture; blend. Gently fold in egg whites.

Drop by spoonfuls on hot, well-greased griddle. Fry until nicely browned. Makes 4 servings.

NOTE: Chances are you'll want to double this recipe.

COLORFUL CORN BAKE

Perfect blending of flavors makes this delicious—
color adds appeal

¼ c. butter
3 c. corn, cut from cob, or 2
(12 oz.) cans whole
kernel corn, drained
½ c. chopped green pepper
½ c. chopped pimiento
½ c. sliced stuffed green
olives
¼ c. chopped parsley

2 tblsp. chopped onion
¼ c. flour
1 tsp. salt
½ tsp. pepper
2 c. milk
3 eggs, slightly beaten
1 c. shredded sharp process
cheese

Melt butter in skillet. Add corn, green pepper, pimiento, olives, parsley and onion. Cook 2 minutes, stirring. Cover and simmer over low heat 10 minutes.

Blend in flour, salt and pepper. Add milk and cook, stirring, until thickened. Gradually stir hot vegetable mixture into eggs. Stir in cheese. Turn into greased 2-qt. casserole.

Set casserole in pan of water and bake in moderate oven (350°) 45 to 50 minutes, or until set. Makes 8 servings.

CORN RAREBIT ON TOAST

For a blue-ribbon supper, serve this, tomato salad,
fresh peach sundae

1½ c. grated fresh corn
3 tblsp. butter
3 tblsp. flour
1 tsp. salt
¼ tsp. dry mustard
⅛ tsp. pepper

1 c. milk
⅔ c. shredded sharp
    Cheddar cheese
6 slices toast
12 slices bacon, diced and
    fried crisp

To fix grated corn, cut corn off cob about two-thirds the depth of the kernel. Scrape cob to remove the remaining corn, but not any of the cob.

Melt butter in skillet; blend in flour and seasonings. Add milk and corn and cook, stirring constantly, until thickened. Stir in cheese and heat only until cheese is melted. Serve over toast. Sprinkle with crisp bacon pieces. Makes 6 servings.

CORN PANCAKES

Golden brown pancakes chock-full of corn—pass butter and maple syrup

1¼ c. flour
1 tsp. baking powder
½ tsp. salt
2 eggs, beaten

1 c. milk
2 tblsp. salad oil
2 c. corn, cut from cob

Sift together dry ingredients.

Combine eggs, milk and oil. Mix into dry ingredients. Stir in corn.

Bake on preheated, lightly greased griddle as for pancakes. Serve with butter and honey or syrup. Makes 16 (4") pancakes.

SUPPERTIME CORN SCRAMBLE

Speedy, satisfying supper main dish featuring bacon, eggs and sweet corn

12 slices bacon, diced
2 c. corn, cut from cob
½ c. milk
12 eggs, slightly beaten

1½ tsp. salt
½ tsp. pepper
½ c. grated Cheddar cheese

Fry bacon in 10″ skillet until crisp. Drain, reserving fat. Return 3 tblsp. fat to skillet. Add corn and cook 8 to 10 minutes, or until golden brown. Stir in milk; simmer 2 to 3 minutes.

Add eggs, salt and pepper. Cook and stir until set. Serve topped with bacon and cheese. Makes 8 servings.

GOLDEN CORN FRY

Ideal way to fix sweet corn that has passed its flavor peak—good!

2 tblsp. butter or margarine	½ tsp. salt
3 c. corn, cut from cob	⅛ tsp. pepper
½ c. light cream	¼ c. grated Parmesan
2 tblsp. chopped chives	cheese
1 clove garlic, minced	

Melt butter in skillet. Add remaining ingredients, except cheese. Cover and simmer until corn is tender, 10 to 15 minutes. Stir in Parmesan cheese. Makes 5 to 6 servings.

CREAMED CORN

This old-country dish bakes in oven

8 ears corn	2 tsp. sugar (optional)
1 c. milk or dairy	⅛ tsp. pepper
half-and-half	2 tblsp. butter
1 tsp. salt	

Cut corn off cob about two-thirds the depth of the kernel. Scrape cob to remove the remaining corn, but not any of cob. (You'll have about 4 c.)

Combine corn with milk, salt, sugar and pepper. Place in greased 1½-qt. casserole. Dot with butter. Bake in moderate oven (350°) until corn is tender, 40 to 50 minutes. Serve in individual small bowls or sauce dishes. Makes 6 servings.

Tight little bouquets of curly parsley make an attractive impromptu centerpiece for a luncheon table.

QUICHE LORRAINE WITH CORN

American corn in France's cheese pie makes a wonderful snack or main dish

Unbaked 9" pie shell	1 tblsp. minced onion, or 1
½ c. milk	tsp. instant minced onion
1½ c. corn, cut from cob	1 tsp. seasoned salt
⅓ c. grated Swiss cheese	⅛ tsp. white pepper
5 eggs	5 slices crisp bacon,
1½ c. light cream	crumbled
½ tsp. sugar	Paprika

Chill pie shell in refrigerator until ready to use.

Add milk to corn and cook over low heat 15 minutes, stirring occasionally. Mix corn with cheese and spread in bottom of pie shell.

Beat eggs and add cream, sugar, onion, seasoned salt and pepper; pour over corn mixture. Sprinkle with bacon, then paprika.

Bake in hot oven (400°) 25 minutes; reduce heat to slow (325°) and bake 20 minutes longer, or until custard is set in center of pie. Remove from oven and let stand 5 minutes, then cut and serve hot. Makes 8 snack servings or 6 luncheon or dinner servings.

OVEN-ROASTED CORN

Let it rain—corn roasted in oven tastes like corn cooked over coals

12 ears sweet corn, including	Savory Butter (see Index)
husks	

Pull back husks on freshly picked sweet corn, leaving husks fastened to the stem end. Remove silk.

Spread kernels generously with Savory Butter. Pull husks around corn and tie a string snugly around ear, close to open end.

Lay corn ears in a large roasting pan. Bake in moderate oven (350°) 40 minutes. Remove strings; remove husks, if you wish, and serve. Makes 12 ears.

Eggplant

Eggplant, a native of China and India, is almost always a deep purple in color in this country; but white eggplant is common in Asia. While the vegetable is available the year around, July, August and September are the months of greatest abundance.

Select firm eggplants, heavy for their size, with smooth, shiny purple skin free from rust spots.

Allow 1 medium eggplant for 4 servings.

Store in a cool place, 50°. It will hold 4 to 5 days.

When ready to cook, use a vegetable peeler or knife to remove the skin if tough. If skin is tender, you need not peel. Cut in ½″ slices or ½ to 1″ strips.

To cook, dip in flour or fine bread or cracker crumbs, in an egg beaten with 2 tblsp. milk, and again in flour or crumbs. Cook in skillet containing hot fat until brown on one side, turn and brown on other side. Serve hot, sprinkled with salt and grated Parmesan cheese.

EGGPLANT PATTIES

*These brown, crisp-coated patties ranked high
with taste-testers*

1 medium eggplant	⅛ tsp. pepper
1 small onion, diced	1½ c. cracker crumbs
1 egg	Corn meal
½ tsp. salt	Shortening

Peel eggplant; slice ¼″ thick. Cook with onion in small amount of boiling salted water (½ tsp. salt to 1 c. water) until very tender. Drain; discard liquid. Cool.

Add egg and mix well, mashing eggplant. Add salt, pepper and cracker crumbs; mix.

Pat rounded tablespoonfuls of mixture into patties on board sprinkled heavily with corn meal; turn patties and press very thin.

Pan-fry quickly in generous amount of hot shortening until brown and crisp. Makes 8 servings.

EGGPLANT SIMPLICITY

Crush oyster crackers for the crumbs in this mushroom-eggplant casserole

1 medium eggplant, cut in cubes (4 c.)
2 eggs, beaten
1 (5⅓ oz.) can evaporated milk
1 can condensed cream of mushroom soup

1 tblsp. minced fresh or frozen onion
1 c. coarse cracker crumbs
Salt to taste
Coarse grind pepper
Paprika

Cook eggplant cubes (peeled or unpeeled) by steaming, if possible; or in boiling salted water in a covered saucepan 5 to 6 minutes. Drain and set aside.

Combine eggs, evaporated milk, soup and onion. Add eggplant; mix gently to avoid breaking up eggplant. Turn into greased 1½-qt. casserole; fold in crumbs. Taste and add salt if needed. Add a few grains pepper and sprinkle with a little paprika.

Bake in moderate oven (350°) 40 to 45 minutes, or until set. Makes 6 servings.

Golden Eggplant Casserole

In some kitchens eggplant is a wonder-what-to-do-with-it vegetable. In other homes it is considered one of the garden's best gifts. Certainly, its shiny blue-purple color contributes beauty to the garden. And it's easy to grow. If there's a problem, it's how to persuade the family unfamiliar with this vegetable how tasty it really is. This need not be a concern because eggplant can be the major ingredient in many superlative dishes.

We sent some eggplant recipes, developed in our Test Kitchens, to members of the FARM JOURNAL Family Test Group, asking them to make the dishes and report on how they and their families liked them.

The reactions to Golden Eggplant Casserole were cheers. Here are two comments, typical of many others: "I never knew eggplant could taste so good" . . . "our kids asked me to fix Golden Eggplant Casserole again."

Use the eggplant recipes in this cookbook and you'll convert tasters to its garden-fresh goodness.

GOLDEN EGGPLANT CASSEROLE

Cheese is the golden flavor touch

2½ c. cubed peeled eggplant	1 tblsp. melted butter or
18 saltine crackers,	margarine
crumbled	½ tsp. salt
½ c. shredded sharp cheese	⅛ tsp. pepper
¼ c. chopped celery	1 c. light cream, or
2 tblsp. chopped pimiento	evaporated milk

Cook eggplant in boiling salted water 10 minutes; drain. Combine with remaining ingredients.

Turn into 1-qt. casserole. Bake in moderate oven (350°) 45 minutes. Makes 6 servings.

EGGPLANT PARMIGIANA

Our taste-testers voted this the blue ribbon eggplant dish. Make and taste it once and you'll know why

2 medium eggplants (2 lbs.)	2 (8 oz.) cans tomato sauce
½ c. flour	(2 c.)
½ tsp. salt	1 (8 oz.) pkg. mozzarella
⅛ tsp. pepper	cheese, thinly sliced
¼ to ½ c. olive oil	½ c. grated Parmesan
	cheese

Peel eggplants and cut in ½" slices. Sprinkle with salt. Spread out in layer on board or paper toweling; let stand 20 minutes. Pat dry with paper toweling.

Dip each slice in mixture of flour, ½ tsp. salt and pepper.

Heat ¼ c. olive oil. Brown eggplant quickly. Cooking quickly over medium high heat will keep eggplant from absorbing a lot of oil. Drain on paper toweling. Continue cooking eggplant slices, adding more oil if necessary.

Pour ¼" tomato sauce in bottom of greased 2-qt. casserole. Top with one-third of eggplant slices, one-third of remaining tomato sauce and one-third of cheeses. Continue layers. Cover and bake in hot oven (400°) 20 minutes. Remove cover and continue baking 10 minutes. Makes 6 servings.

KENTUCKY-STYLE EGGPLANT

The stuffing does the seasoning

1 large eggplant, or 2 small
   ones
¼ c. chopped onion, or 1
   tblsp. instant minced
   onion
3 tblsp. chopped fresh
   parsley, or 2 tsp. parsley
   flakes
1 can condensed cream of
   mushroom soup

½ to 1 tsp. Worcestershire
   sauce
½ tsp. salt
⅛ tsp. pepper
1 c. (about) cracker crumbs
   (from round buttery
   crackers)
2 tblsp. butter or margarine

Remove stem end of eggplant and cut in half lengthwise.
Cut and remove inside pulp, being careful to leave about
¼" at outside of shell (use a curved grapefruit knife).
Cook pulp in just enough boiling salted water to avoid
scorching, about 10 minutes, or until barely tender. Drain
thoroughly.

Mix eggplant pulp with remaining ingredients, except
butter, using only enough cracker crumbs to make a filling
of stuffing consistency. Return filling to eggplant shells;
cover with cracker crumbs, dot with butter and put into a
baking dish with ½" boiling water.

Bake in moderate oven (375°) 45 minutes. Makes 6 to
8 servings.

EASY-BAKE EGGPLANT

*Really a snap to fix eggplant this way and it's
deliciously seasoned*

½ c. salad or olive oil
1 clove garlic, minced
1 tsp. salt
¼ tsp. pepper

½ tsp. basil leaves
1 large eggplant (or 2 small
   ones)

Combine oil, garlic, salt, pepper and basil in a cup. Let
stand while you fix eggplant.

Peel eggplant and cut in ½" crosswise slices. Spread in
an oiled 15½ × 10½ × 1" jelly roll pan, or other large
shallow pan.

Pour on the oil marinade, distributing it evenly over eggplant.

Bake in moderate oven (375°) 30 minutes, or until barely tender. Makes 6 to 8 servings.

If you've been peeling and chopping onions or garlic, rub your hands with salt and rinse under cold water. The odor on your hands will disappear like magic.

FRENCH FRIED EGGPLANT

Even people who are not eggplant fans praise it fixed this way

1 large eggplant	1 tblsp. salad oil
1 c. sifted flour	Fat or oil for deep-fat frying
1 tsp. onion salt	Salt
⅛ tsp. pepper	Grated Parmesan cheese
1 egg, slightly beaten	(optional)
1 c. milk	

Peel eggplant. Cut in ½" slices. Cut slices in ½" strips.

Mix together flour, onion salt and pepper. Combine egg, milk and oil; gradually add to flour mixture, beating until smooth.

Dip eggplant strips into batter. Drain well on wire rack. Fry in deep hot fat (375°) 2 to 3 minutes. Or fry in shallow fat (½" deep) from 2 to 5 minutes. Turn once.

Drain on paper toweling. Sprinkle with salt. Serve immediately with grated Parmesan cheese, if desired. Makes 6 servings.

EGGPLANT-CHEESE SANDWICHES

Cheese melts deliciously between eggplant slices while they brown

1 eggplant (1¼ lb.)	1 tblsp. water
1 c. grated sharp process cheese	1 c. cracker crumbs
2 eggs	¼ to ½ c. salad oil

Peel eggplant; cut in slices ¼" thick (makes 12 slices).

Lay on platter or large plate and sprinkle with salt; let stand 20 minutes. Pat dry on both sides with paper towel.

Combine cheese and 1 egg, beaten. Spoon over 6 eggplant slices, spreading almost to edge. Top with remaining slices.

Dip each eggplant sandwich in mixture of water and remaining egg, beaten, then in cracker crumbs. Fry in hot salad oil until brown and crisp on both sides. Serve immediately. Makes 6 sandwiches.

VARIATION

Eggplant Pockets: You can make Eggplant Pockets filled with cheese, the Italian way: Begin as above, to cut slices of eggplant ¼″ thick. Hold back on the first cut and each alternate cut you make, though—do not cut through eggplant—and you'll have a "pocket" between two slices. Put cheese-egg mixture in the pockets and proceed as for Eggplant-Cheese Sandwiches. If you like, you can substitute slices of mozzarella cheese for the grated process cheese mixed with egg.

Garlic

Garlic plays an important role in seasoning other vegetables and many dishes. It is available throughout the year.

Select plump, firm garlic with the outer skin, which encloses the cloves, unbroken.

Buy 1 root at a time.

Keep garlic in a cool dry place. If you put it in a covered jar, punch holes in the lid to provide ventilation.

When ready to use in cooking, break outer skin and remove the number of cloves needed. Peel garlic cloves (one way is to sandwich cloves in a paper towel, crush with the handle of a knife and remove meat from skin); mince or chop very fine. Or use a garlic press which will purée a whole unpeeled clove. Be cautious—garlic pushed through a press is much stronger than minced or chopped garlic, because the press releases all the volatile oils.

To add to vegetable-meat stews, impale whole, peeled garlic clove on a toothpick for easy removal after cooking.

Greens

Among vegetable leaves cooked for greens are beet tops, collards, dandelion, kale, mustard greens, young Swiss chard, turnip tops. (In spring, country people gather the leaves of many plants that grow on the farm or along the edge of woods. Every area has its favorites: In Maine, it's fiddleheads, the uncoiled fronds of ostrich ferns. Field cress is a great favorite in North Carolina and Virginia, lamb's quarter in the Midwest, wild mustard, narrow leaf dock, wild cabbage, cowslip, marsh marigold.) The market affords some kind of greens throughout the year.

Select fresh, green, tender leaves that have bright color and few wilted or yellow leaves.

Allow 2½ lbs. for 4 servings.

Rinse leaves in cool water, drain and place in the refrigerator crisper. Use very soon.

When ready to cook, cut off roots and remove any damaged leaves. Strip leaves from stiff, thick midribs. Wash leaves thoroughly in running cold water.

Cook, covered, in ¼ to ½" boiling salted water 10 to 20 minutes for dandelion greens, 3 to 10 minutes for Swiss chard, 7 to 10 minutes for mustard greens, 8 to 15 minutes for beet tops and turnip greens and 10 to 15 minutes for kale or collards. Or put greens in a colander over a pan of boiling water, cover and let the steam wilt and tenderize leaves. It takes from 10 to 25 minutes, depending on the kind of leaves. Slash through cooked greens a few times with kitchen shears or two knives. Season with salt, pepper, butter or margarine, bacon or ham drippings. Add vinegar or lemon juice if you like.

CREAMED KALE AND ONIONS

Good with pork chops

1½ lbs. kale, cleaned	3 tblsp. flour
2 lbs. small white onions, peeled (about 12)	1½ c. milk
¼ c. shortening	Seasonings

Cook kale in boiling salted water (enough to come halfway up on layer of the vegetable) until tender, about 15 minutes.

Cook onions in boiling salted water until tender, about 15 minutes.

Drain; combine vegetables.

Make white sauce of shortening, flour, milk and seasonings you prefer (salt, pepper, etc.). Pour over kale and onions. Serve hot. Makes 6 servings.

NOTE: You can use liquid drained from cooked vegetables for all or part of milk in making the sauce.

Swiss Chard with Cheese

When you look at a seed catalogue on a wintry day, cheering yourself by dreaming what to plant next spring in your garden, do consider Swiss chard. Its generous, tender, rich green leaves contain an exceedingly bountiful supply of vitamins and minerals. What may appeal more to your family is this good-for-you vegetable's good taste. Milder or more delicate than spinach, due to a lower acid content, the flavor surprises and delights many people unfamiliar with chard. One of our testers, eating Swiss Chard with Cheese, exclaimed: "I've never tasted spinach half as good as this."

Another merit of this vegetable is that the plants bear their large leaves throughout the summer if you make frequent cuttings. You can gather chard long after the spinach is gone from your garden.

SWISS CHARD WITH CHEESE

*Once you team chard with cheese they'll go steady
in your kitchen*

2 lbs. Swiss chard	½ lb. diced pasteurized
2 tblsp. butter or margarine	process cheese
2 tblsp. flour	½ c. bread crumbs
1 tsp. salt	2 tblsp. melted butter
½ c. milk	

Cut stalks from washed chard leaves in 1″ pieces. Place in bottom of large kettle; cover with boiling salted water

(½ tsp. salt to 2 c. water). Cover; cook 5 minutes. Add torn leaves and continue cooking until tender, about 5 minutes. Drain thoroughly in colander, pressing out liquid. You should have 5 c. chard.

Meanwhile, melt butter. Blend in flour and salt. Add milk and cook, stirring constantly, until mixture comes to a boil. Add cheese, stirring until cheese is melted and blended. Place chard in greased 2-qt. casserole. Stir in sauce.

Toss crumbs with melted butter; sprinkle over casserole. Bake in moderate oven (350°) until bubbly, about 25 minutes. Makes 6 servings.

SWISS CHARD CASSEROLE

The Swiss chard and chicken flavors complement each other beautifully

2 lbs. Swiss chard	⅛ tsp. pepper
1 can condensed cream of	1½ c. herb-seasoned
chicken soup	croutons
½ tsp. salt	3 tblsp. melted butter

Cut stalks from washed chard in 1″ pieces. Cook in boiling salted water in large kettle 5 minutes (½ tsp. salt to 2 c. water). Tear leaves, add to kettle and continue cooking until tender. Drain thoroughly. (You'll have 5 c. chard.)

Combine with undiluted soup, salt and pepper in greased 2-qt. casserole.

Toss croutons in melted butter. Sprinkle on top of chard. Bake in moderate oven (350°) 25 minutes. Makes 6 servings.

Kohlrabi

Kohlrabi has a delicate turnip-like flavor and can be cooked in the same ways as turnips. It is available throughout summer and autumn, but its peak season is June and July.

Select small to medium bulbs with fresh green leaves and with a rind that you can pierce easily with a fingernail. Avoid deeply scarred or blemished bulbs.

Allow 1 medium bulb for each person.

Remove tops to store; keep bulbs in a cool, moist place or in the refrigerator crisper. Kohlrabi holds several days.

When ready to cook, peel, wash and cut bulbs into cubes, slices or strips.

Cook, covered, in 1″ boiling salted water until tender, 12 to 30 minutes. (One variety of kohlrabi has bulbs the size of a grapefruit, which, when mature, contain some woody fiber. Put this kohlrabi through a food mill after cooking to remove the fiber.) Drain and season with salt, pepper and butter or margarine. If you like, sprinkle lightly with lemon juice or vinegar.

KOHLRABI IN CREAM SAUCE

Select small to medium bulbs with fresh green leaves to make this

1 qt. cubed peeled kohlrabi bulbs (4 to 6)	3 tblsp. flour
	½ c. milk
Kohlrabi leaves	Salt and pepper to taste
2 tblsp. butter or margarine	

Cook kohlrabi cubes in boiling salted water until tender, 15 to 20 minutes.

Cook the leaves in boiling salted water in another pan, discarding any that appear old and tough, for 20 minutes.

Drain kohlrabi cubes, reserving ½ c. liquid. Drain greens and chop coarsely (use blender, if available).

In another saucepan, melt butter, add flour and cook, stirring in reserved vegetable liquid and milk gradually. When thickened, add kohlrabi cubes and greens. Check for seasonings, adding more salt, if needed, and pepper. Makes 4 to 6 servings.

NOTE: Use 2 tblsp. flour for sauce when leaves are not used (they tend to thin the sauce).

Leeks

Many people are confused about the differences between leeks, shallots and green onions—all members of the onion family. They have similarities but do not look or taste the same. Leeks are the most delicate and least pungent; they have a sweet flavor. They look like large green onions, with a long, thick, blanched neck about ½ to 1½" in diameter, and only a slight bulb formation at the base. Their leaves are broad, flat and dark gray-green.

Shallots are small bulbs; under the dry reddish-brown outer skin you'll find two or three separate cloves with a purplish skin. Flavor is somewhere between that of green onions and garlic, but mild. They are often specified in French recipes, but are not easily available in U.S. stores. Green onions may be substituted for shallots in recipes (and vice versa).

You can find leeks in some markets the year around, but the peak season extends from October to June. They are sold in bunches.

Select leeks with a white neck and fresh-looking dark green tops.

Allow 2 bunches for 4 servings.

Wrap in plastic bag and store in refrigerator crisper. They will keep several days.

When ready to cook, cut off green tops and roots, wash white part, separating layers and letting water run between them to remove all traces of dirt (leeks tend to be very gritty).

Cook, covered, in chicken broth or water until tender, 15 to 20 minutes; drain. Season with salt, pepper and butter or margarine.

Mushrooms

Mushrooms grow in houses, cellars and caves in many states, although Pennsylvania produces the largest amounts. Mushrooms are available the year around. They have three parts: the stem, the cap, which is the wide portion at the top, and the gills or rows of paper-thin tissues under the cap.

Select young, plump mushrooms that are small to medium in size, with caps closed around the stem or only moderately opened with pink or light tan gills. Creamy white caps, free from spots, are desirable, although mushrooms grown in some regions have a light brown color, which is satisfactory.

Allow 1 lb. mushrooms for 6 servings.

Keep mushrooms on a shallow tray or rack on refrigerator shelf where cold air can move freely around them. Lay a moistened paper towel over mushrooms. Moisten towel each day; mushrooms will hold for several days. As long as they feel dry and firm, they are perfectly fresh.

Or, pile mushrooms loosely into a tall plastic container; refrigerate uncovered, so air can circulate.

When ready to cook, wash mushrooms gently and quickly under a light stream of cold water, wiping dry immediately—never let mushrooms soak in water. Or simply wipe them off with a paper towel dipped in water containing a few drops of lemon juice—the lemon juice helps keep them white. Do not peel mushrooms if fresh and tender. Cut a thin slice off the end of stem and use the remainder of the mushroom. To slice, cut parallel with the stem.

Mushrooms usually are cooked in a little butter or margarine instead of water (see recipe that follows for Sautéed Mushrooms). If you want to cook them ahead for later use, here are directions from the American Mushroom Institute:

Put ¼ c. water into a small saucepan along wtih 1 tblsp. lemon juice, a bit of lemon peel and a dash of salt. Add ½ lb. whole or quartered mushrooms and heat just until bubbles form around the edge—do not boil. Reduce heat to simmer and cover pan. Simmer about 5 minutes. Cool and store in refrigerator. Serve with other vegetables, such as peas, and with steaks, chops and chicken.

Sautéed Mushrooms

If you want to taste mushrooms at their best, follow our directions to the letter. The American Mushroom Institute cautions, do not overcook mushrooms. It should take you only 3 to 4 minutes to sauté sliced mushrooms. Cooking them quickly, over high heat, helps them retain their moisture; this is what keeps them from shrinking and makes them so tender and delicious.

Use a big skillet, or do the mushrooms in two batches. You must not crowd the mushrooms in the pan, else they'll steam instead of brown. When they go into the pan, the mushrooms must be dry and the butter very hot. Olive oil added with the butter helps keep the butter from burning while you get it hot enough.

SAUTÉED MUSHROOMS

A delicacy to serve with steak

2 tblsp. butter	½ tsp. lemon juice
1 tblsp. olive oil	¼ tsp. seasoned salt
½ lb. mushrooms, left whole if small, quartered or sliced	Dash pepper

Put butter and oil in a large skillet over high heat. Butter will foam. When foam begins to subside, butter is hot enough. Add mushrooms (they should be dry). Toss them and shake the pan, or keep them moving with a wooden spoon or spatula until lightly browned, about 4 minutes. Remove from heat.

Sprinkle with lemon juice, seasoned salt and pepper. Toss to distribute seasonings. Serve as accompaniment to broiled steak or add to 1 (10 oz.) pkg. frozen peas, cooked and buttered. Makes 2 to 3 servings with steak, 4 servings with peas.

NOTE: Make this recipe twice instead of doubling it, to get more servings.

MUSHROOMS BRAISED IN BUTTER

Midwesterners like them this way

¼ c. butter or margarine	1 tsp. lemon juice
2 tblsp. minced onion	½ tsp. seasoned salt
1 lb. mushrooms	⅛ tsp. pepper

Melt butter in large skillet; add onion and cook over low heat until tender, not browned.

Add mushrooms, cut through caps and stems in thick lengthwise slices; cover and cook over medium heat 10 minutes, stirring occasionally. Turn off heat and let stand, covered, about 5 minutes, or until mushrooms absorb pan juices.

Sprinkle with lemon juice, seasoned salt and pepper and toss to distribute seasonings. Serve as accompaniment to broiled steak or add to 2 (10 oz.) pkgs. frozen green beans or peas, cooked and buttered. Makes 5 to 6 servings with steak, 8 servings with vegetables.

Mushrooms in Cream: Omit lemon juice and stir in ⅓ c. dairy half-and-half or light cream. Serve on buttered toast. Makes 5 to 6 servings.

BROILED MUSHROOMS

Allow 3 broiled mushrooms per person; serve with steak or vegetables

18 fresh mushrooms	**Pepper**
¼ c. butter or margarine	**Lemon juice**
Salt	

Remove stems from mushrooms (see Note).

Place mushroom caps, tops down, in shallow baking pan. In cavities of upturned mushrooms place butter (about ½ tsp. for each mushroom cap) and sprinkle with salt, pepper and lemon juice. Brush with melted butter and broil 6 to 8 minutes. Serve with steak or on plate as a vegetable. Makes 6 servings.

NOTE: Save stems from mushrooms to slice crosswise and cook in butter or margarine, as for Sautéed Mushrooms (see Index), to add to cooked vegetables, such as peas or green beans.

Okra

Okra, a special favorite in Carolina Low Country and throughout the South, is the immature pod of the okra plant. It's available the year around with the peak season from June through November.

Select crisp, tender, small or medium-size pods with tips that bend under light pressure from the finger. Choose pods free from blemishes.

Allow 1 lb. for 4 servings.

Store in a cool, moist place (50°) or in refrigerator crisper.

When ready to cook, wash; do not cut off stems or tips of small pods. Larger pods should be sliced thickly.

Cook in ½″ boiling salted water, uncovered, for 5 minutes; then cover and cook 5 minutes longer. Season with salt, pepper and butter or margarine. Add a little vinegar, lemon juice or French dressing, or combine with seasoned cooked tomatoes.

Onions

Dry Onions: Like green onions, the dry ones are available throughout the year. They boost the flavors of many foods and naturally rate as kitchen friends.

Select onions that are bright, clean, hard and well shaped, with dry skins and small necks. Avoid onions with blemishes or green sunburned patches.

Allow 1½ lbs. for 4 servings.

When ready to cook, pour boiling water over onions; rinse in cold water. Slit skin with knife from stem to root end and remove one or two layers of skin. Leave whole, quarter or slice and separate into rings. If left whole, cut a slice from one side so onion will not roll.

Cook, uncovered, in enough boiling salted water to cover onions. Small onions cook in 5 to 20 minutes, larger ones in 20 to 30 minutes and slices in 10 minutes. Drain and season with salt, pepper and butter or margarine or thin cream and, if you like, toss in a little grated Romano cheese.

You'll find dry onions ranging in size from small to large and including white, yellow and red varieties. Most of the dry onions grown in the United States are either the yellow varieties, with pungent flavor, or the small white onions, which are far more delicate for cooking—your choice for creamed onions or in stews or vegetable combinations. Some other commonly used onions are:

Bermuda: This is a big onion, imported, with a somewhat flattened shape and a yellow skin. It has a mild, delicate flavor.

Italian: This red onion, an import, is mild and sweet, which makes it a good choice for salads. The red rings are also attractive as a garnish.

Pearl: This is a very small round white onion about the size of a large pea. It is usually pickled and used as a garnish.

Spanish: A large, fleshy yellow-skinned onion, it usually has a mild flavor.

Green Onions: There are many varieties of green onions (also called scallions) and some of them are available around the year. The peak months are May through August.

Select onions with crisp, green tops with 2 to 3″ of well-blanched white medium-sized roots.

Allow 2 bunches for 4 servings.

Wrap onions in plastic bag and store in refrigerator crisper. They will hold several days.

When ready to cook, wash well, remove any loose layers of skin and cut off tops, leaving about 3″ of stem.

Cook, covered, in boiling salted water until barely tender, 8 to 10 minutes. Drain and season with salt, pepper and butter or margarine.

You may substitute green onions in recipes calling for shallots.

PANNED GREEN ONIONS

These fried onions add the taste and look of spring to meat platters

30 green onions	½ tsp. salt
¼ c. butter	⅛ tsp. pepper

Partially cut off tops of onions, leaving onions about 4″ long. Peel off tough layers and wash. Drain on paper toweling.

Melt butter in skillet; add onions and cook over medium heat until soft, turning occasionally. Sprinkle with salt and pepper. Serve as a garnish with thick broiled hamburgers or steak. Makes 6 servings.

ONION PIE
(Zwiebel Kuchen)

A main-dish pie of German origin—a great
FARM JOURNAL favorite

Pastry for baked 10" shell:

1½ c. sifted flour
¾ tsp. salt
1½ tsp. caraway seeds

½ c. shortening
2 to 3 tblsp. water

Filling:

3 c. thinly sliced peeled
  onions
3 tblsp. melted butter,
  margarine or fat
½ c. milk

1½ c. dairy sour cream
1 tsp. salt
2 eggs, well beaten
3 tblsp. flour
Bacon slices

Combine flour, salt and caraway seeds. Add shortening; cut into flour until mixture resembles coarse corn meal.

Stir water in lightly with fork until mixture adheres and follows fork around bowl.

Turn onto floured board; roll to ⅛" thickness. Fit into 10" pie pan.

Bake in hot oven (425°) 10 minutes, or until lightly browned.

Cook onions in fat until lightly browned. Spoon into pastry shell.

Add milk, 1¼ c. sour cream and salt to eggs.

Blend flour with ¼ c. sour cream. Combine with egg mixture; pour over onion mixture.

Bake in slow oven (325°) 30 minutes, or until firm in center.

Garnish with slices of crisp-fried bacon. Makes 8 servings.

FRENCH ONIONS AND RICE

Absolutely delicious with poultry

¼ c. long grain rice
2 qts. boiling water
1 tsp. salt
¼ c. butter or margarine
4 c. thinly sliced large white
  or yellow onions (about 3)

½ tsp. salt
⅛ tsp. paprika
2 tblsp. grated Parmesan
  cheese

Drop rice into rapidly boiling water with 1 tsp. salt added; boil uncovered 5 minutes; drain at once.

Melt butter in 2-qt. casserole in oven; stir in onions.

Add ½ tsp. salt and stir onions in butter until nicely yellowed and coated. Then add rice and stir to distribute evenly. Cover and bake in slow oven (325°) 1 hour. Sprinkle with paprika and cheese. Makes 8 servings.

NOTE: Large onions are easier to slice if first cut in halves lengthwise and then placed on a flat surface and sliced. (Cut a thick slice from top and bottom, enough to remove top and root growth; save this for seasoning another dish.)

ONION CUSTARD

Dill weed seasons this rich dish that's good with chicken or turkey

2 slices bacon	⅓ c. water
3 c. sliced and quartered onions	1 tsp. salt
	⅛ tsp. pepper
1 c. water	1 tsp. crushed dill weed or dill seeds
2 eggs	
1 (13 oz.) can evaporated milk (1⅔ c.)	

Fry bacon; remove from skillet and crumble. Pour bacon fat from skillet. Add onions and 1 c. water; cook 10 minutes; drain.

In mixing bowl, combine remaining ingredients; stir in bacon and onions.

Pour into 1½-qt. casserole. Set in pan of water. Bake in moderate oven (375°) 35 to 40 minutes, or until knife inserted halfway between edge and center comes out clean. Makes 6 servings.

Parsley

Parsley ranks at the top of vegetables in vitamin A wealth. While most people consider it a garnish, it deserves to be eaten on two counts. It tastes good and it *is* a food. It's almost always available.

Select crisp, fresh, bright green leaves for both curly and plain leaf types. You can freshen wilted parsley somewhat by cutting off stem ends and placing stems in cold water.

Store in plastic bag in refrigerator crisper. It will keep at least a week.

Prepare and use as recipes direct. Usually you chop parsley. If you need a lot of it, bunch it tight together, lay it on a chopping board and chop with a large knife. If you need only a sprinkling, snip the leaves with scissors.

Parsnips

Although parsnips are available to some extent throughout the year, they are primarily a winter vegetable because their flavors sweeten after exposure to cold temperatures. The peak season is January, February and March. Home gardeners in New England leave them in the ground until spring. After the ground thaws they dig their parsnips, which are wonderfully sweet.

Select parsnips of small to medium width that are smooth, firm, well shaped and free from decay. Large parsnips sometimes are woody.

Allow 1½ lbs. for 4 servings.

If you buy parsnips in cellophane wrapping, leave them wrapped; otherwise wrap them in plastic bag and store them in refrigerator crisper. If kept moist, they hold 1 to 2 weeks. Sometimes storage parsnips, also white turnips and rutabagas, are coated with a thin layer of paraffin to prevent loss of moisture.

When ready to cook, scrape or peel skin (and paraffin) with vegetable peeler. Leave whole, or cut in half or in slices. Cut out core. Cook covered in boiling salted water to cover until tender, 10 to 15 minutes for slices, 20 minutes for halves and 30 to 40 minutes for whole parsnips. If cooked whole, remove cores after cooking. Drain and season with salt, pepper and butter or margarine. Or brown lightly in butter or bacon drippings.

GLAZED PARSNIPS

Honey-orange glazed parsnips tempt appetites
with a gourmet flavor

3 c. diagonally sliced (½″)	2 tblsp. butter
parsnips	1 tblsp. honey
¾ c. water	¼ c. orange juice
½ tsp. salt	1 tsp. grated orange peel

Cook parsnips in water and salt until tender, about 10 minutes. Drain and remove from saucepan.

Heat remaining ingredients together in saucepan. Combine with parsnips. Serve hot. Makes 6 servings.

PARSNIP FRITTERS

Parsnips couldn't be better any other way—truly delicious and different

4 to 5 medium parsnips	⅛ tsp. salt
½ c. milk	Flour
1 egg	Fat or oil for deep-fat frying
½ tsp. baking powder	

Scrape parsnips clean, cut in lengthwise slices and cook in boiling salted water until tender. Drain.

Combine remaining ingredients, adding enough flour to make a batter the consistency of griddle cakes.

Dip parsnips in batter; fry in deep hot fat (370° to 390°) until golden brown. Makes 6 servings.

PARSNIPS COUNTRY-STYLE

If you're fond of parsnips, you'll like these golden brown patties

8 to 10 medium parsnips	⅛ tsp. pepper
(2 lbs.)	1 egg, beaten
½ tsp. onion salt	⅓ c. fine bread crumbs
½ tsp. salt	2 tblsp. butter or margarine

Peel parsnips. Cut in halves crosswise. Then halve or quarter lengthwise to make strips about the same size. Cook in boiling salted water until tender. Remove cores if woody.

Mash parsnips. Beat in seasonings and egg. Chill well.

Make 6 patties. Coat with bread crumbs. Cook patties on both sides in melted butter until golden brown. Makes 6 servings.

PARSNIP PATTIES

What could be better with roast beef? You'll want to double this one

6 medium parsnips, scrubbed	**1½ tsp. salt**
½ c. light cream	**Pepper**
2 tblsp. flour	**Butter or fat**

Cook parsnips in a little boiling salted water until tender. Cool, peel and mash. (If parsnips have woody cores, cut in halves lengthwise and strip out the tough fibers.) Should make 2 cups.

Mix cream with flour until smooth; add salt and pepper. Stir into parsnips; shape into 8 patties.

Brown slowly in small amount of butter for a nice crisp crust. Makes 4 to 5 servings.

ORANGE-BUTTERED PARSNIPS

Orange juice glamorizes this old-time dish and improves its taste

8 to 10 medium parsnips	**⅛ tsp. pepper**
2 tblsp. butter	**¼ c. orange juice**
⅓ c. brown sugar	**1 tsp. grated orange peel**
½ tsp. salt	

Wash and peel parsnips. Cook in boiling salted water until tender. Cut in sticks 3″ long and about ¼″ thick, discarding center core if woody.

Melt butter in saucepan; blend in remaining ingredients. Heat to boiling. Add parsnips and simmer until parsnips are hot, stirring occasionally to coat each parsnip with orange-sugar mixture. Makes 6 servings.

Peas, Green

June is the time of roses and garden peas in the Midwest and it's difficult to determine which are more anticipated and enjoyed, the flowers or vegetables. Peas come from home gardens in some areas as early as April and from commercial fields throughout the year. The peak months are from the last half of March through June.

Select filled, fresh, bright green pods. Farmers judge freshness by gently rubbing a handful of peas between their hands. If they squeak, they say the peas are fresh.

Allow 3 lbs. for 4 servings.

Store peas unshelled in the refrigerator crisper, but use quickly.

When ready to cook, wash pods and shell.

Cook peas, covered, in 1" boiling salted water with 1 tsp. sugar and 2 or 3 empty pods added, until tender, 8 to 10 minutes. Drain and discard cooked pods, season with salt, pepper and butter or margarine, or with heated cream.

GREEN PEAS LORRAINE

Peas cooked by the best French chefs cannot surpass this recipe

3 tblsp. butter	½ tsp. salt
⅓ c. water	⅛ tsp. pepper
2 c. shelled fresh peas (about 2 lbs. in pods)	¼ tsp. ground nutmeg (optional)
2 tblsp. finely chopped onion	4 to 6 outside lettuce leaves, finely shredded
1 tblsp. finely chopped fresh parsley	½ c. light cream
1 tsp. sugar	

Heat butter, water and peas together. Add onion, parsley, sugar and seasonings. Cover and simmer until peas are almost tender.

Stir in lettuce. Continue cooking 5 minutes longer. Blend in cream. Heat and serve. Makes 5 to 6 servings.

NOTE: You can substitute frozen peas for the fresh vegetable.

NEW PEAS IN CREAM

A FARM JOURNAL master recipe

4 c. shelled peas	Water
2 tsp. sugar	2 tblsp. butter
2 tsp. salt	½ tsp. pepper
Pea pods	1 c. light cream
1 small green onion with top, chopped	

Cook peas with sugar, salt, 5 or 6 pea pods, onion and enough water to cover for 10 to 15 minutes, or until just tender (water should almost evaporate). Add butter and hold over heat to melt. Add pepper and cream. Heat but do not cook. Makes 6 to 8 servings.

NEW PEAS, 12 WAYS

With Mint: Cook 2 or 3 fresh mint leaves with the peas.

With Mint Jelly: Omit sugar and add 3 to 4 tblsp. mint jelly to peas with butter. Hold over heat to melt. Add pepper and cream and heat to warm.

With Pimiento: Add ¼ c. chopped pimiento to peas just before adding cream.

With Sour Cream and Chives: Add 3 tblsp. chopped chives to peas before buttering. Then add 1 c. dairy sour cream instead of light cream and heat to warm; do not cook.

With Potatoes: Cook 12 small new peeled whole potatoes until just tender. Mix with peas before adding cream.

With Mushrooms: Sauté 1 c. drained canned sliced mushrooms in 1 tblsp. butter. Mix with peas before adding cream.

With Onions: Cook 1 c. sliced small green onions (use tops, too), until just tender. Add to peas before buttering.

With Carrots: Cook 1½ c. thinly sliced carrots until just tender. Add to peas before buttering.

With Celery: Cook ¼ c. chopped celery in small amount of water until tender. Add to peas before buttering.

With Bacon: Sprinkle ½ c. finely crumbled bacon over top of peas just before serving.

With Ham: Cut ham slices (boiled or baked) in thin strips 1″ in length. Mix with peas just before serving.

With Lettuce Leaves: Line saucepan with several leaves of leaf lettuce, wet from washing. In center place peas, salt, pepper, sugar, tops of small green onions and 3 or 4 tblsp. water. Cover and cook until tender. Discard lettuce; season peas with cream.

Pattypans and Peas: *Cook small, young whole pattypan*

squash (cymlings) in boiling salted water until tender. Drain and scoop out a little pulp from the center. Fill with buttered peas. Serve as an edible garnish on a meat platter.

PEAS IN PATTY SHELLS

Patty shells give creamed peas a setting—serve them at your next party

¼ c. chopped green onion	1 c. milk
1 tblsp. butter or margarine	2 tsp. lemon juice
½ tsp. sugar	2 c. cooked peas, fresh or
2 tblsp. flour	frozen
½ tsp. salt	12 (2¾") patty shells (or 12
⅛ tsp. pepper	slices toast)
1 c. dairy half-and-half	

Cook onion in butter until golden. Combine sugar and flour and add to onion mixture; add salt and pepper, stirring to mix.

Add half-and-half and milk, and stir over low heat until mixture thickens. Add lemon juice and peas.

Serve in patty shells, or oven crisp toast. Makes enough to fill 12 patty shells.

VARIATION

Peas with Dairy Sour Cream: Substitute dairy sour cream for half-and-half.

Chinese-Style Pod Peas

More home gardeners are getting to know edible pod peas—and liking them. Look in your seed catalogues and consider giving at least a row or two in your garden to this vegetable, which commands a premium price in Chinese restaurants.

You don't have to shell them, and both the peas and their pods are very tasty if you don't let the vegetable mature too long in the garden. Gather and use them while the peas in the pods are still tiny, recommends a Wisconsin farm gardener.

Chinese-Style Pea Pods are a fine accompaniment for pork and chicken. They are favorites in meals composed of American versions of Chinese dishes, but it would be a pity to limit them to restaurant meals.

Soy sauce helps to season the vegetable and to make it special. If you don't add this salty sauce, be sure to check the seasonings before serving the peas—you will need more salt.

CHINESE-STYLE PEA PODS

Give interest and color to your meal by featuring these edible pod peas

4 green onions with tops, chopped	**½ tsp. salt**
¼ c. salad oil	**1 c. chicken stock**
4 c. fresh pea pods (1 lb.), or 2 (7 oz.) pkgs. frozen Chinese pea pods	**1 tblsp. cornstarch, mixed with an additional ¼ c. chicken stock**
2 (5 oz.) cans water chestnuts, drained and sliced	**1 to 2 tblsp. soy sauce (optional)**

Cook green onions in oil in skillet 2 minutes. Add peas and water chestnuts. Cook, stirring, another 2 minutes.

Add remaining ingredients. Cook, stirring until mixture comes to a boil and is transparent. Simmer briefly until pea pods are barely tender—still crispy. Makes 6 servings.

Chinese Peas and Fried Rice: *In a skillet, cook a package of frozen fried rice according to package directions. Two or three minutes before serving, add fresh Chinese-style pod peas, cover and steam until pods are tender-crisp.*

Peppers, Green

These peppers, which Hoosiers call Mangoes, are sweet, rather than hot; they are available throughout the year, with the peak supply in late summer. (Some fully mature peppers turn a brilliant red in color. They will be a bit sweeter than green peppers, but delicious.)

Select peppers which are thick-fleshed, medium to dark green in color and glossy, heavy for their size. Choose those with firm walls.

Allow 1 pepper per serving unless they are unusually large.

Hold them in a cool, moist place or in the refrigerator crisper. They will hold for a week or two.

When ready to cook, wash, cut slice from top or stem end and remove seeds and fibrous portion. Wash inside and out and cut as recipe directs. Leave whole to stuff and bake (wide, chunky peppers are best for stuffing). Parboil peppers 5 minutes and drain before stuffing. Drop slices, rings or strips in boiling salted water to cover and cook 3 to 5 minutes. Drain, season with salt, pepper and butter. (Or cook raw slices or strips in a little butter or margarine until tender and crispy.)

ITALIAN ROASTED PEPPERS

Broil both mature red and green peppers
for a gorgeous color effect

6 large green peppers	½ tsp. salt
⅓ c. salad oil	⅛ tsp. pepper
½ tsp. orégano leaves	1 large clove garlic, sliced

Wash large, thick-fleshed peppers; dry and cut stems so peppers can be turned and broiled on all sides. Place in pan 5″ from broiler heat. Keep turning with tongs as heat turns peppers from green to brown and then to black; this takes 15 to 18 minutes (do not let burn). The peppers will be dark and the skin wrinkled.

Remove from oven; place peppers in a paper bag, close and let stand 5 minutes. Steam forms and loosens the skins.

Peel skins from peppers and cut in 1″ strips. Place in bowl.

Meanwhile, combine remaining ingredients; pour over pepper strips and toss to mix well. Let stand at least 2 hours (they will keep in refrigerator at least 1 week). Leave a few slices garlic in the bowl; discard remaining garlic.

Toss just before serving. Sprinkle with chopped parsley and serve as a relish with hot or cold meats, or add to sandwiches made with luncheon meats. Makes 4 servings when used as a dinner accompaniment.

NOTE: These peppers are a delicious addition to antipasto plates.

FRIED PEPPERS WITH EGGS

*Try this Italian special for a main dish or for a
sandwich filling*

4 large green peppers	¼ tsp. pepper
3 tblsp. salad oil	4 eggs
½ tsp. salt	¼ tsp. salt
¼ tsp. garlic salt	1 tblsp. water

Wash peppers, cut off stem ends and remove seeds. Cut
in strips.

Add peppers to heated oil in skillet and cook over medium heat, stirring with a fork, until they are heated. Do
not let peppers brown.

Sprinkle with ½ tsp. salt, garlic salt and pepper. Lower
heat; cover and cook 3 to 5 minutes, stirring occasionally.
Uncover, increase heat to medium and cook to desired
tenderness. For best flavor, do not overcook.

Beat eggs, ¼ tsp. salt and water together slightly. Pour
over peppers in skillet; do not stir mixture until eggs start
to set; then, with fork or spatula, move mixture to allow
all liquid to set. Do not let eggs overcook. Turn onto warm
platter. Makes 4 main dish servings, or enough for 6
sandwiches.

LAYERED STUFFED PEPPERS

*The stuffing bakes between bright-colored pepper halves—
truly delicious*

8 large red peppers	¼ tsp. finely chopped garlic
6 c. day-old bread crumbs	1 tblsp. chopped parsley
⅓ c. salad oil	1 (4½ oz.) can deviled ham
¼ tsp. salt	Salad oil
⅛ tsp. pepper	⅛ tsp. salt
½ tsp. orégano leaves	

Select thick-fleshed peppers that have turned red when
they matured, or use green peppers. Fix as for Italian
Roasted Peppers (see Index), except do not cut in strips;
cut peppers in halves after roasting.

Put bread crumbs in a bowl; add ⅓ c. salad oil, ¼ tsp.

salt, pepper, orégano, garlic and parsley. Mix thoroughly to distribute oil and garlic with the crumbs.

Grease bottom of 11¾ × 7½" baking dish. Place a layer of 4 peppers, overlapping, to cover bottom of dish. Place half the bread stuffing over peppers; spread evenly to corners. Dot with deviled ham, cut in pieces. Lay other half of stuffing over top; spread evenly to corners. Lay remaining pepper halves over stuffing to cover it. Brush lightly with oil and sprinkle with ⅛ tsp. salt.

Bake in moderate oven (350°) 25 minutes, or until heated throughout. Serve for supper or a luncheon main dish. Cut into squares to make 6 servings.

NOTE: You can use other meats instead of deviled ham. Try cooked ham, leftover meat loaf or meatballs, and roasted meats. Cut meat in small pieces (about 1 to 1½ c.), season and arrange between layers of stuffing.

MACARONI IN GREEN CUPS

Sour cream and green peppers do something good for macaroni and cheese

6 large green peppers	½ tsp. salt
1 (8 oz.) pkg. elbow macaroni, cooked	¼ tsp. pepper
	⅛ tsp. dry mustard
1 c. dairy sour cream	2¼ c. grated sharp process cheese
1 tblsp. grated onion	

Cut tops off peppers; remove and discard seeds and membrane. Cook in boiling salted water 5 minutes. Drain and stand upright in muffin-pan cups.

Combine macaroni, sour cream, onion, salt, pepper, mustard and 2 c. cheese. Spoon into green peppers. Top with remaining ¼ c. cheese.

Bake in moderate oven (350°) 25 minutes. Makes 6 servings.

Potatoes

Sweet Potatoes: The varieties of sweet potatoes with a yellowish, fawn-colored skin have pale-colored flesh and are dry and mealy when cooked. Yams, another variety of sweet potato, are very sweet and moist. They have a reddish skin and the flesh is orange in color. (True yams grow on a tropical vine and are not produced in the United States.) The production of the light-colored sweet potatoes has dwindled, while that of yams has increased. Some kind of sweet potato is available most of the year, but they are in greatest supply from September through winter.

Select well-shaped, firm sweet potatoes with smooth, bright, uniformly colored skin free from signs of decay.

Allow 1½ to 2 lbs. for 4 servings (3 medium to 1 lb.).

Store only in small quantities for sweet potatoes are highly perishable. Never put them in the refrigerator.

When ready to cook, scrub well.

Cook, without peeling, in 1″ boiling salted water, covered, until tender, 30 to 35 minutes. Drain, spread out to cool enough to peel. Season as recipe directs. Brown sugar, syrup, salt, pepper and butter or margarine are favorite seasonings. Cooked sweet potatoes often are mashed and seasoned.

SWEET POTATO PIE

Why look further for the best sweet potato dish to team with roast pork?

3 lbs. sweet potatoes (8 to 9 medium)	¾ tsp. salt
3 tblsp. light cream	¾ c. chopped dates or pineapple
¼ tsp. ground cinnamon	Marshmallows

Cook sweet potatoes until tender; peel and mash while hot. Add cream, seasonings and dates; mix well.

Put in shallow casserole or 10″ pie pan; top with marshmallows. Bake in moderate oven (350°) just until brown, about 15 to 20 minutes. Makes 8 to 10 servings.

STUFFED BAKED SWEET POTATOES

You can stuff and refrigerate these a few hours before baking them

6 medium sweet potatoes	1 (8 oz.) can crushed pineapple
3 tblsp. butter	½ c. chopped pecans
½ c. orange juice	
1 tsp. salt	

Bake scrubbed sweet potatoes in moderate oven (375°) until tender, 45 minutes to 1 hour. Cut strip off top of each potato. Spoon potato out of shell. Combine with butter, orange juice and salt, and whip.

Stir in pineapple. Spoon back into sweet potato shells. Sprinkle with nuts. Bake in moderate oven (375°) until thoroughly hot, about 12 minutes. Makes 6 servings.

Fluffy Sweet Potatoes: *Fold a little whipped cream into the mashed potatoes and season with salt and a touch of nutmeg or cinnamon.*

BAKED SWEET POTATOES WITH ORANGE MARMALADE

Bake these sweets alongside your pork roast—
they're good oven partners

8 medium sweet potatoes, cooked and peeled	1 c. light cream or evaporated milk
¼ c. brown sugar	½ c. orange marmalade
½ tsp. salt	16 large marshmallows

Cut potatoes in 1″ slices. Place in greased 13 × 9 × 2″ pan. Sprinkle with brown sugar and salt. Pour cream over. Bake in moderate oven (350°) 45 minutes.

Spread marmalade over potatoes; top with marshmallows. Return to oven and bake until marshmallows are lightly browned, 15 to 20 minutes. Makes 8 servings.

SWEET POTATO-APPLE TREAT

Sweet potatoes and apples are a fine combination
especially good with pork

6 medium sweet potatoes, cooked and peeled	½ c. brown sugar
	½ tsp. salt
2 peeled apples, cored and sliced	6 tblsp. melted butter or margarine

Slice potatoes. Put half in greased 2-qt. casserole. Top with half of each: apples, brown sugar, salt and butter; repeat layers.

Cover and bake in moderate oven (350°) 60 minutes. Makes 8 servings.

PECAN SWEET POTATOES

You can fix these in the morning and refrigerate them until baking time

6 medium sweet potatoes,
  cooked and peeled
½ c. brown sugar
⅓ c. chopped pecans

1 tblsp. grated orange peel
1 c. orange juice
2 tblsp. butter
½ tsp. salt

Slice potatoes and put one layer deep in greased 13 × 9 × 2" pan. Sprinkle with brown sugar, nuts and orange peel. Pour over orange juice. Dot with butter and sprinkle with salt.

Bake in moderate oven (350°) 1 hour. Makes 8 servings.

OVEN-CANDIED SWEET POTATOES

Fine escort for ham or pork chops

¼ c. butter
½ c. dark corn syrup
2 tblsp. water
¼ c. brown sugar

½ tsp. salt
6 medium sweet potatoes,
  cooked and peeled

Melt butter. Stir in corn syrup, water, brown sugar and salt.

Cut potatoes in halves lengthwise. Dip in corn syrup mixture, coating all sides. Place in 13 × 9 × 2" pan. Pour remaining syrup over top.

Bake in slow oven (325°) until tender and glazed, about 1 hour and 15 minutes. Baste occasionally. Makes 6 servings.

YAM FLOWERETTES

Pretty vegetable combination that tastes wonderful— try it with pork

2 c. mashed yams, cooked
  or canned
2 tblsp. evaporated milk,
  undiluted
1 tblsp. butter or margarine

½ tsp. salt
⅛ tsp. pepper
6 large onions, cooked
⅛ tsp. paprika
Butter

73

Mix together yams, milk, 1 tblsp. butter, salt and pepper.

Remove centers from onions; spread "petals" to enlarge onion cavity. Fill with yam mixture. Place onion centers on top; sprinkle with paprika. Dot with butter.

Bake in buttered baking dish in hot oven (400°) about 20 minutes; add a little boiling water to prevent sticking. Makes 6 servings.

NOTE: To complete menu, serve Yam Flowerettes with pork roast or fresh ham, a buttered green vegetable, relishes, hot muffins and pineapple upside-down cake.

SPICED SWEET POTATOES IN PEACHES

The whiff of cloves gives a pleasing, faint taste of spiced peaches

1½ c. mashed cooked sweet potatoes
2 tsp. lemon juice
2 tblsp. light brown sugar
¼ tsp. ground cloves
1 (1 lb. 13 oz.) can peach halves
1 tblsp. butter or margarine

Combine sweet potatoes, lemon juice, brown sugar and cloves.

Drain peach halves and arrange in buttered baking dish. Fill centers with sweet potatoes; dot tops with butter.

Bake in hot oven (400°) 20 minutes. Serve on platter with pork chops or ham, or in a shallow serving dish. Makes 8 servings.

SWEET POTATO BAKE

Make a day ahead to save time

3 lbs. sweet potatoes
1 c. firmly packed brown sugar
1½ tblsp. cornstarch
¼ tsp. salt
⅛ tsp. ground cinnamon
1 c. apricot nectar
½ c. hot water
2 tsp. grated orange peel
2 tblsp. butter
½ c. chopped pecans

Peel sweet potatoes. Cook in boiling salted water until tender but not mushy. Drain and cool.

Combine brown sugar, cornstarch, salt and cinnamon in medium saucepan. Stir in apricot nectar, hot water and orange peel. Bring to full boil, stirring constantly. Remove from heat. Stir in butter. Cool slightly; stir in pecans.

Cut sweet potatoes in halves and place in 12 × 7½″ casserole. Pour sauce over potatoes so all are glazed. If you wish, cover and refrigerate overnight.

Bake, covered, in moderate oven (375°) 25 minutes, or until sauce is bubbling. Makes 6 to 8 servings.

YAMS WITH ORANGE SAUCE

Orange complements yam flavors

6 medium-large yams	2 tblsp. cornstarch
1 c. orange juice	Salt and pepper to taste
⅓ c. brown sugar	1 tsp. grated orange peel
⅓ c. white sugar	(optional)
2 tblsp. butter	

Bake yams in moderate oven (375°) until tender, 45 minutes to 1 hour. Remove skins and slice into greased 2-qt. casserole.

Combine remaining ingredients and pour over yams. Bake in moderate oven (350°) 30 minutes. Makes 6 to 8 servings.

SUNSHINE POTATO BALLS

A Christmas special as pretty on the table as glitter balls on the tree

¼ c. butter, melted	4 c. mashed cooked sweet
¼ c. milk	potatoes
2 tblsp. sugar	18 to 20 miniature
½ tsp. salt	marshmallows
¼ tsp. pepper	3 c. coarsely crushed corn
	flakes

Beat butter, milk, sugar, salt and pepper into potatoes; form 2″ balls with marshmallow centers; roll in corn flakes.

Place in greased 13 × 9 × 2″ baking pan. Bake in moderate oven (375°) 25 to 35 minutes. Or freeze; then bake without defrosting 45 minutes. Makes 18 to 20.

White Potatoes: White potatoes, like meat, are so highly favored by farmers and most other men that wives often say, "My husband's a meat-and-potato man!" Certainly, no vegetable plays the supporting role to meats so successfully as do the tubers. Sometimes called Irish potatoes because they're a favorite food in Ireland, white potatoes are native to Peru. From their beginning in South America, potatoes have spread to all parts of the world. They are harvested and shipped to our markets every month. Winter potatoes are harvested and marketed during January, February and March. The spring harvest extends from April to June, the early summer potatoes from June to August and the late crop from mid-August to late September. Fall-crop potatoes make up about three-quarters of the total crop and are harvested after October 1. New potatoes are those harvested before they are fully mature, beginning in the spring.

For cooking purposes, potatoes can be put into three groups, although the distinctions between them are not clear-cut and there is much overlapping. The best use of *new potatoes* is boiling or creaming; they also make a good potato salad. They vary widely in size and shape, depending upon variety.

General purpose potatoes include the great majority of supplies offered for sale in the markets, both round and long types. As the term implies, they are used for boiling, frying and baking, although many of the common varieties are not considered to be best for baking.

In *baking potatoes,* both the variety and the area where grown are important factors affecting baking quality. The Russet Burbank, a long variety with fine, scaly netting on the skin, is the most widely grown and best known.

Select potatoes that are reasonably clean, smooth, well shaped, firm and free from blemishes, sunburn and decay. Avoid potatoes with green color (caused by sunburn or exposure to light), for the green portions are bitter and must be cut off.

Allow 1½ to 2 lbs. (about 6 medium or 12 small) for 4 servings.

Store potatoes in a cool place, the best temperature being 45 to 50°. Higher temperatures cause sprouting and shriveling. If stored in 70 to 80° temperature, use within 1 week. When stored more than a week in temperatures lower than 45°, potatoes take on a sweetish taste as some of their starch turns to sugar. Then, if stored for a week or two in temperatures 70 to 80°, the flavor improves. Store potatoes in a dark place—light causes the skin and flesh under it to turn green, lowering eating quality. And store potatoes in a place with good ventilation, never in an airtight container.

When ready to cook, wash and leave skins on, or peel thinly. Leave whole, cut in quarters, or dice. Cook, covered, in 1" boiling salted water 35 to 45 minutes if whole, 20 to 25 minutes if cut up. Boil gently; vigorous boiling frequently causes potatoes to disintegrate. Drain and serve plain, or mash and season.

REFRIGERATOR MASHED POTATOES

Taste good, like baked potatoes served with sour cream and chives . . . one of the best recipes in this book

5 lbs. potatoes (9 large)	1 tsp. salt
2 (3 oz.) pkgs. cream cheese	¼ tsp. pepper
1 c. dairy sour cream	2 tblsp. butter or margarine
2 tsp. onion salt	

Cook peeled potatoes in boiling salted water until tender. Drain.

Mash until smooth (no lumps). Add remaining ingredients and beat until light and fluffy. Cool.

Cover and place in refrigerator. May be used any time within two weeks.

To use, place desired amount in greased casserole, dot with butter and bake in moderate oven (350°) until heated through, about 30 minutes. Makes 8 cups, or 12 servings.

NOTE: If you use the full amount, heat in a 2-qt. casserole and dot with 2 tblsp. butter.

BAKED BARBECUE POTATOES

Good with hamburgers and a green salad

1 tblsp. flour	⅓ c. ketchup
1½ tsp. salt	1 tsp. Worcestershire sauce
¼ tsp. pepper	3 drops Tabasco sauce
5 c. thinly sliced raw potatoes	1½ c. scalded milk
½ c. chopped onion	2 tblsp. butter
1 c. shredded process American cheese	4 slices bacon, diced, fried crisp and drained

77

Combine flour, salt and pepper; mix. Arrange potatoes, onions, flour mixture and half of cheese in layers in 2-qt. casserole.

Combine ketchup, Worcestershire sauce, Tabasco sauce and scalded milk; mix. Pour over potatoes; dot with butter.

Cover and bake in moderate oven (375°) 50 minutes. Uncover and stir; continue baking until potatoes are tender, about 20 minutes. Sprinkle with remaining cheese and bacon. Makes 6 servings.

RANCHO MASHED POTATOES

Wonderful to serve with steak

9 medium potatoes, peeled	½ tsp. salt
1 clove garlic	¼ tsp. pepper
¼ c. melted butter or margarine	1 (4 oz.) can mushroom slices, drained
2 egg yolks	2 tblsp. butter
½ c. heavy cream	¼ c. finely chopped parsley

Cook potatoes in salted water with clove of garlic until just tender. Drain; remove garlic.

Mash potatoes with ¼ c. butter. Blend in egg yolks, cream, salt and pepper.

Cook mushrooms in 2 tblsp. butter; add with parsley to potatoes and mix.

Place in 3-qt. casserole. Bake in moderate oven (375°) 35 minutes. Makes 8 servings.

NEW POTATO CASSEROLE

Quick dress-up for new potatoes

24 small new potatoes	1 c. grated process American cheese
2 cans condensed cream of chicken soup	

Cook potatoes; peel. Place in greased 2-qt. casserole. Pour soup over potatoes; sprinkle with cheese.

Bake in hot oven (400°) about 15 minutes. Makes 8 servings.

DANISH SUGAR-BROWNED POTATOES

24 small new potatoes	6 tblsp. sugar
¼ c. butter or margarine	2 tsp. salt

Cook scrubbed potatoes in their jackets in boiling water until tender. Drain and peel.

Melt butter in skillet; stir in sugar and cook, stirring constantly, until mixture is a light caramel color.

Add potatoes; continue cooking, shaking the potatoes to roll about until lightly browned. Sprinkle with salt during cooking. Makes 8 servings.

Perfect mashed potatoes: *Take a minute or two to shake cooked, drained potatoes over heat to dry them out. This makes them mealy and good. Mash them until no lumps are left, then add milk and butter, warmed together (don't let milk boil), and whip potatoes until fluffy. Taste for seasoning.*

BAKED CREAMED POTATOES

This dilled version is good with fish

4 c. diced potatoes	1 tblsp. minced fresh dill
2 tsp. salt	leaves
½ tsp. pepper	1 c. heavy cream
	1 c. milk

Place potatoes in shallow baking dish; sprinkle with salt, pepper and dill.

Combine cream and milk; pour over potatoes. Bake in moderate oven (350°) 30 minutes. Makes 6 servings.

POTATO CASSEROLE

*Potatoes are an attractive apricot-orange color—
they're really good*

6 medium potatoes	1 can condensed tomato
¼ c. butter	soup
	½ c. grated Cheddar cheese

Peel and cook potatoes; mash and season with butter.

Heat tomato soup and add. (Mixture is rather thin but it thickens during baking.)

Spoon into 1½-qt. casserole; sprinkle with cheese. Bake in moderate oven (350°) 25 minutes, until top is browned. Makes 5 to 6 servings.

CHEESE-STUFFED BAKED POTATOES

This new version of an old favorite is tasty—
an easy recipe to double

4 large baking potatoes
¼ c. soft butter or
   margarine
1 c. chive creamed cottage
   cheese

2 tblsp. mayonnaise
Salt and pepper to taste
½ c. grated American
   cheese
Paprika

Scrub, then bake potatoes in hot oven (400°) 1 hour.

When done, cut a thin lengthwise slice from top of each. Scoop out insides into mixing bowl. Mash well with fork and blend in butter, cottage cheese, mayonnaise, salt and pepper. Blend thoroughly.

Pile lightly into potato shells, leaving top surface rough. Sprinkle with grated cheese, then paprika.

Bake in very hot oven (450°) 10 to 12 minutes, or until cheese melts and potatoes are heated through. Makes 4 servings.

SWISS POTATOES

All the men say these are great

5 boiled potatoes, peeled
   and cubed
2 tblsp. chopped green
   onions with tops
2 tblsp. salad oil

2 tblsp. butter
2 tblsp. grated Swiss cheese
1 tsp. salt
¼ tsp. pepper

Cook potatoes and onions in mixture of salad oil and melted butter in skillet until potatoes are lightly browned. Add cheese, salt and pepper and toss. Serve immediately, or place in casserole and keep warm in oven until ready to serve. Makes 6 servings.

SWISS POTATO PIE

Bake these cheese-flavored potatoes in a pie pan and cut in wedges to serve

4 c. peeled diced cold
   boiled potatoes
2 tblsp. butter or margarine
3 eggs, separated
½ c. dairy sour cream

Salt and pepper to taste
¼ c. grated Swiss cheese
3 tblsp. bread or corn flake
   crumbs

Place potatoes in a mixing bowl.

Cream butter. Beat egg yolks and blend with sour cream; combine with butter. Add to potatoes; season with salt and pepper.

Beat egg whites until stiff, but not dry; fold into potato mixture. Pour into greased 10″ pie pan.

Combine cheese and crumbs; sprinkle over top of potatoes. Bake in moderate oven (350°) 25 to 30 minutes. Makes 8 to 10 servings.

FLUFFY POTATO SPECIAL

Mashed potato mounds, gold-tipped with cheese-whipped cream topping

6 medium potatoes
2 tblsp. butter or margarine
1 egg, beaten
½ tsp. salt
⅛ tsp. pepper
¾ c. dairy half-and-half,
   heated

½ c. heavy cream
⅛ tsp. salt
⅛ tsp. ground red pepper
   (cayenne)
½ c. grated Cheddar
   cheese
Parsley flakes or dill weed

Boil peeled potatoes until tender; mash with butter (there should be about 6 c.).

Combine egg, ½ tsp. salt, pepper and half-and-half; add to potatoes and whip until fluffy. Shape potatoes into 6 or more mounds on greased ovenproof platter.

Whip cream until stiff; add salt and red pepper; fold in cheese and spread over potatoes. Sprinkle with parsley.

Bake in moderate oven (375°) until cheese is melted and potatoes lightly browned, 12 to 15 minutes. Serve piping hot. Makes 6 to 8 servings.

Exciting Potato-Nut Dishes

Southern women for a long time have teamed their native nut, the pecan, with sweet potatoes in elegant dishes. And now recipes teaming other nuts with white potatoes are coming from far Western kitchens. Potato-Filbert Scallop is an Oregon special, where filberts are native. Potato-Macadamia Nut Puffs are Californian, as well as Hawaiian. The macadamia is an Australian nut that grows on the Hawaiian Islands. Most of these nuts in our markets come from there—expensive but superior in flavor.

You can substitute walnuts for filberts or macadamias in areas where they are more available. (They're also less expensive.) Walnuts have a special affinity for carrots, too —see Index for Oregon Carrot Casserole and Walnut Carrots.

POTATO-FILBERT SCALLOP

New extra-good way to fix potatoes

3 c. diced peeled raw potatoes
¾ c. chopped filberts or walnuts
1 c. grated Cheddar cheese
2 tblsp. finely chopped onion

2 tblsp. butter or margarine
½ can condensed cream of mushroom soup
¾ c. milk
1 tsp. salt
½ tsp. coarse grind pepper
Corn flake or bread crumbs

In a greased 1½- to 2-qt. casserole arrange alternate layers of potatoes, filberts and cheese; sprinkle with onion. Dot with butter, or melt and drizzle over.

Combine soup, milk, salt and pepper; spoon over casserole. Sprinkle with crumbs.

Bake in moderate oven (350°) 40 minutes, until potatoes are done. Makes 5 to 6 servings.

POTATO-MACADAMIA NUT PUFF

Consider these distinctive potato puffs when you want to splurge a bit

6 medium potatoes	½ c. finely chopped
½ c. milk	macadamia nuts or
1 egg	walnuts
¼ c. soft butter or	2 tsp. salt
margarine	2 tsp. baking powder
	¼ tsp. white pepper

Cook peeled potatoes in boiling water until done; drain. Put through a ricer or mash well. Turn into large bowl of electric mixer; add remaining ingredients and whip at medium speed until fluffy.

Drop large spoonfuls onto well-greased baking sheet. Bake in moderate oven (375°) 10 to 15 minutes. Makes 8 servings.

ROLLED POTATO PANCAKES (BOHEMIAN)

Serve for brunch or supper with tiny pork sausages or ham and a green salad or vegetable relish tray

3 c. cold seasoned mashed	Melted butter
potatoes	Grape jelly or other fruit
¾ c. flour	spread
¼ tsp. salt (about)	

Combine potatoes, ¾ c. flour and salt (amount of salt depends on mashed potato seasonings). Knead with hand to blend thoroughly; divide in 12 equal parts.

Roll each piece of dough on a heavily floured board with floured rolling pin to make a 7" circle.

Heat a heavy griddle or skillet; do not grease. Bake each pancake over medium heat, turning once, until golden brown spots appear on both sides. If bubbles form while pancakes are baking, pierce them with a fork.

Remove from griddle, brush one side with melted butter, spread with jelly and roll up. Place, seam side down, in shallow pan and keep warm in very slow oven (275°) until all pancakes are baked. Makes 12 pancakes.

Potato Treats to Fix in Blender

Electric blenders do wonders with potatoes—and fast. We give you three fine examples: Potato Puff Casserole, Potato-Bacon Casserole and Speedy Potato Pancakes. If your kitchen has a blender, do put it to work on these treats and watch your family and friends enjoy them. Their enthusiasm will please you.

POTATO PUFF CASSEROLE

You can double this recipe, but fix half the potato mixture at a time, combine and bake in a 3-qt. casserole

3 eggs	1½ tsp. salt
1 c. milk	¼ tsp. white pepper
3 c. cubed peeled raw potatoes (4 medium)	⅔ c. cubed Cheddar cheese
2 tblsp. butter or margarine	3 tblsp. corn flake crumbs
1 medium onion, sliced	3 tblsp. melted butter
½ medium green pepper, sliced	

In a 4- or 5-cup blender put 1 egg, ½ c. milk and 1 c. potatoes; blend at grate speed until potatoes are finely grated. Place in 1½-qt. casserole greased with 2 tblsp. butter.

Put in blender remaining eggs, milk and potatoes, onion, green pepper, salt, pepper and cheese; blend until vegetables are finely grated. Add to potatoes in casserole; stir to combine.

Toss crumbs with 3 tblsp. melted butter; sprinkle over top of casserole. Bake in moderate oven (350°) 1 hour. Makes 4 servings.

POTATO-BACON CASSEROLE

There's bacon both on top and bottom to distribute the smoky flavor

1½ qts. cubed peeled raw potatoes (about 6 medium)	¼ c. firmly packed parsley sprigs or 2 tsp. parsley flakes
3 eggs	2 tblsp. flour
1½ tsp. salt	1 tsp. baking powder
¼ tsp. coarse grind pepper	¼ c. milk
1 small onion, sliced, or 2 green onions	6 slices bacon, cut in 1″ pieces

Place 3 c. potatoes in blender; add enough water nearly to cover, about 1 c. Blend at grate speed about 1 minute;

84

work potato pieces down and around the side *above area of the blades*. Potato pieces not grated finely enough can be grated with remaining potatoes. Empty grated potatoes immediately into a colander over a bowl to save potato water.

Grate remaining potatoes in water (re-use the water saved from the first grating, adding more as necessary). Again drain grated potatoes; let stand. (Potato starch will settle in bowl; this can be used in final combination.)

Place remaining ingredients, except bacon, in blender and process at chop, then mix speeds.

Measure ½ c. potato water; add to ingredients in blender. Pour off any remaining potato water, leaving potato starch in bowl. Add grated potatoes and other blended ingredients to bowl.

Lay half of bacon pieces in bottom of 2-qt. casserole. Add potato mixture; top with remaining bacon pieces. Bake in moderate oven (350°) 1 hour, keeping casserole covered the first 20 minutes. Makes 8 servings.

SPEEDY POTATO PANCAKES

Pass butter and table syrup with these hot cakes— it's a feast

2 eggs
½ small onion
1 tsp. salt
2 tblsp. flour

½ tsp. baking powder
3 c. cubed peeled raw
   potatoes

Put eggs, onion, salt, flour and baking powder into blender container; add ½ c. potato cubes; cover and blend at grate speed about 1 minute.

Add remaining potatoes and blend at chop, or low speed, until potatoes are of medium grated consistency, about 1 minute.

Bake like pancakes on a hot well-greased griddle. Drain on paper toweling and place in warm oven until all cakes are baked. Makes about 12 (2 to 3") cakes.

BAKED POTATO STICKS

Serve with hamburgers or steak—potatoes absorb cream and taste rich

6 medium potatoes	¾ c. dairy half-and-half or
1 tsp. salt	light cream
1 tsp. parsley flakes	3 tblsp. butter
1 tsp. instant minced onion	½ c. grated process cheese
¼ tsp. pepper	

Peel potatoes and cut in lengthwise strips as for French fries. Place in greased 2-qt. casserole. Sprinkle with salt, parsley, onion and pepper. Pour cream over. Dot with butter and sprinkle with cheese.

Cover; bake in hot oven (425°) 50 minutes, or until tender. Makes 6 servings.

BUTTER-CRUMB POTATOES

Potatoes come from the oven brown and crisp-coated.
Select for meal with fish or meat cooked on range top

6 medium potatoes, peeled	1 tsp. salt
3 tblsp. melted butter	¼ tsp. pepper
½ c. bread crumbs	

Roll potatoes in melted butter, then in mixture of remaining ingredients.

Place in greased 2½-qt. casserole. Pour any remaining butter over top.

Cover and bake in hot oven (400°) 45 minutes. Uncover and bake until tender, 15 to 20 minutes. Makes 6 servings.

DUCHESS POTATOES

These golden brown potato balls will please the family
and guests

Hot potatoes to make 3 c.	2 drops Tabasco sauce, or
mashed	a few grains ground red
Milk	pepper (cayenne)
2 egg yolks, slightly beaten	Salt to taste
¼ c. butter or margarine	Evaporated milk
½ tsp. prepared mustard	Corn flake crumbs

Mash hot potatoes until no lumps remain; then whip with enough milk to make them fluffy. Add egg yolks, butter, mustard, Tabasco and salt; let mixture cool briefly, then shape in 8 to 12 potato balls on lightly floured board.

About 15 minutes before serving, brush potato balls with evaporated milk, then roll in crumbs. Bake in hot oven (425°) 5 to 6 minutes. Serve at once. Makes 4 to 6 servings.

NOTE: You can use instant mashed potatoes instead of fresh ones in this recipe, if you wish. Follow package directions for reconstituting potatoes, adding 2 egg yolks, slightly beaten, to the amount of milk called for in directions.

KENTUCKY POTATOES

Tuck these in oven to bake with ham for your next buffet supper. Long, slow cooking develops super flavors

¼ c. butter or margarine
¼ c. flour
4 c. milk
2 tsp. salt

Pepper to taste (about ¼ tsp.)
7 large potatoes (about 6 c. grated)
¼ c. finely chopped onion

Melt butter in a large saucepan over low heat; remove from heat and blend in flour. Add a little milk slowly, blending until smooth; then add rest of milk and boil 1 minute, stirring constantly. Add salt, pepper and grated potatoes.

Pour into greased 15½ × 10½ × 1″ jelly roll pan, or shallow casserole (jelly roll pan fits neatly on oven shelf below ham). Bake in slow oven (300°) about 3 hours. Makes 10 servings.

COUNTRY POTATO PATTIES

You shred partly cooked potatoes, shape them in patties and brown quickly in this modernized recipe

6 medium potatoes (1½ lbs.)
2 tblsp. chopped fresh or frozen onion
2 tblsp. chopped pimiento or parsley

2 tblsp. flour
1 tsp. salt
3 tblsp. bacon drippings, butter or margarine

87

Parboil unpeeled potatoes 15 to 20 minutes (they will still be hard in the center). Turn at once into a colander and cool under running water.

As soon as they can be handled, peel potatoes and shred with a coarse grater. Toss with onion, pimiento, flour and salt, using 2 forks to mix ingredients.

Shape into patties, using about ½ c. for each; brown in hot fat about 5 minutes on each side. Makes 6 servings.

FRENCH FRIED POTATO BALLS

Teen-agers—and men—like French fries; they'll also like these. To save time start with instant potatoes

1½ c. warm, unseasoned mashed potatoes	1 tsp. parsley flakes, or 3 tblsp. finely chopped fresh parsley
2 eggs, beaten	
Milk	¾ c. dry bread crumbs
1 tsp. grated onion	3 to 4 c. salad oil or fat for deep-fat frying
½ tsp. salt	

Combine potatoes, eggs, beaten with a little milk, onion, salt and parsley. Mix in ¼ c. crumbs.

Shape mixture in small balls, about 1 tblsp. each, and roll in remaining crumbs; you should have 18 to 24, depending on size. Fry, a third at a time, in hot fat (380°) 1 minute, or until golden brown. Drain on paper toweling and keep hot in warm oven until all potatoes are cooked. Makes 6 servings of 3 or 4 balls each.

FARM POTATOES WITH EGGS

Give thanks to Pennsylvania Dutch women who invented this simple treat

4 c. sliced boiled potatoes	2 tblsp. minced parsley, or 1 tsp. parsley flakes
¼ c. butter, margarine or bacon drippings	
Salt and freshly ground pepper to taste	2 eggs, slightly beaten

Fry potatoes in butter until nicely browned; taste to judge for proper seasoning.

Combine parsley and eggs; stir into potatoes at the moment they are being dished up (do not let pan remain on heat after eggs are in). Serve as a breakfast dish with broiled ham or bacon. Makes 4 servings.

POTATOES IN BUTTERMILK

These potatoes are a perfect ham or bacon go-with for breakfast—or any meal

2 tblsp. butter or margarine
2 c. chopped peeled raw
   potatoes
½ tsp. salt

⅛ tsp. coarse grind pepper
1 c. thick buttermilk
Paprika

Heat butter in a skillet (electric one is excellent); add potatoes and toss and cook until potatoes begin to brown. Add salt, pepper and buttermilk; simmer slowly until potatoes are tender and liquid thickened. Sprinkle a little paprika on each serving. Makes 4 servings.

POTATO ROSES

A new shape for mashed potatoes. Make the day before and refrigerate

4 lbs. baking potatoes
¼ c. butter
1 tblsp. minced onion
1½ tsp. salt
⅛ tsp. pepper
1 tblsp. minced parsley

2 tblsp. grated Parmesan or
   Romano cheese
1 egg
Paprika
½ c. melted butter

Peel potatoes; cut in halves and cook in boiling, lightly salted water until tender. Mash slightly.

Place potatoes in large mixer bowl; beat until light and fluffy. Add ¼ c. butter, onion, salt, pepper, parsley, cheese and egg. Whip until well mixed. Cool.

Moisten hands; shape potato mixture into balls, about ¾ c. each. Place on greased baking sheet; flatten slightly on bottom.

To form roses, dip forefinger in water; make an indentation in center of each potato ball. Swirl finger clockwise to make a spiral. If you wish, cover and chill overnight.

Before baking, sprinkle lightly with paprika and drizzle

½ c. melted butter over roses. Bake in very hot oven (450°) 8 minutes. Let set a few minutes. Makes 10 servings.

POTATO-CHEESE SCALLOP

You won't go wrong on this

1 medium onion, thinly
   sliced
2 tblsp. melted butter or
   margarine
6 medium potatoes (about
   2 lbs.)
1 c. grated sharp process
   cheese

2 tblsp. flour
2 tsp. salt
⅛ tsp. pepper
2½ c. milk
¼ c. finely crushed cracker
   crumbs or potato chips

Cook onion slices in butter until lightly browned.

Peel and slice potatoes. Place one-quarter of potatoes in bottom of greased 2-qt. baking dish. Add one-quarter each: onion slices, cheese, flour, salt and pepper. Repeat layers. Pour milk over top. Sprinkle with crumbs.

Cover and bake in moderate oven (350°) 1 hour. Remove cover the last 15 minutes of baking time. Makes 6 servings.

TWO-STEP CHEESE-BAKED POTATOES

You fix and freeze these potatoes a week before you want to serve them

7 baking potatoes
Milk
2 tsp. finely chopped onion
2 tblsp. butter

Salt and pepper to taste
Mild Cheddar cheese,
   shredded
Paprika

Bake potatoes in hot oven (425°) 1 hour, or until tender. Cool; cut in halves. Scrape pulp from shells and mash; add a little milk to make a light and fluffy mixture.

Cook onion in butter; stir into potato mixture along with salt and pepper. Pile mixture into 12 potato shells (discard 2 shells).

Cover tops with shredded cheese; sprinkle on paprika.

Place shells in flat freezing container or pan. Cover tightly. Freeze.

To serve, place frozen potatoes on baking sheet; bake in very hot oven (450°) about 25 minutes. Makes 12 servings.

Pumpkin

If you grow pumpkins, nine chances out of ten most of them end up in spicy pumpkin pies. October is the big pumpkin month, although a few are available in September and November.

Select bright-colored, firm, unblemished pumpkins.

Three pounds raw pumpkin makes 3 c. cooked, mashed pumpkin.

Store in a cool, dry place away from frost danger.

When ready to cook, cut in half and remove seeds and stringy portion. Cut in small pieces and peel.

Cook, covered, in 1" boiling salted water 25 to 30 minutes or until tender. Drain and mash. Season as recipe directs.

Salsify

This root vegetable boasts of two other names, oyster plant and oyster vegetable. As its names imply, the vegetable has a faint oyster taste. It looks something like a parsnip, but the skin is darker. It is available in October and November.

Select plump, firm, well-shaped, medium-sized, fresh-looking roots free from blemishes.

Allow 1½ lbs. for 6 servings.

Store salsify in a dry, cool place or in the refrigerator crisper. Use within a few days.

When ready to cook, cut off tops, scrub, scrape or peel, slice or sliver. Plunge at once into cold water containing 1 tblsp. lemon juice or vinegar (to each quart of water) to prevent discoloration.

Cook, covered, in 1" boiling salted water until tender, 15 to 20 minutes. Drain and season with salt, pepper and butter or margarine. Or reheat in cream or white sauce.

SALSIFY-OYSTER CASSEROLE

*Oyster stew bolsters salsify's faint oyster taste
in this delightful dish*

1½ lbs. salsify (about
    6 roots)
1 tsp. vinegar
½ tsp. salt
2 eggs
1 (6 oz.) can evaporated
    milk, undiluted

1 can condensed oyster
    stew
1 c. coarse cracker crumbs
Salt and pepper to taste
1 tblsp. butter or
    margarine
⅛ tsp. paprika

Cut off tops of salsify; wash and peel thinly with vegetable peeler. Cut in ½″ slices (you'll have 3½ to 4 c.), and plunge into cold water containing a little vinegar to prevent discoloration. Drain. Barely cover with boiling water; add ½ tsp. salt and cook until tender, about 15 minutes. Drain, and cool.

Beat eggs; add evaporated milk and oyster stew (there should be 12 to 15 small oysters, actually tiny ones).

Place salsify in greased 1½-qt. casserole or baking dish. Pour oyster stew mixture over, distributing the oysters about. Add crumbs and fold in slightly. Add more salt, if necessary, and a little pepper. Dot with butter and sprinkle with paprika. Bake in moderate oven (350°) 40 to 45 minutes, or until set. Makes 6 to 8 servings.

FRENCH FRIED SALSIFY

If you like fried oysters, you'll like this "oyster plant" dish

1½ lbs. salsify (about
    6 roots)
1 tsp. vinegar
½ tsp. salt
2 peppercorns
1 c. flour

½ tsp. salt
⅔ c. milk
2 eggs, beaten
Fat or oil for deep-fat
    frying

Cut off tops and wash salsify; peel thinly with vegetable peeler; cut in 3″ lengths. Drop at once in cold water to cover with vinegar added. Add ½ tsp. salt and peppercorns; bring to a boil and cook, covered, until salsify is barely tender, 15 to 20 minutes. Remove peppercorns; drain and pat dry with paper towels.

Prepare batter: Sift together flour and ½ tsp. salt. Combine milk and eggs, and add to flour.

Heat fat to 375°. Place 6 to 8 salsify pieces (about half) in batter, lowering one at a time into the hot fat so temperature does not lower. As each browns, lift out and drain on paper toweling, then place on ovenproof platter. Keep hot in warm oven. Continue until all salsify pieces are fried. Any leftover batter can be fried and served with the salsify. Makes 6 servings.

SALSIFY AU GRATIN

What a great main dish for a women's luncheon!
Sure to get compliments

1½ lbs. salsify (about 6 roots)	3 tblsp. flour
1 tsp. vinegar	1½ c. milk
½ tsp. salt	½ c. bread crumbs
¼ tsp. celery salt	2 tblsp. butter or margarine
Dash white pepper	Dash paprika
1 egg, beaten	6 rolled anchovies (optional)
3 tblsp. butter	

Cut off tops and wash salsify; peel thinly with vegetable peeler; cut in 1″ lengths. Drop into cold water to cover with vinegar added. Add salt, celery salt and pepper; bring to a boil and cook, covered, until tender, 15 to 20 minutes. Drain thoroughly and mash. Add egg all at once and stir to combine.

Meanwhile, make white sauce: Melt 3 tblsp. butter in saucepan, add flour and stir until smooth. Gradually add milk; cook and stir over low heat until smooth and thick (you'll have 1½ c.). Stir in salsify mixture.

Lightly grease 6 large scallop shells or individual casseroles and place on baking sheet for easy handling. Turn salsify mixture into shells.

Heat crumbs in 2 tblsp. butter; sprinkle salsify with crumbs, then paprika; center an anchovy in each shell. Place under broiler, about 5 to 7″ from heat, for 5 minutes; turn off heat. Remove to lower shelf in oven and let stand 5 minutes more. Makes 6 servings.

SALSIFY CAKES

Serve these with ham and eggs, or with maple syrup or honey

1½ lbs. salsify (about   3 to 4 tblsp. butter or
   6 roots)   margarine
1 tsp. vinegar   ⅛ tsp. garlic powder
½ tsp. salt   Flour
⅛ tsp. pepper

Cut off tops and wash salsify; peel thinly with vegetable peeler; cut in 1″ lengths. Drop immediately in cold water to cover with vinegar and salt added. Bring to a boil and cook, covered, until tender enough to mash, 15 to 20 minutes. Drain thoroughly.

Mash salsify, adding pepper, 1 tblsp. butter and garlic powder. Form in flat cakes about 3″ in diameter; dredge lightly with flour. Cook in remaining butter. Makes 12 cakes, or 6 servings.

SALSIFY WITH HERBS

For a change of pace serve this with chicken instead of potatoes

1½ lbs. salsify (about   2 tsp. chopped parsley
   6 roots)   1 tsp. chopped chives
1 tsp. vinegar   ½ tsp. dill weed (optional)
½ tsp. salt   ½ tsp. salt
3 to 4 tblsp. butter or   Flour
   margarine   1 tblsp. lemon juice

Cut off tops and wash salsify; peel as thinly as possible, using a vegetable peeler; cut in 1″ lengths. Drop immediately in cold water to cover with vinegar added. Add ½ tsp. salt, and bring to a boil. Cook, covered, 15 to 20 minutes, until barely tender. Drain.

Melt butter. Add parsley, chives, dill weed and salt; keep warm over low heat.

Dredge salsify lightly with flour; add to butter and cook to brown lightly, shaking pan occasionally. Add lemon juice just before serving. Makes 6 servings.

Spinach

The dark green leaves are well known in most homes. They are available throughout the year.

Select leaves that are young, fresh, tender and free of blemishes. Look for that attractive green color.

Allow 2 lbs. for 4 servings.

Rinse leaves in cool water; drain. Put in refrigerator crisper, but use very soon.

When ready to cook, wash thoroughly in running cold water or through several changes of water, lifting the leaves out of the water so the sand and grit will stay in the pan. Discard yellow and damaged leaves and tear out the thick bottom midribs.

Put spinach in saucepan, sprinkle on 1 tsp. salt for each pound of spinach. Cover and cook in the water that clings to the leaves after washing, until tender and wilted, 6 to 10 minutes. Or steam in colander as described under Greens (see Index). Season with salt, pepper and butter or margarine and, if you like, a sprinkling of lemon juice. Sliced hard-cooked eggs or grated egg yolks are a pretty garnish.

HERBED SPINACH

Spinach is no common vegetable when cooked and seasoned like this

3 slices bacon, cut in slivers	½ tsp. rosemary leaves, or a 1″ tip of fresh rosemary, broken in bits
2 medium onions, thinly sliced	1 tsp. salt
2 lbs. washed spinach	¼ tsp. pepper
1 c. parsley, or ½ c. coarsely chopped parsley	2 tblsp. wine vinegar or lemon juice

Cook bacon bits in large skillet until barely crisp; remove with slotted spoon. Remove all but 1 tblsp. drippings; to this add onions, spinach, parsley and seasonings. Cover and cook over medium heat a few minutes (not more than 10), until wilted, stirring once or twice.

Add vinegar; sprinkle with bacon bits and serve. Makes 6 servings.

GREEN RICE

An old friend—as popular as ever and a perfect companion to chicken

3 c. cooked rice (1 c. uncooked)
1 c. chopped spinach
2 eggs, well beaten
1 c. milk

1 tsp. Worcestershire sauce
1¼ tsp. salt
2 tsp. grated onion
¼ c. butter or margarine
½ c. grated sharp cheese

Toss rice and spinach together with fork. Add eggs, milk, Worcestershire sauce, salt and onion. Toss gently to mix, using care not to mash rice.

Pour into greased 2-qt. baking dish; dot with butter and sprinkle cheese on top.

Bake in slow oven (325°) 30 to 40 minutes. Makes 8 servings.

NOTE: Add a few chopped blanched almonds, if you like. You can substitute ½ c. chopped parsley for half of the spinach.

Squash

Summer Squash: Summer squash grows fast and you eat it before the rind and seeds begin to harden—that means when it is really young. While some squashes are available throughout the year, the peak season extends from May throughout summer.

Select fresh, bright-looking squash heavy for its size and with smooth skin. A tender squash has a glossy rather than dull look; it is never hard or tough.

Allow 2 lbs. for 4 servings.

Store squash in plastic bag in refrigerator crisper. It keeps for a week or longer.

When ready to cook, wash and scrub well with a brush; cut off stem and blossom ends, but do not peel. Slice or dice.

Cook, covered, in ½ to 1" boiling salted water until

tender, 8 to 10 minutes. (You can cook a garlic clove, peeled, or 1 tsp. chopped green onion with squash to add flavor.) Drain, season with salt, pepper and butter or margarine and sprinkle with grated Parmesan cheese if you like.

The different summer squashes may be substituted for one another in most recipes. Here are some of the most widely available and best-liked summer squashes. Look for them in your markets and at roadside vegetable stands.

Zucchini: A straight-sided cylindrical squash, zucchini may be slightly larger at the tip end. The skin is shiny and dark green. Flesh is creamy white and tender. Zucchini is at best eating stage when 6 to 8″ long.

Scallop or Pattypan: This squash is rather flat (about 7″ across and 3″ deep), disk-shaped, like a flared bowl, with a scalloped edge. It is pale green when immature, changing to white later. Flesh is milk-white.

Cocozelle: There are two kinds of cocozelle squash, short and long. They are straight, almost cylindrical; when young, the tips are slightly enlarged. The soft, smooth skin is very dark green striped with a pale yellowish green, appearing as a lacy pattern. Cocozelle is at its best when 6 to 8″ long and 1½ to 2″ in diameter. Flesh is greenish white and firm; it tastes like zucchini.

Caserta: This is one of the cocozelle types of squash. It is widely grown and is in the markets the year around. It is cylindrical, but slightly thicker at the tip and has a yellowish-green skin irregularly mottled with dark green. The squash 6 to 7″ in diameter makes the best eating. Flesh is yellowish white, tender and delicious.

Yellow Crookneck: In some parts of the country this squash grows throughout the year; it does not store well. The squash curves at the neck and is larger at the tip than at the base. It has a thin, moderately warted skin that is light yellow at the edible stage, turning a deeper color as it matures. The flesh is creamy yellow, rather fine. It grows 8 to 10″ long and has a diameter of 2½ to 3″ at the widest part. There are other larger crooknecks that grow 20″ long and 4½″ thick.

Yellow Straightneck: This squash is the same as the yellow crookneck, but it is relatively straight, with a smooth skin. It also is available throughout the year.

Chayote: While the chayote is not so widely used as some of the other squashes, its popularity is increasing. It is about the size of an acorn squash and is shaped something like a pear. The skin is soft pale green; its flesh is faintly tinged with green and it has one large seed in the center. When it is young and tender you cook it like other summer squash without peeling; the cooked seed is edible.

The summer squash varieties are generally called vegetable marrows in all the English-speaking countries other than the United States.

CREOLE ZUCCHINI

Sprinkle on parsley and cheese at serving time as a bow to good looks

1 c. chopped onion (1 medium)	4 tomatoes, peeled and chopped
1 clove garlic, minced	1½ tsp. salt
¾ c. chopped green pepper	¼ tsp. pepper
¼ c. salad oil, butter or margarine	¼ c. chopped parsley
2 lbs. zucchini, sliced	¼ c. grated Parmesan cheese

In skillet, cook onion, garlic and green pepper in oil until soft. Add zucchini, tomatoes, salt and pepper; cover, cook over medium heat until zucchini is tender, about 20 minutes. Serve topped with chopped parsley and Parmesan cheese. Makes 8 servings.

ZUCCHINI CASSEROLE WITH SOUR CREAM

Sauce makes casserole a standout!

2 lbs. zucchini, sliced (3 medium)	½ tsp. salt
1 tblsp. butter	⅛ tsp. paprika
¼ c. dairy sour cream	1 egg yolk, beaten
1 tblsp. grated process cheese	1 tblsp. chopped chives
	½ c. cracker crumbs
	2 tblsp. melted butter

Cook zucchini in a small amount of boiling salted water

until tender-crisp. Drain and place in greased 1½-qt. casserole.

Meanwhile, melt butter. Stir in sour cream, cheese, salt and paprika; cook over low heat, stirring constantly, until cheese is melted. Remove from heat and stir in egg yolk and chives. Stir into zucchini.

Toss crumbs with melted butter. Place over zucchini. Bake in moderate oven (350°) 20 minutes. Makes 6 servings.

CHEESE-STUFFED ZUCCHINI

Cheese-filled squash has a new look and taste—
this is expertly seasoned

6 zucchini, 6 to 7″ long	2 tblsp. chopped onion
2 eggs, well beaten	½ tsp. salt
1½ c. sharp Cheddar cheese	⅛ tsp. pepper
½ c. small curd creamed cottage cheese	½ c. cracker crumbs
	2 tblsp. melted butter
2 tblsp. chopped parsley	

Cut off ends and scrub zucchini well. Cook whole in boiling salted water to cover about 12 minutes, or until barely tender. Remove from water and cut in halves lengthwise. Scoop out center pulp. Invert on paper toweling to drain.

Combine eggs, Cheddar cheese, cottage cheese, parsley, onion, salt and pepper. Fill zucchini shells.

Toss crumbs with butter; sprinkle over zucchini. Arrange in greased 15½ × 10½ × 1″ jelly roll pan. Bake in moderate oven (350°) 25 minutes. If desired, run under broiler a few minutes to brown topping. Makes 12 servings.

STUFFED ZUCCHINI

Squash boats hold flavorful stuffing that browns prettily
as it bakes

4 zucchini, 6 to 7″ long	⅛ tsp. pepper
1¾ c. soft bread crumbs	2 eggs, beaten
½ c. grated process cheese	¼ tsp. salt
¼ c. chopped onion	2 tblsp. butter
2 tblsp. chopped parsley	3 tblsp. grated Parmesan cheese
1¼ tsp. salt	

Scrub zucchini well. Cut off ends; do not peel. Cook in boiling salted water until just tender (½ tsp. salt to 2 c. water); do not overcook.

Cut squashes in halves lengthwise. Carefully remove center part of squash with tip of spoon. Turn squashes hollow side down on paper toweling to drain.

Chop center part of squashes and combine with bread crumbs, grated cheese, onion, parsley, 1¼ tsp. salt, pepper and eggs.

Place squashes hollow side up in greased 13 × 9 × 2" baking pan. Sprinkle with ¼ tsp. salt. Fill with bread mixture. Dot with butter and sprinkle with Parmesan cheese. Bake in moderate oven (350°) 35 to 45 minutes, or until browned on top. Makes 8 servings.

NOTE: Stuffed Zucchini may be prepared in advance and refrigerated until time to start meal preparations. Then bake 10 to 15 minutes longer.

ITALIAN ZUCCHINI

Seasoned the Roman way with olive oil, garlic, orégano, tomatoes

3 medium zucchini (about 2 lbs.)	¼ tsp. garlic salt
¼ c. olive or salad oil	¼ tsp. pepper
1½ c. chopped onion	⅛ tsp. orégano leaves
1½ tsp. salt	3 c. canned or chopped fresh tomatoes

Cut ends from zucchini, then cut in halves lengthwise. Cut each half in thirds crosswise. Place cut side down in hot oil in large skillet. Add onion. Cook until cut side of zucchini is lightly browned. If skillet is not large enough for all of squash, push browned pieces to one side and add more squash.

Sprinkle with seasonings. Top with tomatoes. Cover and cook over medium heat until squash is tender and juice forms a fairly thick sauce. Serve in sauce dishes or small bowls. Makes 8 servings.

PAN-FRIED ZUCCHINI

Zucchini strips come from the fry pan tender, golden and crisp-crusted

3 medium zucchini (about	2 eggs
2 lbs.)	2 tblsp. lemon juice
¼ c. flour	Cracker crumbs
1 tsp. salt	½ c. butter or margarine
½ tsp. pepper	

Wash unpeeled zucchini; trim off stem and blossom ends. Cut in lengthwise quarters, then slice quarters in strips about 2½″ long and ½″ thick.

Combine flour, salt and pepper on a sheet of waxed paper. Beat eggs and lemon juice together in a bowl. Put cracker crumbs on another piece of waxed paper.

Roll zucchini in flour mixture, then in eggs, then coat with crumbs. Fry in butter in skillet until brown on all sides and tender. (Add 2 tblsp. more butter, if necessary.) Drain on paper toweling. Makes 6 servings.

STUFFED ZUCCHINI SWISS-STYLE

Zucchini that grows a little bigger than you like
is fine eating when stuffed and baked this way

6 small to medium, or	2 tblsp. finely chopped
3 large zucchini (3 lbs.)	parsley
1½ c. bread crumbs	½ tsp. salt
½ c. milk	⅛ tsp. coarse grind pepper
¾ c. grated Swiss cheese	Paprika
¾ c. slivered almonds	Butter or margarine
3 hard-cooked eggs, diced	
or chopped	

Cut zucchini in halves lengthwise; scoop out pulp with a teaspoon, leaving a ½″ shell; reserve pulp.

Simmer shells in salted water 10 minutes; drain, cut side down, on paper toweling.

In a mixing bowl combine bread crumbs and milk; let stand for a minute, then squeeze out any excess milk.

Chop pulp and add to bread mixture along with cheese, almonds, eggs, parsley, salt and pepper. Mound stuffing in center of each zucchini shell; place shells close together in a greased baking dish. Sprinkle with paprika and dot with about 1 tsp. butter for the large shells (less for smaller ones).

101

Bake in moderate oven (350°) 20 minutes, or until hot and nicely browned on top. Makes 6 servings.

When a recipe calls for chopped parsley, chop the leaf sprigs, not the stems. Thrifty cooks use bundles of stems to flavor soups—they get the parsley flavor without adding the distinctive parsley color.

SOUTHWESTERN ZUCCHINI

*Give zucchini zip as Southwesterners do—
add hot green chili peppers*

1½ to 2 lbs. zucchini, sliced crosswise	1 tblsp. chopped green chili (canned)
½ tsp. salt	3 tblsp. melted butter
½ medium onion, chopped	1 c. grated American cheese

Cook zucchini in small amount of water with salt and onion added, until barely tender. Drain thoroughly.

Mix zucchini gently with chili; place in buttered casserole. Pour butter over top.

Bake in moderate oven (350°) about 30 minutes. Top with grated cheese and turn off oven at same time; leave in oven until cheese melts. Makes 4 to 6 servings.

Speedy Squash au Gratin

Herb-seasoned croutons and a generous sprinkle of cheese turn yellow summer squash into a delicious vegetable. While this excellent dish is a summer specialty, the Montana farm woman who contributed the recipe for Speedy Squash au Gratin cans the vegetable so she can treat family and friends to it all winter, too. Make this squash special for dinner some day soon and you'll understand why she lengthened the season.

SPEEDY SQUASH AU GRATIN

Easy enough to fix for family meals, and special enough for company

3 medium yellow squash	¼ tsp. pepper
(2 lbs.)	3 tblsp. butter
½ c. chopped onion	1 c. herb-seasoned croutons
(1 small)	½ c. grated Cheddar
¼ c. water	cheese
1 tsp. salt	

Wash squash; trim ends and slice ¼" thick. Place in skillet with onion, water, salt and pepper; cover. Cook, stirring once or twice, until just tender, 10 to 12 minutes. Drain. Season with 1 tblsp. butter.

Meanwhile, melt 2 tblsp. butter in small skillet. Stir in croutons. Heat over very low heat.

Spoon squash into serving bowl. Top with croutons and cheese. Makes 6 servings.

Winter Squash: Winter squash has a hard rind and you eat it when it is fully mature. It is most plentiful from early autumn until late winter.

Select squash of full maturity; that is, with a hard, tough rind and one that is heavy for its size. Heaviness indicates the wall is thick with edible flesh.

Allow 2 to 3 lbs. for 4 servings.

Store in a cool, dry place. If cut, wrap in plastic bag and store in the refrigerator crisper.

When ready to cook, wash, cut in half and then in serving pieces with a heavy-bladed knife or a hand saw. Remove and discard seeds and stringy portions.

Cook, covered, in 1" boiling salted water until tender, 25 to 30 minutes. Butternut squash cooks in 12 to 15 minutes. Season with salt, pepper and butter or margarine and if you wish, with syrup or brown sugar. Or you can bake squash: Place pieces in a covered pan (or cut-side down on a baking sheet) and bake in a hot oven (400°) until tender, 30 to 45 minutes. Leave the flesh in the rind or scoop it out and mash. Season as for squash cooked in water.

Among the widely favored winter squash are these:

Hubbard: This squash grows 10 to 16" long and 9 to 12" thick at the largest diameter. It is globular in shape with a slight tapering at neck and blossom ends. The warted skin is ridged and has a dark bronze, blue-green or orange-red color; the flesh is thick, sweet and orange-yellow.

Butternut: This squash has a smooth skin, is 9 to 12" long and 3½ to 5" thick at the widest diameter. It is turban-shaped with the seed cavity contained in the slightly bulbous blossom end. The skin is light creamy brown or dark yellow and the flesh is fine-grained and yellow to orange in color.

Banana: Many banana squash are large, from 18 to 24″ long and 5 to 6½″ thick. This squash is available from August through March. It is almost cylindrical, but tapers moderately at both ends. The skin is pale olive-gray, changing to a creamy pink in storage. The shell is thick and medium hard and its flesh is thick, orange-buff and moderately dry. The flesh has a fine texture; the seed cavity is large.

Acorn, Table Queen, Danish or Des Moines: A widely grown squash, it is available the year round. It is 5 to 8″ long and 2 to 5½″ thick. The shell is hard-thin and widely ribbed. The dark green rind changes to a dull orange with some dull green during storage. The flesh is pale orange, tender, moderately dry and often fibrous. The squash has a smooth surface except for the ribbing; the seed cavity is large.

Delicious: Shaped like a top, with the stem end largest in diameter, this squash is available from August through March. It is believed to be a derivative of the Hubbard squash introduced in 1905. It is 8 to 12″ long and 8 to 10″ thick; its skin is dark green striped with light green near the blossom end, although it sometimes is a bright reddish or tangerine color with green splotches and cream-colored stripes at the blossom end. Its rind is hard-thin and it is slightly warted and ridged. The flesh is thick, yellow and dry.

Marblehead: Available from September through March, this squash is nearly globular to short-oval in shape. It tapers toward both ends and is 11 to 16″ long and 9 to 10″ thick at the largest diameter. The rind is very hard; it is 1″ thick with a bumpy surface that is bluish gray to creamy gray or pinkish buff. The flesh is light orange-yellow, medium thick, slightly tough, and moderately dry with fair flavor. The seed cavity is large.

Gold Nugget: The nutty flavor of this squash develops when it is fully mature. Thanks to its hard skin, it will store for a long time; you'll find it in markets from October until spring. About the size of a cantaloupe, and a bright orange color, it looks like a miniature pumpkin. It has deep orange flesh that is thick, dry, fine-textured and free from fiber.

Warren Turban: This squash has a turban-like swelling at the blossom end. It is drum-shaped, 8 to 10″ long and 12 to 15″ in diameter. The shell is thick and completely covered with fine warting. The skin is bright reddish orange with some scattered stripes at the stem end; the turban end is blue. The flesh is bright orange, thick, sweet, quite dry and often stringy. The seed cavity is large.

Buttercup: This late summer turban squash is available in autumn and winter. It is 4 to 5″ long, 6 to 8″ wide and the turban is 2 to 3″ in diameter. The skin is moderately thin, dark ivy green to blackish green and has grayish pock marks and faint gray stripes. The turban either is light gray or blue gray. The flesh is orange, dry, sweet and fine-textured. And the seed cavity is small.

BUTTERNUT SQUASH BAKE

Really sweet—almost like a pudding, but really good!
Spoon raisin sauce on each serving

2 c. cooked mashed butternut squash	⅓ c. nonfat dry milk
1 c. sugar	½ c. raisins
2 eggs, beaten	½ tsp. salt
⅓ c. orange juice	¼ c. melted butter

Combine all ingredients and mix well. Pour into greased 1½-qt. casserole. Bake in moderate oven (350°) until set, 60 to 65 minutes. To serve, spoon out so every serving contains raisins (they sink to bottom of casserole). Makes 6 servings.

MAPLE BUTTERED SQUASH

Country cooking at its best—squash flavored with butter and maple syrup

1 (3 to 3½ lb.) Hubbard squash	1 tsp. salt
2 tblsp. maple syrup	Dash pepper
2 tblsp. butter or margarine	Chopped chives or green onion

Cut squash in large pieces; place in large baking pan. Cover with foil and bake in moderate oven (350°) about 1¼ hours, or until squash is tender.

Scoop out pulp and put through a sieve. Stir in syrup, butter, salt and pepper. If mixture is thin, simmer gently to reduce moisture. Otherwise, heat just to boiling; turn into serving dish and garnish with chopped chives. Makes 4 to 6 servings.

SQUASH PATTIES

Pretty Green Pepper Sauce adds zest and salted peanuts give crunchiness to these winter squashburgers

1½ c. chopped salted peanuts	2 tblsp. melted butter
	1½ tsp. salt
2 c. sieved cooked squash	¼ tsp. pepper
1 tsp. onion juice	½ c. water
1c. fine, dry bread crumbs	Fat or oil for deep-fat frying
1 egg, separated	
1 tblsp. milk	Green Pepper Sauce

Combine peanuts, squash, onion juice and ½ c. bread crumbs. Add egg yolk, milk, butter, salt and pepper; mix well. Form into patties.

Mix slightly beaten egg white with water. Dip patties into egg white mixture, then in remaining crumbs. Fry in deep hot fat (365°) about 1 minute, or until brown and heated through. Drain. Serve with Green Pepper Sauce. Makes 12 (2″) patties.

Green Pepper Sauce: Cook 1 medium green pepper, seeded and chopped, in 3 tblsp. melted butter 3 minutes, or until pepper is soft but not browned. Stir in 3 tblsp. flour, 1 tsp. salt and ⅛ tsp. pepper; mix until smooth. Gradually add 2 c. milk; cook 5 minutes, stirring constantly, until thickened. Makes 2 cups.

SQUASH CASSEROLE SPECIAL

Serve orange-yellow squash and green peas with chicken— a real feast

3 c. hot mashed butternut squash	1 tsp. minced onion
¼ c. butter	¼ c. milk
1 tsp. salt	3 eggs, well beaten
⅛ tsp. pepper	¼ c. buttered bread crumbs

To hot squash add butter; beat until butter melts. Stir in salt, pepper and onion. Blend milk into eggs; add to squash mixture.

Pour into greased 1½-qt. casserole; top with buttered bread crumbs. Set in pan of warm water and bake in moderate oven (350°) until knife inserted in center comes out clean, about 45 minutes. Makes 6 servings.

BAKED BUTTERNUT SQUASH

Squash bakes to delicious perfection with practically no oven-watching

1 (3 to 3½ lb.) butternut squash	1 tblsp. butter or margarine
Salt and pepper to taste	3 to 4 tblsp. water
	⅓ c. toasted pecan halves

Wash squash; remove seeds at full, rounded end; cut in ½" slices. Overlap slices in shallow baking dish. Sprinkle with salt and pepper; dot with butter. Add water; cover tightly with foil.

Bake in hot oven (400°) 35 to 40 minutes, or until squash is tender. Serve topped with pecans. Makes about 4 servings.

NOTE: This is an easy recipe to double if you need more servings. Just bake two pans of squash.

CHEESE-SQUASH SCALLOP

Here's a good way to serve squash—bake it in a well-seasoned custard

9 c. yellow squash slices, ½" thick (about 3 lbs.)	½ c. cracker crumbs
1 c. chopped onion (1 medium)	¼ c. chopped parsley
1 clove garlic, minced	4 eggs
1 tblsp. salad oil	1 c. milk
1 c. grated Swiss cheese	2 tsp. salt
	¼ tsp. pepper

Cook squash in boiling salted water until barely tender. Drain well.

Meanwhile, cook onion and garlic in oil until onion is soft.

Place half of onion mixture on bottom of greased 2-qt. casserole. Top with half of cheese, cracker crumbs and parsley. Add all the squash, then remaining onion, cheese, crumbs and parsley.

Beat eggs, blend in milk, salt and pepper. Pour over squash. Place casserole in pan of hot water and bake in slow oven (325°) 50 to 55 minutes, or until set. Makes 8 servings.

Tomatoes

Even a farm family without a garden usually grows a few tomato plants, home-grown and vine-ripened tomatoes are so superior. But the supply offered at produce counters during winter and early spring has improved in recent years. Tomatoes are available in moderate supply throughout the year.

In selecting ripe tomatoes, look for a rich red color and slight softness. For tomatoes slightly less than fully ripe, look for firm texture with color ranging from pink to light red. Choose well-formed, smooth tomatoes that are reasonably free from blemishes.

Allow 2 lbs. for 4 servings (8 small).

If tomatoes are fully ripe, keep them in the refrigerator. They will hold several days. If they need further ripening, lay them stem-end down at room temperature or in a cool place, to ripen slowly. You can keep them blemish-free if you lay them on a padded surface only one layer deep.

When ready to cook, peel tomatoes. There are two quick ways to do this. Dip the tomato in boiling water for ½ to 1 minute. Plunge into cold water and slip off the skin. Or hold the tomato on a fork over heat and rotate until it wrinkles and splits. Pull off the skin and cut out core.

To cook, put quartered tomatoes in saucepan with a little finely chopped onion and 1 to 2 tsp. sugar (for 6 to 8 medium tomatoes). Usually no water is required. Simmer, covered, 5 to 15 minutes. Season with celery salt, salt, pepper and butter or margarine. If tomatoes are very juicy, add toasted bread cubes. Serve hot.

BROILED TOMATOES WITH SOUR CREAM

Nice bright taste treat on the dinner plates for company

4 tomatoes
Salt and pepper to taste
⅓ c. dairy sour cream

⅓ c. mayonnaise
⅛ tsp. curry powder

Wash tomatoes; core, but do not peel. Cut in halves crosswise. Sprinkle with salt and pepper. Blend together remaining ingredients; spread on cut sides of tomatoes. Broil until mixture is bubbly, 5 to 10 minutes. Makes 8 servings.

SAVORY TOMATO SKILLET

*Ripe tomatoes cook to perfection in buttery sauce
for this country treat*

¼ c. butter or margarine
½ c. finely chopped onion
2 tblsp. chopped parsley
½ tsp. salt

¼ tsp. thyme leaves
⅛ tsp. pepper
6 whole tomatoes, peeled
  and cored

Melt butter in skillet. Add onion, parsley, salt, thyme and pepper. Add tomatoes, cored side down.

Cover and cook 5 minutes. Turn tomatoes carefully, basting with butter mixture. Cover and continue cooking 5 minutes. Serve in sauce dishes with sauce spooned over. Makes 6 servings.

COUNTRY-SCALLOPED TOMATOES

*When tomatoes are ripe, it's time to turn to this great
country favorite*

¼ c. chopped onion
¼ c. chopped green pepper
¼ c. butter
6 medium tomatoes, peeled
  and sliced
½ tsp. salt

¼ tsp. pepper
1 tblsp. sugar
⅛ tsp. basil leaves
  (optional)
1½ c. toasted bread cubes

Cook onion and green pepper in butter until soft. Place half of tomatoes in 2-qt. casserole. Top with half of seasonings and bread cubes, and all of green pepper mixture.

Top with remaining tomatoes, seasonings and bread cubes. Bake in moderate oven (350°) 30 minutes. Makes 6 servings.

BAKED TOMATO HALVES

*Just bake these seasoned tomatoes in the oven—
no last-minute fuss*

6 tomatoes	2 tblsp. chopped parsley
2 tblsp. chopped onion	½ tsp. salt
2 tblsp. butter	⅛ tsp. pepper
½ c. bread crumbs	

Cut stem end out of tomatoes. Cut tomatoes in halves and place in shallow baking pan.

Cook onion in butter until soft. Add remaining ingredients and toss. Spread mixture on top of tomato halves.

Bake in hot oven (400°) until lightly browned, about 25 minutes. Makes 6 servings as a vegetable, 12 as a garnish.

TOMATOES WITH RICE

*Use ripe, juicy tomatoes in this easy,
but French-gourmet creation*

1 c. rice	3 medium tomatoes,
2 bay leaves	chopped
2 c. water	¼ c. grated Parmesan
½ tsp. salt	cheese

Cook rice and bay leaves, covered, in salted water until rice is tender.

Remove bay leaves. Stir in tomatoes. Cook until all liquid is absorbed. Stir in cheese. Makes 6 servings.

Tomatoes in Cream: *Dip thick tomato slices in batter and brown on both sides in butter or bacon drippings. Remove to hot serving dish. Stir ½ c. light cream into drippings and let simmer over low heat until brown. Serve over hot tomatoes.*

Autumn's Green Tomato Slices

Autumn in country kitchens means many good-tasting dishes, such as the garden's last green tomatoes, sliced and browned in bacon drippings. What you dip the slices in to encourage browning and the development of a crunchy coating influences the way they taste.

Some farm women like to use half and half corn meal and flour. An Ohio homemaker prefers corn muffin mix, which she buys, a cupful at a time, in a little plastic bag. We tested her suggestion and tasted the results, and agreed that this gives the tomatoes a special flavor. Get out your skillet and try the recipe for Green Tomato Slices and see if your family and friends don't like them. They're a wonderful accompaniment served with meat on the platter. To serve the tomatoes as a separate vegetable, you'll want to double the recipe to make 6 servings.

GREEN TOMATO SLICES

They're a marvelous garnish for meats

3 green tomatoes, sliced	**3 tblsp. bacon or other fat**
½" thick	**¼ tsp. salt**
½ c. prepared corn muffin	**⅛ tsp. pepper**
mix	

Dip tomato slices in corn muffin mix. Fry in bacon fat until brown on both sides, turning once. Sprinkle with salt and pepper. Makes 6 servings when used as a meat garnish.

COUNTRY-FRIED GREEN TOMATOES

If you don't count calories, you'll like these tomatoes with hot, rich cream gravy poured over the top

6 medium green tomatoes,	**½ tsp. salt**
sliced	**¼ tsp. pepper**
1 tblsp. sugar	**¼ c. butter**
½ c. flour	

Sprinkle tomatoes with sugar; let stand about 15 minutes. Combine flour, salt and pepper. Dip tomato slices in mixture.

Melt 2 tblsp. butter in skillet. Brown tomatoes slowly on both sides. Remove each batch to ovenproof platter and keep hot in oven until all tomatoes are cooked. Add more butter if needed. For crisp slices, serve as is. Or add ½ c. light cream or dairy half-and-half to skillet. Heat, stirring into drippings, and pour over tomatoes. Makes 6 servings.

Try cooking cherry tomatoes. Sauté them in a skillet in butter or margarine for only 2 or 3 minutes. Season with salt and pepper and a sprinkle of sugar to make them shine. A bright and tasty addition to a dinner plate.

Turnips

White Turnips: The most popular turnip has white flesh and a purple tint or collar at the top. It is available throughout the year.

Select roots that are smooth and heavy for their size. If the tops have not been removed, they should be green, young and tender.

Allow 2 lbs. for 4 servings (6 medium).

Store, with tops removed, in a cool moist place or enclose in plastic bag and put in refrigerator crisper. Cook turnip tops like greens if they're young (see Index).

When ready to cook, peel off thin skin with knife or vegetable peeler. Wash and leave whole, cut in strips or dice for quicker cooking.

Cook them, covered, in 1" boiling salted water 10 to 20 minutes for cut pieces, 30 minutes for whole turnips. Drain and season with salt, pepper and butter or margarine. If you like, sprinkle with a few drops of lemon juice.

Yellow Turnips: Rutabagas are a variety of Swedish turnips and a member of the cabbage family. They grow partly above and partly below the ground. Their flesh is yellow and they have a stronger flavor than white turnips. They are not available in summer.

Select smooth, firm, heavy roots of small to medium size with a minimum of deep scars at the top and of fibrous roots at the bottom. Lightweight rutabagas often are woody, pithy and strong in flavor. All rutabagas come to market without tops.

Allow 2 lbs. for 4 servings.

When ready to cook, scrub well and peel. Sometimes storage rutabagas, also white turnips and parsnips, are coated with a thin layer of paraffin to prevent loss of moisture and shriveling. Remove paraffin and skin with a vegetable peeler and cut the rutabaga into 2″ pieces or into strips or ½″ cubes.

Cook, covered, in 1″ boiling salted water until tender, about 35 to 40 minutes for 2″ pieces, 20 to 25 minutes for strips or ½″ cubes. Drain and season with salt, pepper and butter or margarine. Or cook rutabagas in consommé instead of water. For a classic dish, combine equal parts cooked rutabagas and potatoes, mash, add a little hot milk and seasonings, and whip until fluffy.

WHIPPED TURNIPS

Taste-testers named this the best turnip dish
they ever tasted—mild

4 c. mashed cooked turnips	2 tsp. salt
2 c. soft bread crumbs	¼ tsp. pepper
½ c. melted butter	4 eggs, slightly beaten
2 tblsp. sugar	

Combine turnips with bread crumbs. (To prepare soft bread crumbs, remove crusts from fresh bread; cut or tear in tiny cubes.)

Blend in remaining ingredients. Place in greased 2-qt. casserole. Bake in moderate oven (350°) 1 hour and 15 minutes, or until set. Makes 8 servings.

TURNIPS IN CHEESE SAUCE

If your family doesn't fancy turnips, try this
and win them over

3 c. sliced peeled turnips	1 c. shredded process
¼ c. butter or margarine	cheese
¼ c. flour	1 tblsp. minced chives
1½ c. light cream	

Cook sliced turnips in boiling salted water 8 to 10 minutes. Drain; cover to keep hot.

Melt butter in saucepan; stir in flour. Add cream; cook, stirring, until thickened. Add cheese, and stir until melted.

Add turnips to sauce. Sprinkle with chives. Makes 6 servings.

NOTE: New Englanders refer to yellow and white turnips, but in some areas the yellow ones are called rutabagas. White turnips are more delicate in flavor, but they may be used interchangeably.

FRENCH-STYLE TURNIPS

The seasonings do something special to turnips—
taste-testers approved

2½ lbs. medium turnips	or 1 bouillon cube
(about 9)	dissolved in ¾ c. water
¼ lb. bacon in one piece	½ to 1 tsp. salt
⅔ c. minced onion	1 tsp. sugar
1 tblsp. flour	¼ tsp. rubbed sage
¾ c. canned beef bouillon,	¼ tsp. pepper

Peel, quarter and cook turnips in 1" boiling salted water 5 minutes. Drain.

Cut bacon in ¼" cubes; you should have ¾ c. Cook bacon 4 minutes in skillet, stirring constantly. Add onion and cook 5 minutes (do not let brown). Blend in flour; add bouillon, salt (the exact amount depending on saltiness of bacon), sugar, sage and pepper. Cook 2 minutes, stirring constantly.

Add turnips; cover and simmer 15 to 20 minutes, or until turnips are tender. Makes 6 to 7 servings.

SWEDISH RUTABAGAS

An heirloom recipe shared by the granddaughter
of a good Swedish cook

2 medium rutabagas, peeled, quartered and sliced ¼" thick	½ tsp. ground ginger
2 tblsp. brown sugar	½ tsp. salt
	⅛ tsp. pepper
	2 tblsp. butter

Cook rutabagas in boiling salted water; drain.

Meanwhile, combine brown sugar, ginger, salt and pepper; mix thoroughly. Add with butter to rutabagas. Stir gently over low heat until sugar melts, 2 to 3 minutes. Makes 6 servings.

Vegetables in Cheese Sauce

In talking with farm women and reading their letters, you learn how they strive to fix vegetables so their families will enjoy them. Cheese sauce is the magic many mothers depend on to dress up vegetables so that they appeal to children—husbands, too. There's a plus value in this custom—the sauce adds calcium, one of the big nutritional deficiencies in our diets.

Here is the simple sauce one reader shares, along with her ways to use it to make vegetables inviting. Start out by making the simple, basic sauce.

VEGETABLES IN CHEESE SAUCE

At first, try the plain sauce on vegetables for color and tastiness; then try our additions to it in the recipes that follow—they are extra-special

2 tblsp. butter or margarine	1 c. grated process cheese
2 tblsp. flour	Salt and pepper to taste
1 c. milk	Paprika

Melt butter; blend in flour. Remove from heat and add milk slowly, stirring constantly, until smooth and blended. Return to heat and cook and stir until thick. Turn off heat; add cheese and let stand until cheese is melted. Stir enough to blend; add salt, pepper and a little paprika. Makes 1 cup.

Zucchini in Cheese Sauce: Add ½ tsp. Worcestershire sauce to 1 c. Cheese Sauce. Wash 2 lbs. unpeeled young zucchini and cut in ½" slices. Cook in small amount boiling salted water until just tender. Drain. Place in serving dish and pour sauce over. Serve at once. Makes 4 to 6 servings.

Scalloped Cabbage: Add 1 to 2 tblsp. vinegar to 1 c. Cheese Sauce. Shred 1 medium head cabbage and cook until just tender in boiling salted water, 5 to 8 minutes. Drain. Mix gently with sauce and serve immediately. Or, if desired, place cabbage and Cheese Sauce in greased 1½-qt. casserole, top with buttered cracker crumbs and brown under the broiler; or bake in moderate oven (375°) until bubbly. Makes 4 to 6 servings.

Green Beans with Mustard Sauce: Add prepared mustard to taste to 1 c. Cheese Sauce. Serve over 3 c. green beans that have been cooked in boiling salted water until just tender. Garnish with sliced pimiento, if desired, or sprinkle with paprika. Makes 6 servings.

Cauliflower with Almonds: Trim leaves from stalk of 1 medium head cauliflower, leaving 1" of stem for support. Steam, tightly covered, using enough boiling salted water to cover stem but not touching head, until tender, about 25 minutes. To serve, cut off stalk and place cauliflower in serving dish. Stick ⅓ c. slivered blanched almonds into cauliflower, then pour 1 c. Cheese Sauce over top. Sprinkle with paprika or chopped parsley. Makes 6 servings.

Cooking Vegetables at High Altitudes

If you live in high country, you may wish to use a pressure cooker to shorten the longer cooking time altitude makes necessary for fresh vegetables. Put in your pressure cooker the amount of water that the manufacturer recommends. Add the prepared vegetable and ¼ tsp. salt. Over high heat, bring the pressure to the point recommended by the manufacturer. Then reduce heat to maintain that pressure throughout cooking. When cooking time is up, reduce the pressure at once as the manufacturer recommends.

TIMETABLE FOR COOKING VEGETABLES
IN A PRESSURE COOKER

Vegetable	Approximate Cooking Time in Minutes (15 lbs. pressure)
Artichokes	
Globe, French or Italian	6 to 10
Jerusalem	
Sliced	8
Whole	14
Asparagus	
Whole stalks	2
Cut up	1 to 2
Beans, Green and Wax	
Sliced crosswise	2 to 3
French-style	1 to 2
Beans, Green Lima	
Small	2
Large	3 to 5
Beets	
Diced	5
Whole, young	10 to 12
Whole, old	12 to 18
Broccoli	1½ to 2
Brussels sprouts	2
Cabbage	
Shredded	2
Quartered (wedges)	4 to 6
Carrots	
Sliced	2 to 3
Whole	5 to 6
Cauliflower flowerets	2
Celeriac sliced or diced	5
Celery sliced	3
Corn on cob	4 to 5
Greens	3 to 5
Kohlrabi sliced or quartered	5
Mushrooms	
Small	3 to 4
Large	5 to 7
Okra	
Whole	3
Cut up	2
Onions	
Sliced ¼" thick	3 to 4

Vegetable	Approximate Cooking Time in Minutes (15 lbs. pressure)
Sliced ½" thick	6 to 7
Whole (small white)	5 to 6
Parsnips	
Diced	2
Whole, small	8
Peas shelled	1
(Cook with a few pods for flavor)	
Potatoes	
Sweet	
Unpeeled	8 to 10
White	
Whole	10 to 20
Sliced	1½
Pumpkin unpeeled, cut up	15
Salsify sliced	4 to 9
Spinach	1
Squash	
Acorn cut in half	10
Hubbard cut up	12 to 13
Summer	2 to 3
Turnips	
Sliced ¼" thick	5 to 6
Strips	3 to 5
Rutabagas (yellow turnips)	
Sliced 2" thick	15
Strips or ½" cubes	9 to 12

Chapter Two

Frozen Vegetables

Let the snow whirl around the back steps or rain make music on the kitchen windowpanes. The time of year need have no influence on availability of vegetables. Open the freezer door and take your pick of several vegetables; some may have been home-grown, others from the supermarket. Rejoice that you live in a time when you can serve foods with summer flavors the year around.

Frozen vegetables cook fast—from around 3 minutes for whole kernel corn to about 12 minutes for Fordhook lima beans. If you live at a high altitude, it takes a few minutes longer. (This chapter tells how to cook frozen vegetables the easiest way if you live in mountainous country.)

Because you are busy, this wonderful quick cooking may lead to monotonous vegetable dishes. All you need do to get more exciting dishes is spend a very few extra minutes on seasonings. This chapter contains the recipes. Use them and listen to your family: "Mom, these green beans taste so good!" And the drop-in neighbor, whom you persuade to stay for dinner, will wonder, "Why does your corn taste so much better than the corn I froze?" The answers may be as simple as dressing the beans with frozen Tomato Sauce Cubes and adding a hint of garlic salt or chili powder to the corn.

All frozen vegetable cookery need not be fast. When you have meat, chicken or a main dish casserole baking in the oven, it may be more convenient to cook frozen vegetables alongside. This chapter gives a timetable for oven-cooking frozen vegetables.

You'll like the new recipes for frozen vegetables from Farm Journal Family Test Group members and from our Test Kitchens. Read the recipe for Jiffy Scalloped Potatoes that bake in 30 minutes (you start with frozen potatoes). And do make Potato Pizza to please the teenagers—a snap to fix with frozen French fries. Young people actually rave about this main dish pie. These recipes are samples of the treats that await you in this chapter.

A GUIDE TO
FROZEN VEGETABLE MEASUREMENTS

Vegetable	Weight per Package	Contents
Asparagus, cuts and spears	10 oz.	2 c.
Beans		
Green	9 oz.	2 c.
Limas, green	10 oz.	1¾ c.
Broccoli, spears, chopped	10 oz.	1¾ c.
Brussels sprouts	10 oz.	19 sprouts
Cauliflower	10 oz.	2 c.
Corn, cut	10 oz.	1¾ c.
Greens	10 oz.	1⅔ c.
Mixed Vegetables	10 oz.	2 c.
Okra	10 oz.	2 c.
Onions, chopped	12 oz.	3¼ c.
Peas, black-eyed	10 oz.	2 c.
Peas, green, shelled	10 oz.	2 c.
Spinach	10 oz.	1½ c.
Squash		
Summer, sliced	10 oz.	1½ c.
Winter, cooked	12 oz.	1½ c.

COOKING FROZEN VEGETABLES
AT HIGH ALTITUDES

Put unthawed frozen vegetable in saucepan. It's important to use a pan with a tight-fitting lid to reduce evaporation of moisture. Follow cooking directions on package, but add a little more water and allow more time for cooking.

Cover saucepan and place over low heat. When water starts to simmer, separate vegetable with a fork. Then cover and simmer very gently until vegetable is tender, stirring occasionally. If necessary, add a little more water. Corn is tender in about 8 minutes, Fordhook limas in 18 to 20 minutes.

COOKING FROZEN VEGETABLES
OVER COALS

Place unthawed frozen vegetables on foil and top with pats of butter. Wrap securely in the foil, making a flat, long package or individual packages. Place on grill over coals for 10 to 15 minutes; turn occasionally. Open package, fold edges back, season with salt and pepper and serve. Mixed frozen vegetables are especially nice fixed this way for meals cooked outdoors.

COOK FROZEN VEGETABLES IN YOUR OVEN

When you're busy, you'll find it convenient to cook frozen vegetables in your oven alongside meat loaf, a main-dish casserole, meat or chicken. You need not thaw the vegetable. Just place the frozen block in a greased casserole, add 1 to 2 tblsp. butter or margarine on top and sprinkle on ¼ tsp. salt. There are two exceptions: Add 2 tblsp. water with butter and salt to baby lima beans, ¼ c. water to Fordhooks. Cover with tight-fitting lid and place in the oven. Stir about 15 minutes before end of cooking time and again just before serving. Check for seasonings, adding more salt and a little pepper if needed.

Here is a guide to how long to bake frozen vegetables in a moderate oven (350°). If you are using a slower heat (325°), increase cooking time about 10 minutes, and decrease time about 10 minutes if the oven heat is 375°.

TIMETABLE FOR
BAKING FROZEN VEGETABLES

9 to 12 oz. Package Frozen Vegetable	Minutes (Approximate)
Asparagus, cut and spears	55 to 60
Broccoli, chopped	45 to 50
Broccoli, spears	40 to 45
Brussels sprouts	40 to 45
Cauliflower	50 to 55
Corn, cut or whole kernel	45 to 50
Green beans, cut and French-style	45 to 50

9 to 12 oz. Package Frozen Vegetable	Minutes (Approximate)
Green limas, baby	40 to 50
Green limas, Fordhook	45 to 50
Italian and whole beans	55 to 60
Mixed vegetables	60
Peas	40 to 50
Peas and carrots	55 to 60
Spinach, chopped	45 to 50
Succotash	50 to 60
Wax beans	60

Elegant Asparagus Almondaise

You're on the right track, when you decide to serve Asparagus Almondaise for the hot green vegetable in your company dinner. It's delicious . . . and it's different. Cook frozen asparagus by package directions, drain and place in a warm serving dish. Then top with the sauce that converts the plain vegetable into an elegant one.

ASPARAGUS ALMONDAISE

The sauce is as great on broccoli and cauliflower as on asparagus

3 egg yolks
1 tsp. cornstarch
½ c. cold water
1 tblsp. lemon juice
¼ c. melted butter or margarine
Salt to taste

Ground red pepper (cayenne) to taste
½ c. toasted slivered almonds
2 (10 oz.) pkgs. frozen asparagus spears, cooked and drained

Beat egg yolks slightly in top of double boiler. Blend in cornstarch, then stir in water, lemon juice and butter. Cook over simmering water, stirring constantly, until thickened, 2 to 3 minutes.

Add salt and red pepper. Stir in almonds. Serve over hot cooked asparagus spears. Makes 6 servings.

WINTER TAKE-ALONG CASSEROLE

This tasty dish is popular at potluck suppers
in the country

2 (10 oz.) pkgs. frozen asparagus	2 tsp. salt
1 c. chopped onion	¼ tsp. pepper
¼ c. butter or margarine	4 hard-cooked eggs, sliced
6 tblsp. flour	½ c. shredded Cheddar cheese
3 c. milk	½ c. dry bread crumbs

Cook asparagus as directed on package until barely tender; drain.

In a large skillet, cook onion in butter until tender (not brown). Stir in flour. Add milk and cook, stirring constantly, until thickened. Mix in salt, pepper, eggs and asparagus.

Turn into a 2-qt. casserole. Top with cheese and crumbs. Bake in moderate oven (350°) until hot and bubbly, about 30 minutes. Makes 8 servings.

NORTHWEST ASPARAGUS

"Be ready for compliments when you serve this,"
a farm woman revealed when she sent us her recipe

2 (10 oz.) pkgs. frozen cut asparagus	⅓ c. slivered toasted almonds
6 hard-cooked eggs	1 c. Cheese Sauce (see Index)
½ tsp. salt	
⅛ tsp. pepper	

Cook asparagus by package directions; drain. Place half of asparagus in greased 1½-qt. casserole. Top with half of hard-cooked eggs, sliced. Sprinkle with half of salt and pepper.

Repeat layers of asparagus, eggs and seasonings. Top with almonds, then Cheese Sauce.

Bake in moderate oven (350°) 25 minutes. Makes 6 servings.

NOTE: You can use sauce made from 1 (1¾ oz.) pkg. cheese sauce mix instead of Cheese Sauce, if you wish.

In the earliest spring, in the eastern United States, people who know good eating search for fiddleheads, the young sprouting leaves of the ostrich fern. The tightly curled sprouts are picked when they are about two inches long, cooked quickly in salted water and served with butter, salt and pepper to taste, and maybe a drop of vinegar or lemon juice. This delicacy rates being served as a separate course.

Green Beans with Corn Rosettes: *With a heavy sharp knife, cut uncooked corn on cob crosswise into 1" slices. Cook like corn on cob, drain and add to hot cooked and seasoned green beans. Serve at once. You eat the corn with your fingers. This makes a fine buffet supper dish.*

Green Beans with Oranges

If you're hunting for a new, appetizing and attractive way to fix frozen green beans, do try Green Beans with Oranges. The flavor of the unusual combination pleases almost everyone who tastes it and the color contrast adds eye appeal. The recipe comes from a Midwestern farm woman, who invented it in her kitchen. She brought it to our Test Kitchens when she visited our food editors as a Guest Cook. When she made the dish, our home economists, who sampled it, gave enthusiastic approval.

GREEN BEANS WITH ORANGES

Easy; combines two well-liked foods

2 (10 oz.) pkgs. frozen whole green beans	**3 tblsp. butter**
1 (11 oz.) can mandarin oranges, drained	**Salt and pepper to taste**

Cook beans according to package directions; drain. Add orange sections and butter. Heat through; season with salt and pepper. Makes 6 servings.

DILLED GREEN BEANS

The seasoning's the secret—fix beans this way and you'll agree

2 beef bouillon cubes
1 c. water
2 tblsp. chopped onion
¼ c. chopped green pepper

½ tsp. dill seeds
2 (10 oz.) pkgs. frozen cut
green beans

Dissolve bouillon cubes in water in saucepan. Add onion, green pepper and dill seeds. Cook several minutes.

Add beans; cook, covered, 8 to 10 minutes, until beans are tender. Makes 6 servings.

GREEN BEANS WITH CHEESE

Do try these green beans combined with Swiss cheese and sour cream

2 (10 oz.) pkgs. frozen
French-style green beans
2 tsp. minced onion or leek
2 tblsp. butter or margarine
2 tblsp. flour
1 tsp. sugar
½ tsp. salt

¼ tsp. pepper
1 c. dairy sour cream
6 thin slices Swiss cheese,
cut in strips
½ c. corn flake crumbs
Paprika

Cook beans according to package directions; drain.

Cook onion or leek, using only the white part of latter, in butter 3 minutes. Add flour, sugar, salt and pepper; stir in sour cream and heat thoroughly, but do not boil. Pour over beans, arranged in a well-buttered 11 × 7″ flat baking dish; arrange cheese strips on top. Top with crumbs, then sprinkle generously with paprika.

Bake in moderate oven (350°) 20 minutes. Makes 8 servings.

GREEN BEANS WITH WATER CHESTNUTS

Wonderful way to fix green beans

2 (9 oz.) pkgs. frozen
French-style green beans
1 (3 oz.) can broiled
mushroom crowns,
drained

1 (8 oz.) can water
chestnuts, drained and
sliced
1 can condensed cream of
celery soup

Allow green beans to defrost until they can be separated.

125

Mix in remaining ingredients. Place in greased 2-qt. casserole; cover and bake in moderate oven (350°) 50 minutes, or until green beans are tender. Makes 6 to 8 servings.

PARTY GREEN BEANS

This is a company-special dish, favorite of a home economist

2 (9 oz.) pkgs. frozen
  French-style green beans
3 tblsp. butter or margarine
3 tblsp. flour
1½ c. milk or dairy
  half-and-half
Salt and pepper to taste

Onion salt to taste
Worcestershire sauce to
  taste
1 (6 oz.) can broiled
  mushroom crowns
¼ lb. cashew nuts

Cook beans according to package directions.

Melt butter; blend in flour. Stir in milk and cook, stirring constantly, until sauce is thickened. Season with salt, pepper, onion salt and Worcestershire sauce.

Drain beans and mushrooms; combine with sauce. Stir in cashews and heat through. Makes 6 to 8 servings.

New Green Bean-Onion Bake

One of the most popular casserole combinations going the rounds consists of green beans in mushroom soup topped with French fried onions. Here's a new version that taste-testers gave a high rating.

NEW GREEN BEAN-ONION BAKE

Sour cream adds tang, water chestnuts crispness. Spring this on guests

2 (9 oz.) pkgs. frozen
  French-style green beans
1 c. dairy sour cream
½ can condensed cream of
  mushroom soup

1 (5 oz.) can water
  chestnuts, drained and
  thinly sliced
1 (3½ oz.) can French fried
  onions

126

Cook beans according to package directions until tender-crisp. Drain thoroughly and pour onto paper toweling so all liquid is absorbed.

In a 1-qt. casserole combine beans with sour cream, mushroom soup and water chestnuts. Bake in slow oven (325°) about 20 minutes, or until bubbly. Sprinkle onions over top and continue baking 5 to 10 minutes, or until onions are crisp and heated through. Makes 4 servings.

GREEN BEANS PROVENÇALE

*No need to wonder what vegetable to serve guests
if you have this recipe*

2 (9 oz.) pkgs. frozen cut green beans	1 clove garlic, minced
2 tblsp. butter or margarine	1 tsp. salt
1 c. finely diced cooked ham	Dash pepper
	2 medium tomatoes, cut in wedges

Cook green beans according to package directions; drain.

In same saucepan, melt butter; add ham and garlic, and cook until garlic is golden brown.

Stir in beans, salt and pepper. Top with tomato wedges; cover and heat through. Makes 8 servings.

GREEN BEAN CAKES

Here's proof there's something new in the old standby, pancakes

1 (10 oz.) pkg. frozen green beans	½ c. milk
2 eggs	2 tblsp. butter or margarine (about)
¼ c. flour	Whipped butter
¼ tsp. salt	

Cook green beans according to package directions; drain thoroughly and cool.

Place beans, eggs, flour, salt and milk in blender container; put on lid and process at chop speed a few seconds, then blend at medium speed.

Melt 1 tsp. butter on griddle or in fry pan. Pour a small

127

amount of batter onto griddle to make cakes about 2½"
in diameter; fry a little slower than regular hot cakes.
Serve with whipped butter. Makes 12 (2½") cakes.

NOTE: If you do not have a blender, make batter as follows: Chop cooked beans very fine (putting them through
a sieve or food mill after chopping gives a better consistency). Beat eggs; combine with flour, salt and milk, beating until smooth. Add beans to batter and mix.

VARIATION

Filled Green Bean Cakes: Instead of the small cakes, make
5" cakes, cooking one at a time, and rolling after browning
on both sides. When all cakes are baked, unroll and add a
hot filling of creamed chicken, ham or small link sausages;
then roll up again and serve. Makes 6 (5") cakes.

ORIENTAL GREEN BEANS

*Family tired of green beans? We guarantee
this recipe for new appeal*

2 (10 oz.) pkgs. frozen French-style green beans	**1 clove garlic, crushed**
½ lb. fresh mushrooms, sliced	**¼ c. soy sauce**
	2 tblsp. wine vinegar
¼ c. butter or margarine	**Salt to taste**
2 tblsp. olive oil	**½ c. croutons**

Cook frozen beans according to package directions;
drain.

Cook mushrooms in butter 5 minutes, until barely trans-
lucent; add to beans.

Heat olive oil and garlic; add to combined mushrooms
and beans. Add soy sauce and vinegar; mix well and heat
together for a few minutes. Discard garlic; add salt.

Turn into a serving dish and scatter croutons on top.
Makes 8 servings.

GREEN BEANS GOLDENROD

*This so-good green and yellow treat
fits into a spring color scheme*

2 (10 oz.) pkgs. frozen cut green beans	¼ tsp. salt
2 hard-cooked eggs	⅛ tsp. pepper
2 tsp. butter	½ c. milk
2 tsp. flour	½ c. mayonnaise

Cook beans in boiling salted water by package directions. Chop egg whites; press yolks through sieve.

While beans cook, make sauce by melting butter in saucepan; blend in flour, salt and pepper. Gradually stir in milk. Cook over medium heat, stirring constantly until thickened. Stir in chopped egg whites. Remove from heat; stir in mayonnaise.

Drain beans; place in serving dish. Spoon on sauce; sprinkle top with sieved egg yolks. Makes 8 servings.

GREEN BEAN CASSEROLE

A fine vegetable dish for a buffet. It bakes without attention during the last-minute rush at mealtime

3 tblsp. butter, melted	2 (12 oz.) pkgs. frozen French-style green beans, cooked
2 tblsp. flour	
1 tsp. salt	
¼ tsp. pepper	½ lb. grated Cheddar cheese
1 tsp. sugar	
½ tsp. grated onion	½ c. corn flake crumbs
1 c. dairy sour cream	

Combine 2 tblsp. butter and flour; cook gently. Remove from heat; stir in salt, pepper, sugar, onion and sour cream. Fold in beans. Place in shallow 2-qt. casserole.

Cover with cheese, then with crumbs mixed with remaining 1 tblsp. butter. Bake in moderate oven (350°) 30 minutes. Makes 8 servings.

Italian Green Beans Sesame

More gardeners every year grow Italian green beans and freeze the summer surplus to contribute variety to meals the remainder of the year. Many women depend on the freezer cases in their supermarkets to provide packages of this broad-podded, tender vegetable, which they keep in their home freezers for a quick change in vegetable dishes. Toasted Sesame Seeds add fascinating flavor and a touch of crunchiness to Italian Green Beans Sesame.

ITALIAN GREEN BEANS SESAME

Every woman who entertains friends at dinners
will want this recipe

2 (9 oz.) pkgs. frozen Italian green beans	1 tblsp. soy sauce
1 tblsp. salad oil	4 tsp. sugar
1 tblsp. lemon juice	1 tblsp. Toasted Sesame Seeds

Cook green beans according to package directions; drain.

In a small saucepan, combine remaining ingredients; heat to boiling. Pour sauce over hot green beans and serve at once. Makes 5 to 6 servings.

Toasted Sesame Seeds: Spread sesame seeds in shallow pan and place in moderate oven (350°). Remove pan when seeds are a pale brown. It will take about 20 minutes, but watch them to prevent overbrowning, which destroys the seeds' finest flavors.

BEANS AU GRATIN

Three kinds of beans with a cheese topper
make this a buffet special

1 (10 oz.) pkg. frozen lima beans	2 tblsp. flour
1¼ c. boiling water	1¼ c. light cream
1 tsp. salt	½ tsp. salt
1 (10 oz.) pkg. frozen green beans	⅛ tsp. pepper
1 (9 oz.) pkg. frozen wax beans	¼ tsp. Worcestershire sauce
4 tblsp. butter	½ c. grated Parmesan cheese

Place lima beans, boiling water and salt in large saucepan; bring to a boil; reduce heat, cover and cook 5 minutes. Add green and wax beans. Continue cooking 8 to 10

130

minutes, breaking up frozen block of beans once during cooking. Drain.

Meanwhile, melt 2 tblsp. butter. Blend in flour. Add cream and cook, stirring constantly, until mixture comes to a boil. Add salt, pepper and Worcestershire sauce. Combine with beans.

Spoon mixture into greased 1½-qt. casserole. Top with cheese; dot with remaining 2 tblsp. butter. Bake in moderate oven (350°) 30 minutes, or until heated bubbling hot. Makes 8 servings.

NOTE: You can make this ahead and refrigerate it. Then bake 35 to 45 minutes before mealtime.

BAKED LIMA BEANS

Frozen limas bake fast—sour cream
gives them an extra-good taste

2 (10 oz.) pkgs. frozen lima beans	¼ c. brown sugar
½ c. chopped onion (1 small)	1 c. dairy sour cream
	¼ c. ketchup
2 tblsp. butter	½ tsp. salt
	⅛ tsp. pepper

Cook beans in boiling salted water until tender. Drain. Meanwhile, cook onion in butter until soft. Stir in remaining ingredients and blend. Stir in lima beans.

Place in 1½-qt. casserole and bake in moderate oven (350°) 25 minutes. Makes 6 servings.

PIQUANT LIMA BEANS

Bacon, herbs and vinegar add extra-special
flavor to frozen limas

2 (10 oz.) pkgs. frozen lima beans	2 tsp. minced fresh parsley, or ½ tsp. parsley flakes
2 slices bacon, cut in ½" strips	¼ tsp. seasoned salt
	¼ tsp. dill weed
2 tblsp. garlic red wine vinegar	Salt and white pepper to taste

Cook beans according to package directions, adding

bacon at beginning of cooking time. Uncover toward end of cooking period to reduce liquid as much as possible. Add remaining ingredients. Makes 8 servings.

Chopped Broccoli Favorites

Frozen chopped broccoli is easy to fix. Its popularity and its rich vitamin content makes this a great selection for family and guest meals. One reason many mothers depend on frozen broccoli is that fresh broccoli is so perishable. If stored too long in the refrigerator, the green to purplish green buds turn yellow and lose some of their best flavors.

Baked Broccoli Ring and Broccoli Almond look festive on the buffet or dining table. The recipes for these and other country favorites in this chapter call for frozen chopped broccoli, a country kitchen favorite. Be sure to look for Broccoli-Chicken in the chapter on Vegetable Main Dishes, which features frozen broccoli stalks.

BAKED BROCCOLI RING

This tasty vegetable ring decorates any meal—
cheese sauce enhances it

2 (10 oz.) pkgs. frozen chopped broccoli	1 tsp. salt
	Dash pepper
2 tblsp. butter or margarine	1¼ c. milk
2 tblsp. flour	3 eggs, slightly beaten
1½ tsp. instant minced onion	

Let broccoli stand at room temperature while preparing sauce.

Melt butter; blend in flour, onion, salt and pepper. Add milk all at once and cook, stirring constantly, until sauce is thickened. Add broccoli and stir over heat to thaw.

Stir a little of the hot mixture into eggs, then stir egg mixture into broccoli. Blend well; turn into well-greased 5½-c. ring mold, or a 1½-qt. greased casserole.

Bake in slow oven (325°) about 45 minutes, until firm. Insert sharp knife around sides, and shake gently to loosen ring. Turn onto hot platter. Serve plain or with cheese or mushroom sauce. Makes 6 to 8 servings.

BROCCOLI ALMOND

*Broccoli and cheese combine in many fine dishes—
this is a good example*

2 (10 oz.) pkgs. frozen
   chopped broccoli
¼ c. chopped onion
¼ c. butter
2 tblsp. flour
½ c. milk
1 (8 oz.) jar pasteurized
   process cheese spread

½ tsp. salt
⅛ tsp. pepper
2 eggs, well beaten
½ c. bread crumbs
2 tblsp. melted butter
¼ c. toasted slivered
   almonds

Cook broccoli in boiling salted water. Drain thoroughly.
Cook onion in ¼ c. butter until soft. Blend in flour,
then milk. Cook, stirring constantly, until thickened. Stir
in cheese spread, salt and pepper until thoroughly blended.
Remove from heat.

Add cheese mixture to eggs, a little at a time, stirring
constantly. Stir in broccoli. Place in greased 1½-qt. casserole. Toss crumbs with melted butter and sprinkle on
top. Top with almonds. Bake in a slow oven (325°) until
set, 40 to 45 minutes. Makes 6 servings.

BROCCOLI BAKE

Two kinds of cheese add fine flavor

2 (10 oz.) pkgs. frozen
   chopped broccoli
2 tblsp. butter
2 tblsp. flour
1½ c. milk

2 oz. Roquefort or blue
   cheese, crumbled
1 (3 oz.) pkg. cream cheese,
   cut in cubes
½ c. cracker crumbs
1 tblsp. melted butter

Cook broccoli in boiling salted water according to package directions. Drain well; set aside.

Melt 2 tblsp. butter in small saucepan. Stir in flour, then
gradually stir in milk, Roquefort and cream cheese; cook,
stirring until slightly thickened and smooth. Allow to cool;
add broccoli. Spoon into 2-qt. casserole.

Bake in moderate oven (350°) 30 minutes. Remove

from oven; top with crumbs mixed with 1 tblsp. melted butter. Return to oven and bake 10 minutes before. Makes 6 to 7 servings.

BROCCOLI-RICE MÉLANGE

*This dish is a specialty of a gracious
Missouri hostess. Try it*

3 c. fluffy cooked rice (1 c. before cooking)
1 (10 oz.) pkg. frozen chopped broccoli, thawed, heated and drained
1 egg
2 tblsp. instant minced onion
1 tsp. Worcestershire sauce

1¼ tsp. salt
1 c. milk
2 tblsp. melted butter or margarine
½ c. shredded sharp Cheddar cheese
Paprika

Combine rice and broccoli.

Mix egg, onion, Worcestershire sauce, salt and milk. Stir into the rice-broccoli mixture. Pour into a greased 2-qt. casserole.

Top with melted butter and shredded cheese. Sprinkle with paprika. Bake in slow oven (325°) 30 to 40 minutes. Makes 6 generous servings.

VARIATION

Spinach-Rice Mélange: Substitute 1 (10 oz.) pkg. frozen chopped spinach, thawed, heated and drained, for broccoli in Broccoli-Rice Mélange.

BROCCOLI SOUFFLÉ

*This soufflé falls slightly during baking—
it's light and flavorful*

1 (10 oz.) pkg. frozen chopped broccoli
3 tblsp. butter or margarine
3 tblsp. flour
1 c. milk
½ tsp. salt

⅛ tsp. ground nutmeg
1 tsp. lemon juice
4 egg yolks, beaten
4 egg whites, beaten until stiff

Cook broccoli according to package directions; drain. Meanwhile, melt butter in saucepan; blend in flour; add milk gradually, stirring constantly. Cook and stir until thick and smooth. Add salt, nutmeg and lemon juice; mix sauce into broccoli. Add egg yolks and let stand to cool.

About 30 minutes before serving time, turn broccoli mixture into greased 1½-qt. casserole. Carefully fold in egg whites. Bake in hot oven (400°) 25 minutes. Makes 4 to 6 servings.

BROCCOLI-SOUR CREAM PUFF

Sour cream lends a subtle tang to this
puffed-up broccoli favorite

1 (10 oz.) pkg. frozen
  chopped broccoli
2 eggs, separated
¼ tsp. cream of tartar
½ tsp. salt
⅛ tsp. pepper

2 tblsp. flour
1 c. dairy sour cream
¼ c. bread crumbs
¼ c. shredded Cheddar
  cheese

Cook broccoli according to package directions; drain.

Beat egg whites and cream of tartar until stiff, but not dry.

Combine egg yolks, salt, pepper, flour and sour cream in mixing bowl; beat until well blended. Fold in broccoli, then beaten egg whites.

Turn into 1½-qt. casserole or soufflé dish. Sprinkle with mixture of bread crumbs and cheese. Bake in moderate oven (375°) 30 to 35 minutes, or until knife inserted in center comes out clean. Makes 6 servings.

Popular Broccoli-Rice Bake

Good recipes travel. When a Kansas woman took Broccoli-Rice Bake to a potluck luncheon for a women's group, everyone asked her about the recipe. She told her friends that her daughter, who lives in Oklahoma, sent it to her—everyone there liked the dish.

The broccoli appears as bright green flecks in the yellow-with-cheese rice. The broccoli and cheese flavors stand up to each other and the mild-tasting rice complements them. This is an easy main dish for luncheon or supper because you use convenience foods, such as frozen broccoli, process cheese foods, precooked rice and canned cream of mushroom soup, to make it.

BROCCOLI-RICE BAKE

*If you tote this to a potluck meal
you'll get requests for the recipe*

½ c. chopped celery
½ c. chopped onion
½ c. margarine (1 stick)
1 can condensed cream of
  mushroom soup
½ c. water

1 (8 oz.) jar pasteurized
  process cheese spread
1 (10 oz.) pkg. frozen
  chopped broccoli
1 (7 oz.) pkg. precooked
  rice

Cook celery and onion in melted margarine until golden.
Combine soup, water and cheese spread.
Thaw broccoli over hot water in top of double boiler.
Cook rice according to package directions.
Combine all ingredients; place in greased 2-qt. casserole.
Bake in moderate oven (350°) 45 minutes. Makes 6 servings.

BRUSSELS SPROUTS SUPREME

*Give it the spotlight in the Thanksgiving dinner—
it's extra-good*

1 (10 oz.) pkg. quick-frozen
  Brussels sprouts
1½ tblsp. flour
⅔ c. water
⅔ c. light cream
½ tsp. salt

¼ tsp. thyme leaves
⅓ lb. chestnuts, cooked
  and chopped (optional)
2 tblsp. buttered bread
  crumbs

Cook Brussels sprouts as directed on package; drain.
Blend flour and water until smooth. Add cream and seasonings; bring to a boil, stirring constantly. Boil 2 minutes, or until slightly thickened.
Add Brussels sprouts and chestnuts (about ¾ c.); pour

mixture into serving dish. Sprinkle buttered crumbs over top. Serve immediately. Makes 4 servings.

NOTE: To cook chestnuts, slit shells with two gashes made to form an "x". Place in heavy skillet with a little salad oil. Cover and shake over low heat until shells loosen. Peel, removing shell and skin. Place chestnuts in salted water to cover; boil 15 to 20 minutes, or until tender. Drain and chop coarsely. You can substitute ½ c. chopped cashew nuts for the chestnuts, if you like.

Corn Custard Pudding

Fresh corn flavor in January and other winter months is one joy that frozen corn brings to our meals. For a superb treat on a blustery, cold day, serve Corn Custard Pudding. No vegetable dish more successfully complements chicken. And there are men who pronounce it the perfect dish with tender, brown pork chops.

CORN CUSTARD PUDDING

*They'll want second helpings—you'd better
bake two casseroles of this*

2 c. frozen loose-pack whole kernel corn	1 tblsp. sugar
2 c. milk or dairy half-and-half	1 tsp. salt
	⅛ tsp. white pepper
2 tblsp. melted butter or margarine	3 eggs, beaten

Add corn, milk, butter, sugar, salt and pepper to eggs; stir to combine well. Turn into a well-greased 1½-qt. casserole. Place in pan of hot water; bake in moderate oven (350°) 45 minutes, or until pudding is set. Makes 4 servings.

NOTE: You can substitute 1 (1 lb.) can cream-style corn for frozen whole kernel corn, but use 1 c. milk or dairy half-and-half instead of 2 c.

VARIATIONS

To the ingredients for Corn Custard Pudding make the following additions:

Cheese-Pepper Corn Pudding: Add ½ c. grated sharp process cheese and ¼ c. finely chopped green pepper.

Ham-Corn Custard Pudding: Add ½ c. finely chopped cooked ham.

Mushroom-Corn Custard Pudding: Add ½ c. chopped mushrooms.

CORN CURRY

A favorite in our Test Kitchens; mild curry flavor makes it special

¼ c. butter or margarine	3 tblsp. chopped onion
3 c. frozen or canned corn	½ tsp. curry powder
2 tblsp. chopped green pepper	¾ c. dairy sour cream
	½ tsp. salt
2 tblsp. chopped red pepper or pimiento	⅛ tsp. pepper

Melt butter in skillet. Add vegetables and curry powder; cook over low heat until vegetables are just tender (8 to 10 minutes).

Stir in sour cream, salt and pepper. Heat through, stirring constantly. Makes 6 servings.

KALE CASSEROLE

A grand way to fix kale—you bake it with eggs and cheese in a sauce

2 (10 oz.) pkgs. frozen chopped kale	1 tsp. salt
	⅛ tsp. pepper
¼ c. butter	4 hard-cooked eggs, chopped
¼ c. flour	
2 c. milk	½ c. bread crumbs
1 c. grated Cheddar cheese	2 tblsp. melted butter

Cook kale according to package directions; drain.

Melt butter; blend in flour, then milk. Cook, stirring constantly, until mixture comes to a boil. Stir in cheese, salt and pepper; continue stirring until cheese is melted. Stir in hard-cooked eggs and kale.

Place in greased 1½-qt. casserole. Toss crumbs with melted butter. Sprinkle on top. Bake in moderate oven (350°) 30 minutes. Makes 8 servings.

Luscious Holiday Peas

For the Christmas or other Yuletide dinner, serve luscious Holiday Peas. Mushrooms, onion, celery and pimientos do something wonderful to bright green frozen peas. You might classify this as a mixed vegetable dish, but the small amounts of the other vegetables are really seasonings. You'll want to double this recipe if there are more than three or possibly four hungry people around your table. And you'll also want to look in the chapter on mixed vegetables for exceptionally good recipes in which frozen peas play an important part.

HOLIDAY PEAS

Serve this beauty to company

1 (4 oz.) can mushroom stems and pieces
1 (10 oz.) pkg. frozen peas
1 small onion, chopped
½ c. chopped celery
3 tblsp. butter
1 (2 oz.) jar pimientos, chopped
½ tsp. salt
⅛ tsp. pepper

Drain mushrooms, reserving liquid. If not enough liquid to cook peas as directed on package, add water to make enough. Cook peas as directed; drain.

Cook onion and celery in butter until soft. Add pimientos and mushrooms and heat thoroughly. Add to peas along with seasonings. Heat. Makes 3 to 4 servings.

GOURMET PEAS

Very good and very simple to fix

1 (10 oz.) pkg. frozen peas
¼ c. consommé
2 to 4 tblsp. dairy sour cream
Salt

Cook frozen peas in consommé until barely tender. Drain off consommé; reserve for later use, if desired. Stir sour cream into peas; heat only until cream is hot and peas are coated. Add a little salt, if necessary. Makes 4 servings.

TEXAS BLACK-EYED PEAS AND RICE

Barbecue sauce adds the right zip

2 (10 oz.) pkgs. frozen black-eyed peas	⅔ c. rice
1 c. chopped onion	10 slices bacon, diced
1 qt. water	⅔ c. barbecue sauce
1 tblsp. salt	¼ tsp. pepper
	2 tblsp. bacon drippings

Place peas, onion, water and salt in large saucepan. Cover; bring to a boil. Reduce heat and simmer 30 minutes. Add rice and continue simmering until rice is tender, 20 to 25 minutes. Stir occasionally.

Cook bacon; remove from skillet.

Combine pea mixture, barbecue sauce, half of bacon, pepper and bacon drippings. Place in greased 2-qt. casserole. Top with remaining bacon.

Bake in moderate oven (350°) 30 minutes. Makes 8 servings.

Frozen Potato Specialties

Nothing in today's kitchens would surprise our grandmothers more than the frozen potatoes kept on hand in freezers. They're one of the most appreciated frozen foods in many households, especially if the men and boys are potato-meat fans. It's not only that the potatoes taste so good, but also that they help so many times when you need to get a meal in a jiffy. There's no washing and no peeling and cutting, which saves minutes. And no worry that potatoes stored in bulk will sprout.

If you grow potatoes and sometimes have a surplus, you will be interested in our FARM JOURNAL way of freezing them, described in the chapter on Freezing and Canning. Most women depend on the freezer cases in supermarkets for potatoes in boxes and loose-packed in plastic bags.

A Colorado mother says she tries to keep frozen French fries on hand to make Potato Pizza for her three sons when they come off the ski slopes and say they're starving. "It takes a lot of replenishing," she adds, "because my boys really like the pizza and think it's a weekend necessity."

POTATO PIZZA

You'll want to keep frozen potatoes on hand
to make this teen-age treat

2 (1 lb.) pkgs. frozen
   French fries
2 (6 oz.) pkgs. mozzarella
   cheese slices
1 (8 oz.) can tomato sauce

1 c. cut-up salami
1 c. cut-up pepperoni
1 c. cooked pork sausage
¼ tsp. orégano leaves

Arrange French fries in a single layer in 15½ × 10½ × 1″ jelly roll pan. Lay cheese slices over potatoes, then spread with tomato sauce. Place meat evenly over top; sprinkle with orégano.

Bake in very hot oven (450°) 15 to 20 minutes. Cut in squares and serve immediately. Makes 6 to 8 servings.

QUICK SCALLOPED POTATOES

Convenient frozen hashed browns are good
scalloped—also fast and easy

1 (32 oz.) pkg. frozen
   shredded potatoes for
   hashed browns
1 tblsp. instant minced
   onion, or 3 tblsp. chopped
   fresh onion
¾ tsp. salt

Few grains coarse grind
   pepper
3 tblsp. butter
3 tblsp. flour
1½ c. milk
3 tblsp. corn flake crumbs

Grease a flat 7½ × 12″ or 9″ square baking dish.

Break potatoes apart in the plastic bag while still frozen; turn into baking dish, spreading evenly. Add onion, spreading evenly, salt and pepper.

Prepare thin white sauce by melting butter over heat; add flour and blend. Slowly add milk and cook about 5 minutes. Pour over potatoes. Sprinkle with crumbs.

Bake in moderate oven (375°) 30 minutes. Makes 8 to 12 servings.

NOTE: You can give variety to Quick Scalloped Potatoes by adding one of the following to the white sauce: ½ to ⅔ c. grated cheese, ¼ c. chopped parsley (or 1 tblsp. parsley flakes) or 1 (2 oz.) jar pimiento strips, drained.

VARIATION

Quick Scalloped Potatoes and Ham: For a hearty casserole, add 1 to 1½ c. cubed cooked ham to potatoes before adding white sauce.

JIFFY SCALLOPED POTATOES

*When you get home late and want to get
dinner fast, try these potatoes*

4 c. frozen shredded potatoes for hashed browns	¼ tsp. pepper
	1 c. condensed cream of celery soup
1 tblsp. instant minced onion	½ c. milk
1 tsp. salt	¾ c. grated sharp process cheese

Place potatoes in greased 9 × 9 × 2″ pan. Sprinkle with onion, salt and pepper.

Blend soup and milk together in saucepan. Heat to boiling. Pour over potatoes.

Bake in moderate oven (375°) 15 minutes. Remove from oven and stir. Sprinkle with cheese. Return to oven and continue baking 15 minutes. Makes 6 servings.

ZIPPY FRENCH FRIES

*Easy to fix, different and tasty—
keep frozen potatoes ready to go*

1 (2 lb.) bag frozen French fries	1 tsp. salt
	½ tsp. onion salt
2 tblsp. grated Parmesan cheese	¼ tsp. pepper
	¼ tsp. chili powder

142

Cook French fries according to package directions. Combine remaining ingredients. Sprinkle over piping hot French fries and serve immediately. Makes 6 servings.

HASHED BROWN POTATO BAKE

Easy, new potato dish

½ c. chopped onion
1 can condensed cream of
  celery soup
1 (3 oz.) pkg. cream cheese,
  cut in cubes

4 c. frozen shredded
  potatoes for hashed
  browns
⅓ c. shredded Cheddar
  cheese

Cook onion in a little water until tender. Drain. Combine soup and cream cheese in saucepan and heat, stirring, until mixture is smooth.

Combine frozen potatoes and onion in a 2-qt. casserole. Stir in hot soup mixture.

Cover and bake in moderate oven (350°) 1 hour and 15 minutes. Remove lid, sprinkle Cheddar cheese on potatoes and return to oven long enough to melt cheese. Makes 6 to 7 servings.

CHEESE-CREAMED SPINACH

*The kind of vegetable dish you'll be proud
to offer guests—it's distinctive*

3 (10 oz.) pkgs. frozen
  chopped spinach
1 (1 to 1½ oz.) envelope
  onion soup mix

2 c. dairy sour cream
½ c. grated Cheddar cheese

Cook spinach as directed on package; drain. Combine with onion soup mix and dairy sour cream. Spoon into greased 2-qt. casserole. Top with cheese.

Bake in moderate oven (350°) until heated throughout, about 25 minutes. Makes 8 to 10 servings.

SPINACH PARMESAN

A glorified version of spinach

**2 (10 oz.) pkgs. frozen
chopped spinach**
½ tsp. instant minced onion
½ c. heavy cream, whipped

Salt and pepper to taste
**½ c. grated Parmesan
cheese**

Cook spinach according to package directions until just tender. Drain through sieve until very dry.

Fold in onion, whipped cream, salt and pepper. Turn into shallow baking dish; sprinkle with cheese.

Bake in slow oven (325°) about 15 minutes, until heated through. Makes 6 servings.

SPINACH-PECAN RING

*Give spinach eye and taste appeal—
bake it this way in a ring mold*

**2 (10 oz.) pkgs. frozen
chopped spinach**
3 eggs, beaten
½ c. bread crumbs
¾ c. chopped pecans

**¼ c. melted butter or
margarine**
½ tsp. salt
⅛ tsp. pepper
½ tsp. ground nutmeg

Cook spinach according to package directions, using smallest amount of water possible. Remove from heat and cool (do not drain).

Add eggs, bread crumbs, pecans and 2 tblsp. melted butter to cooled spinach. Add seasonings and mix well. Turn into 9″ ring mold greased generously with remaining butter; bake in moderate oven (350°) 30 minutes, or until firm. Turn out on hot platter or chop plate; fill center as desired —with parslied small potatoes, frozen potato balls heated until brown and crispy, or a creamed vegetable or meat. Makes 8 servings.

BAKED SPINACH COUNTRY-STYLE

They'll like spinach this new way

2 (10 oz.) pkgs. frozen	1 tsp. salt
chopped spinach	¼ tsp. pepper
2 tblsp. minced onion	½ c. cracker crumbs
3 tblsp. butter	2 tblsp. melted butter
3 tblsp. flour	½ c. shredded process
2 c. milk	cheese
3 hard-cooked eggs, finely	
chopped	

Cook spinach in boiling salted water until tender; drain thoroughly in sieve.

Meanwhile, cook onion in 3 tblsp. butter until soft. Stir in flour, then milk. Cook, stirring constantly, until mixture comes to a boil. Remove from heat and add eggs, salt and pepper.

Stir in spinach. Place in greased 1½-qt. casserole. Toss cracker crumbs with melted butter, then cheese; sprinkle over top of casserole. Bake in moderate oven (350°) 25 minutes, or until bubbling. Makes 6 servings.

When you cook small white onions, here's how to keep them whole: After peeling, cut an "x" into the root end with the tip of a small sharp knife. Simmer them gently, and don't overcook.

SQUASH VERONIQUE

Green grapes and candied ginger
win gourmet rating for frozen squash

2 (10 or 12 oz.) pkgs.	1 c. halved seedless green
frozen squash	grapes
1 tblsp. finely slivered	1 tblsp. butter
candied ginger, or ½ tsp.	1 tblsp. brown sugar
ground ginger	

Cook squash according to package directions. Stir in ginger and grapes. Turn into 1-qt. casserole; dot with butter; sprinkle brown sugar over top.

Bake in moderate oven (350°) 25 to 30 minutes, until thoroughly heated. Makes about 6 servings.

MEXICAN CORN CHIP SQUASH

Try this South-of-the-Border squash dish:
quick, easy, different, delicious

2 (12 oz.) pkgs. frozen
  squash
2 tblsp. butter or margarine
1 tsp. instant minced onion
1 tblsp. minced pimiento
Salt and pepper to taste

⅛ tsp. ground nutmeg or
  ground mace
⅔ c. crushed corn chips
  (hot Mexican type, if
  available)

Thaw and cook squash according to package directions, adding butter. Add onion, pimiento and seasonings; turn into a greased shallow baking dish or large pie pan. Sprinkle with corn chips.

Bake in moderate oven (350°) 20 to 25 minutes. Makes 6 servings.

HAWAIIAN SQUASH

Pineapple and winter squash are
flavor mates in this ham go-with

2 (12 oz.) pkgs. frozen
  squash
6 tblsp. butter or margarine
1 (9 oz.) can crushed
  pineapple, drained
  (reserve juice)

1 tsp. salt
⅛ tsp. white pepper
⅛ tsp. ground nutmeg or
  ground mace
½ c. chopped macadamia
  nuts or pecans

Thaw and cook squash in saucepan according to package directions. When hot, add butter, pineapple and seasonings.

Heat; beat until well mixed, adding just enough of the pineapple syrup to make mixture fluffy and light. Turn into a hot vegetable dish; sprinkle nuts over top and serve. Makes 6 to 8 servings.

CHAPTER THREE

Canned Vegetables

CANNED VEGETABLES, both home preserved and purchased, are such reliable old friends in country kitchens that we tend to take them for granted. Too often, we open them quickly with an electric can opener, heat them, give them a dash of seasoning and serve them with scant ceremony and a dab of butter, grateful that they're so fast to fix.

If they're to continue to please your family, canned vegetables deserve a little more attention. Look over the recipes you use. Are they always the same? To produce pleasing surprises in flavor and looks, you need some new ideas. We asked the Home Economics staff of the National Canners Association (specialists in working with canned foods) to share with you their best recipes featuring canned vegetables. You'll find many of them in this chapter, including updated versions of old-time favorites our grandmothers cherished.

Try Honey Scalloped Corn the next time you want to take something delicious to the church supper or family reunion. Set a dish of Honeyed Beets or Honey-Glazed Sweet Potatoes on the buffet table when you entertain. If you want to cater to the men, fix Mustard Buttered Beans.

Have you tried sliced salad tomatoes in cans? These tomato varieties not only stand up to mechanical packing and handling, but they also retain their firmer texture when canned. Their flavor is excellent. And have you noticed how tender-crisp canned beans are today? They, too, are the result of painstaking research to develop varieties of superior flavor that can be picked mechanically and hurried into cans. There's a fabulous story of scientific agriculture behind today's canned vegetables. It has much to do with the superior products you buy at a reasonable cost.

The progress made in vegetable fields challenges homemakers in their kitchens to keep up to date in the ways to fix canned vegetables. This chapter will lead you to more delicious, easy-to-fix vegetable dishes without straining your food budget or adding to your work load.

GUIDE TO COMMON CAN SIZES

Trade Term	Weight (Approximate)	Cups (Approximate)
8 ounce	8 oz.	1
Picnic	10½ to 12 oz	1¼
12 ounce (vacuum)	12 oz.	1½
No. 300	14 to 16 oz.	1¾
No. 303	16 to 17 oz.	2
No. 2	1 lb. 4 oz., or 1 pt. 2 fl. oz.	2½
No. 2½	1 lb. 13 oz.	3½
No. 3	3 lb. 3 oz., or	5¾
Cylindrical	1 qt. 14 fl. oz.	
No. 10	6½ lb. to 7 lb. 5 oz.	12 to 13

NOTE: The 12 oz. vacuum can is used primarily for corn. The 3 lb. 3 oz. and 6½ lb. to 7 lb. 5 oz. sizes are for restaurant and institutional use, but come in handy when planning and serving meals to a large crowd.

SUBSTITUTIONS YOU CAN MAKE: For one 6½ lb. to 7 lb. 5 oz. can you can use seven 1 lb. cans, five 1 lb. 4 oz. cans, four 1 lb. 13 oz. cans and two 3 lb. 3 oz. cans.

Asparagus for Company

When a country woman opens a can or two of asparagus, chances are good that company is coming. While people today do not divide vegetables into Sunday and everyday foods, as Pennsylvania Dutch women once did, asparagus still rates as a Sunday-best or special occasion vegetable. It vies with peas as the top green vegetable in chicken dinners.

Cheese and asparagus flavors complement each other. That explains why you'll find cheese listed among the seasonings in several asparagus recipes in this chapter. Be adventuresome. Also try the asparagus dishes with more off-beat seasonings, such as lemon juice, herbs and mushrooms.

ASPARAGUS AND EGG CASSEROLE

Team mates: asparagus and cheese

1 (1 lb.) can asparagus (cut lengths or whole)
¼ c. butter or margarine
3 tblsp. flour
½ tsp. salt
1½ c. asparagus liquid and milk

½ c. sharp Cheddar cheese cubes
5 hard-cooked eggs, sliced
Corn flake crumbs, or buttered bread crumbs
Paprika

Drain asparagus, reserving liquid.

In saucepan, melt butter; blend in flour and salt. Add enough milk to asparagus liquid to make 1½ c.; add to saucepan. Stir and cook until sauce is thickened slightly; add cheese, continue cooking over low heat until cheese is melted.

Arrange asparagus pieces in greased 1-qt. casserole; cover with egg slices; pour hot cheese sauce over. Sprinkle with córn flake crumbs and paprika.

Bake in moderate oven (375°) 20 minutes, or until sauce bubbles up around edges. Makes 4 to 6 servings.

BAKED ASPARAGUS AND CHEESE

Pretty yellow and green treat

2 (14½ oz.) cans asparagus, drained (you'll have 2½ c.)
2 c. toasted bread cubes
2 c. shredded sharp process cheese

3 eggs, slightly beaten
2 c. milk
½ tsp. salt
½ tsp. celery salt
⅛ tsp. pepper
1 tsp. instant minced onion

Place half of each in greased 8″ square pan: asparagus, bread cubes and cheese; repeat layers.

Combine remaining ingredients and pour over asparagus mixture. Bake in slow oven (325°) until set, 60 to 70 minutes. Makes 8 servings.

ASPARAGUS AU GRATIN

*This dish brings spring to the table
even if a blizzard is raging*

1 (16 or 17 oz.) can
  asparagus spears
1½ c. crushed potato chips
1 can condensed cream of
  mushroom soup

⅔ c. grated Cheddar cheese
⅛ tsp. paprika
Bread crumbs

Drain asparagus, reserving ½ c. liquid.

Arrange asparagus spears in a circle, bases at center, like spokes of a wheel, in greased 8″ glass pie pan. Add half the potato chips; spread half the soup over top. Add remaining potato chips in a layer. Add asparagus liquid to remaining soup; pour over potato chips. Top with cheese and sprinkle with paprika and a few bread crumbs.

Bake in moderate oven (350°) until bubbly and lightly browned, 20 to 25 minutes. Makes 4 to 6 servings.

ASPARAGUS WITH CHEESE-BACON SAUCE

*The dash of nutmeg is just right—
use less than ⅛ teaspoonful*

2 tblsp. flour
2 tblsp. butter or margarine
1 c. milk
¾ c. grated sharp Cheddar
  cheese
¼ tsp. salt

⅛ tsp. pepper
Ground nutmeg (less than
  ⅛ tsp.)
2 slices bacon, cooked
2 (14½ oz.) cans or jars
  asparagus spears

In heavy saucepan stir flour into melted butter until smooth; cook over low heat 3 minutes (do not brown). Add milk; continue cooking over low heat, stirring constantly, until nearly thickened.

Add cheese; stir until cheese is melted and sauce is bubbling. Add salt, pepper, nutmeg and crumbled bacon. Serve over hot drained asparagus. Makes 6 servings.

Baked Bean Casseroles: *Turn canned baked beans into in-*

*dividual casseroles. Arrange canned Vienna sausages on
top of the beans and heat in oven.*

*Use up leftover vegetables in an omelet. Grate some cheese
to toss with the vegetables and stir them into egg mixture
in the skillet.*

ASPARAGUS WITH CELERY HOLLANDAISE

Quick to fix, a pleasure to serve

2 (13 to 14½ oz.) cans or
    jars asparagus spears
½ c. condensed cream of
    celery soup

1 tsp. fresh or canned lemon
    juice
2 tblsp. mayonnaise

Heat undrained asparagus in skillet.

Blend soup, lemon juice and mayonnaise; stir over low
heat until bubbling and hot.

Lift hot asparagus from skillet with a slotted spoon and
place in warm serving bowl. Pour sauce over asparagus.
Makes 6 servings.

ASPARAGUS WITH MUSHROOMS

*Lemon juice points up the wonderful
asparagus-mushroom flavor blend*

1 (4 oz.) can mushroom
    slices, drained
2 tblsp. butter
2 (1 lb.) cans cut asparagus

½ c. chopped parsley
¼ tsp. savory (optional)
1 tsp. canned or fresh lemon
    juice

Brown mushrooms in butter. Add ½ c. liquid drained
from vegetables. Stir in remaining ingredients. Mix gently
and heat. Makes 6 servings.

LAYERED ASPARAGUS CASSEROLE

*Here's the right vegetable dish
for the chicken dinner—really good*

2 (13 to 14½ oz.) cans or
jars asparagus spears,
drained
1 (3¾ oz.) can French fried
onions

1 can condensed cream of
mushroom soup
½ tsp. rosemary leaves

Put asparagus in bottom of shallow casserole. Layer onions over top.

Blend soup with rosemary; pour over vegetables. Bake in moderate oven (350°) 20 minutes. Makes 6 servings.

ASPARAGUS OLYMPIAN

*Garlic, lemon juice and olive oil, hallmarks
of Grecian cooking, highlight the
delicious asparagus taste*

1 small clove garlic, minced
1 tblsp. olive or salad oil
2 (14 or 15 oz.) cans
asparagus spears

1 egg, beaten
1 tblsp. canned or fresh
lemon juice

Cook garlic in oil a few minutes. Add ¼ c. liquid from asparagus, egg and lemon juice, mixing well. Cook over low heat, stirring constantly, until thickened. Pour over heated drained asparagus. Makes 6 small servings.

Green Beans

Canned green beans head the list of favorite vegetables in many homes. Perhaps their popularity explains why women often use less imagination in fixing them than other vegetables.

Recipes for Aloha Green Beans and Green Beans Caesar will help you get out of this cooking rut, if you're in it, and they'll produce two distinctive dishes that taste exceptionally good.

These recipes greeted many friends of a former home economics teacher, now a homemaker in North Dakota, when they opened one of her annual Christmas letters. Every year this home economist encloses the year's favorite recipes with her Yuletide letter.

The lucky recipients promptly tried these recipes with pleasing response from people who tasted. Once you try them, you'll understand why anticipation builds up for this home economist's next holiday letter.

ALOHA GREEN BEANS

Second time you make this dish
you'll double the recipe—it's tasty

1 (1 lb.) can cut green beans	1 tblsp. cornstarch
1 (6 oz.) can pineapple tidbits, drained (reserve liquid)	⅛ tsp. freshly ground pepper
3 tblsp. vinegar	¼ tsp. salt
2 tblsp. sugar	2 tblsp. butter or margarine

Drain green beans, reserving ⅓ c. liquid.

Combine bean liquid, pineapple juice and vinegar in a saucepan. Blend dry ingredients and add to liquids in pan. Boil 3 minutes, stirring constantly.

Add beans, pineapple tidbits and butter. Heat thoroughly. Makes 4 to 6 servings.

GREEN BEANS CAESAR

Bread cubes make this unusual

1 c. bread cubes	¼ tsp. salt
2 tblsp. salad oil	1 (1 lb.) can green beans, drained
1 tblsp. vinegar	
1 tblsp. salad oil	2 tblsp. grated Parmesan cheese
1 tsp. instant minced onion	

Lightly brown bread cubes in 2 tblsp. oil in skillet; remove cubes and keep hot.

In the same skillet, combine vinegar, 1 tblsp. oil, onion and salt; heat. Add beans and cook until thoroughly heated through. When ready to serve, add bread cubes; toss gently, then sprinkle with cheese. Makes 4 servings.

GREEN BEANS IN TANGY SAUCE

Mayonnaise and lemon juice give the beans
that marvelous tangy taste

2 tblsp. flour
½ tsp. salt
2 tblsp. butter
1 c. milk

¼ c. mayonnaise
2 tsp. fresh or canned lemon
juice
2 (1 lb.) cans green beans

Stir flour and salt into melted butter. Add milk and cook until thickened, stirring. Blend in mayonnaise and lemon juice. Serve hot over heated drained green beans. Makes 6 servings.

GREEN BEANS WITH BACON

You can't surpass the green bean-bacon
team, as this recipe proves

2 to 3 slices bacon, cut in
½" pieces
1 (16 or 17 oz.) can
French-style green beans
2 green onions, finely cut

1 tsp. lemon juice
2 tsp. cornstarch
½ tsp. sugar
Salt and pepper to taste

Fry bacon until crisp; drain off fat.

Drain beans, reserving ½ c. liquid; add beans and onions to bacon.

Combine bean liquid and lemon juice; stir in cornstarch. Add to beans; heat together until sauce is thickened; add sugar, salt and pepper. Makes 4 to 6 servings.

PLANTATION GREEN BEANS

Perfect to serve with fried chicken

1 large onion, thinly sliced
(about 1 c.)
1 branch green celery, thinly
sliced (about 1 c.)
1 tblsp. parsley flakes
1 tblsp. butter or margarine

¼ tsp. garlic salt
¾ tsp. salt
⅛ tsp. coarse grind pepper
1 tblsp. cornstarch
1 (16 to 17 oz.) can cut
green beans

Cook onion, celery and parsley in butter until onion is golden and celery tender-crisp.

Combine garlic salt, salt, pepper and cornstarch.

Drain beans; add enough water to bean liquid to make 1 c.; slowly stir into dry ingredients to form a thin smooth paste.

Combine cooked vegetables with beans over heat and add sauce. Stir; let simmer 10 minutes, or until sauce has thickened slightly. Makes 4 to 6 servings.

GREEN BEANS WITH FILBERTS

Women in the Northwest add crunch
to vegetables with nuts—tasty idea

2 tblsp. minced onion
2 tblsp. thinly sliced celery
2 tblsp. butter or margarine
1 (16 to 17 oz.) can green beans, drained
1 can condensed cream of chicken soup

¾ c. Chopped Toasted Filberts
1 tblsp. grated Parmesan or Romano cheese
Paprika

Cook onion and celery in butter until golden brown and tender.

Add beans and soup to onions and celery, then add filberts. Mix; turn into greased 1-qt. casserole. Sprinkle with cheese and paprika.

Bake in moderate oven (350°) 25 minutes. Makes 6 servings.

Chopped Toasted Filberts: Spread about 1 c. shelled filberts in shallow pan; toast in very slow oven (275°) 20 minutes; remove and let cool slightly. Rub filberts between layers of terry cloth or nylon net to remove most of the brown skins, then chop coarsely. (Filberts prepared this way have a superior flavor.) If you do not have filberts, substitute chopped toasted pecans or almonds for them. Toast them, also, for about 20 minutes in a slow oven; cool slightly and chop.

GREEN BEAN POTATO CASSEROLE

So good, and so quick to fix—
potato sticks add crunchiness

1 (16 to 17 oz.) can green
  beans, drained
¾ c. Cheese Sauce (see
  Index)

½ (1⅛ oz.) can potato
  sticks

Combine green beans and cheese sauce. Put in shallow casserole. Bake in moderate oven (350°) 20 minutes.

Remove from oven and top with broken potato sticks. Continue baking 5 minutes more. Makes 4 to 5 servings.

NOTE: You can melt process cheese in milk to make the cheese sauce. Melt cheese over water in double boiler. Or prepare sauce from a mix.

MIXED BEANS PARMESAN

This bean duet has cheese-olive overtones.
No wonder it's a winner

1 (1 lb.) can cut green beans
1 (1 lb.) can cut wax beans
2 tblsp. butter or margarine

½ c. sliced pitted ripe olives
½ c. grated Parmesan
  cheese

Combine drained beans with ¼ c. bean liquid and butter in saucepan; heat.

To serve, toss gently with olives and sprinkle with cheese. Makes 6 to 8 servings.

SWEET-SOUR BEANS ROQUEFORT

You get a flavor of France in this bean dish—
serve it with beef

2 slices bacon, cut in pieces
1 small onion, chopped
1 (1 lb.) can green beans
2 tsp. sugar

2 tblsp. vinegar
Salt and pepper to taste
2 tblsp. crumbled Roquefort
  or blue cheese

Brown bacon and onion lightly. Add 2 tblsp. liquid drained from beans, drained beans, sugar, vinegar, salt and pepper. Heat. Put hot beans in serving dish, sprinkle crumbled cheese on top. Makes 4 servings.

QUICK AND EASY GREEN BEANS

*This recipe's name fits the well-seasoned
dish you make with it*

1 tblsp. butter or margarine	**1 (1 lb.) can cut green beans**
¼ c. dry bread crumbs	**1 tblsp. salad oil**
½ tsp. paprika	**¼ tsp. salt**
3 tblsp. grated Parmesan cheese	**⅛ tsp. garlic powder**

Melt butter in saucepan; stir in crumbs and paprika and mix together. Remove from heat and add cheese.

Drain beans; combine with salad oil, salt and garlic powder in another saucepan. Heat thoroughly and serve topped with the crumb mixtures. Makes 4 servings.

Elegant Beans and Mushrooms Amandine

The commercial pack of canned green beans has steadily increased in recent years. Blue Lake beans contributed to the increased interest. No doubt you've noticed on can labels this descriptive name, Blue Lake. This variety of beans first grew in the Pacific Northwest. The pods are large, round and firm; they have a fine flavor and hold their shape well in the canning process.

Exceptionally good recipes for canned green beans have had something to do with the skyrocketing popularity of the vegetable—Beans and Mushrooms Amandine, for instance. Indeed this regal dish is ideal to offer on the buffet or in other company dinners.

This cookbook is rich in splendid green bean recipes. So treat your family and friends to the vegetable fixed many different, tasty ways.

BEANS AND MUSHROOMS AMANDINE

*An elegant dish the entire family will like,
as well as guests*

157

1 tblsp. finely chopped
chives or green onions
2 tblsp. butter or margarine
2 tsp. flour
¼ tsp. salt
⅛ tsp. pepper
¼ c. light cream, dairy half-
and-half or undiluted
evaporated milk

1 (1 lb.) can or jar green
beans
1 (3 to 4 oz.) can
mushroms, drained
2 tblsp. toasted slivered
almonds

Cook chives in butter a few minutes. Add flour, salt and pepper, stirring until smooth. Add cream and ¼ c. liquid from beans. Cook until thickened, stirring constantly.

Add drained beans and mushrooms and heat. Serve sprinkled with almonds. Makes 6 servings.

CURRIED BLUE LAKE BEANS

Try ½ tsp. curry powder first, then ¾ tsp.
next time if you like it—excellent with chicken

1 (1 lb.) can cut Blue Lake
green beans
1 can condensed cream of
celery soup

2 tsp. instant minced onion
1 tsp. Worcestershire sauce
½ to ¾ tsp. curry powder
¼ tsp. salt

Drain beans.

Blend together remaining ingredients and heat, stirring, until mixture bubbles. Add beans and heat through slowly to allow flavors to blend. Makes 4 servings.

PARTY LIMAS

Orégano does something good to limas,
as do cheese, bacon and garlic

3 slices bacon
1 to 2 cloves garlic, minced
⅛ tsp. orégano leaves
1 (1 lb.) can green lima
beans

Salt and pepper to taste
¼ c. grated Parmesan
cheese

Cook bacon until crisp; remove and drain. Add garlic to

bacon fat; cook 1 to 2 minutes. Add orégano, 2 tblsp. liquid from limas and drained limas; heat. Season with salt and pepper. Just before serving, stir in crumbled bacon and cheese. Makes 4 servings.

LIMA BEANS DE LUXE

An easy way to make cheese sauce
is to use packaged cheese sauce mix

1 (1 lb.) can green lima
    beans, drained
1 (2 oz.) can or jar
    pimientos, drained and
    chopped

½ c. Cheese Sauce (see
    Index)
½ tsp. salt
⅛ tsp. pepper

Blend lima beans with pimientos, cheese sauce (your favorite recipe, or made from a mix) and seasonings; heat. Makes 4 servings.

PIMIENTO-WAX BEANS LYONNAISE

Serve this flavorful red, yellow and green treat
to brighten your meals

2 slices bacon
1 small onion, thinly sliced
¼ medium green pepper,
    cut in slivers

1 (1 lb.) jar pimientos,
    drained and diced
Salt and pepper to taste

Cook bacon until crisp; remove and drain. Add onion and green pepper to bacon fat; cook until tender but not brown. Add 2 tblsp. liquid from beans, drained beans, pimientos and crumbled bacon; mix lightly and heat. Season with salt and pepper. Makes 4 servings.

MUSTARD BUTTERED BEANS

The mustard-sugar-lemon juice combination
is the seasoning trick

1 (1 lb.) can whole wax	1 tsp. sugar
beans	¼ tsp. salt
1 tblsp. butter or margarine	1 tsp. fresh or canned lemon
2 tsp. prepared mustard	juice

Combine ¼ c. liquid drained from beans, butter, mustard, sugar, salt and lemon juice; heat. Add drained beans; mix lightly and heat. Makes 4 servings.

Baked Beans from the Cupboard

Although most country cupboards hold a few cans of dried beans, baked, you almost never eat baked beans that taste alike even in the same neighborhood. That's because most women open the cans and add their own special touches. Usually they stir in favorite seasonings, which frequently include a little smoked or highly seasoned meat. Then they bake the casserole long enough to blend the seasonings.

Some city families consider hearty canned beans and pork a main dish, but active farm people with big appetites frequently like the substantial dish as an accompaniment to meat, especially ham or frankfurters.

Here are a few recipes for baked bean dishes that start with canned beans, "doctored up," as farm women say, with seasonings their families really enjoy.

SPECIAL BAKED BEANS

*You start with canned beans and come out
with your own distinctive version*

3 (1 lb. 12 oz.) cans pork	1 tsp. prepared mustard
and beans in tomato	¾ c. plus 1 tblsp. ketchup
sauce (about 10½ c.)	1½ c. firmly packed light or
1 medium onion, chopped,	dark brown sugar
or 1 tblsp. instant minced	5 slices bacon, diced,
onion	browned and drained

Combine all ingredients in large mixing bowl; mix well. Turn mixture into greased 3-qt. baking dish. Cover and bake in slow oven (300°) 3½ to 4 hours. Remove cover and bake 30 minutes more. Stir two or three times during baking. Makes 12 generous servings.

NOTE: These beans freeze well. Pack in aluminum foil baking pans that can go directly from freezer to oven. Recommended storage time: 3 to 4 months. When ready to serve, place beans in moderate oven (350°); bake 45 minutes for pint containers, about 1 hour for quarts.

PIQUANT BAKED BEANS

No wonder these beans taste so good—
look at the interesting seasonings

½ c. chopped onion
1 tblsp. butter or margarine
2 (1 lb.) cans pork and beans in tomato sauce (4 c.)
1 (3 oz.) can deviled ham

1½ tsp. prepared mustard
1 tblsp. brown sugar
½ tsp. salt
Dash pepper

Cook onion in butter until golden and tender. Combine with remaining ingredients. Turn into 1½-qt. casserole; cover and bake in moderate oven (350°) 1¼ to 1½ hours. Makes 4 to 6 servings.

SAVORY BAKED BEANS

Here is a baked bean recipe that's a favorite
in the Rocky Mountain area

2 (1 lb. 13 oz.) cans pork and beans
1 lb. lean bacon, cut in pieces
2 medium onions, cut in chunks

2 large green peppers, cut in chunks
2 tsp. Worcestershire sauce
1 c. ketchup
1 c. brown sugar

Combine all ingredients and put into 2 medium-size or 1 large casserole.

Bake, covered, in slow oven (325°) 3 hours, stirring occasionally. Uncover the last 30 minutes of cooking. Makes about 20 servings.

NOTE: You can use less bacon, but a full pound makes these baked beans unforgettable and a conversation piece whenever served.

SAUCY BAKED BEANS

The recipe to use when you're pressed for time.
Don't miss the variations

2 strips lean bacon, cut in pieces	**2 tblsp. prepared mustard**
	¼ c. dark molasses
2 (1 lb.) cans baked beans in tomato sauce	**1 tblsp. brown sugar**
	¼ tsp. allspice
1 small onion, peeled and chopped	**2 tsp. Worcestershire sauce**

Brown the bacon lightly, drain and crumble. Combine all the ingredients and pour into a 1½-qt. casserole or 2-qt. bean pot. Cover.

Bake in a moderate oven (350°) 1½ hours. Uncover the last half hour to brown. Makes 8 servings.

VARIATIONS

Pineapple Baked Beans: Add 1 (13½ oz.) can drained pineapple chunks to the bean mixture and bake.

Cheese Baked Beans: Omit bacon from Saucy Baked Beans. Add ½ c. grated sharp Cheddar cheese and 1 c. cooked ham or salami, cut in cubes, to the bean mixture and bake.

WESTERN BAKED BEANS

Four-in-one baked beans. Use 1 cup sugar
for beans on the sweet side

8 slices bacon	**2 (15 oz.) cans dried lima beans, drained**
4 large onions, peeled and separated in rings	
½ to 1 c. brown sugar	**1 (1 lb.) can green lima beans, drained**
1 tsp. dry mustard	
½ tsp. garlic powder (optional)	**1 (1 lb.) can dark red kidney beans, drained**
1 tsp. salt	**1 (1 lb. 11 oz.) jar New England style baked beans, undrained**
½ c. cider vinegar	

162

Pan-fry bacon until crisp, drain on paper towels and set aside.

Place onion rings in a large skillet and add the sugar, mustard, garlic powder, salt and vinegar. Cover and cook 20 minutes.

Add onion mixture to the beans and stir in the bacon, crumbled. Pour into a 3-qt. casserole.

Bake, covered, ½ hour in a moderate oven (350°). Uncover, bake ½ hour longer. Makes 12 servings.

PORK AND BEANS QUICKIE

Fast to fix and fast to disappear

2 tblsp. minced onion	½ c. ketchup
¼ c. bacon drippings	¼ c. dark corn syrup
2 (1 lb.) cans pork and beans	2 tsp. dry mustard

Cook onion in bacon drippings until limp, but do not brown.

Combine beans, cooked onion and bacon drippings; place in greased 1½-qt. casserole.

Stir together ketchup, corn syrup and dry mustard; mix well; add to casserole. Cover and bake in moderate oven (350°) 30 minutes. Makes 6 generous servings.

BEAN AND SALAMI SANDWICH FILLING

Boys like sandwiches made with this—
good with dill pickles

1 (1 lb.) can baked beans (2 c.)	2 tblsp. chili sauce
¼ lb. cooked salami, chopped fine (1 c.)	2 tsp. prepared mustard

Combine ingredients and mix well. Makes about 2¾ cups.

163

Baked Kidney Beans

No kind of canned dried beans appears in a greater variety of dishes than the red kidney bean. The two recipes that follow are for kidney beans, delightfully seasoned and baked briefly. While they, like all beans, are a splendid escort for baked ham, these baked kidney beans taste wonderful with hamburgers and also with crusty ham or beef loaves.

FARM-STYLE KIDNEY BEANS

Farm-style means wonderful tasting—
an apt description of this recipe

2 (1 lb.) cans kidney beans
⅓ c. chopped onion
⅓ c. chopped green pepper
1 tsp. sugar

¼ c. chopped cooked ham
   or luncheon meat
¼ c. red wine vinegar
2 to 3 tblsp. buttered bread
   crumbs

Drain beans, reserving ½ c. liquid. Turn half of beans into greased 1½-qt. casserole; cover with onion and green pepper; sprinkle with sugar. Add ham, then remaining beans.

Mix together vinegar and bean liquid; pour over beans. Sprinkle with crumbs. Bake, uncovered, in moderate oven (350°) 30 to 40 minutes. Makes 8 servings.

NOTE: You can use ¾ c. dry red wine instead of the red wine vinegar and bean liquid. And you can substitute 3 strips thick sliced bacon, fried and crumbled, for the chopped ham.

KIDNEY BEAN BAKE

Pickle relish adds a new flavor

2 (1 lb.) cans red kidney
   beans
½ tsp. salt
½ c. chili sauce

¼ c. pickle relish
1 medium onion, thinly
   sliced
1 tblsp. butter or margarine

Drain 1 can beans and add to entire contents of second can. Add salt, chili sauce, relish and onion. Mix well. Put in 1½-qt. casserole; dot with butter. Cover and bake in moderate oven (375°) 35 minutes. Makes 4 servings.

KIDNEY BEAN RABBIT

Serve with a green or tomato salad

¼ c. chopped onion
½ c. chopped green pepper
2 tblsp. butter or margarine
1 (1 lb. 4 oz.) can kidney
  beans, drained (2½ c.)
2 tblsp. ketchup

1 tsp. Worcestershire sauce
½ tsp. salt
⅛ tsp. pepper
½ lb. process American
  cheese, diced

Cook onion and green pepper in butter until soft. Add beans, ketchup, Worcestershire sauce and seasonings.

Alternate layers of bean mixture and cheese in greased 1-qt. casserole. Bake in slow oven (350°) about 20 minutes. Makes 4 servings.

Colorful Beets

Many homemakers give canned beets a workout in winter meals. The vegetable adds the bright color that provides interest and appetite appeal.

Another merit of beet dishes is the tart note they supply, even though subtle at times. In Family Choice Beets, lemon juice furnishes the tartness; in Honeyed Beets, it's vinegar. Both recipes are a good starting point for women who crusade against drab, colorless and monotonous meals.

RAISIN-SAUCED BEETS

Give winter meals brightness with these beets
that excel in flavor— they're a fine companion to ham

1 (1 lb.) can beets
½ c. raisins
1 tblsp. cornstarch
¼ c. sugar

3 tblsp. lemon juice
2 tblsp. butter
½ tsp. salt
⅛ tsp. pepper

Drain liquid from beets into saucepan. Add raisins and simmer a few minutes until raisins are plumped.

Combine cornstarch and sugar. Add to mixture in saucepan along with lemon juice, butter, salt and pepper. Cook, stirring constantly, until mixture comes to a boil and is thickened. Stir in beets and simmer just until beets are hot. Makes 4 servings.

NOTE: You may want to double this recipe.

FAMILY CHOICE BEETS

Apple slices are the new idea

1 (1 lb.) can or jar sliced
    beets
½ tsp. salt
1 tblsp. firmly packed brown
    sugar

1 tsp. cornstarch
2 tsp. canned or fresh lemon
    juice
1 tart apple, peeled and
    sliced

Drain beets, saving liquid.

Combine salt, brown sugar and cornstarch; blend in ½ c. beet liquid and lemon juice. Cook, stirring, until thickened and clear. Add beets and apple; simmer gently 15 minutes. Makes 4 servings.

HONEYED BEETS

Honey, vinegar and onion—
no wonder these beets taste extra-good

½ c. honey
2 tblsp. vinegar
2 (1 lb.) cans sliced beets

2 tblsp. butter
1 medium onion, sliced and
    separated into rings

In a saucepan blend honey, vinegar and 2 tblsp. beet liquid. Add butter, beets and onion rings. Simmer until heated through, stirring occasionally. Do not overcook as onion rings should remain crisp. Makes 8 servings.

Piquant Juno Carrots

For a color-bright vegetable dish with a faint piquant taste, fix Juno Carrots. The tiny amount of lemon juice has remarkable ability to bring out the best flavors in the vegetable. A Michigan farm woman says: "It's wonderful what a squirt of lemon juice does in seasoning carrots. And adding chopped parsley or sprinkling the green flecks over the vegetables steps up eye appeal."

JUNO CARROTS

These carrots carry a tart-tingling lemon flavor—
they're fine with fish

1 (1 lb.) can diced carrots	2 tsp. butter
1 tsp. sugar	½ tsp. grated lemon peel
1 tsp. fresh or canned lemon juice	

Drain carrots. Combine ¼ c. liquid from carrots, carrots, sugar, lemon juice and butter; heat. Serve sprinkled with grated lemon peel. Makes 4 servings.

NOTE: This is an easy recipe to double.

Homey Scalloped Corn

Not all appetites are fickle, but change of pace in taste is an American tradition. Some dishes make a spectacular rise to popular acclaim and then fade into the background. Scalloped corn has escaped such a fate. It's one of the farm favorites that holds its own through the years.

There are many ways to make scalloped corn, but in most country kitchens two ingredients almost always find their way into the baking dish—corn and cracker crumbs. Homey Scalloped Corn also carries the taste of bacon and cheese. You'll find it an excellent dish to take to church and community suppers.

HOMEY SCALLOPED CORN

Watch the traffic when they spy scalloped corn at the church supper

4 slices bacon, chopped
1¼ c. crushed saltine
    crackers
1 medium onion, chopped
2 eggs, beaten
1 (1 lb.) can cream-style
    corn

1 (4 oz.) can pimientos,
    drained and chopped
1 c. milk
1 c. grated Cheddar cheese
¼ tsp. salt
¼ tsp. pepper

Cook bacon until crisp; remove from skillet. Combine 2 tblsp. bacon fat with ¼ c. cracker crumbs; set aside for topping.

Cook onion in remaining bacon drippings until tender. Add remaining crumbs; mix and brown slightly.

Combine onion-crumb mixture with eggs, corn, pimientos, milk, cheese, bacon, salt and pepper. Pour into greased shallow 1½-qt. casserole. Top with reserved crumbs. Bake in moderate oven (350°) about 45 minutes. Makes 6 servings.

CORN SCALLOP

It's a well-seasoned corn scallop

¼ c. butter
⅓ c. flour
1 tsp. salt
¾ tsp. dry mustard
¼ tsp. paprika
1½ c. scalded milk

1 (1 lb. 4 oz.) can
    cream-style corn
1 egg, slightly beaten
1 tblsp. Worcestershire
    sauce
¾ c. buttered cracker
    crumbs

Melt butter, add flour and dry seasonings; mix together. Add scalded milk gradually and cook, stirring constantly, until thick.

Add corn, egg and Worcestershire sauce. Pour into buttered 1½-qt. casserole; cover with crumbs.

Bake in slow oven (325°) 30 minutes, or until crumbs are brown. Makes 6 servings.

SOUTHWESTERN CORN BAKE

*A vegetable dish that's highly prized by
Southwestern hostesses—do try it*

2 (16 to 17 oz.) cans
  cream-style corn
2 eggs, beaten
¾ c. yellow corn meal
1 tsp. garlic salt

6 tblsp. salad oil
1 (4 oz.) can green chili
  peppers finely cut
2 c. grated Cheddar cheese

Mix together all ingredients except chili and cheese.

Divide mixture in half. Place one half in a greased
8 × 8 × 2″ baking dish.

Mix together chili and cheese; lay on top of corn mixture in dish. Cover with the remaining corn mixture.

Bake in moderate oven (350°) 35 minutes. Makes 8
servings.

SOUTHWESTERN CORN SCALLOP

*Different scalloped corn—chili peppers give this
a lively taste*

2 eggs, slightly beaten
1 (1 lb.) can cream-style
  corn
⅔ c. milk
½ c. coarsely crushed soda
  crackers
1 tsp. sugar

1 tsp. salt
⅛ tsp. pepper
1 c. grated sharp Cheddar
  cheese
1 tblsp. chopped canned
  green chili peppers

Combine all ingredients. Place in greased 1-qt. casserole.
Bake in moderate oven (350°) until set, 60 to 70 minutes.
Makes 6 servings.

SPANISH SCALLOPED CORN

*They'll say "Olé" when they taste—that's approval
in Spanish*

1 medium onion, chopped	1 tsp. salt
½ medium green pepper, chopped	¼ tsp. pepper
	1 (16 to 17 oz.) can cream-style corn
¼ c. butter or margarine	
1 c. coarse cracker crumbs	⅔ c. milk
¼ c. diced pimiento	2 eggs, beaten

Cook onion and green pepper in butter until tender. Add crumbs and cook until lightly browned. Add remaining ingredients; mix.

Pour into greased 1-qt. casserole and bake in moderate oven (375°) about 35 minutes, or until firm. Makes 4 to 6 servings.

CORN-OYSTER SCALLOP

Serve this tasty dressed-up corn with fried chicken or pork chops

2 (10 oz.) cans frozen condensed oyster stew	1 egg, slightly beaten
	½ tsp. salt
1 (1 lb.) can cream-style corn	⅛ tsp. pepper
	2 tblsp. pimiento strips
1 (1 lb.) can whole kernel corn, drained	2 tblsp. melted butter
	½ c. cracker crumbs
1¼ c. cracker crumbs, crushed medium fine	

Place unopened cans of oyster stew in hot water 10 minutes.

Combine oyster stew, corn, 1¼ c. cracker crumbs, egg, salt, pepper and pimiento. Pour into greased 2-qt. casserole. Combine butter and ½ c. cracker crumbs. Sprinkle around edge of corn mixture.

Bake in moderate oven (350°) 1 hour, or until knife inserted halfway between center and edge comes out clean. Makes 8 servings.

CORN-OYSTER PUDDING

As American as apple pie, this dish makes any chicken dinner special

¼ c. chopped onion	1 c. coarsely crushed soda
3 tblsp. melted butter	crackers
1 (1 lb.) can cream-style	2 eggs, beaten
corn	⅔ c. milk
½ lb. oysters (about 1 c.)	½ tsp. salt
	⅛ tsp. pepper

Cook onion in butter until soft. Combine with remaining ingredients.

Place in greased 1½-qt. casserole. Bake in moderate oven (350°) until set, about 1 hour. Makes 6 servings.

Corn/Celery Mix-Up: *Combine equal parts diced, cooked celery and whole kernel corn. Heat and season with butter and salt to taste. Fold in chopped sweet green pepper, cooked in butter until tender-crisp.*

BUTTERED CORN

Dream up seasonings to add to this basic—we give you a few tips

| 1 (12 oz. or 1 lb.) can whole | 1 tblsp. butter or margarine |
| kernel corn | Salt and pepper to taste |

Combine 2 tblsp. liquid drained from corn, drained corn and butter; heat. Add salt and pepper. Makes 4 servings.

VARIATIONS

Dilly Corn: Add ½ tsp. dried dill weed to basic recipe.

Parslied Corn: Add 2 tblsp. minced parsley to basic recipe.

Pepper Corn: Cook 2 tblsp. minced green pepper in butter until soft; add 2 tblsp. liquid drained from corn and drained corn; heat. Season with salt and pepper.

Delicate Creamy Corn Pudding

Some blustery, snowy morning when you're glad to stay in the house and want to treat the family at noon, bake this Creamy Corn Pudding. While it needs to spend about

171

1¼ hours in a slow oven, you don't have to watch it until the last 15 minutes when you start testing it for doneness.

Few vegetables can touch this kind of corn pudding for delicacy and taste. It's the perfect companion to either pork chops or fried chicken and indeed to most meats cooked on top of the range, including ham. You'll discover this vegetable dish won't go begging.

CREAMY CORN PUDDING

For success, bake this delicate corn custard
in a shallow casserole

3 eggs, well beaten
1 (1 lb.) can cream-style corn
1¼ tsp. salt
¼ tsp. pepper
1 tblsp. instant minced onion

2 tblsp. cracker meal
1 (14½ oz.) can evaporated milk
⅓ c. water
2 tblsp. butter or margarine
Paprika

Combine eggs, corn, salt, pepper, onion and cracker meal.

Put evaporated milk, water and butter in a saucepan; heat slowly until butter is melted. Add to corn and mix well. Pour into a buttered 1½-qt. *shallow* casserole. Sprinkle with paprika. Set in pan of warm water.

Bake in slow oven (325°) about 1¼ hours, or until an inserted knife blade comes out clean. Makes 6 servings.

HERBED CORN BAKE

This hot dish wins almost everyone's approval
with its special seasonings

1 c. milk
½ c. mayonnaise
1 egg, well beaten
1 (12 oz. or 1 lb.) can whole kernel corn, drained

1 c. herb-seasoned bread stuffing
1 small onion, minced
1 tsp. parsley flakes
1 c. dry bread crumbs
2 tblsp. butter or margarine

Combine milk and mayonnaise; mix well. Add egg, corn,

stuffing, onion and parsley. Pour into greased and floured 8″ round baking dish.

Toss bread crumbs with melted butter; sprinkle over corn mixture. Bake in moderate oven (350°) 30 minutes. Makes 6 servings.

CORN WITH CREAM CHEESE

This creamy corn is the company special
of a busy Iowa farm woman

¼ c. milk	⅛ tsp. pepper
1 (3 oz.) pkg. cream cheese	2 (12 oz.) cans whole kernel
1 tblsp. butter	corn, drained (3 c.)
½ tsp. salt	

Combine milk, cream cheese, butter, salt and pepper in saucepan. Cook over low heat, stirring constantly, until cheese melts and is blended. Add corn and heat. Makes 6 servings.

SPICY HOT CORN

A hot relish-vegetable combination to serve
with roast pork or ham

2 tblsp. butter or margarine	2 whole cloves
⅓ c. minced onion	2 tblsp. sugar
½ c. diced or thinly sliced	1 tsp. salt
green celery	1 (16 to 17 oz.) can cream-
¼ c. white wine vinegar	style corn
1 tsp. Tabasco sauce	1 tsp. grated lemon peel

Melt butter in heavy saucepan; add onion, celery, vinegar, Tabasco sauce, cloves, sugar and salt. Cover and simmer 20 minutes.

Add corn and lemon peel during last 5 minutes of cooking, stirring occasionally to prevent sticking. Remove cloves before serving. Makes 4 to 6 servings.

NOTE: You can use 1 (16 to 17 oz.) can succotash (corn and lima beans) or 2 c. frozen corn instead of the cream-style corn.

Hominy Goes Fancy

Look what's happening to hominy, a member of the corn family, in today's kitchens. Hostesses are glamorizing this pioneer food in expertly seasoned casserole dishes. These new combinations have something in common with the skillet-fried hominy our grandmothers served in their frontier homes. Serve either of the casseroles—Scalloped Hominy or Hominy-Almond Casserole—with tender, golden brown pork chops. Your dinner will be a success.

HOMINY-ALMOND CASSEROLE

Hominy goes fancy for the ham or pork chop
company dinner. Delicious—you'll want
to double this recipe

1 can condensed cream of
  mushroom soup
½ c. light cream or
  evaporated milk,
  undiluted
1 tsp. celery seeds
1 tblsp. Worcestershire
  sauce

4 drops Tabasco sauce
  (about)
1 (14½ oz.) can hominy,
  yellow or white whole
  kernel
½ c. slivered almonds
2 tblsp. corn flake crumbs
1 tblsp. melted butter or
  margarine

In a saucepan, combine soup, cream, celery seeds, Worcestershire sauce and Tabasco. Simmer gently a few minutes to blend flavors.

Meanwhile, drain hominy; add to hot sauce together with almonds. Turn into greased 1-qt. casserole.

Combine crumbs and melted butter; sprinkle over casserole. Bake in moderate oven (350°) 25 to 30 minutes. Makes 4 servings.

SCALLOPED HOMINY

Easy dress-up for plain-Jane hominy that makes it
a company special

174

¾ c. chopped green pepper
(1 large)
2 tblsp. butter
2 (1 lb.) cans hominy,
drained
1 c. grated Cheddar cheese

1 can condensed cream of
celery soup
⅓ c. milk
¼ tsp. salt
⅛ tsp. pepper
½ c. cracker crumbs
2 tblsp. melted butter

Cook green pepper in butter until soft. Combine with hominy, cheese, soup, milk, salt and pepper. Turn into greased 1½-qt. casserole. Toss cracker crumbs with melted butter. Sprinkle over hominy.

Bake in moderate oven (350°) 35 minutes, or until mixture is bubbly and lightly browned. Makes 6 servings.

MUSHROOMS POLONAISE

*Watch after you add sour cream—heat but
don't let mixture boil*

2 (8 oz.) cans sliced
mushrooms
1 medium green pepper,
chopped

½ tsp. salt
¼ tsp. pepper
1 tblsp. butter
1 c. dairy sour cream

Combine mushrooms and their liquid, green pepper, salt and pepper in saucepan. Bring to a boil and simmer, uncovered, until green pepper is tender. Drain and save juice to add to gravy or soup.

Add butter and sour cream. Heat, but do not boil. Makes 6 servings.

NOTE: This is a company-special dish. Good with steak, grilled hamburgers or other meats.

Mushrooms on Toast: *Heat canned broiled mushrooms in their liquid until piping hot; drain. Serve them on slices of toast spread with deviled ham.*

MUSHROOM-NOODLE BAKE

Mushrooms make noodles special

1 (8 oz.) can sliced
  mushrooms, drained
½ c. finely chopped onion
1 clove garlic, minced
3 tblsp. butter
3 c. fine noodles (uncooked)

1 c. small curd creamed
  cottage cheese
1 c. dairy sour cream
1 tsp. Worcestershire sauce
½ tsp. salt
¼ tsp. pepper

Cook mushrooms, onion and garlic in butter until onion is soft.

Meanwhile, cook noodles in boiling salted water until tender; drain.

Combine all ingredients; mix together by lifting with 2 forks. Bake in greased 1½-qt. casserole in moderate oven (350°) 30 minutes. Makes 6 servings.

MUSHROOM-SEASONED RICE

*Splendid escort for roast beef and steaks—
something really special*

1 c. brown rice
½ c. butter
1 can condensed beef broth

½ soup can water
1 (4 oz.) can button
  mushrooms, drained

Brown rice in melted butter in heavy skillet, stirring constantly.

In 1½-qt. casserole, combine rice and butter with beef broth and water. Cover; bake in moderate oven (375°) 1¼ hours. Stir in mushrooms and continue to bake 15 minutes longer. Makes 6 servings.

HONEY LEMON-GLAZED ONIONS

*Saucy-sweet glaze glistens on tiny onions—
they're excellent with pork*

1 tblsp. butter or margarine
2 tblsp. honey
¼ tsp. grated lemon peel
1 tsp. fresh or canned lemon
  juice

1 (1 lb.) can small whole
  onions, drained
⅛ tsp. ground mace
  (optional)

Melt butter; mix with honey, lemon peel and juice in

skillet; cook until thickened. Add onions and cook over low heat until glazed, turning onions often.

Put in serving bowl and sprinkle lightly with mace. Makes 3 servings.

NOTE: You can double this recipe to make 6 servings.

Creamed Peas in Chicken Dinners

If you travel the side roads in Pennsylvania Dutch country, you are likely to hear how wonderful sugar peas taste. This is a local name for the vegetable Southerners call English peas and people in other parts of the country refer to only as peas. Dishes made with the vegetable, regardless of how you designate it, can be tempting and rewarding in taste.

It's understandable why some people underestimate the appeal creamed canned peas have in many farm homes when gardens are out of season. They've never had them as served in country chicken dinners. Many farm women make mounds of fluffy mashed winter squash, sweet potatoes or white potatoes, scoop out a hollow in each with a spoon and fill with creamed peas. If you've never known the combination or have forgotten how marvelous it tastes, try this recipe.

CREAMED PEAS

Spoon creamed peas into nests of mashed potatoes, pass chicken and cranberries—a country feast

1 tblsp. flour	⅓ c. light cream or dairy
½ tsp. salt	half-and-half
⅛ tsp. pepper	1 (16 to 17 oz.) can peas
1 tblsp. butter or margarine	½ tsp. Worcestershire sauce

Blend flour, salt and pepper with melted butter. Add cream and ⅓ c. liquid from peas; cook until thickened, stirring constantly. Add drained peas and Worcestershire sauce; heat. Serve garnished with garlic buttered croutons, toasted almonds, chopped salted peanuts or canned French fried onions. Makes 4 servings.

NOTE: For variety, add one of the following to the cream sauce before adding the peas: grated cheese, cooked canned mushrooms, sliced water chestnuts, chopped ripe olives or diced pimiento.

FIESTA PEAS AU GRATIN

Rich, creamy and delicious

½ c. process cheese spread	1 (4 oz.) can sliced
1 egg, beaten	mushrooms, drained
1 small onion, minced	1 (16 to 17 oz.) can peas,
	drained

Have cheese spread at room temperature; mix thoroughly with egg. Add onion.

Put mushrooms and peas in shallow 1½-qt. baking dish; top with cheese mixture. Bake in moderate oven (350°) 30 minutes. Makes 4 servings.

NEW PEAS LORRAINE

Water chestnuts give extra crunch

2 slices bacon	1 c. light cream or dairy
1 (4 oz.) can mushrooms	half-and-half
¼ c. chopped green onions	1 (5 oz.) can water
1 tblsp. flour	chestnuts, drained
	2 (1 lb.) cans peas, drained

Cook bacon until crisp; remove. Add mushrooms and onions to bacon fat; cook until onions are tender. Stir in flour; add cream and cook, stirring, until thickened.

Add water chestnuts, sliced, and peas; mix lightly and heat. Serve sprinkled with crumbled bacon. Makes 6 to 8 servings.

PEAS FRANÇAISE

A truly French dish quickly made from foods in most farm kitchens

4 small green onions with
1" of tops
2 tblsp. butter or margarine
1½ c. shredded iceberg
lettuce

2 tblsp. minced parsley
⅛ tsp. chervil leaves
(optional)
1 (1 lb.) can peas, drained
Salt and pepper to taste

Cut onions in ½" pieces; cook in butter until lightly browned. Add lettuce, parsley, chervil and peas; cover and cook gently just until lettuce is wilted and peas are hot. Add salt and pepper. Makes 4 to 6 servings.

SPICED BLACK-EYED PEAS

*A taste of Texas that's welcome in all states—
it's that good*

2 slices bacon
1 (16 to 17 oz.) can
black-eyed peas
¼ tsp. onion salt

¼ tsp. celery salt
1 tsp. minced parsley
⅛ tsp. orégano leaves

Fry bacon until crisp; remove and drain on absorbent paper.
Add 2 tblsp. liquid drained from peas, seasonings and drained peas to bacon fat; heat. Serve sprinkled with crumbled bacon. Makes 4 servings.

HASHED BROWN POTATOES

*Easy-do hashed browns which are crisp,
delicious and please the men*

2 (15 to 16 oz.) cans whole
potatoes

3 tblsp. butter or margarine
Salt and pepper to taste

Drain and grate potatoes. Brown until crisp in melted butter; turning with a spatula. Season with salt and pepper. Makes 4 servings.

Summer Favorite Sweet Potatoes

During summer months canned sweet potatoes enjoy their heyday. That's when the fresh vegetable disappears from most markets for several weeks. With canned "sweets" on hand, you can quickly and easily provide this popular vegetable, especially when you have a collection of superior recipes for fixing them, such as Honey-Glazed, Maple and the other tasty sweet potato dishes that follow.

Canned sweet potatoes help busy women the year around. You take them cooked and peeled from the can. All you have to do is season and heat them, which takes little time and effort.

HONEY-GLAZED SWEET POTATOES

Take your choice of candying sweet potatoes in oven
or on top of range

¼ c. strained honey
2 tblsp. brown sugar
2 tblsp. butter or margarine

¼ tsp. salt
1 (17 oz.) can vacuum pack
  sweet potatoes, drained

Combine honey, brown sugar, butter, and salt and liquid drained from sweet potatoes in saucepan. Boil until thickened. Add sweet potatoes and heat; spoon glaze over potatoes occasionally. Or put sweet potatoes in an oiled shallow baking dish (if sweet potatoes are large, cut in halves). Pour the syrup over and bake in moderate oven (375°) about 30 minutes. Makes 4 servings.

GLAZED SWEET POTATOES

Easy to fix, extra-good, attractive—pink glaze glistens
over sweets

½ c. apple jelly
1 tsp. red cinnamon candies
  (red hots)
2 tblsp. butter

½ tsp. salt
7 (17 oz.) cans vacuum pack
  sweet potatoes, drained

180

Melt apple jelly, candies and butter in skillet. Add salt and stir to blend.

Add sweet potatoes. Turn to coat thoroughly with mixture. Cover and cook over low heat 5 minutes. Uncover. Turn potatoes again and continue cooking until thoroughly heated, 2 or 3 minutes. Makes 6 to 8 servings.

MARMALADE-GLAZED SWEET POTATOES

Marmalade does double duty—it adds both orange taste and sweetness

2 tblsp. butter or margarine
⅓ c. orange marmalade
¼ tsp. salt
1 tblsp. fresh or canned lemon juice
1 (17 oz.) can vacuum pack sweet potatoes, drained

Combine butter, marmalade, salt and lemon juice in skillet. Cook a few minutes until thickened, stirring. Add sweet potatoes and cook slowly, turning frequently, until they are glazed. Makes 4 to 6 servings.

MAPLE SWEET POTATOES

The maple flavor complements sweet potatoes, gives them a nice glaze

½ c. maple syrup
¼ c. butter or margarine
1 (17 oz.) can vacuum pack sweet potatoes, drained

Combine syrup and butter in saucepan; bring to a boil and cook until thickened.

Add sweet potatoes; simmer until hot, basting occasionally with glaze. Makes 4 servings.

SWEET POTATOES WITH RAISIN-NUT SAUCE

Perfect companion for baked ham

¾ c. water
¼ c. seedless raisins
2 tblsp. sugar
⅛ tsp. salt
1 tblsp. butter or margarine
1 tsp. flour
¼ tsp. ground cinnamon
¼ c. chopped nuts
1 (17 oz.) can vacuum pack sweet potatoes, drained

Combine water, raisins, sugar and salt; boil 10 minutes.

Blend softened butter with flour and cinnamon. Add to raisins; cook until thickened, stirring. Add nuts.

Put sweet potatoes in shallow 8″ square baking dish; pour over sauce. Bake in moderate oven (350°) about 30 minutes, until heated through. Makes 4 to 5 servings.

PLUMP SWEET POTATO CROQUETTES

*Cranberry sauce gives color—the tart taste is nice
with the sweets*

1 (17 oz.) can vacuum pack
  sweet potatoes, drained
  and mashed
1 egg, slightly beaten
1 tsp. grated orange peel
1 tblsp. brown sugar

½ tsp. salt
¾ c. finely chopped pecans
1 tblsp. melted butter or
  margarine
Canned whole cranberry
  sauce

Combine sweet potatoes, egg, orange peel, brown sugar and salt. Form into 12 balls by rolling heaping tablespoonfuls of the mixture in the nuts. Place on greased baking sheet. Make a large thumbprint in each ball to form a nest. Dribble with butter.

Bake in hot oven (425°) 20 minutes, or until brown. Place a spoonful of cranberry sauce in center of each. Makes 12 croquettes.

SPINACH WITH FLUFFY SAUCE

Also serve this sauce on drained green beans or asparagus

2 (15 oz.) cans spinach
2 hard-cooked eggs
¼ c. butter or margarine

1 tblsp. fresh or canned
  lemon juice
⅛ tsp. salt

Drain and heat spinach.

Force hard-cooked eggs through sieve or food mill. Put in a small bowl with soft butter, lemon juice and salt; beat with rotary beater until fluffy.

Put spinach in serving bowl and top with sauce. Makes 6 servings.

Refreshing Tomatoes au Jus

Sometimes the simple dishes taste best—Tomatoes au Jus, for instance. Certainly, carefully and delicately seasoned canned tomatoes have a loyal following. Aside from their characteristic taste, which most people like, they frequently are the lightest dish in an otherwise heavy meal. This makes them especially refreshing.

The helpfulness of canned tomatoes in country kitchens doesn't end with this simple dish, however. Tomatoes, along with onions, are the great diplomats of the vegetables—they know how to get along with and improve a wide variety of foods. When you look at the many recipes in this cookbook that list tomatoes with the ingredients, it may be difficult for you to decide which one to try first. Give each one its turn and in so doing find the favorites of your family and friends.

TOMATOES AU JUS

Old-time favorite always in style

2 tblsp. butter or margarine	1 (28 oz.) can tomatoes
1 small onion, finely	⅛ tsp. pepper
chopped	1 tsp. Worcestershire sauce
2 tblsp. minced parsley	Salt to taste

Combine butter, onion, parsley and juice drained from tomatoes; cook down to about half.

Add tomatoes, pepper, Worcestershire sauce and salt; heat. Serve in sauce dishes. Makes 5 servings.

TOMATOES COUNTRY-STYLE

*Seasoning tomatoes with celery seeds is a
favored farm kitchen custom*

2 slices bacon	¼ tsp. celery seeds
1 small onion	Salt and pepper to taste
1 (1 lb.) can tomatoes	

Cook bacon until crisp; remove from skillet and drain.

Slice onion and separate into rings; cook in bacon fat until tender, but not brown. Add tomatoes and celery seeds; heat. Season with salt and pepper. Serve topped with crumbled bacon. Makes 4 servings.

STEWED TOMATOES SUPREME

The parsley decorates, the crackers add crispness and a taste of cheese

1 (1 lb.) can stewed tomatoes　**1 tblsp. chopped parsley**
¼ c. crushed appetizer
**　cheese crackers**

Heat tomatoes in saucepan. Serve in individual sauce dishes, topping each serving with a spoonful of crackers and a sprinkling of parsley. Makes 4 servings.

TOMATOES ITALIENNE

Skillful seasoning is the difference

1 small onion, finely　**1 (1 lb.) can tomatoes**
**　chopped**　**½ tsp. sugar**
1 clove garlic, finely　**⅛ tsp. orégano leaves**
**　chopped**　**Salt and pepper to taste**
2 tblsp. butter or margarine

Cook onion and garlic in butter until tender but not brown. Add tomatoes, sugar and orégano; heat. Season with salt and pepper. Makes 4 servings.

TOMATO-CHEESE CASSEROLE

The bacon, cheese and onion flavors make these tomatoes extra-special

1 small onion, sliced　**1 c. grated sharp cheese**
2 tblsp. bacon fat　**1 c. crushed potato chips**
1 (1 lb.) can tomatoes

184

Cook onion in bacon fat until tender; add tomatoes. Put layers of tomato mixture, cheese and potato chips in a casserole, ending with a layer of potato chips.

Bake in hot oven (400°) about 20 minutes. Makes 4 servings.

CHAPTER FOUR

Dried Vegetables

"WE'RE HAVING a bean supper tomorrow. Won't you folks come?" If you live in New England, this invitation for Saturday evening is not unusual. When you see an earthen pot of brown beans steaming in their rich juices on the buffet table and get a whiff of their aroma, you'll know why baked beans never will go out of style. The pages in this chapter will help you entertain in this friendly, gracious way regardless of where you live.

Beans are not the only vegetable preserved by drying, but they're what country people think of first. The kind you like depends largely on where you live and what you find in your supermarket. Among the popular favorites are small white pea or navy, the larger white Great Northern, yellow-eye, dark red kidney, red and white marrow, giant and small lima, white cranberry speckled with red, small pink and red Mexican, buff-colored pinto with brown spots, huge horse or fava, green and yellow garden soy and black or turtle beans. Black-eyed peas or cowpeas also are beans. Then there are dried lentils and split peas that make marvelous soups (see Index).

Do try our recipe for Superior Baked Beans, a recipe contributed by a New York farm woman who features them in her family's big picnics that celebrate the end of the harvesting season. Their superb flavors develop during 48 hours in a spicy marinade before baking. Ranch-Style Lentil Casserole deserves an honorable mention; the recipe for this hearty dish came from an Idaho lentil grower's wife. And Indian Beans feature pintos in a true South-western special.

Instant potatoes (a form of dried vegetable) speedily won acceptance in farm kitchens and most women now keep them on hand for quick mashed potatoes and other dishes. You'll like the recipe for Party Potato Casserole—potatoes and cottage cheese unite in this delicious dish.

You'll find extra-good recipes for other dried vegetables

in this chapter. This collection of recipes contains the farm and ranch favorites of our readers. And don't overlook recipes in the chapters on soups, main dishes and mixed vegetables, which also call for dried vegetables.

How to Soak Dried Beans

It is necessary to soak dried beans in water before cooking to restore the water they lost in drying. This helps them to cook tender. The old-fashioned way was to let the beans soak overnight in cold water. You may still find this method the most convenient to follow, but if you want to speed things up, cover the beans with cold water, bring to a boil and boil 2 minutes; remove from heat, cover and soak 1 hour in the water in which they boiled. This gives you the same results as soaking 15 hours at room temperature!

To Soften Hard Water

The minerals naturally occurring in hard water affect the softening of beans and other dried vegetables during cooking. If the water is very hard, the cooked vegetables will be hard, no matter how long they cook. You can shorten the cooking time greatly by adding a small amount of baking soda (sodium bicarbonate) to the water in which you bring dried beans to a boil. Avoid adding more than a pinch of soda. It's all you need to soften the water, and B vitamins are destroyed by an excess of soda.

Homespun Baked Beans

There's something about a pot of beans baking that speaks of home. It's a part of our heritage. Baked beans are a historical food and as American as the Fourth of July. The Indians, who baked their pots of beans over coals in holes covered by earth, taught early colonists how satisfying and tasty this long- and slow-cooked vegetable was. Through the years women experimented with seasonings in beans they baked; this brought great variety to the vegetable dish.

New York and Michigan country women frequently include apples with beans in the pot—see our recipe for Baked Beans Michigan. Many Middle Western and Pacific Northwestern homemakers add tomatoes or ketchup to the bean pot. You'll find the taste of tomatoes in our Oregon Ranch Beans and Indiana Baked Beans, for instance. But the traditional dish, Boston Baked Beans, has no substitute to this day in New England.

New versions continue to come from country kitchens. One of the delightful ones is Superior Baked Beans. When you read the recipe, you'll notice that the beans soak in a wonderfully seasoned marinade in the refrigerator before you bake them. Do try fixing them; they're really good.

All baked beans are at their best when every bean is tender and juicy without being mushy. If you are cooking dry beans, taste for doneness while they cook. When they're done, remove them from the oven. If necessary, you can reheat them.

While a bean pot is ideal for baking beans and adds a homey touch to the buffet or table, you can use a casserole if you don't have a pot. Deep casseroles, those nearest the shape of bean pots, are best choice.

SUPERIOR BAKED BEANS

No wonder these beans taste so good. They soak in a rich-in-flavor liquid for 48 hours before you bake them

1 lb. dried navy beans	1 bay leaf, crushed
3 c. water	1 clove garlic, minced
¾ c. firmly packed brown sugar	1 tsp. dry mustard
¼ c. light molasses	1½ tsp. salt
1 c. water	¼ tsp. pepper
¼ c. finely chopped celery tops	¼ tsp. ground cinnamon
	⅛ tsp. ground allspice
1 onion, finely chopped	¼ tsp. ground nutmeg
	½ lb. ham or salt pork

Wash and sort beans. Place beans and 3 c. water in a large earthenware pot.

Mix rest of ingredients, except ham. Pour over beans in pot; stir to mix (liquid should cover beans). Refrigerate 48 hours.

Add cut-up ham or salt pork just before cooking.

Bake, covered, in slow oven (300°) 6 hours. Then uncover, add ½ c. hot water if liquid does not cover beans, and bake 1 hour longer. Recipe makes about 8 servings.

NOTE: Double this recipe for a crowd.

The Indian squaws added deer fat and an onion to their bean pots. As the recipe evolved in New England kitchens, pork replaced the deer fat, and brown sugar and molasses became favorite seasonings.

BAKED BEANS MICHIGAN

It's easy to understand why this is a favorite of bean growers' families. Apples are unusual tasty addition

2 lbs. dried navy beans	½ c. brown sugar
9 c. water	½ c. molasses
1 lb. salt pork, diced	3 tsp. dry mustard
3 tart apples, peeled, cored and coarsely cut	3 tblsp. vinegar
	¼ tsp. pepper
1 medium onion, chopped	

Wash beans. Add water to them; cover and let soak overnight. Or bring to a boil and boil 2 minutes; remove from heat, cover and let stand 1 hour.

Add salt pork to beans and cook in the water in which they soaked until beans are tender, about 1 hour.

Pour bean mixture into a bean pot; add remaining ingredients. Cover and bake in slow oven (300°) 6 hours. Add more warm water during cooking, if necessary. Makes 10 servings.

BOSTON BAKED BEANS

Stick a few whole cloves in the onion for subtle spicy taste—really good

1 lb. dried navy beans (2 c.)	1 medium onion, peeled
6 c. cold water	2 tsp. dry mustard
1 tsp. salt	⅓ c. brown sugar
¼ lb. salt pork	¼ c. molasses

Wash beans and add cold water to them. Cover and let soak overnight. Or bring to a boil and boil 2 minutes, remove from heat, cover and let stand 1 hour.

Add salt to beans and liquid and simmer until tender, about 1 hour. Drain, reserving liquid. Measure 1¾ c. bean liquid; add water if necessary.

Cut a slice from the salt pork and put it in bottom of bean pot. Add beans; place the onion in the center of beans.

Mix mustard, sugar and molasses in with bean liquid; pour over beans.

Cut 3 gashes in remaining salt pork, and place on beans, rind side on top.

Cover and bake 5 to 7 hours in slow oven (300°), adding more water as needed. Remove cover from bean pot the last half hour of baking so the pork rind will brown and become crisp. Makes 6 servings.

Indiana Baked Beans

Women today frequently bake a large quantity of beans to freeze for quick reheating on busy days. The recipe for Indiana Baked Beans tells how to bake about 8 quarts! You can, of course, serve part of them and freeze the remainder—we give you directions in the recipe.

INDIANA BAKED BEANS

Full-meal, brown beauty beans that can be baked ahead and kept in freezer, handy to serve on busy days

4 lbs. dried navy beans or	3½ tsp. prepared mustard
pea beans	2 c. ketchup
4 qts. water	1 c. molasses
1 c. brown sugar	1½ c. chopped onion
2 tblsp. salt	¾ lb. salt pork, sliced

Soak beans, covered, in large kettle overnight. Or bring

them to a boil and boil 2 minutes. Remove from heat and let them stand, covered, 1 hour.

Simmer beans in water in which they soaked until almost tender, about 1 hour.

Combine sugar, salt, mustard, ketchup, molasses and onion. Add to beans; bring to a boil.

Pour beans into casseroles or bean pots or leave them in the kettle. Mix some of the salt pork slices into the beans; lay remaining pork on top.

Bake, covered, in slow oven (300°) 6 hours; remove cover the last 30 minutes of cooking. Add boiling water during cooking if necessary to keep beans from becoming dry. Makes about 20 servings.

To Freeze: Cook beans 5 hours, covered. Pack in freezer containers, seal, label, date and freeze. (Some cooks like to remove the salt pork before freezing, as it tends to become rancid.) Recommended storage time: 4 to 6 months.

To Serve: Partially thaw at room temperature about 2 hours; then heat in saucepan with a little water added, or in the top of a double boiler. Or bake beans in moderate oven (350°) until they are heated, about 45 minutes for a pint, 1 hour for a quart.

OREGON RANCH BEANS

If you like the taste of tomato in baked beans,
this is your recipe

2 lbs. small dried white
   beans (navy or pea)
1 to 2 tsp. salt
1 lb. salt pork, diced or
   coarsely ground
2 medium onions, chopped

½ tsp. coarse grind pepper
1 (1 lb. 12 oz.) can
   tomatoes
2 tblsp. prepared mustard
1 lb. brown sugar

Soak beans overnight in water to cover. Or bring to a boil and boil 2 minutes; remove from heat, cover and let stand 1 hour. Add 1 tsp. salt and simmer in same water until tender, about 1 hour. Drain, reserving liquid.

Place layers of pork, beans, onions and pepper in large bean pot, or two 1½-qt. casseroles.

Combine tomatoes, mustard, brown sugar and 1 c. bean liquid. Add more salt, if needed; add to bean pot.

Bake, covered, in slow oven (300°) 4 hours, stirring occasionally. Remove cover and bake 4 hours longer. Add more bean liquid or water to keep moisture visible at all times. Makes 15 to 30 servings, depending on accompaniments.

Western Bean Roundup

Recipes for different kinds of beans baked together come from Western ranch country. This one for Baked Beans Roundup is a splendid example. Look also for Western Baked Beans (see Index), which calls for four kinds of beans from cans baked in a casserole. "One variety of beans baked in a pot makes good eating," says a Washington State rancher's wife, "but several kinds cooked together are that much better." You can depend on an enthusiastic reception for these ranch specials.

BAKED BEANS ROUNDUP

*Four kinds of beans blend flavors in this special
for a hungry crowd*

1 c. dried navy beans	1 c. chopped onion
1 c. dried lima beans	½ tsp. coarse grind pepper
1 c. dried kidney beans	1 tblsp. dry mustard
1 c. dried black-eyed peas	1 tblsp. ground ginger
2 tsp. salt	½ c. light molasses
½ lb. salt pork in 1 piece	½ c. light brown sugar

Wash beans, including black-eyed peas; cover with water (about 2 qts.) and soak overnight. Or cover with cold water, bring to a boil and boil 2 minutes; then remove from heat and let stand, covered, 1 hour before cooking. Add salt; bring to a boil in the water in which they soaked and simmer 15 to 20 minutes. Drain, reserving liquid.

Cut a fourth of the pork in ½" cubes; place in bottom of 5-qt. casserole or bean pot. Cover with a 1" layer of beans and peas, then onion; alternate beans, peas and onion, ending with beans and peas.

Score remaining piece of pork, making ½" cuts to the rind; press into beans until only the rind shows.

Combine reserved bean liquid, pepper, dry mustard, ginger, molasses and brown sugar. Heat and pour over beans. Add more water, if needed, to cover.

Cover and bake in slow oven (250°) 6 to 7 hours. Makes 12 to 16 servings.

Barbecued Lima Beans

If you live in high altitude country, here's a recipe made to order for you. You cook Barbecued Lima Beans in a pressure saucepan. A Wyoming homemaker likes to serve them at summer barbecues and for family meals during the cold months. Try them when you want to fix something different to serve with hamburgers or steak and a molded fruit salad. You'll find the beans unusually well seasoned.

BARBECUED LIMA BEANS

A good pressure saucepan recipe

1 lb. dried lima beans	2 c. tomato juice
5 c. cold water	¼ c. vinegar
¼ lb. salt pork, diced	3 tblsp. brown sugar
1 onion, sliced	2 tsp. Worcestershire sauce
1 clove garlic, minced	½ tsp. chili powder
2 branches celery, chopped	1 tblsp. prepared mustard
1 green pepper, chopped	½ tsp. salt

Sort and wash lima beans; soak overnight in 5 c. water. Or bring to a boil and boil 2 minutes; remove from heat, cover and let stand 1 hour.

Heat pressure saucepan and brown salt pork. Add onion, garlic, celery and green pepper; brown lightly.

Drain beans; add with remaining ingredients to saucepan; mix well. Cover saucepan and cook at 15 pounds pressure 30 minutes. Allow pressure to reduce normally. Makes 6 servings.

NOTE: Be sure to follow manufacturer's directions for operation of pressure cooker.

OVEN BAKED LIMAS

*An easy way to get the barbecue flavor—
it develops while beans bake*

2 c. dried lima beans	2 tsp. Worcestershire sauce
5 c. cold water	1½ tsp. chili powder
¼ lb. salt pork, cubed	1 tsp. salt
1 small onion, sliced	1 can condensed tomato
1 clove garlic, chopped	soup
¼ c. shortening	⅓ c. vinegar
1½ tblsp. prepared mustard	¼ lb. salt pork, diced

Sort and wash limas. Soak overnight in 5 c. water. In the morning add more water, if needed, to cover beans. Or bring to a boil and boil 2 minutes; remove from heat, cover and let stand 1 hour. Add cubed salt pork; simmer slowly in the water in which beans soaked until tender, about 30 minutes. Drain, reserving 1½ c. bean liquid.

Brown onion and garlic in shortening. Add bean liquid, mustard, Worcestershire sauce, chili powder, salt, tomato soup and vinegar; cook about 5 minutes.

Alternate lima beans and sauce in greased 1½- to 2-qt. casserole. Top with ¼ lb. diced salt pork.

Bake in moderate oven (350°) 50 to 60 minutes. Makes 6 servings.

BAKED LIMA BEANS

Sweet-sour flavor complements beans

2 c. cooked dried baby lima	½ tsp. dry mustard
beans	⅛ tsp. pepper
¼ c. mild molasses	1 tsp. salt
1 c. dairy sour cream	1 tsp. Worcestershire sauce
1 tblsp. minced onion	3 slices bacon

Drain beans, saving ½ c. liquid. Combine with molasses, sour cream, onion, mustard, pepper, salt and Worcestershire sauce.

Place beans in 3-qt. casserole. Add liquid. Arrange bacon slices on top.

Bake in slow oven (325°) 1 hour. Makes 8 servings.

BAKED LIMA CASSEROLE

Beginners can bake this hearty dish that pinch-hits tastily for potatoes

1 lb. dried lima beans
1 qt. water (more if
  necessary)
1 c. light cream, or dairy
  half-and-half

1 can condensed bean with
  bacon soup
2 tblsp. sugar
1 tsp. salt
½ tsp. pepper
¼ c. butter or margarine

Boil beans in water 2 minutes. Let set 1 hour; simmer 30 minutes; drain.

Add cream to soup, mixing well.

Place a fourth of beans in 2-qt. casserole; top with a fourth of sugar, salt, pepper, butter and soup mixture. Repeat layers three times.

Bake, covered, in slow oven (325°) 1½ hours; uncover and bake 30 minutes more. Makes 8 servings.

Mexican Bean Pot

Something good-tasting and unusual—that description fits our recipe for Mexican Bean Pot. The expertly seasoned dish, featuring red kidney beans, has made many friends since FARM JOURNAL first printed the recipe. The secret to the success of this hearty treat is the variety of seasonings, which includes herbs, spices, sweet pickle juice and strong coffee!

MEXICAN BEAN POT

*Mighty good—serve with tomato, pineapple
or a tossed green salad*

2 c. dried kidney beans (or
  4 c. cooked or canned)
6 c. water
1 tblsp. salt
6 slices bacon
1 clove garlic, minced or
  crushed
⅛ tsp. thyme leaves
2 whole cloves
Small bay leaf

2 tsp. dry mustard
⅛ tsp. ground pepper
  (cayenne)
2 tblsp. vinegar
½ c. spicy juice (from
  sweet pickles, spiced
  fruit)
¼ c. strong coffee
6 onion slices

195

Cover beans with 6 c. water and 1 tblsp. salt. Bring to a boil and boil 2 minutes; then soak 1 hour, covered.

Fry bacon until half cooked; drain fat to make ¼ c. Add fat to beans (fat keeps beans from foaming).

Simmer beans in water in which they have been soaked until tender, about 2 hours.

Drain beans; combine with other ingredients except bacon, coffee and sliced onion.

Place in 1½-qt. casserole. Bake in moderate oven (350°) 1 hour.

Pour coffee over beans. Garnish top with bacon and onion slices.

Bake in hot oven (400°) about 20 minutes, until bacon is crisp. Makes 6 servings.

KIDNEY BEANS AND ONIONS

Man, this is a dish for a cold day!

4 c. drained red kidney beans (cooked or canned)	2½ tsp. salt
	¼ c. mild molasses
1½ c. shredded sharp cheese	1½ tsp. dry mustard
	⅛ tsp. pepper
6 medium or 12 small white onions, cooked	1 tsp. Worcestershire sauce
	2 tblsp. melted butter or margarine
½ c. liquid drained from beans	

Put half of beans in 2-qt. casserole. Sprinkle with 1 c. cheese. Add remaining beans. Arrange onions over top. Sprinkle remaining cheese in center and over onions.

Combine remaining ingredients. Pour half of mixture over beans. Bake in moderate oven (350°) 20 minutes. Spoon remaining liquid over top, and bake 5 minutes longer. Makes 6 servings.

Indian Pinto Beans

Pinto beans are important crops in Colorado and New Mexico, where they are great favorites. You find them for sale in many states, however. The spotted beans take the spotlight in Indian Beans, an unusual and delicious dish.

It's the long and easy cooking that makes them taste so good.

INDIAN BEANS

It takes time to cook pinto beans—their taste
makes it time well spent

1 lb. dried pinto beans	¾ c. sliced celery
3 qts. water	1½ tsp. salt
1 (1 lb.) can tomatoes	¾ tsp. ground cinnamon
1 large onion, chopped	6 tblsp. sugar
8 slices bacon, cut in 2″ lengths	3 tblsp. vinegar

Wash beans; place in 6-qt. kettle with 3 qts. water and bring to a simmer. Cover; cook beans about 4 hours, or until tender.

Mix remaining ingredients with beans and cooking water. Place in 4-qt. casserole; cover and bake in moderate oven (350°) 2 to 3 hours, or until done. Add a little water if necessary. Makes 10 to 12 servings.

TEXAS RICE-BEAN CASSEROLE

Serve this at barbecues—people love it
and it fills them up!

1 lb. dried pinto or red kidney beans	1 c. chopped onion
6 c. water	⅓ c. bacon drippings
2 (1 lb. 13 oz.) cans tomatoes (7 c.)	1 tblsp. parsley flakes
2 c. rice	1 tblsp. salt
2 tsp. salt	2 tsp. chili powder
1 c. chopped green pepper	¼ tsp. pepper
	2 tsp. Worcestershire sauce

Wash beans. Add water and bring to a boil. Boil 2 minutes. Remove from heat and let stand 1 hour. Cover and simmer until tender, about 2 hours.

Drain beans, reserving liquid. Drain tomatoes, reserving liquid. Combine bean and tomato liquid; add water to make enough liquid to cook rice according to package directions. Add rice and 2 tsp. salt; cook rice according to package directions.

Meanwhile, cook green pepper and onion in bacon drippings until soft; do not brown. Add to beans along with rice and remaining ingredients. Place in 4-qt. casserole. Bake in moderate oven (350°) 45 minutes. Makes 15 servings.

Baked Swedish Brown Beans

Swedish brown beans have a hold on a large group of loyal Scandinavians in Wisconsin, Minnesota, the Dakotas, Iowa and other neighborhoods where people of this ancestry live. Taste the delicately spiced Baked Swedish Brown Beans and you'll understand why. Our recipe makes a big batch because the beans are ideal for potluck suppers and entertaining a crowd.

BAKED SWEDISH BROWN BEANS FOR A CROWD

Watch the men take second helpings when these beans are on the buffet

2 lbs. dried Swedish brown beans	1 c. dark molasses
	1 (3″) stick cinnamon
2 tsp. salt	¼ tsp. ground nutmeg
1 lb. lean salt pork, cut in cubes	1 medium onion, sliced

Wash beans and soak overnight in cold water to cover. Or bring to a boil and boil 2 minutes; remove from heat, cover and let stand 1 hour.

Add salt and salt pork; simmer about 2 hours. Stir in remaining ingredients. Place in deep bean pot.

Bake, covered, in slow oven (325°) 4 to 5 hours, adding more water if beans become too dry. Makes 12 to 14 servings.

Ranch-Style Lentil Casserole

Lentils have an advantage over dried beans: they cook tender much faster. And they require no presoaking. Ranch-style Lentil Casserole is an example of a substantial dish in which the dried vegetable takes an important role. Be sure also to try Idaho Lentil Soup and Vegetable Lentil Chowder (see Index).

RANCH-STYLE LENTIL CASSEROLE

Serve these barbecue-flavored lentils with a
crisp green salad

2 c. lentils, washed	1 (1⅜ oz.) pkg. onion soup
1 qt. water	mix
1 lb. ground beef	1 tsp. cider vinegar
½ c. salad oil	1 tsp. prepared mustard
1 c. ketchup	⅛ tsp. pepper
	1 c. water

Combine lentils and 1 qt. water in saucepan. Cook, uncovered, over medium heat 30 minutes.

Brown beef in oil. Stir in lentils and remaining ingredients. Pour into 2½-qt. casserole. Bake, uncovered, in hot oven (400°) 30 minutes. Makes 8 servings.

Party Potato Casserole

Instant mashed potatoes occupy shelf space in most country kitchens. They're such a convenience when time is at a premium. You can use them in any recipe in this cookbook that calls for mashed potatoes. Party Potato Casserole takes honors in any meal in which it appears. The sour cream and cottage cheese give the potatoes fascinating flavor.

PARTY POTATO CASSEROLE

Cottage cheese adds flavor, protein

199

Instant mashed potatoes	½ tsp. salt
for 8 servings	⅛ tsp. pepper
1 tblsp. onion flakes	2 tblsp. butter
1 c. dairy sour cream	⅛ tsp. paprika (optional)
2 c. small curd creamed	
cottage cheese	

Prepare instant potatoes according to package directions, but use only half the amount of milk specified and add dried onion flakes to the water before heating.

Add sour cream, cottage cheese, which has been sieved or creamed in blender, salt and pepper. Spoon into greased 2-qt. casserole. Dot top with butter and sprinkle with paprika. Bake in moderate oven (350°) 30 minutes. If desired, place under broiler a few seconds to brown lightly. (Potatoes brown a little on peaks without broiling.) Makes 8 servings.

NOTE: You can make this in advance and refrigerate. Then add 5 minutes to the baking time. You also can cook and mash 6 medium potatoes and substitute them for the instant mashed potatoes.

CAMPER FRIED POTATOES

Vinegar gives these camp-style potatoes an intriguing tart flavor

6 thick slices bacon	¼ c. vinegar
1½ c. instant mashed	¼ c. sugar
potato flakes (not	1 tsp. salt
reconstituted)	⅛ tsp. pepper
1 small to medium onion,	
finely chopped	

Fry bacon slices in skillet over medium heat.

Meanwhile, have potato flakes soaking in enough water barely to cover; they should soak about 20 minutes.

When bacon is crisp remove from skillet, reserving about ¼ c. fat in pan. Add onion and toss in hot fat until it is limp and yellow; then add potatoes, vinegar, sugar, salt and pepper. Let simmer over low heat.

Just before serving, add bacon, broken into bite-size pieces. Makes 4 servings.

CHAPTER FIVE

Mixed Vegetables

THERE'S ALMOST no limit to the vegetable twosomes or trios you can serve in the same bowl or on the same platter. Two vegetables often taste better than one, and sometimes three or more taste better than two. And they look more appetizing, too, if you consider color and shape as well as harmonious flavors, when you combine them. Midget carrot strips and green lima beans look much more decorative, for example, if you toss them together in one bowl, rather than present them in separate bowls. Cook separately the vegetables you plan to combine (unless they require the same cooking time); then combine them, add butter and seasonings and toss gently.

If you're having a buffet supper, try serving two or three vegetables arranged on a large platter or in an oblong baking dish. You might center the platter with a snowy white cauliflower and spoon buttered limas and julienne carrots in two colorful rings around the cauliflower—or in crescents at each end of the platter. Or you could line up three strips of color in a flat baking dish: sautéed cherry tomatoes, diced creamed potatoes and green peas, for example. Or arrange several pie-shaped wedges of color on a round chop plate.

Still another way of serving vegetables together is to fill one with another. Some vegetables make their own "serving shells." Thus, you can stuff cooked green peppers with cooked carrots or onions; or large cooked onions with chopped sautéed mushrooms; or acorn squash with tiny green peas. You could mash cooked carrots or squash with baked potatoes when you make baked stuffed potatoes . . . or stir a little crumbled French-fried onion rings into the potatoes.

And do look through this chapter for new recipes, many from farm and ranch kitchens, for the best mixed vegetable dishes you'll ever taste: Cabbage and Peas, Corn-Tomato Skillet, Okra with Corn and a red-green-yellow special called Bean-Duet Casserole, in which green and wax beans join tomato sauce. Once you start teaming different cooked vegetables together, you'll dream up many appealing variations of your own.

Good Vegetable Companions

Everyone knows the traditional vegetable combinations —peas and mushrooms, peas and pearl onions, corn and lima beans. If you check the frozen food case at your supermarket, you'll find other combinations, too—which makes this a good place to look for ideas for serving your own fresh garden vegetables.

Here are a few more suggestions for cooked vegetable combinations that contrast pleasantly in flavor, color and texture.

Asparagus pieces with whole kernel corn.

Cut green beans with whole kernel or creamed corn, or with diagonally cut celery pieces.

Lima beans with cauliflower flowerets, or buttered limas in baked acorn squash halves.

Sliced beets with tiny whole onions.

Brussels sprouts with midget carrot strips.

Carrot pennies with cauliflower flowerets.

Cauliflower flowerets with sautéed sliced mushrooms.

Diced carrots wreathed by French-style green beans.

Whole kernel corn with zucchini slices.

Small whole onions with thin green pepper strips.

Mashed parsnip nest filled with peas.

Peas with cubed summer squash.

Sliced summer squash with red cherry tomatoes sautéed briefly in butter. Or for subtle color contrast, yellow crookneck slices with zucchini slices.

Mashed winter squash spooned into a ring shape on chop plate and filled with Brussels sprouts.

Spinach nest filled with creamed onions.

Tomato wedges, sautéed in butter, tossed with cut green beans.

Baked tomatoes with bread crumb stuffing, served on a platter with broccoli spears.

Turnips mashed half-and-half with potatoes, shaped into a nest and filled with green lima beans.

Broiled large mushroom caps stuffed with mashed carrots and garnished with chopped parsley.

Peas (or any vegetable) mixed with rice, with bits of ham and/or pimiento added for bright color.

Green Bean-Tomato Bake

Farm women say they're in luck when their gardens generously yield green beans and tomatoes. They like to combine the two favorite vegetables in many delightful dishes. Sometimes they add cheese and bacon to this red and green combination, as in Green Bean-Tomato Bake, to heighten delicious flavors. Another pet country custom is to serve cooked green and wax beans, buttered, in the same vegetable dish. And if green lima beans are available, they are often added, cooked and buttered, for a triple bean treat. The contrast in color, shape and flavor is pleasing.

GREEN BEAN-TOMATO BAKE

Two vegetables, big in most gardens, pair off
in this men's favorite

2 c. cooked green beans, cut in 1½″ pieces	½ c. chopped onion
2 c. diced peeled tomatoes (2 large)	½ tsp. salt
3 slices bacon, diced	⅛ tsp. pepper
	½ c. grated Cheddar cheese

Combine green beans and tomatoes in 1½-qt. casserole. Cook diced bacon until crisp; drain, reserving fat.

Return 2 tblsp. bacon fat to skillet. Add onion and cook until soft. Add to beans along with salt and pepper.

Top with grated cheese and bacon. Bake in moderate oven (350°) until tomatoes are cooked, 20 to 25 minutes. Makes 6 servings.

EVERYDAY GREEN BEANS

Simple, unusual way to season beans when you have
a big garden crop

4 c. cut green beans (1 lb.)
2 tblsp. salad or olive oil
1 tblsp. minced onion
1 clove garlic (whole)
1 tblsp. minced celery

1 tblsp. minced green pepper
1 c. diced peeled tomato (1 large)
½ tsp. salt
⅛ tsp. pepper

Cook beans in boiling salted water until barely tender. Drain.

Heat oil. Add onion, garlic, celery and green pepper; cook over medium heat until soft. Add tomato, salt and pepper, and cook until tomato is soft, 8 to 10 minutes, stirring occasionally; remove garlic. Add beans and heat. Makes 6 servings.

GREEN BEAN BAKE

You can use home-canned green beans and tomatoes in this oven dish

2 onions, thinly sliced
½ c. uncooked rice
1 (1 lb.) can tomatoes (2 c.)
1 (1 lb.) can cut green beans, drained (2 c.)

⅓ c. water or broth
1 tsp. salt
⅛ tsp. pepper
⅛ tsp. Tabasco sauce

Make layer of onions in buttered 2-qt. casserole. Cover with rice.

Combine remaining ingredients and heat to boiling; pour over rice.

Cover tightly. Bake in moderate oven (350°) 30 minutes, or until rice is tender. Makes 6 servings.

Bean-Duet Casserole

From a California ranch kitchen comes this easy and quick casserole recipe that makes weight-watchers happy. The vegetables bake in only 20 minutes. And if your family likes highly seasoned vegetables, you'll get their approval on this dish.

If you're not interested in low calorie dishes, top the food, just before putting it into the oven, with grated or shredded process cheese. If you omit the cheese, snip parsley over the top just before serving the casserole.

204

BEAN-DUET CASSEROLE

*High in flavor and low in calories. No fat
in this bean dish*

2 c. cooked green beans,
fresh, frozen or canned
2 c. cooked wax beans,
fresh, frozen or canned

1 (8 oz.) can tomato sauce
(1 c.)
1 (1⅜ oz.) pkg. onion soup
mix
¼ tsp. pepper

Combine all ingredients in 1½-qt. casserole. Bake in
moderate oven (350°) 20 minutes, or until bubbly. Makes
6 servings.

COMPANY GREEN BEANS

*You'll be proud to serve guests green beans fixed
this distinctive way*

2 (10 oz.) pkgs. frozen
French-style green beans
¼ c. butter
2 tblsp. flour
1¼ tsp. salt
¼ tsp. pepper
¼ tsp. Worcestershire sauce
2 c. dairy half-and-half or
milk

1 (1 lb.) can bean sprouts,
drained
1 (5 oz.) can water
chestnuts, drained and
sliced
½ c. grated Parmesan
cheese
½ c. slivered toasted
almonds

Cook green beans in boiling salted water until barely
tender. Drain.

Meanwhile, melt butter; blend in flour. Add seasonings
and half-and-half and cook, stirring constantly, until mixture comes to a boil and is thickened.

Place half of beans in greased 2-qt. casserole. Add half
of each: bean sprouts, water chestnuts, cheese and white
sauce. Repeat layers. Top with almonds.

Bake in moderate oven (350°) until bubbly, about 30
minutes. Makes 8 servings.

GREEN BEAN BUFFET CASSEROLE

*Rich, luscious, special-occasion dish to serve a crowd
at a buffet supper*

3 (10 oz.) pkgs. frozen
French-style green beans
3 (5 oz.) cans water
chestnuts, drained and
sliced
½ c. butter
1 medium onion, diced
1 (8 oz.) can mushroom
stems and pieces, drained

¼ c. flour
3 c. milk
2 c. shredded sharp Cheddar
cheese
1 tsp. salt
¼ tsp. pepper
⅛ tsp. Tabasco sauce
2 tsp. soy sauce
½ c. toasted sliced almonds

Cook green beans in boiling salted water, according to
package directions, until tender. Alternate beans in 3-qt.
baking dish with water chestnuts.

Melt butter in heavy skillet or saucepan. Add onion and
cook until golden; add mushrooms. Blend in flour. Add
milk and stir until thick.

Blend in cheese, salt, pepper, Tabasco and soy sauce.
Pour over beans in casserole; top with almonds. Bake in
slow oven (300°) 1 hour, or until slightly browned and
bubbly. Makes 12 servings.

FAST-FIX BEANS AND ONIONS

*Open two cans and you're well on the way to fixing
this busy day dish*

1 (1 lb.) can Blue Lake
green beans
1 (1 lb.) can small whole
onions
⅛ tsp. ground nutmeg
3 tblsp. butter or margarine

3 tblsp. flour
½ tsp. salt
1 c. milk
⅛ tsp. white pepper
1 tsp. white wine vinegar

Drain vegetables well and combine, adding nutmeg.

Meanwhile, melt butter in saucepan. Add flour and salt
and combine over heat; slowly add milk and cook to make
a medium-thick white sauce. Add pepper and vinegar.
Combine with beans and onions over heat, stirring as little
as possible so onions remain whole. Makes 8 servings.

CRUNCHY BEAN CASSEROLE

*The flavors that distinguish Chinese food do the same
for this bean dish*

2 (10 oz.) pkgs. frozen
   French-style green beans,
   thawed
1 tsp. salt
1 (5 oz.) can water
   chestnuts, drained and
   sliced

1 (1 lb. 3 oz.) can bean
   sprouts, drained
2 cans condensed cream of
   mushroom soup
1 (3½ oz.) can French fried
   onions, crumbled

Place 1 pkg. beans in a greased 2-qt. casserole; sprinkle
with ½ tsp. salt. Add water chestnuts and bean sprouts;
cover with 1 can of soup. Top with remaining beans, salt
and soup.

Bake in moderate oven (350°) 20 minutes; then sprinkle
with French fried onions and bake 10 minutes more.
Makes 12 servings.

NOTE: This casserole can be made ahead and refrigerated.
Then bake 20 minutes before adding the onions.

GERMAN GREEN BEANS

*Tastes like good old German potato salad—
serve with cold meats*

4 c. green beans, cut in 1″
   lengths (1 lb.)
4 strips bacon
1½ tblsp. flour
2 tblsp. sugar
2 tblsp. vinegar

2 tblsp. chopped onion
¼ tsp. dill seeds
1 tsp. salt
¼ tsp. pepper
2 c. cooked diced potatoes

Cook beans in boiling salted water until just tender;
drain, reserving liquid.

Cook bacon until crisp; drain reserving fat. Return 2
tblsp. fat to skillet. Blend in flour and sugar. Add vinegar
and 1 c. bean liquid (add water if necessary to make
1 c.). Cook, stirring constantly, until mixture is thickened
and comes to a boil. Add onion, dill seeds, salt and
pepper.

Combine green beans and potatoes in saucepan. Add

207

sauce and heat just until potatoes and beans are hot, stirring occasionally. Serve at once, or keep warm in oven until mealtime. Spoon into serving dish and top with bacon. Makes 8 servings.

FAR EAST BEANS

Wonderful way to dress up frozen green beans quickly—and deliciously

1 (10 oz.) pkg. frozen cut green beans
1 (1 lb.) can bean sprouts
2 tblsp. butter or margarine

¼ c. chopped blanched almonds (optional)
Salt and pepper to taste

Cook beans according to package directions. About 2 minutes before they are done, add bean sprouts (sprouts only need heating).

Drain, add butter and almonds; season and serve. Makes 6 to 8 servings.

SPANISH GREEN BEANS

Green pepper, onions and tomatoes glorify beans.
Do try this

1 qt. green beans
1 sweet bell pepper
2 c. chopped fresh tomatoes
2 small onions, chopped

1 tblsp. flour
2 tsp. salt
¼ c. butter

Wash and break beans; cook until tender in a little boiling salted water; drain.

Cook pepper, tomatoes and onions together until tender, 5 to 10 minutes. Add flour, salt and butter, blended, to tomato mixture. Mix with beans. Place in 1½-qt. casserole.

Bake in moderate oven (350°) 10 minutes. Makes 6 to 8 servings.

LIMAS AND CARROTS

Carrots and limas share honors in this imaginative vegetable dish

1 medium onion, sliced
1 tblsp. butter or margarine
1 (1 lb.) can green lima
  beans, drained

1 (8 oz.) can sliced carrots
¼ c. light cream or dairy
  half-and-half
¼ tsp. seasoned pepper

Cook onion in butter until tender; add lima beans and carrots; heat. Remove from heat, stir in cream and pepper. Makes 6 servings.

LIMA-CHEDDAR CASSEROLES

This is a good way to glamorize lima beans
for a luncheon party main dish

¼ c. minced onion
2 tblsp. butter or margarine
1 (1 lb. 12 oz.) can tomatoes
  (3½ c.)
2 (10 oz.) pkgs. frozen green
  lima beans, cooked and
  drained
¾ tsp. salt

Dash garlic salt
1½ tsp. chili powder
3 tblsp. flour
¼ c. cold water
2 c. shredded sharp or
  medium aged Cheddar
  cheese

Cook onion in butter. Stir in vegetables and seasonings. Simmer, uncovered, about 10 minutes.

Blend flour into water; stir into hot mixture. Cook and stir over low heat until mixture is thickened.

Divide half of mixture evenly among 6 greased shallow individual casseroles. Sprinkle 1 c. cheese evenly on top of bean mixture in casseroles. Add remaining bean mixture to casseroles.

Bake in moderate oven (350°) about 20 minutes. Sprinkle casseroles evenly with remaining 1 c. cheese. Bake 3 to 4 minutes longer, until cheese is melted. Makes 6 servings.

Companionable Cabbage and Peas

Do you give vegetables a fair chance in your kitchen? That's the question a Minnesota farmer's wife, who puts on food demonstrations for her local power company, asks the women in her audience. She emphasizes the importance of *planning* vegetables for meals—not just tacking them on at the last minute.

When one of our food editors enjoyed luncheon in this farm woman's home, she ate Cabbage and Peas for the first time. It wasn't long before we invited this busy homemaker to come to our Test Kitchens as a Guest Cook, to prepare a variety of her favorite vegetable dishes. You will find recipes for some of them in this cookbook, in addition to Cabbage and Peas, which follows. (See Index for Green Beans with Oranges; Corn Curry, Carrot Pickles and Cauliflower Pickles.)

This Guest Cook has a few rules for handling vegetables in the kitchen. Two of the most important ones are: Avoid cooking the life out of vegetables—cook them only until tender-crisp; and cook them in *little* water.

CABBAGE AND PEAS

People are surprised to find this simple combination so tasty

1½ c. fresh peas, or 1 (10 oz.) pkg. frozen peas	Salt and pepper to taste
1 small head cabbage, chopped	2 tblsp. butter

Cook peas in boiling salted water in saucepan until tender; drain. Cook cabbage in another saucepan in a small amount of water until tender-crisp; drain.

Combine vegetables; season with salt, pepper and butter. Makes 6 servings.

CABBAGE-TOMATO SKILLET

Taste-testers say this simple, homey country dish is rich in fine flavors

¼ c. butter	½ c. chopped onion
5 c. shredded cabbage	1 tsp. salt
2 c. chopped peeled tomatoes	1 tsp. sugar
	⅛ tsp. pepper

Melt butter in skillet. Stir in remaining ingredients. Cover, bring to a boil and cook 5 minutes, stirring once.

210

Uncover and simmer a few minutes to reduce liquid.
Makes 6 servings.

Surprise Sweets: *Scrub sweet potatoes and bake in a
moderately hot oven (375° to 400°) until tender, about
45 minutes. Cut a cross in top of each potato and press
down on the four corners. Insert a pat of butter and
1 tblsp. orange marmalade in each potato.*

BUTTERED CARROTS AND CELERY HEARTS

You can get this ready in a jiffy

1 (1 lb.) can tiny whole carrots	½ tsp. seasoned salt
1 (1 lb.) can celery hearts, drained	⅛ tsp. pepper
	½ tsp. marjoram leaves
3 tblsp. butter or margarine	Minced parsley

Drain carrots reserving 2 tblsp. liquid. Heat carrots and
celery hearts in skillet with 2 tblsp. liquid, butter and
seasonings. Serve sprinkled with parsley. Makes 6 to 8
servings.

Minted Carrots and Peas

A Utah home economist, a mother of four children,
contributes this favorite recipe of her family. In her part
of the country, where mint grows generously along the
banks of irrigation ditches, the fragrant leaves play a leading role in seasoning many dishes. Minted Carrots and
Peas are one fine example. They can't be surpassed as a
companion to roasted or broiled lamb.

MINTED CARROTS AND PEAS

Simple, but elegant and easy to fix

8 small carrots	½ tsp. salt
3 c. fresh or frozen peas	3 tblsp. chopped fresh mint
¼ c. butter	leaves

211

Cook whole carrots in small amount of boiling salted water, covered, 15 minutes, or until tender. Cook peas in boiling salted water until tender. Drain vegetables; reserve liquids for soup or sauce.

Brown butter slightly; add vegetables, salt and mint. Toss lightly. Makes 6 to 8 servings.

CELERY STUFFING

This recipe makes enough stuffing to fill a 12-lb. ready-to-cook turkey

1 c. chopped onion	½ tsp. pepper
2 c. finely chopped celery	1½ tsp. rubbed sage
⅔ c. melted butter or margarine	½ tsp. poultry seasoning
	1⅓ c. milk
7 c. dry bread crumbs	1¼ c. turkey broth
2 tsp. salt	2 eggs, slightly beaten

Simmer onion and celery in butter until soft, but do not brown.

Combine with bread crumbs and seasonings.

Add milk, broth and eggs; toss lightly to blend.

Stuff loosely into cavities of bird. Makes 6½ cups stuffing.

NOTE: Cook turkey giblets and neck in water to make broth.

Corn and Tomatoes

This is one favorite twosome that unites in marvelous dishes, such as Corn-Tomato Skillet and Scalloped Corn and Tomatoes. Both red and yellow combinations look as good as they taste. Their cheerful color certainly contributes to their popularity.

CORN-TOMATO SKILLET

Get out your skillet and treat the family to this so-good farm special

1 green pepper, chopped
½ c. chopped onion
2 tblsp. butter
1 tsp. salt
1 tsp. sugar
⅛ tsp. pepper
4 tomatoes, peeled and
sliced
2 c. corn, cut from cob

Cook green pepper and onion in butter until soft. Add remaining ingredients and cook until tomatoes and corn are tender, about 10 to 15 minutes. Makes 6 servings.

SCALLOPED CORN AND TOMATOES

An extra-delicious way to glamorize ordinary canned vegetables

3 slices bacon, chopped
2 c. chopped onion
¼ c. chopped green pepper
1 (1 lb. 12 oz.) can tomatoes
(3½ c.)
1 (8 oz.) can cream-style
corn (1 c.)
1 c. packaged stuffing mix
2 tsp. sugar
½ tsp. salt
⅛ tsp. pepper
⅛ tsp. thyme leaves

Cook bacon until crisp. Remove bacon. Add onion and green pepper to skillet and cook until soft.

Combine all ingredients. Place in 2-qt. casserole. Bake in moderate oven (350°) 45 minutes. Or omit baking and simmer 10 minutes in skillet to blend flavors. Serve in individual sauce dishes. Makes 8 servings.

New Corn Combinations

Did you ever combine corn and celery and add a dash of brilliant red pimiento and other seasonings? Or have you teamed corn with cabbage? If you haven't, you'll welcome the next two recipes; they're tops in vegetable eating.

CORN 'N' CELERY SAUTÉ

Tastes like fresh buttered corn on the cob. Try it soon

¼ c. butter	1 (10 oz.) pkg. frozen whole
2 c. diagonally sliced celery	kernel corn
(very thin)	2 tblsp. sliced pimiento
	½ tsp. salt

Melt butter in saucepan. Add celery; cover and cook 5 minutes. Add remaining ingredients and cook until corn is tender, about 10 minutes. Stir to combine. Makes 5 servings.

DUTCH CORN AND CABBAGE

Quick cooking saves delicate flavor

5 slices bacon	2 c. shredded cabbage
½ c. water	½ tsp. salt
2½ c. corn, cut from the	⅛ tsp. pepper
cob	1 tsp. sugar

Fry bacon until crisp in skillet. Remove bacon; drain, crumble. Reserve 2 tblsp. drippings in skillet.

Add water, corn and cabbage to bacon drippings. Cook, covered, until cabbage is tender, about 5 minutes. Add salt, pepper, sugar and bacon. Mix lightly and serve. Makes 6 servings.

Kohlrabi Takes the Spotlight

Kohlrabi is one of today's neglected vegetables. Gardeners who grow it and gather the bulbs when tender and young frequently rave about its delicate or mild turnip flavor. Combined with color-bright carrots (see Kohlrabi and Carrots in Cream Sauce), it pleases most people. This is especially good served with venison. Kohlrabi-Potato Custard is another country-kitchen special. With seasonings of bacon, a touch of cayenne pepper and Worcestershire sauce, the dish contributes zip to otherwise commonplace meals.

KOHLRABI AND CARROTS IN CREAM SAUCE

A Colorado farmer says this is the perfect vegetable dish to serve with roast venison or fried ham

2 c. cubed peeled kohlrabi
bulbs (2 medium)
2 c. cubed carrots
1½ tsp. chicken-seasoned
stock base, or 1 chicken
bouillon cube
3 tblsp. butter or margarine
3 tblsp. flour

½ c. light cream or
evaporated milk
2 egg yolks, beaten
1 tblsp. lemon juice
½ tsp. salt
⅛ tsp. pepper
⅛ tsp. ground red pepper
(cayenne)
⅛ tsp. ground ginger

Cook kohlrabi and carrots separately in boiling salted water; drain, reserving 1 c. liquid from carrots and ½ c. from kohlrabi. Combine liquids, add chicken stock base and dissolve.

In a saucepan, melt butter; add flour and vegetable liquid; cook until thickened.

Combine cream and egg yolks; pour a little of the hot sauce into egg yolk mixture, thoroughly mixing; then add to the sauce quickly, stirring well. Cook over low heat (do not boil) until thickened, stirring constantly. Add lemon juice, salt, pepper, red pepper and ginger; stir to mix.

Pour sauce over hot vegetables and serve at once. Makes 8 servings.

KOHLRABI-POTATO CUSTARD

Just right to serve with ham or pork

2 c. cubed peeled kohlrabi
bulbs (2 medium)
3 medium potatoes
¼ tsp. paprika
6 drops Worcestershire
sauce

3 to 4 slices bacon
3 eggs, separated
⅓ c. milk
⅛ tsp. ground red pepper
(cayenne)

Cook kohlrabi in boiling salted water until tender, about 20 minutes.

Peel and halve potatoes; cook in boiling salted water until tender. Drain vegetables; combine and mash, or put through ricer. Add paprika and Worcestershire sauce.

Broil or fry bacon until crisp; crumble into the vegetable along with ¼ c. drippings.

Beat egg yolks; add milk and red pepper; thoroughly

215

mix with vegetables, whipping as for mashed potatoes. Let cool slightly.

Beat egg whites stiff and fold into vegetables. Heap lightly into greased 2-qt. baking dish, set in pan of hot water, and bake in slow oven (325°) 40 to 50 minutes, or until risen and delicately browned. Makes 8 servings.

Spicy Okra and Tomatoes

Okra came to America from Africa. It won popularity first in the South, especially when teamed with juicy tomatoes. Its succulence depends primarily on the age and size of the pods; the small, young ones which you find in cans are the most desirable.

Spicy Okra and Tomatoes is a lively version that many people consider tops. If you want to make it a company special, sprinkle with crumbled crisp bacon at serving time.

SPICY OKRA AND TOMATOES

The spot of hot sauce and bit of spice enliven
this Southern dish

1 (1 lb.) can okra and tomatoes	½ tsp. barbecue spice
	⅛ tsp. hot pepper sauce
½ tsp. onion salt	2 tblsp. butter or margarine

Combine okra and tomatoes with remaining ingredients, mixing gently. Heat. Serve in sauce dishes. Makes 4 servings.

OKRA AND TOMATOES

Chose firm tomatoes and tender okra about 2" long
to make this treat

3 c. okra, cut in rounds	¾ c. onion slices
¼ c. butter or margarine	2 tsp. salt
3 c. tomatoes, peeled and cut in wedges or chopped	¼ tsp. pepper

Cook okra in butter until tender.

Add remaining ingredients and simmer gently, covered, 5 minutes (do not overcook). Makes 6 servings.

NOTE: Green tomatoes can be used instead of ripe ones.

OKRA WITH CORN

Tomato and onion flavors blend with okra and corn in this colorful dish

1⅓ c. diced green pepper
   (2 medium)
½ c. chopped onion
¼ c. butter
1½ c. corn, cut from cob
1½ c. sliced okra

1 c. diced peeled tomato
   (1 large)
½ c. boiling water
½ tsp. salt
⅛ tsp. pepper

Cook green pepper and onion in butter in skillet 3 minutes to soften. Add remaining ingredients. Cover and simmer until vegetables are tender, about 10 minutes. Stir occasionally. Makes 6 servings.

ONION-MUSHROOM CASSEROLE

You can use fresh onions, or canned (more expensive, but fewer tears)

2 (1 lb.) cans whole small
   onions
¼ c. butter
1 c. canned mushrooms,
   stems and pieces, or 1½ c.
   sliced fresh mushrooms
½ tsp. salt

1 (3 oz.) pkg. cream cheese
3 tblsp. flour
1½ c. milk
¼ c. shredded Cheddar
   cheese
¼ c. cracker crumbs

Drain onions; combine with butter, mushrooms and salt; simmer 5 minutes. Add cream cheese. When melted, add flour, then milk and reheat.

Turn into 1½- or 2-qt. casserole. Sprinkle with mixture of shredded cheese and crumbs. Bake in hot oven (400°) 25 to 30 minutes. Makes 5 servings.

NOTE: You can use 4 c. sliced and quartered onions instead of canned onions, but you have to cook them in 1 c. water 10 minutes and drain them before combining with other ingredients. And you weep more!

PEAS SCALLOPED WITH POTATOES

Here's how to cook and serve potatoes
and a second vegetable

3 tblsp. butter or margarine
1½ tblsp. flour
½ tsp. salt
¼ tsp. pepper
1½ c. dairy half-and-half
2 (15 oz. cans) potatoes, drained

1 (16 to 17 oz.) can peas, drained
1 medium onion, sliced and separated in rings
Pimiento strips (optional)

Melt butter; blend in flour and seasonings. Add half-and-half; cook over low heat, stirring, until thickened.

Place potatoes, peas and onion rings in alternate layers in greased 1½-qt. casserole. Pour sauce over.

Bake in moderate oven (350°) 30 minutes, or until bubbly. Garnish with pimiento strips, if desired. Makes 6 servings.

PEAS AND CELERY

Celery adds crispness to this well-seasoned vegetable dish

2 beef bouillon cubes
¼ c. water
4 branches celery, sliced diagonally

⅛ tsp. thyme leaves
⅛ tsp. salt
2 (10 oz.) pkgs. frozen peas

Dissolve bouillon cubes in water in skillet. Add celery, thyme and salt. Cook until just tender, but still crisp. Add peas and cook until just tender, about 5 minutes. Makes 6 servings.

FRIED POTATOES AND OKRA

Cut okra thin for this plantation special and cook
until just tender

2 tblsp. butter or margarine	½ tsp. salt
4 c. cubed cold boiled potatoes	Freshly ground pepper to taste
2 c. thinly sliced raw okra	

Melt butter in skillet; add potatoes, okra, salt and pepper. Cover and fry over medium heat (if necessary, use a lower heat to prevent scorching). After 10 minutes test for doneness of okra; turn with a spoon. Add a little water (about 1 tblsp.) and continue cooking until okra is tender. Makes 4 to 6 servings.

NOTE: You can use 1 (10 oz.) pkg. frozen okra for the fresh vegetable. Thaw and cut okra in thin slices, and use 3 c. cubed potatoes instead of 4 c.

IRISH POTATO PUFF

Common potatoes go high-hat in this

2 tblsp. soft butter	1 tsp. salt
2 tblsp. yellow corn meal	¼ tsp. white pepper
4 c. diced peeled potatoes	2 c. cooked buttered carrot sticks
6 eggs, separated	
1 c. butter (2 sticks)	

Coat an 8-cup ring mold well with 2 tblsp. butter; sprinkle with corn meal, then tap out excess.

Cook potatoes in lightly salted boiling water 10 minutes, or until tender. Drain well, then shake pan over low heat to dry; mash (you should have about 3 c.).

Beat egg whites until firm.

In another smaller bowl beat egg yolks until thick. Cream 1 c. butter in large bowl and beat in egg yolks, then potatoes, salt and pepper. Fold in egg whites. Spoon into mold; cover tightly with foil. Set mold on rack or trivet in kettle or steamer; pour in boiling water to half the depth of mold; cover tightly. Steam 45 minutes.

Cool puff in mold 5 minutes. Remove foil. Loosen around edge of tube with a knife; turn out onto serving plate. Fill center with hot buttered carrot sticks. Makes 8 servings.

New Ways with Potato Chips

When you're yearning for a new way to fix potatoes, try scalloping potato chips. Or make beautifully browned potato patties with them. Both are jiffy dishes and both are surprisingly good. The recipes for Potato Special and Quick Potato Patties are the invention of a home economist who shares them with you.

POTATO SPECIAL

Ever scallop potato chips? Try these.
Potatoes are a lovely brown

4 c. potato chips
3 tblsp. flour
¾ tsp. salt
⅛ tsp. pepper
½ c. canned mushrooms, stems and pieces

2 tblsp. chopped parsley or pimiento
2½ c. scalded milk
½ c. shredded Cheddar cheese

Place potato chips in 1½- or 2-qt. casserole. Add flour, salt, pepper, mushrooms and parsley; toss lightly. Pour hot milk over chips; sprinkle with cheese.

Bake in moderate oven (375°) 25 to 30 minutes, or until thickened. Makes 6 servings.

QUICK POTATO PATTIES

Make these patties with potato chips, eggs and seasonings
for a quick meal—a little like Chinese egg foo yung

3 eggs
½ c. milk
½ tsp. salt
⅛ tsp. pepper

¼ c. drained canned mushrooms, stems and pieces (optional)
1 tblsp. minced parsley
3 c. crushed potato chips
1 tblsp. chopped onion

Beat together eggs, milk, salt and pepper. Stir in remaining ingredients.

Place large tablespoonfuls in greased skillet. Fry over

medium heat until golden brown; turn and brown other side. Makes 6 patties.

SPRINGTIME SPINACH

Team mates three—spinach, beets and eggs—
beautiful color and taste

1 lb. fresh spinach, washed	½ tsp. salt
1 tsp. salt	⅛ tsp. pepper
¼ c. bacon fat	2 hard-cooked eggs,
1 c. diced cooked beets	chopped
2 tblsp. vinegar	

Sprinkle spinach with 1 tsp. salt and cook (in water that clings to leaves) in heavy saucepan, covered, 10 minutes. Drain and chop coarsely.

Heat bacon fat in skillet; add beets and heat thoroughly. Add vinegar, ½ tsp. salt, pepper, spinach and eggs. Heat. Makes 5 servings.

RUTABAGA-POTATO CASSEROLE

Complete the main course with pork chops or sausage
and buttered beans

2 medium potatoes	⅛ tsp. pepper
2 medium rutabagas	4 eggs, well beaten
½ c. flour	¼ c. milk
1 tsp. baking powder	¼ c. melted butter or
1 tsp. salt	drippings

Peel potatoes and rutabagas; cover with cold water and let stand.

Sift together flour, baking powder and seasonings.

Blend half of dry ingredients with eggs. Stir in milk and butter; mix.

Drain vegetables; grate fine or use blender.

With wooden spoon, quickly mix remaining dry ingredients with vegetables. Work quickly to avoid dark potatoes!

Place in greased 1-qt. casserole. Set in pan of hot water with level at least ⅔ up side of casserole.

Bake in slow oven (325°) 1 hour. Makes 6 servings.

Zucchini-Corn Bake

Many mothers confess that it takes considerable planning to teach children to enjoy eating plentiful zucchini. A Colorado woman says her most successful way is to team the squash with corn. Early in the season, when there's zucchini in the garden but sweet corn is not ready, she depends on canned corn.

ZUCCHINI-CORN BAKE

Hitch squash with corn for popular vegetable dishes—here's a good one

1 lb. zucchini, sliced	3 eggs, beaten
½ c. chopped onion	¾ tsp. salt
⅓ c. chopped green pepper	¼ tsp. pepper
2 tblsp. butter	⅓ c. grated sharp Cheddar
1 (1 lb.) can cream-style corn	cheese

Cook zucchini in boiling salted water until tender; drain thoroughly.

Meanwhile, cook onion and green pepper in melted butter until soft.

Combine zucchini, onion and green pepper, corn, eggs, salt and pepper. Spoon into greased 1½-qt. casserole. Sprinkle with cheese. Bake in moderate oven (350°) 50 minutes, or until set. Makes 6 servings.

DILLED ZUCCHINI-CORN COMBO

Dill and green pepper do something wonderful to the zucchini-corn team

1 lb. unpeeled zucchini, sliced	1 tsp. salt
	2 tblsp. water
1½ c. whole kernel corn, fresh, frozen or canned	2 tblsp. butter or margarine
	1 tblsp. snipped fresh dill, or
½ c. chopped onion	1 tsp. dried dill weed
½ c. chopped green pepper	

In large skillet, combine zucchini, corn, onion and green pepper. Sprinkle with salt. Add water; cover and simmer, stirring occasionally, 8 to 10 minutes, just until vegetables are tender.

Drain off any liquid. Add butter and dill; toss lightly to coat vegetables. Makes 4 to 6 servings.

SQUASH MEDLEY

A highly praised FARM JOURNAL *vegetable casserole—it's tasty*

4 fresh medium unpeeled summer squash, or 4 c. frozen summer squash
½ green pepper, chopped
2 ripe tomatoes, peeled and chopped
6 slices bacon, fried and chopped

1½ c. shredded process cheese
⅓ c. chopped onion
½ tsp. salt
½ c. fine bread crumbs
2 tblsp. butter

Parboil squash (zucchini for 3 minutes; yellow crooknecks or small white pattypans, 5 minutes; and white scallops, 15 to 20 minutes). If you use frozen squash, do not parboil.

To make filling, combine remaining ingredients except crumbs and butter. Mix well.

Slice parboiled squash thinly. Place in baking dish, alternating squash and filling. Top with bread crumbs and dabs of butter.

Bake in moderate oven (375°) 35 minutes. Makes 6 to 8 servings.

To peel and seed tomatoes, drop them in boiling water for only 10 seconds. Cut out stem; peel off skin. Cut tomatoes crosswise and squeeze gently to remove seeds.

ACORN SQUASH WITH CREAMED ONIONS

Creamed onions de luxe fill baked squash cups for an extra-good dish

3 acorn squash	2 tblsp. butter or margarine
Salt	2 tblsp. flour
2 lbs. small onions, peeled	¼ tsp. salt
(about 4 c.)	1½ c. milk
½ c. light raisins	¼ tsp. ground nutmeg

Wash squash; cut in halves lengthwise, and remove seeds. Place squash, cut side down, in shallow baking pan; add a few tablespoons water to pan. Bake in hot oven (400°) 30 minutes. Turn cut side up; sprinkle with salt and continue baking 25 to 30 minutes, until tender.

Cook onions in boiling salted water, covered, about 30 minutes, or until tender. Drain.

Simmer raisins in water to cover 10 minutes; drain.

Melt butter; blend in flour and ¼ tsp. salt. Add milk all at once. Cook and stir until sauce is thickened. Blend in ¼ tsp. nutmeg. Gently stir in onions and raisins. Spoon into cooked squash halves; sprinkle with additional nutmeg. Makes 6 servings.

SUCCOTASH WITH MUSTARD SAUCE

Two great companions, corn and limas,
with a mustard-flavored sauce

1 (1 lb.) can green lima	¼ c. sugar
beans	2 tblsp. prepared mustard
1 (1 lb.) can whole kernel	¼ c. ketchup
corn	2 tblsp. butter or margarine
2 egg yolks, slightly beaten	1 tblsp. vinegar

Heat drained beans and corn with 2 tblsp. liquid drained from beans.

To make sauce, combine remaining ingredients in saucepan; cook over medium heat, stirring, about 2 to 3 minutes. Serve over hot vegetables. Makes 4 servings.

MEXICAN SUCCOTASH

They call it Colache south of the border—it's good
by any name

1 medium onion, chopped
2 tblsp. butter or margarine
1 tsp. sugar
1 (1 lb.) can Italian-style
  zucchini

1 (12 or 16 oz.) can whole
  kernel corn
Salt and pepper to taste

Cook onion in butter until tender. Add sugar, zucchini and drained corn; mix gently and heat. Season with salt and pepper. Makes 6 to 8 servings.

Ready-to-go Canned Tomato Treats

If a country woman earned a dollar for every can or jar of tomatoes she opens, her bank account would grow fast. Tomatoes, like potatoes, are a staple in most kitchens. Many homemakers confess they wouldn't know how to cook without them.

Scattered throughout this chapter and on other pages in this cookbook, are recipes in which canned tomatoes star. You'll want to try them all. Be sure to make Tomato-Mushroom Soufflé for a new treat . . . an especially good beef or lamb go-with.

TOMATO-MUSHROOM SOUFFLÉ

Airy, delicate, delicious, colorful—apt descriptions of this dish

½ c. mushrooms, stems and
  pieces, or 1 c. sliced
  fresh mushrooms
1 tblsp. chopped onion
¼ c. butter
¼ c. flour

2 c. canned tomatoes
½ tsp. salt
1 tsp. sugar
⅛ tsp. pepper
3 eggs, separated
¼ tsp. cream of tartar

Cook mushrooms and onion in butter in saucepan. Stir in flour. Break up any large pieces of tomatoes; add to saucepan along with salt, sugar and pepper. Cook until very thick.

Beat egg yolks slightly with fork. Add ½ c. hot mixture to yolks; mix well. Return to mixture in saucepan; cook 1 minute.

225

Beat egg whites and cream of tartar until stiff; fold into tomato mixture. Turn into 1½-qt. casserole or soufflé dish. Set in pan of hot water.

Bake in hot oven (400°) 30 to 35 minutes, or until set. Makes 6 servings.

NOTE: You can serve a cheese sauce with this soufflé, but it's good without, too. (See Index for sauce recipes.)

SOUTHERN TOMATOES AND OKRA

Speedy, easy and tasty—cloves give tantalizing fragrance and flavor to this long-popular vegetable duo

1 large onion, sliced	1 tblsp. sugar
2 tblsp. butter	4 drops Tabasco sauce
1 (1 lb. 12 oz.) can tomatoes (3½ c.)	¼ tsp. ground cloves
	6 to 8 whole cloves
1 (1 lb.) can sliced okra (2 c.)	Salt and pepper to taste

Cook onion in butter until yellow and limp. Add remaining ingredients and simmer gently 15 minutes. Serve in individual vegetable dishes or soup plates. Makes 6 to 8 servings.

TOMATO, OKRA AND RICE BAKE

Perfect meat or poultry accompaniment to serve for a change

3 slices bacon, diced	1½ tsp. salt
½ c. chopped onion	¼ tsp. pepper
1 c. sliced okra	Few drops Tabasco sauce
1 c. rice	½ c. water
2 (1 lb.) cans tomatoes (1 qt.)	Chopped parsley (optional)

Cook bacon until crisp; remove from skillet. Cook onion and okra in bacon fat until onion is soft.

Add rice, canned tomatoes, salt, pepper, Tabasco sauce and water. Bring to a boil. Pour into greased 2-qt. casserole.

Bake in moderate oven (350°) about 1 hour, or until rice is tender. Serve sprinkled with chopped parsley, if desired. Makes 8 servings.

TOMATO-GREEN BEAN CASSEROLE

Put tomatoes and green beans in a casserole, season well and bake—you'll be proud of the results

1 c. herb-seasoned bread
  stuffing
¼ c. butter or margarine
1 (14½ oz.) can sliced
  tomatoes, drained

1 (1 lb.) can cut green
  beans, drained
½ tsp. sugar
½ tsp. seasoned salt
⅛ tsp. basil leaves or
  orégano leaves

Mix stuffing with melted butter; set aside ½ c. for topping.

Combine remaining stuffing, tomatoes, green beans, sugar and seasonings. Mix and put in shallow 10 × 6″ baking dish. Sprinkle with reserved stuffing.

Cover with foil and bake in moderate oven (350°) 25 minutes; remove foil and bake about 10 minutes more. Makes 4 to 5 servings.

TOMATO AND CELERY CASSEROLE

Celery remains crisp and provides contrast to juicy tomatoes

¼ c. butter or margarine
3 slices day-old bread, cut
  in cubes
½ c. sliced celery

1 (28 oz.) can solid pack
  tomatoes
½ tsp. salt
⅛ tsp. pepper
1 medium onion

Brown butter lightly; add bread and cook until browned. Combine with celery and tomatoes. Season with salt and pepper and put in 1½-qt. casserole.

Slice onion and separate into rings. Arrange on top of tomatoes. Bake in moderate oven (375°) about 45 minutes. Serve in individual sauce dishes. Makes 4 servings.

NOTE: The onion rings retain some crispness. If you prefer, sprinkle top just before serving with chopped parsley. Double the recipe to make 8 servings, and bake in a 2-qt. casserole.

Juicy Ripe Tomatoes

Many country gardeners become impatient for ripe tomatoes almost as soon as the small yellow blossoms appear on the dark green vines. The weeks of waiting seem long. That's a tribute to their esteem for the vegetable.

After the family enjoys red tomatoes sliced and in salads for a time, they'll praise Broiled Tomatoes and Mushrooms and Tomatoes with Bread Stuffing. If you're looking for a treat for guests, these two tomato specials give you a delicious choice.

BROILED TOMATOES AND MUSHROOMS

Glamorize hamburger sandwiches for guests
with this extra-good go-with

4 large, firm, ripe tomatoes
3 tblsp. minced onion
Salt and pepper to taste
½ c. soft bread crumbs

¼ c. butter or margarine (about)
8 large mushrooms

Start broiler heating 10 minutes before ready to cook tomatoes and mushrooms. Or preheat broiler as range manufacturer directs.

Cut stem ends from washed tomatoes, then cut in halves. Arrange in large shallow pan. Sprinkle on onion; season with salt and pepper, and top with crumbs. Dot with 2 tblsp. butter.

Remove stems from cleaned mushrooms and reserve for later use. Arrange mushroom caps, rounded side down, around tomatoes in pan. Sprinkle with salt and pepper; dot with butter, allowing about 1 tsp. butter to each mushroom cap.

Broil 4" from heat 12 to 15 minutes, or until nicely browned. Serve mushrooms on top of tomato halves. Makes 8 servings.

*For a flavor change, dissolve a bouillon cube in the hot
milk you use to make mashed potatoes.*

TOMATOES WITH BREAD STUFFING

*Red tomatoes hold expertly seasoned stuffing—
pretty and delectable*

8 tomatoes	½ tsp. basil leaves
1 c. chopped onion	¼ tsp. instant minced garlic
½ c. chopped celery with leaves	1 tsp. salt
¼ c. butter	⅛ tsp. pepper
1 tblsp. parsley flakes	5 c. bread cubes

Cut slice off top of each tomato. Scoop out center and
save. Turn tomatoes upside down to drain.

Cook onion and celery in butter until soft. Chop tomato centers and add to onion mixture along with parsley,
basil, garlic, salt and pepper. Cook until mixture thickens,
about 15 minutes. Stir occasionally.

Add bread cubes. Place tomato shells in muffin-pan
cups. Fill with bread stuffing. Bake in moderate oven
(350°) 30 minutes. Makes 8 servings.

Delicious Vegetable Mix-ups

Many dishes made by recipes in the remainder of this
chapter owe their superior flavors to cooking several vegetables together. We borrow two splendid examples from
French and Italian kitchens, making our own adaptations.
Ratatouille (pronounced ra-ta-tōoy′) is one of the famous
French eggplant specialties, but it contains five other vegetables as well as parsley and basil leaves. The harmonious
blending of flavors explains its marvelous taste.

One of the talented recipe testers in the FARM JOURNAL
Test Kitchens, who is of Italian descent, said that when
she made Mixed Vegetables Italienne, everyone who sniffed
the come-hither aroma of the simmering vegetables hurried
in to find out what was cooking. "It wasn't a surprise to
me," she said, "because when I fix this dish at home, my
husband always wanders into the kitchen and wants to
know how long until dinner."

Do try many of the recipes using mixed vegetables that follow. Several of our recipe testers consider them among the top best in this book.

RATATOUILLE

Taste this late summer dish and you will know why
it's famous in Nice and other places in Southern France

2 medium onions, sliced
2 cloves garlic, chopped
¼ c. olive oil
2 small zucchini, cut in
   ½″ slices
3 tomatoes, peeled and
   diced

1 small eggplant, peeled and
   cut in 1″ cubes
1 large green pepper, cut in
   strips
2 tblsp. chopped parsley
2 tsp. salt
½ tsp. basil leaves
⅛ tsp. pepper

Cook onions and garlic in hot olive oil in bottom of Dutch oven. Add remaining ingredients. Cover and cook 15 minutes. Uncover and continue cooking until vegetables are tender and juice is thickened. Stir occasionally. Makes 8 servings.

MIXED VEGETABLES ITALIENNE

"What's cooking that smells so good?" they'll ask
when you fix this

¼ c. salad oil
1 (1 lb.) can stewed
   tomatoes
1 beef bouillon cube
4 c. zucchini, cut in 1″
   cubes
1½ c. green pepper, cut in
   1″ pieces
1 c. frozen peas

1 c. frozen whole kernel
   corn
1 c. sliced carrots
1 c. diced potatoes
1 c. coarsely chopped onion
1 tsp. orégano leaves
1½ tsp. salt
⅛ tsp. pepper

Put all ingredients in a 10″ skillet. (Zucchini, if young, need not be peeled; just scrub them.) Cover and simmer 25 to 30 minutes, or until vegetables are tender-crisp. Makes 6 servings.

NOTE: If there is too much liquid in skillet, dissolve ½ tsp. cornstarch in 1 tsp. water and stir into vegetables to thicken juices.

VARIATIONS

Vegetables Italienne with Poached Eggs: For a luncheon or supper main dish, break eggs into vegetable stew when almost done; cover and simmer until eggs are set to desired stage of doneness. With a broad spatula, lift eggs and vegetables to serving plates. Sprinkle with grated cheese and serve with crusty bread.

Vegetables Italienne in Pressure Pan: Put all ingredients in pressure cooker (no extra water is needed). Close cover securely. Place over high heat. Bring to 15 lb. pressure, according to manufacturer's directions for your pressure cooker. When pressure is reached (control will begin to jiggle or rock), reduce heat immediately and continue to cook at 15 lbs. pressure for just 2 minutes. Remove from heat. Reduce pressure instantly by placing cooker under running faucet or in pan of cold water. If you wish, thicken juices in pressure-cooked vegetables with a paste of 1 to 2 tsp. cornstarch and 1 tblsp. water.

VEGETABLE JUMBLE

Tastes like summer—that means good

1 large green pepper, sliced
  lengthwise
3 tblsp. butter or margarine
6 medium tomatoes, peeled
  and cut in wedges

2 c. corn cut from cob, or
  canned whole kernel corn
1 tsp. salt
1 tblsp. sugar
⅛ tsp. coarse grind pepper

Cook green pepper in butter about 5 minutes; do not brown. Add tomatoes, corn and seasonings and simmer 10 minutes. Makes 6 servings.

MIXED VEGETABLES IN CHEESE SAUCE

Keep waffles in freezer to reheat in toaster for use under these sauced, color-bright vegetables

1 c. sliced celery
2 tblsp. minced green
  pepper
⅔ c. water
2 (10 oz.) pkgs. frozen
  carrots and peas
3 tblsp. butter or margarine

3 tblsp. flour
½ tsp. salt
½ tsp. Worcestershire sauce
1½ c. milk
1 c. cubed Cheddar cheese
  (1 lb.)

In bottom of double boiler of saucepan, cook celery and green pepper in ⅔ c. salted water 5 minutes. Add frozen carrots and peas and cook the time designated on package.

Melt butter in top of double boiler or saucepan; blend in flour and salt. Add Worcestershire sauce and milk. Cook and stir until mixture thickens. Add cheese and stir until cheese melts to make a thick sauce. Drain vegetables and add to the sauce.

To serve, spoon vegetables on toasted English muffins or crisp waffles. Makes 6 to 8 servings.

VARIATION

Vegetable Pies: Line individual casseroles or ramekins with mashed potatoes (you can use instant mashed potatoes). Fill centers with Mixed Vegetables in Cheese Sauce. Top with corn flake crumbs and run under the broiler (place on second shelf below heat) to reheat pies.

VEGETABLES ROMA

*No one should miss this vegetable recipe imported
from Rome*

1 eggplant (1 to 1½ lbs.)
½ c. salad oil
2 tsp. seasoned salt
1 clove garlic, crushed
¼ c. canned tomato paste
1 (1 lb.) can tomatoes

1 (1 lb.) can cut wax beans
2 slices bread
½ c. grated Parmesan
  cheese
½ lb. mozzarella cheese,
  sliced

Peel eggplant; cut in 1" cubes. Cook in oil until browned, stirring occasionally. Add seasoned salt, garlic, tomato paste, tomatoes and drained wax beans. Cook slowly 15 minutes.

Put half of mixture in baking dish. Sprinkle with bread, torn into crumbs, and Parmesan cheese. Cover with remaining vegetable mixture. Top with mozzarella cheese. Bake in moderate oven (350°) about 30 minutes, until hot and cheese melts and browns. Makes 8 servings.

VEGETABLE COMBO

Bacon highlights vegetable flavors

3 slices bacon, cut in ½"
  bits
1 large white sweet onion,
  sliced lengthwise
2 branches celery, cut in
  ½" bias slices
1 large green pepper, sliced
  lengthwise

1 large firm tomato, cut in
  wedges
3 medium zucchini, cut in
  ½" slices
1 tsp. seasoned salt
⅛ tsp. coarse grind pepper
1 tsp. sugar
¼ tsp. garlic powder

Place bacon in electric or other skillet; cook until crisp. Remove bacon with slotted spoon. Add vegetables to drippings and sprinkle with seasonings and bacon bits; stir well and cover. Cook at medium-low heat 15 minutes, or until barely tender. Avoid stirring any more than necessary to keep vegetables from sticking. Uncover and keep hot until serving time. Makes 6 servings.

VEGETABLE MEDLEY

Three vegetables in one generous dish—
perfect with fried chicken

2 (10 oz.) pkgs. frozen peas
3 medium carrots, sliced
3 c. sliced celery

Salt and pepper to taste
Butter or margarine

Cook peas as directed on package.

Simmer carrots and celery in just enough water to cover, until tender. Don't overcook; celery should be a bit crisp.

Combine vegetables. Season with salt and pepper. Serve with melted butter. Makes 10 to 12 servings.

VEGETABLE HOT DISH

Cucumbers give the unusual flavor

3 slices bacon
3 small cucumbers, peeled and sliced
1 medium onion, diced
¾ c. chopped green pepper

¾ tsp. crushed dried orégano
4 tomatoes, cut into large wedges
1½ tsp. salt
⅛ tsp. pepper

Fry bacon in skillet until crisp. Remove bacon; drain, crumble. Reserve 2 tblsp. drippings in skillet.

Add cucumbers, onion, green pepper and orégano to bacon drippings. Cook until vegetables are just tender. Add tomatoes, salt and pepper; heat through. Garnish with crumbled bacon and serve. Makes 6 servings.

TRIPLE VEGETABLE CASSEROLE

*The taste of Italy makes 3 canned vegetables,
onion-seasoned, so good*

3 slices bacon, chopped
1 onion, chopped
2 tblsp. flour
1 (1 lb.) can tomatoes (2 c.)
1 tsp. Italian herb blend
1 tsp. salt
⅛ tsp. pepper

1 (1 lb.) can whole kernel corn, drained (2 c.)
1 (1 lb.) can green beans, drained (2 c.)
½ c. sliced ripe olives
½ c. bread crumbs
1 c. grated sharp process cheese

Cook bacon until crisp; remove from skillet and drain. Cook onion in bacon fat until soft. Stir in flour. Add tomatoes with juice and cook, stirring constantly, until mixture comes to a boil. Stir in seasonings, corn, green beans and olives. Place in greased 2-qt. casserole. Top with mixture of crumbs and cheese.

Bake in moderate oven (350°) 30 minutes, until mixture is bubbly and cheese is melted. Sprinkle with bacon and serve. Makes 8 servings.

VEGETABLE HARVEST

Ideal for carrying to potluck suppers

1 (9 oz.) pkg. frozen green
    beans
1 (10 oz.) pkg. frozen
    cauliflower
1 (10 oz.) pkg. frozen peas
1 can condensed cream of
    chicken soup
½ c. milk

1 c. shredded Cheddar
    cheese
1 (2 oz.) jar pimientos,
    . drained and chopped
1 (1 lb.) can onions, drained
½ tsp. salt
⅛ tsp. pepper
½ c. toasted slivered
    almonds

Cook frozen vegetables in same pan, as follows: Place beans in large saucepan with boiling salted water; cover and cook 5 minutes. Stir to break beans apart. Add cauliflower; cover and cook 5 minutes; stir. Add peas; cover and cook 3 minutes, or until peas can be separated. Drain.

Blend together soup and milk. Add cooked vegetables, cheese, pimientos, onions, salt and pepper. Place in greased 2-qt. casserole. Sprinkle with almonds.

Bake in moderate oven (350°) 30 minutes. Makes 8 servings.

ORIENTAL CASSEROLE

*Crunchy celery and cheese-tomato taste make this more
an adult party dish than family fare—
good with fried chicken*

¼ c. butter
2 tblsp. water
1 tsp. instant chicken
    bouillon granules
4 c. diagonally sliced celery
½ tsp. salt
1 tsp. sugar

2 tblsp. flour
1 (8 oz.) can tomato sauce
½ c. water
1½ c. shredded Cheddar
    cheese
2 tblsp. bread crumbs

Heat butter, 2 tblsp. water and chicken bouillon granules in saucepan. Add celery and cook 10 minutes. Stir in salt, sugar and flour, then tomato sauce and ½ c. water; cook until hot.

Alternate layers of celery mixture and cheese in 1½-qt. casserole, ending with cheese. Top with crumbs.

Bake in moderate oven (350°) 30 to 35 minutes. Makes 6 servings.

NOTE: You can substitute 1 (1 lb.) can tomatoes or 1½ c. sliced fresh tomatoes for the tomato sauce and ½ c. water.

MIXED VEGETABLE CASSEROLE

Emerald-green pepper rings top three favorite vegetables in this tasty dish

1 (1 lb.) can cream-style corn	⅛ tsp. ground red pepper (cayenne)
1 (1 lb.) can carrots and peas, drained	1 small green pepper, sliced in rings
¼ c. cracker crumbs	

Combine corn, carrots and peas, cracker crumbs and red pepper in shallow casserole. Top with green pepper rings.

Bake in moderate oven (350°) about 30 minutes, or until heated through. Makes 4 to 6 servings.

PARTY VEGETABLE MIX-UP

Your dinner guests will praise this

2 (10 oz.) pkgs. frozen mixed vegetables	1 can condensed cream of chicken soup
1 (4 oz.) can mushroom stems and pieces, drained	1 c. shredded sharp cheese
1 (5 oz.) can water chestnuts, drained and sliced	½ tsp. salt
	⅛ tsp. pepper
	1 c. crushed potato chips

Cook frozen vegetables in boiling salted water just until they can be separated. Combine with mushrooms, water chestnuts, soup, cheese, salt and pepper. Place in greased 1½-qt. casserole; top with potato chips.

Bake in moderate oven (350°) until bubbly, 25 to 30 minutes. Makes 8 servings.

HOLIDAY VEGETABLE CASSEROLE

This medley vegetable is good with meats
for special-occasion meals :

1 (1 lb.) can wax beans
1 (1 lb.) can or jar small
  whole onions
1 (8 oz.) can carrots

1 can condensed cream of
  mushroom soup
½ c. cracker crumbs
Butter or margarine

Combine drained wax beans, onions, carrots and soup in casserole. Top with crumbs and dot with butter. Bake in moderate oven (350°) until heated through. Makes 6 servings.

SPRING VEGETABLE À LA KING

Serve to guests in tulip time

⅓ c. butter or margarine
⅓ c. flour
2 c. light cream
1 c. chicken stock or broth
2 tsp. salt
⅛ tsp. pepper
1 (6 oz.) can broiled
  mushrooms, drained and
  sliced

2 c. cooked asparagus tips
2 c. cooked peas
1 c. cooked sliced carrots
2 to 3 tblsp. chopped green
  onions
1 egg yolk, slightly beaten

Melt butter; add flour and blend. Stir in cream and chicken stock; cook over low heat until thick, stirring constantly. Add salt and pepper.

Add remaining ingredients and heat thoroughly. Serve on toast, fluffy rice or Chinese noodles. Makes 6 servings.

Pretty Rings for the Hostess

Vegetables served in a ring are a feast to the eye, as well as to the palate. Carrots and peas with celery (the crisp note) and yellow-and-white quartered hard-cooked eggs in a flavorful sauce are colorful heaped in a rice ring.

The home economist-homemaker who contributed the recipe likes to serve this for supper or luncheon with very thin slices of ham and golden peach pickles. It's no wonder her friends brag about her food.

CURRIED VEGETABLES IN RICE RING

Looking for a glamorous luncheon or supper dish?
Here's a beauty

¼ c. butter or margarine
1 c. chopped onion
¼ c. flour
½ tsp. curry powder
½ tsp. salt
2 c. milk (or meat or chicken broth)
1 tsp. Worcestershire sauce
1 c. cooked sliced carrots

1 c. cooked diced celery
1 c. cooked green beans or peas
3 hard-cooked eggs, quartered
1½ c. rice
2 tblsp. melted butter or margarine

Melt ¼ c. butter in heavy saucepan. Add onion and cook over low heat until onion is golden. Blend in flour, curry powder and salt. Add milk all at once. Cook, stirring, until sauce is thickened.

Stir in Worcestershire sauce, carrots, celery and green beans; cook until heated through. Gently stir in eggs.

Cook rice, covered, in 3 c. boiling salted water until tender, about 20 minutes. Drain. Add 2 tblsp. melted butter. Press into buttered 1¼- to 2-qt. ring mold. Place in pan of hot water and keep in warm place until serving time.

Unmold rice ring on heated plate; fill center with vegetables. Makes 6 servings.

GOLDEN RUTABAGA RING

Limas in cheese sauce fill the ring

4 to 6 c. mashed rutabagas
3 tblsp. butter
½ to ¾ tsp. salt
⅛ tsp. pepper

2 (10 oz.) pkgs. frozen lima beans
¼ lb. pasteurized process cheese spread
½ tsp. salt
⅛ tsp. pepper

Whip mashed rutabagas with butter, ½ to ¾ tsp. salt and ⅛ tsp. pepper. Arrange on round serving platter around a form. An empty 1 lb. 13 oz. can from which both ends have been removed, and stood upright, makes a good form.

Meanwhile, cook limas in boiling salted water; drain. Add cheese, stirring until cheese is melted. Add ½ tsp. salt and ⅛ tsp. pepper.

Place vegetables in center of can on platter. Carefully lift can; serve immediately. Makes 8 servings.

CARROT-CHEESE-RICE RING

Gold-flecked rice holds green peas—a pretty, tasty combination

1½ c. shredded raw carrots	Salt and pepper to taste
1 tblsp. chopped onion	1 c. grated process cheese
1½ c. cooked rice	2 c. cooked peas
1 or 2 eggs, beaten	

Cook carrots 3 minutes in boiling salted water. Drain thoroughly and add onion, rice, eggs, salt and pepper. Fold in cheese.

Turn into buttered 4-cup ring mold; bake in moderate oven (350°) 30 minutes. Unmold on large platter and serve hot with cooked buttered peas in center. Makes 6 servings.

Wear a large thimble or rubber thumb guard (like secretaries use) on your thumb when you grate or peel vegetables—saves cuts and scratches.

Party Vegetable Ring

You'll be proud of the way this Party Vegetable Ring looks on your buffet, and your guests will be enthusiastic. Keep the ring warm the last few minutes before serving— just leave it in the mold and put it in a slow oven (300°).

Set out a bowl of the right size to fit into the center of the unmolded ring. Fill it either with All-Purpose Mushroom Sauce or try the Tomato-Orange Sauce, which has an unusually fine flavor and fiesta-gay color.

PARTY VEGETABLE RING

Mixed vegetables dot rice in ring, adding elegant touch to the buffet

1 tsp. salt	2 (10 oz.) pkgs. frozen
¼ tsp. curry powder	mixed vegetables
2½ c. water	1 tsp. salt
1 c. uncooked rice	Tomato-Orange Sauce or
⅓ c. butter	All-Purpose Mushroom
2 tblsp. water	Sauce

Add 1 tsp. salt and curry powder to 2½ c. water; add rice and cook according to package directions. (You'll have 4 c. cooked rice.)

Melt butter in saucepan. Add 2 tblsp. water, frozen vegetables and 1 tsp. salt; cover and cook until vegetables are tender, about 15 minutes.

Stir in hot rice. Press firmly into buttered 6½-cup ring mold. Turn out on serving plate. Place bowl with Tomato-Orange Sauce in center. Makes 8 to 10 servings.

Don't peel your garden cucumbers. The skins are not only good to eat, they're very decorative. If your recipe calls for sliced cucumbers, score the skin with the tines of a dinner fork before you slice them; this makes a pretty fluted edge. Cucumbers in the supermarket are sprayed with a harmless wax to keep them from wilting. This makes the skin seem tougher, and you may want to peel them, although it is not necessary.

TOMATO-ORANGE SAUCE

The tomato-orange flavor is luscious on vegetables; its color is festive

⅓ c. diagonally sliced	½ c. orange juice
celery (very thin)	½ tsp. sugar
2 tblsp. butter	½ tsp. salt
2 tblsp. flour	1 tsp. grated orange peel
1 c. canned tomatoes	⅛ tsp. ground nutmeg
½ c. water	

Cook celery in butter until tender. Stir in flour, then tomatoes and water. Cook until thick.

Add remaining ingredients and reheat. Makes about 2 cups.

ALL-PURPOSE MUSHROOM SAUCE

Always a favorite! It complements the taste
of the food it accompanies

½ c. mushrooms, stems and pieces, or 1 c. sliced fresh mushrooms
3 tblsp. butter
2 tblsp. flour

1½ tsp. instant beef bouillon granules, or 2 beef bouillon cubes
¾ c. water
¾ c. light cream or dairy half-and-half
⅛ tsp. ground nutmeg

Cook mushrooms in butter. Stir in flour, then remaining ingredients. Cook until thick. Makes about 1½ cups.

CHAPTER SIX

Vegetable Main Dishes

IF MEAT is king of the table, surely vegetables are the queens, beautiful in yellow, orange, red, green and white. Team meat and vegetables together on a big platter and they take the spotlight in meals. Everyone recognizes the importance of these two foods; that's why the combinations are called *"main* dishes." This chapter has a fine collection of such recipes.

While vegetable-meat stews taste good any time, the true stew season starts when gusty autumn winds blow bright leaves off the trees; it extends all through winter, well into spring. You can give plain stew a dramatic look. If you're having company, cut the meat and vegetables in larger pieces than you ordinarily do. Instead of hiding the attractive stew in a deep bowl, serve it on a large platter or in a shallow baking dish to display the chunks of meat and colorful vegetables in rich, brown gravy.

Vegetable-meat stews with crusty tops—such as our biscuit-crowned Vegetable Beef Potpie or our Lamb Pie Supreme, barley thickened, with batter topping—also have eye appeal. Serve them to guests and watch the anticipation that arises when the big serving spoon cuts through the golden crust, letting steam and aroma escape and revealing the contents—how this tantalizes the appetite.

Many of the main dishes in this chapter feature beef or lamb. But Confetti Casserole is one of the ground beef/ vegetable specialties you'll be sure to like. Vegetables 'n' Chicken in Paprika Sauce is a delightful new way to cook chicken and fresh vegetables together. An updated, country kitchen special, Red Flannel Hash, gives beets a chance to show off their vivid coloring in a homespun, delicious dish. Baked acorn squash halves, filled with apple and ham stuffing, are a treat. And there are top-of-the-range skillet specials, tasty at any time but doubly so in summer.

Combining vegetables with the highly favored protein foods, such as meats, poultry, cheese, fish and eggs, as do the recipes in this chapter, is one of the best ways to "sell" vegetables to the family.

Vegetable Casseroles with Ground Beef

Wise mothers know that a good way to persuade their families to eat their full quota of vegetables is to combine them with meat. Among the interesting recipes for these main dishes which some of the FARM JOURNAL readers share with you are several in which ground beef and vegetables get together. You brown the meat first, add the vegetables and bake them together in a casserole. They cook in a relatively brief time, usually in 30 minutes to 1 hour.

Vegetable-Beef Layer Casserole, a California specialty, has a double topping of chili sauce and grated cheese, which contributes to its color and flavor. You need not hesitate to serve this to guests. With crisp relishes or salad, rolls and a luscious dessert, you'll present a meal they'll enjoy.

VEGETABLE-BEEF LAYER CASSEROLE

Spread chili sauce over the top to give color to this meal-in-a-dish

1 lb. ground beef	2 large potatoes, peeled and
1 tsp. salt	thinly sliced (about 2 c.)
¼ tsp. pepper	2 medium onions, thinly
⅛ tsp. orégano or thyme	sliced
leaves	½ c. chili sauce
1 (1 lb.) can kidney beans,	⅔ c. shredded Cheddar
drained	cheese

In a medium skillet combine beef with salt, pepper and orégano, mix lightly but evenly. Cook over medium heat, stirring occasionally, until lightly browned.

In 2-qt. casserole, layer beef and vegetables, beginning and ending with meat. Add chili sauce.

Cover and bake in moderate oven (375°) 40 minutes. Uncover and top with cheese. Continue baking about 20 minutes more. Makes 6 servings.

SQUAW CORN CASSEROLE

Thyme and marjoram lift the taste of this dish above the commonplace

1 lb. ground beef
2 tblsp. fat
1½ tsp. salt
½ tsp. thyme leaves
¼ tsp. marjoram leaves
¼ c. chopped onion
2 eggs, beaten
¼ c. milk
1 c. soft bread crumbs

1 (1 lb.) can cream-style corn
2 tsp. prepared mustard
½ c. bread or cracker crumbs, or crushed potato chips
2 tblsp. butter (omit if using potato chips)

Brown beef in fat. Add seasonings, onion, eggs, milk, 1 c. crumbs, corn and mustard. Mix well and put into a greased 2-qt. casserole. Mix remaining crumbs and butter and sprinkle over casserole.

Bake in moderate oven (350°) 30 to 40 minutes. Makes 8 servings.

NOTE: You can get this dish ready to bake, then refrigerate; cook just before you want to serve it.

HAMBURGER PIE WITH POTATO CRUST

Teen-agers voted this a great dish and promptly asked for a repeat

2 lbs. ground beef
3 c. chopped celery
2 c. chopped onion
2 cans condensed tomato soup

1 c. ketchup
2 tsp. salt
½ tsp. pepper
2 (9 oz.) pkgs. frozen French fries

Brown meat in large skillet; pour off excess fat. Add celery, onion, soup, ketchup, salt and pepper. Cover and simmer 15 minutes.

Place in 13 × 9 × 2″ pan. Top with French fries. Bake in hot oven (425°) 20 to 25 minutes, or until potatoes are brown. Makes 8 servings.

HAMBURGER SUKIYAKI

*A Japanese favorite goes American with hamburger—
nice company dish*

1 (8 oz.) pkg. fine noodles
2 lbs. ground beef
2 c. sliced green onions
   with tops
½ lb. fresh mushrooms,
   washed and sliced

1 lb. fresh spinach, washed
   and torn
½ c. soy sauce
¼ c. water
2 c. chopped celery

Cook noodles as directed on package. Drain and place
in 3-qt. casserole; cover and place in slow oven (325°) to
keep warm.

Meanwhile, brown meat in large skillet until pink color
disappears. Add onions and cook 2 minutes. Add mushrooms, spinach, soy sauce and water. Cover and cook only
until spinach is wilted (cover may not completely fit at
first—will be held up by spinach, but comes down as
spinach wilts). Stir in celery.

Pour over noodles. Toss to combine. Casserole may be
returned to oven to keep warm a few minutes, but celery
should stay crisp, so don't cook. Makes 10 servings.

EGGPLANT BUFFET STYLE

*It takes time to make this dish but every minute
is well spent*

1 medium-size eggplant,
   peeled and sliced ½"
   thick
Salt
1¼ tsp. garlic salt
¼ tsp. pepper
1 egg
1 lb. ground beef
6 tblsp. salad oil
1 egg, slightly beaten
2 tblsp. chopped onion
½ clove garlic, minced

2 tblsp. flour
2½ lbs. tomatoes, peeled
   and chopped, or 2 (1
   lb.) cans tomatoes
½ tsp. salt
½ tsp. crushed dried
   orégano
1 (4 oz.) pkg. mozzarella
   cheese, shredded
½ c. grated Parmesan
   cheese

Lightly salt the eggplant slices and place in a small bowl. Set aside.

Combine garlic salt, pepper, egg and ground beef. Form into 1" balls; brown in 4 tblsp. salad oil in skillet. Remove meat balls; drain. Reserve 4 tblsp. drippings in skillet.

Drain eggplant slices. Dip in beaten egg and brown in drippings; drain on absorbent towel.

Add 2 tblsp. salad oil to skillet. Cook onion and garlic until tender. Blend in flour. Gradually stir in tomatoes, salt and orégano. Simmer until thick, 15 to 20 minutes.

Layer in 2-qt. casserole in following order, one-third each: tomato sauce, meat balls, eggplant and mozzarella cheese. Repeat layers two more times.

Bake, uncovered, in moderate oven (350°) 30 minutes. Let stand 5 to 10 minutes before serving. Makes 6 servings.

SOUTHWEST-INDIAN HOT DISH

Chili powder gives the right zip

1½ lbs. ground beef	1½ tsp. salt
1 c. chopped onion	½ tsp. chili powder
2 (1 lb.) cans golden	¼ tsp. pepper
hominy, drained	1 c. grated process cheese
2 (8 oz.) cans tomato sauce	
(2 c.)	

Cook together ground beef and onion in skillet until beef is browned and onion is soft. Combine with hominy, tomato sauce, salt, chili powder and pepper.

Place in 2½-qt. casserole. Bake in moderate oven (350°) until bubbly, about 30 minutes. Sprinkle with cheese. Continue baking 10 minutes more. Makes 8 servings.

GROUND BEEF CASSEROLE

An Ohio farm woman says this is her special potluck casserole

1 lb. ground beef	1 large onion, chopped
1 (10 oz.) pkg. frozen whole kernel corn, thawed	½ c. chopped green pepper
	¼ c. flour
1 (10 oz.) pkg. frozen lima beans, thawed	1½ tsp. salt
	¼ tsp. pepper
1 (1 lb.) can tomatoes (2 c.)	1 tsp. curry powder
2 c. sliced potatoes	(optional)

Combine ground beef and vegetables in large bowl. Sprinkle with mixture of flour and seasonings; mix.

Spoon into 3-qt. casserole. Cover and bake in moderate oven (350°) 2 hours. Makes 6 large servings.

SEVEN-LAYER DINNER

A homey dish you'll make again and again—
it takes no watching in oven

2 c. sliced raw potatoes	½ c. chopped green pepper
1½ c. sliced raw carrots	1 (1 lb.) can tomatoes (2 c.)
1½ c. sliced celery	2 tsp. salt
1 lb. ground beef	¼ tsp. pepper
1 c. chopped onion	

Place potatoes in bottom of greased 2½-qt. casserole. Top with other vegetables and uncooked meat in order given, sprinkling each layer with a little of the salt and pepper.

Bake in moderate oven (350°) 2 hours. Makes 6 servings.

CONFETTI CASSEROLE

Receives overwhelming approval of family and friends—
quick to fix

2 lbs. ground beef	1 (8 oz.) pkg. cream cheese
½ c. chopped onion	2 (8 oz.) cans tomato sauce
2 tsp. salt	2 (10 oz.) pkgs. frozen mixed vegetables, defrosted
¼ tsp. pepper	
½ tsp. dry mustard	
2 tblsp. brown sugar	Crushed corn chips

Brown meat in skillet; add onion and cook until tender.

Add salt, pepper, dry mustard, brown sugar and cream cheese; stir until cheese melts. Add tomato sauce and defrosted vegetables.

Turn into 3-qt. casserole. Sprinkle with corn chips. Cover and bake in moderate oven (375°) 40 minutes. Uncover; bake 10 minutes longer. Makes 10 to 12 servings.

BAKED BEEF AND LIMAS

Hamburger and limas get together

1 lb. ground beef	¼ tsp. pepper
1 medium onion, chopped	2 (1 lb. 1 oz.) cans green
1 (15 oz.) can tomato sauce	lima beans, drained
with tomato bits	2 slices bacon, cut in
½ c. brown sugar	fourths
1½ tsp. salt	

Cook ground beef and onion in skillet until beef is browned.

Meanwhile, combine tomato sauce, brown sugar, salt and pepper in 2-qt. casserole. Stir in ground beef and limas. Top with bacon strips.

Bake in moderate oven (350°) 1½ hours. Makes 6 servings.

NOTE: Reduce the brown sugar to ¼ c. for less sweetness.

ITALIAN STUFFED PEPPERS

Spaghetti seasonings used in stuffing for peppers produce a taste triumph

6 large green peppers	¼ tsp. pepper
1 lb. ground beef	¼ c. grated Parmesan
1 c. chopped onion	cheese
(1 medium)	1 (15 oz.) can meatless
½ c. rice	spaghetti sauce
1 c. water	Grated Parmesan cheese
1½ tsp. salt	

Cut tops off green peppers. Scoop out and discard seeds and membrane. Cook in boiling salted water 5 minutes. Drain. Place in muffin-pan cups.

Cook ground beef and onion in skillet until onion is soft. Drain off excess fat.

Meanwhile, combine rice, water and ½ tsp. salt in saucepan. Bring to a boil, stir once; cover and cook over low heat until tender, 15 to 20 minutes.

Combine rice with ground beef mixture, 1 tsp. salt, pepper, ¼ c. Parmesan cheese and half the spaghetti sauce.

Spoon into green pepper cups almost to the top. Spoon remaining sauce over meat. Sprinkle with Parmesan cheese. Bake in moderate oven (350°) until bubbly, about 25 minutes. Makes 6 servings.

Skillet Vegetable-Beef Dishes

Cooked-in-the-skillet main dishes free the oven for baking the dinner dessert or other food. A Tennessee homemaker writes that she likes skillet meals because she frequently uses the oven to bake cookies while getting dinner. Her family enjoys the warm cookies served with canned or frozen fruits for dessert. Among her vegetable-ground beef favorites are Okra-Beef Dinner and Vegetable-Beef Stroganoff, which she serves with fluffy hot rice. Both recipes follow.

VEGETABLE-BEEF STROGANOFF

*Serve in individual casseroles or over fluffy rice
or potatoes*

1 lb. lean ground beef	1 tblsp. Worcestershire
1 small onion, chopped	sauce
2 tblsp. shortening	2 (16 oz.) cans cut green
½ tsp. salt	beans, drained
⅛ tsp. pepper	2 canned pimientos
1 can condensed cream of	¼ c. slivered almonds
mushroom soup	1 c. dairy sour cream
1 (4 oz.) can sliced	Chopped parsley
mushrooms, drained	

Brown beef and onion in hot fat in large skillet. Season with salt and pepper. Drain excess fat. Add remaining ingredients, except sour cream and parsley. Mix thoroughly and simmer until steaming.

Add sour cream, heating until just warmed (do not let boil). Sprinkle top with chopped parsley. Makes 6 to 8 servings.

MEXICAN LIMA-BEEF SKILLET

Try this pleasing, substantial dish of dried limas
and ground beef

2 tblsp. butter or margarine	½ tsp. paprika
1 large onion, chopped	¼ tsp. pepper
1 small clove garlic, minced	Dash ground red pepper
1 green pepper, chopped	(cayenne)
1 lb. ground beef	1 tblsp. chili powder
2½ c. canned tomatoes	2½ c. cooked dried lima
1½ tsp. salt	beans (1 c. uncooked)

Melt butter in heavy skillet. Add onion, garlic and green pepper; cook until onion is golden.

Add ground beef and cook until light brown; stir frequently. Stir in remaining ingredients, except limas; simmer, covered, about 1½ hours.

Add lima beans and continue cooking until heated through. Makes 6 to 8 servings.

Before you add chopped onions to meat loaf, hamburgers
or any vegetable dish, cook the onions first in a little butter
or margarine until they wilt and turn transparent or take
on a light yellow color. This develops the good mild onion
flavor and takes away the strong raw taste.

OKRA-BEEF DINNER

Okra, rice, tomatoes and beef star in this Egyptian
meal-in-a-dish

1 lb. ground beef	2 tsp. salt
1 c. chopped onion	¼ tsp. pepper
1 (1 lb. 13 oz.) can	Few drops Tabasco sauce
tomatoes (3½ c.)	2 (10 oz.) pkgs. frozen okra
½ c. uncooked rice	

Cook ground beef and onion in skillet until beef is browned. Add tomatoes and bring to a boil. Add remaining ingredients, except okra. Cover and simmer 20 minutes.

Separate okra and stir into mixture. Cover and simmer until rice is done, 20 to 25 minutes, stirring occasionally. Makes 6 servings.

VARIETY KETTLE MEAL

Fix this double-quick main dish

4 oz. uncooked egg noodles
1 can condensed beef broth
1 medium onion, diced, or
  2 tblsp. instant minced
  onion

2 (15¼ oz.) cans meat balls
  in beef gravy
1 (1 lb.) can kidney beans,
  drained
1 (1 lb.) can sliced or diced
  carrots, drained

Combine noodles, beef broth, onion and gravy drained from meat balls in a kettle or skillet. Cover and bring to a boil. Reduce heat; simmer, covered, 5 to 7 minutes, or until noodles are tender.

Add kidney beans, carrots and meat balls; heat. Makes 6 servings.

Stuffed Cabbage Leaves

Vegetable recipes have traveled far. Take Stuffed Cabbage Leaves, for example: Most food historians believe the dish started out in Hungarian kitchens, but it rates high in popularity throughout all of Eastern Europe. And in America!

Recipes for this main dish vary somewhat from kitchen to kitchen as well as from country to country. Our version, adapted to American tastes, borrows the touch of lemon juice from Balkan cooks. Taste-testers said it brings out good flavors.

When you use our recipe for Stuffed Cabbage Leaves, we believe your family and friends will praise this international main dish.

251

STUFFED CABBAGE LEAVES

*Bring a welcome change to menus
with this meat-vegetable favorite*

1 large head cabbage	1 (8 oz.) can tomato sauce
1½ lbs. ground beef	(1 c.)
½ c. uncooked rice	1 (1 lb. 12 oz.) can
1 small onion, grated	tomatoes (3½ c.)
1 egg, beaten	¼ c. lemon juice
1 tsp. salt	1 tsp. salt
¼ tsp. pepper	¼ tsp. pepper

Remove core from cabbage. Place in boiling salted water; cover and cook until outer leaves are soft, about 5 minutes. Remove 12 large leaves from cabbage. Trim off thick part of each leaf. Reserve remaining cabbage for other use.

Combine meat, rice, onion, egg, 1 tsp. salt and ¼ tsp. pepper. Divide in 12 parts. Put mound of meat mixture in cup part of each leaf. Loosely fold sides over meat; roll up. Place, flap side down, in kettle or Dutch oven. Pour over tomato sauce, canned tomatoes, lemon juice, 1 tsp. salt and ¼ tsp. pepper. Cover and simmer 1 hour. Makes 6 servings.

CHILI-STUFFED PEPPERS

Chili con carne fans will praise this

6 large green peppers	1 (1 lb. 4 oz.) can kidney
¼ c. chopped green pepper	beans, drained
½ c. chopped onion	1 tsp. salt
2 tblsp. butter or margarine	1 tsp. paprika
1 lb. ground beef	1 tblsp. chili powder
1 c. finely chopped celery	1 c. water
2 (8 oz.) cans tomato sauce	

Wash peppers. Cut off tops and save; remove seeds.
Cook chopped green pepper and onion in butter until tender. Add beef and cook until lightly browned. Add

celery, 1 can tomato sauce, beans, salt, paprika and chili powder. Stir and simmer until thoroughly blended, about 5 minutes.

Stuff peppers with hot beef mixture. Cover with pepper tops and place in baking dish.

Combine remaining can of tomato sauce with water; pour around peppers. Bake in moderate oven (350°) about 30 minutes. Makes 6 servings.

TAMALE PIE

Very good, inexpensive main dish

4 c. chicken broth	1 (1 lb.) can tomatoes (2 c.)
1½ c. yellow corn meal	1 (12 oz.) can whole kernel
Salt to taste (about 1 tsp.)	corn
2 eggs, beaten	2½ tsp. salt
⅔ c. grated Parmesan	⅛ tsp. pepper
cheese	1 tblsp. chili powder
1 lb. ground beef	⅓ c. yellow corn meal
1 large onion, chopped	⅔ c. sliced pitted ripe
1 green pepper, chopped	olives
1 clove garlic, minced	

To make crust, heat 3 c. broth. Stir 1½ c. corn meal into remaining 1 c. broth, then stir into hot broth. Add salt (amount depends on saltiness of broth).

Place over boiling water; cover and cook 20 minutes. Stir a little of the hot corn meal mixture into eggs. Then beat this into remaining corn meal mixture. Stir in ⅓ c. cheese.

Meanwhile, prepare filling. Brown meat in skillet; add onion, green pepper and garlic. Drain ⅓ c. liquid from tomatoes and reserve. Add tomatoes, undrained corn, 2½ tsp. salt, ⅛ tsp. pepper and chili powder to mixture. Cover and simmer 10 minutes.

Blend together ⅓ c. reserved tomato liquid and ⅓ c. corn meal. Add to meat mixture, stirring until mixture boils and is thickened. Add olives.

Line bottom and sides of 3-qt. casserole with about two-thirds of corn meal crust. Place filling in center. Spoon remaining corn meal crust over top in mounds. Sprinkle with remaining ⅓ c. cheese.

Bake in moderate oven (350°) 30 minutes, or until thoroughly heated. Makes 8 servings.

POTATO-BEEF ROLL

Potatoes surround beef in this loaf . . .
a winner with the men and boys

2 slices bread, crusts
  removed and cubed
1 egg, beaten
¼ c. milk
1 medium onion, chopped
1 small clove garlic,
  crushed
1 tblsp. salad oil
1 lb. ground beef

1 tsp. salt
¼ tsp. rosemary leaves
¼ tsp. pepper
2 tblsp. dry bread crumbs
Instant mashed potatoes for
  4 servings
1 tblsp. minced parsley
2 slices bacon

Combine cubed bread with egg and milk; let soak.

Cook onion and garlic in salad oil until onion is soft.

Combine bread mixture, onion and garlic, ground beef and seasonings. Blend together thoroughly.

Sprinkle 2 tblsp. bread crumbs on waxed paper, making a 10 × 8″ rectangle. Pat meat mixture into an even layer over crumbs. Spread potatoes, made by package directions, over meat. Sprinkle with parsley.

Using waxed paper as an aid, roll meat and potatoes like a jelly roll. Place in shallow baking pan; lay bacon strips over top. Bake in moderate oven (350°) 1 hour. Makes 5 to 6 servings.

Vegetable-Beef Stews

Vegetables are as important as meat in these homey dishes. It's the combination of the foods in their juices that elevates well-made stews to great main dishes. Some stews go directly from kettle to serving dish, while others take a turn in the oven—like our Vegetable-Beef Potpie. You bake it long enough to turn the biscuit topping golden brown. Try it and other stew recipes in this cookbook.

VEGETABLE-BEEF POTPIE

When the serving spoon cuts through
the golden topping, appetites soar

2 lbs. beef chuck, cut in
  1½" cubes
¼ c. flour
2 tsp. salt
¼ tsp. pepper
2 tblsp. shortening
1 c. tomato juice
2 c. hot water
1 tsp. Worcestershire sauce
1 bay leaf
1 clove garlic

½ c. chopped onion
6 medium carrots, peeled
  and cut in 2" lengths
4 medium potatoes, peeled
  and quartered
4 branches celery, coarsely
  cut
Salt
Flour
Cold water
2 c. prepared biscuit mix

Dredge meat in flour combined with salt and pepper; brown slowly on all sides in hot shortening.

Add tomato juice, hot water, Worcestershire sauce, bay leaf, garlic and onion. Cover and simmer 1½ hours.

Add carrots, potatoes and celery; taste for seasoning, and salt lightly. Cover and cook 20 to 30 minutes, until vegetables are tender. Remove meat and vegetables and place in 2½-qt. casserole.

Thicken liquid with a paste made with a little flour and cold water; season to taste and pour over meat and vegetables.

Make dough for drop biscuits following directions on package, and drop on meat.

Bake in hot oven (425°) about 25 minutes, or until biscuits are golden brown. Makes about 8 servings.

CASSEROLE BEEF STEW

Crunchy-nut biscuits top steaming stew—
keep makings in cupboard

1 (24 oz.) can beef stew
1 (16 oz.) can small whole
  onions
1 (8 oz.) can peas

½ recipe for biscuits (1 c.
  prepared biscuit mix)
½ c. grated American
  cheese
½ c. chopped pecans

Combine stew, drained onions and peas in saucepan; heat.

Prepare biscuit dough as directed on package. Roll into 12 × 9" rectangle; sprinkle with cheese and nuts. Roll like a jelly roll, starting at wide end; cut in 1" slices.

Pour stew into 10 × 6" baking dish; top with cheese-nut biscuits. Bake in hot oven (400°) 20 minutes, or until biscuits are lightly browned. Makes 5 to 6 servings.

HARVEST BEEF CASSEROLE

The vegetables in this baked beef stew
help make it a taste-pleaser

1½ lbs. beef stew meat, cut in 1" cubes	1 c. green pepper, cut in ½" squares
Meat tenderizer	2 c. cubed peeled eggplant
2½ c. chopped onions	½ c. uncooked regular white rice
¼ c. salad oil	
¼ c. water	2 tsp. salt
5 medium tomatoes, peeled	¼ tsp. pepper
2 c. cut-up green beans	⅔ c. water
2 carrots, peeled and sliced	

Place meat on board; sprinkle top side with meat tenderizer. Prick each piece with fork and turn over. Sprinkle again with meat tenderizer.

Cook onions in heavy skillet in hot oil until soft; remove. Add meat to skillet and brown on all sides. Add ¼ c. water; cover and simmer 30 minutes.

Place half of onions in bottom of greased 13 × 9 × 2" pan. Top with 3 tomatoes cut in ½" slices. Cover with half the beans, carrots, green pepper and eggplant. Top with rice, then meat with juices. Top with remaining onions, beans, carrots, green pepper and eggplant. Down center arrange the remaining tomatoes, cut in slices. Sprinkle with salt and pepper. Pour ⅔ c. water over vegetables; cover with foil. Bake in moderate oven (375°) until all vegetables are tender, about 2 hours. Makes 6 servings.

VEGETABLE-BEEF STEW

Vegetables play the leading role in this
exceptionally good stew

2 lbs. stew beef, cut in
  1½″ cubes
¼ c. salad oil
1 medium onion, chopped
2 c. beef broth
2 c. water
1 clove garlic, finely
  chopped
2 tblsp. chopped parsley
1 bay leaf
1½ tblsp. salt
¼ tsp. pepper
⅛ tsp. thyme leaves

6 medium potatoes, peeled
  and cut in halves
6 small onions, peeled
6 medium carrots, peeled
  and cut in halves
  crosswise
3 branches celery, cut in
  halves
1 green pepper, cut in
  strips
1 (8 oz.) can stewed
  tomatoes

Cook beef in oil over medium heat in Dutch oven until all sides are browned. Remove meat from pan and add chopped onion. Cook until soft. Return meat to pan; add beef broth, water, garlic, parsley, bay leaf, salt, pepper and thyme. Cover and simmer 1½ hours.

Add remaining ingredients. Cover and simmer until vegetables are tender, about 1 hour.

Gravy will be thin. To thicken, remove vegetables and meat from Dutch oven and keep warm in oven. Blend mixture of 6 tblsp. flour and 6 tblsp. cold water into meat broth. Cook, stirring constantly, until mixture comes to a boil. Spoon over meat and vegetables. Makes 6 to 8 servings.

NOTE: If you cannot find canned beef broth in your markets, and do not want to make your own, you can use one of the packaged beef flavors, dissolved in hot water by label directions.

QUICK BAKED STEW

If you have 4 minute steaks and need 6
servings, this will fix you up

4 minute cube steaks
(about 1½ lbs.)
½ c. flour
2 tblsp. shortening
2 c. diced potatoes
2 c. sliced carrots
1 c. chopped onions
1 c. sliced celery
1 c. frozen loose-pack green
beans

1 beef bouillon cube, or
1 envelope beef broth mix
1 c. hot water
2 tblsp. lemon juice
½ tsp. salt
¼ tsp. pepper
¼ tsp. thyme leaves
(optional)
1 bay leaf

Cut steaks in strips ½″ wide. Shake in bag with flour. Brown in hot fat. Combine with remaining ingredients (mix bouillon cube with hot water before adding).

Turn into 2½-qt. casserole. Cover and bake in moderate oven (350°) about 1 hour and 15 minutes. Stir once or twice during cooking to mix well. Makes 6 servings.

SONORA STEW

A South-of-the-Border stew of beef,
beans, onions and tomato sauce

1 lb. beef stew meat, cut
in bite-size pieces
1 large onion, cut in eighths
1 clove garlic, crushed
3 tblsp. fat or salad oil
1 (15 or 15½ oz.) can
garbanzos

1 (8 oz.) can tomato sauce
(1 c.)
1 c. water
1 tblsp. chili powder
1½ tsp. salt
½ lb. (or more) cut green
beans, or 1 (10 oz.) pkg.
frozen green beans

Brown meat, onion and garlic in fat.

Add garbanzos with their liquid, tomato sauce and water. Simmer 1 hour, or until meat is almost tender.

Add chili powder, salt and green beans; continue cooking over very low heat 1 hour more; stir occasionally. Add a little more water, if needed, to avoid sticking; however, it should be a thick, almost non-liquid stew when done. Makes 4 to 6 servings.

NOTE: To crush garlic clove easily, place it between a fold

of aluminum foil and strike with flat side of heavy knife or a mallet—keeps odor off hands.

GOULASH

Excellent way to cook venison, but try the
recipe also with beef or veal

2½ to 3 lbs. meat (beef,
  veal or venison), cubed
1 tblsp. paprika
3 tblsp. fat
4 medium onions
½ green pepper, cut in
  squares
1 small clove garlic, crushed
2 c. canned tomatoes, or
  2 c. tomato juice

Meat stock to cover
  (about 1 c.)
1½ tsp. salt
1 tsp. caraway seeds
1 tblsp. red wine vinegar
½ c. water
6 medium potatoes, peeled
  and cut in chunks

Season meat with paprika; brown lightly in hot fat in kettle or large fry pan. Add onions, peeled and cut in thick slices, green pepper and garlic.

Add tomatoes and enough meat stock just to cover meat. Add salt, caraway seeds, vinegar and water. Cover and let simmer gently 30 minutes.

Add potatoes; cook until meat and potatoes are tender, about 30 minutes more. Makes 6 to 8 servings.

NOTE: If you do not have meat stock, make your own by dissolving 2 tsp. beef-seasoned stock base in 1 c. water. You also can substitute ½ c. dry red wine for the wine vinegar and ½ c. water. The European custom of cooking with wine is on the increase in American kitchens. As the food cooks, alcohol in the wine evaporates, leaving the wine flavor.

BROWN STEW WITH VEGETABLES

Round out the feast with piping hot biscuits,
a fine partner for stews

2 lbs. stew meat, cut in cubes
2 tblsp. salad oil
3 c. boiling water
1 tblsp. salt
¼ tsp. pepper
1 tsp. Worcestershire sauce
1 beef bouillon cube

3 c. cubed peeled potatoes (3 medium)
1 c. sliced carrots
1 c. sliced celery
6 small whole onions
1 c. frozen loose-pack green beans

Brown meat thoroughly in hot oil in Dutch oven. Add water, salt, pepper, Worcestershire sauce and bouillon cube. Cover and simmer 2 hours.

Add potatoes, carrots, celery and onions. Simmer 15 minutes.

Add frozen green beans, and continue simmering until all vegetables are tender, 15 to 25 minutes.

Stew may be thickened, if desired. To thicken, blend ¼ c. flour into ½ c. water to make a smooth paste. Stir into stew, and heat until thickened. Makes 6 servings.

Growers refer to vegetables as "truck crops" and you might think it's because many vegetables are hauled to market on trucks. Not so. An old meaning of the word truck is "to barter or exchange." The word developed a special meaning as a synonym for vegetables through the practice of bartering small lots of them in the market.

Chinese Vegetable-Beef Specials

Although Chinese-American vegetable beef main dishes have won greater acceptance in our Western states than elsewhere, they're gaining popularity across the country. Aside from their tastiness, they have other merits. They're fast cooking, largely because you cut the beef in thin narrow strips. And they're attractive: green pepper strips, tomatoes and parsley in Pepper Steak; edible pod peas and tomatoes in Beef Tomato. The vegetables are tender-crisp and the taste is marvelous, especially if you like the flavors of Chinese-style dishes.

PEPPER STEAK

Splendid version of a Chinese favorite

2 lbs. (about) round steak
2 tblsp. salad oil
2 c. chopped onions
1 (10½ oz.) can beef
  bouillon
½ lb. fresh mushrooms,
  sliced
3 green peppers, seeded and
  cut in 1" strips

3 tomatoes, cut in eighths
2 tblsp. cornstarch
¼ c. water
1½ tsp. salt
¼ tsp. pepper
2 tsp. chopped parsley
  (optional)

Cut meat across grain in ¼" strips. Brown quickly in hot oil in skillet. Add onions and cook slightly. Add bouillon. Cover and simmer 30 minutes.

Stir in mushrooms and green peppers. Simmer 5 minutes. Add tomatoes; simmer 2 minutes more.

Meanwhile, blend together cornstarch and water. Add to meat mixture along with salt and pepper. Cook, stirring until thickened. Serve, sprinkled with parsley, with buttered rice. Pass soy sauce. Makes 6 servings.

GREEN BEANS AND BEEF

*This dish has oriental flavors
and crisp textures, and it cooks fast*

2 tblsp. soy sauce
1 tsp. sugar
1 tblsp. cornstarch
1 tblsp. dry sherry (or wine
  vinegar)

½ lb. top round of beef,
  thinly sliced
2 tblsp. salad oil
1½ c. boiling water
½ lb. green beans, washed
  and cut lengthwise

Combine soy sauce, sugar, cornstarch and sherry in shallow dish and mix thoroughly. Add beef and coat pieces evenly.

Heat oil in skillet. Add beef; cook over high heat 1 or 2 minutes.

Pour boiling water over prepared green beans. Bring to a boil; drain immediately, reserving ¼ c. liquid.

Add parboiled beans and reserved liquid to beef. Bring to boil and simmer 1 minute. Do not overcook or flavor and color will not be satisfactory. Serve with hot cooked rice. Makes 4 servings.

NOTE: Instead of the fresh vegetable, you can use 1 (10 oz.) pkg. frozen green beans or 1 (15¼ oz.) can julienne green beans, and reserve only 2 tblsp. of the liquid.

BEEF TOMATO

If you like Chinese food, you'll treasure this recipe and use it

1 lb. flank, top round or sirloin steak	1 c. cooked edible pod peas, fresh or frozen
1 tsp. flour	1 (1 lb. 4 oz.) can solid pack
1 tblsp. soy sauce	tomatoes, or 4 fresh
½ tsp. salt	tomatoes, peeled and cut
3 tblsp. salad oil	in quarters
1 small onion, thinly sliced	½ tsp. salt
1 branch celery, sliced	3 tblsp. sugar
(about ½ c.)	1 tblsp. ketchup
½ green pepper, sliced	1 tblsp. lemon juice

Cut beef in very thin slices, about 1½″ long.

Combine flour, soy sauce and ½ tsp. salt in shallow dish. Add beef and coat evenly.

Heat oil in skillet. Add beef and brown quickly; set aside in dish to be used later.

In same skillet, brown onion, celery and green pepper, cooking only a few minutes. Add peas, tomatoes, ½ tsp. salt and sugar. Cook only until heated through; do not overcook.

Add ketchup and beef; heat about 1 minute. Remove from heat and add lemon juice. Serve with hot cooked rice. Makes 6 servings.

Pot-au-Feu for Dinner

You don't have to be French to relish this dinner from a kettle. (Literally translated from the French, *pot-au-feu* means "pot on the fire.") Everyone who tastes the meat, vegetables and broth or soup blesses the woman who cooked the feast. Served with crusty bread or rolls and a fruit dessert or sherbet, smiles of approval travel around the table.

Be sure to select a beef cut with very little fat, or simmer a fattier cut of meat until tender, chill it in the broth overnight and remove the fat before you add the vegetables. When you divide the meal-getting into two parts, you can fix dinner easily the day you serve it. All you have to do is get the vegetables ready and drop them into the kettle to cook. On busy days or when there's company, this really helps. And it also helps make the dinner a big success if you serve it on a winter day.

POT-AU-FEU

Long simmering of meat and cooking vegetables
only until tender brings out the superlative flavor

4 lbs. beef with bone (rump, plate, chuck or round)	1 onion, chopped
	1½ c. mixed chopped vegetables (carrots, celery, white turnips, parsnips)
3 qts. cold water	
1 tblsp. salt	
1 bouquet garni (1 bay leaf, ¼ tsp. thyme leaves, ½ tsp. peppercorns, 5 sprigs parsley and a few celery leaves tied in a cheesecloth bag)	6 leeks (optional)
	6 carrots
	6 peeled potatoes
	1 head cabbage, cut in 6 wedges

Place meat in large kettle. Add water, salt and bouquet garni. Bring to a boil, reduce heat, and simmer until meat is tender, about 4 hours.

Add onion, chopped vegetables, leeks, carrots and potatoes. Simmer 30 minutes. Add cabbage and continue to simmer until all vegetables are tender, about 20 minutes.

To serve, discard bouquet garni; remove meat to large platter and surround with large pieces of vegetables. Keep warm in oven on low heat. (Serve broth with chopped vegetables as a first course. Or it may be saved and used as a soup later.) Makes 6 servings.

Vegetables Rescue Leftover Beef

Few women complain when they have leftover cooked beef; it's the promise of another good meal. Recipes for two old-time, beloved country dishes, brought up to date, are Shepherd's Pie and Red Flannel Hash. They taste so wonderful that you may want to *plan* for leftover beef in order to make them. That's what country women refer to as "planned-overs."

SHEPHERD'S PIE

An old-fashioned main dish made with new-fashioned ingredients—very good

Instant potatoes for 8 servings	Leftover gravy, or 1 (1¾ oz.) pkg. instant gravy mix
1 tblsp. instant minced onion	2 c. chopped cooked beef
1 egg, beaten	1 tsp. parsley flakes
1 (10 oz.) pkg. frozen peas and carrots	1 tsp. salt
½ c. chopped celery	⅛ tsp. pepper
1 (4 oz.) can mushroom stems and pieces	Grated Parmesan cheese

Prepare instant potatoes according to package directions, but adding instant onion to the water. Cool slightly and beat in egg.

Cook frozen peas and carrots with the celery in boiling salted water. Drain, reserving liquid. Drain mushrooms, reserving liquid. (You may need liquids for gravy.)

You will need 1⅓ c. gravy; if you don't have enough, add reserved liquids to make 1⅓ c. Or prepare gravy mix, using reserved liquids plus water to make 1⅓ c.

Combine beef, peas, carrots, celery, mushrooms, parsley, salt, pepper and gravy.

Place half of potatoes in bottom of greased 2½-qt. casserole. Top with meat mixture. Top with remaining potatoes. Sprinkle with Parmesan cheese.

Bake in hot oven (400°) 25 minutes, or until mixture is bubbly. Makes 6 servings.

RED FLANNEL HASH

For a heartier main dish, top each serving of hash with a poached egg

3 slices salt pork or bacon,
cut in ½" pieces
2 c. finely chopped cooked
beets (about 6 medium)
2 c. finely chopped cooked
potatoes (about 6
medium)

½ c. finely chopped onion
2 c. ground cooked beef or
ham
½ c. meat gravy, meat
stock or water
Salt and pepper to taste
¼ tsp. marjoram leaves

Cook salt pork in skillet until well browned. Remove meat, reserving 2 tblsp. fat.

Combine vegetables and ground meat together with gravy; add salt pork bits, salt, pepper and marjoram. Turn into skillet containing reserved 2 tblsp. fat, cover and bake in moderate oven (375°) 20 minutes. Remove cover and bake 10 minutes more; turn on broiler briefly to crisp top. Makes 6 to 8 servings.

NOTE: Chop vegetables fine with a French chef's knife, if available. To do this, cut vegetables in half and place together in a row on cutting board; make thin slices, turn and slice again. Then, holding knife with both hands, chop quickly in all directions until vegetables are as fine as desired. Do only as many at a time as can be handled easily with knife blade. Meat can be chopped similarly, but putting it through a food chopper, using coarse-grind blade, gives a little better texture for hash.

Dried Beef-Vegetable Treats

Keeping a jar or package of dried beef on hand ensures a pleasing main dish. Hearty Lima Casserole requires little preparation and Broccoli Luncheon Special is pretty and tasty for an informal luncheon. In fact, if you have a bit of chipped beef on hand, stir it into any vegetables in cream sauce—tasty.

HEARTY LIMA CASSEROLE

From start to finish, takes slightly more than half an hour to make this

2 (2½ oz.) jars dried beef,
  shredded
⅓ c. butter
6 tblsp. flour
½ tsp. dry mustard
⅛ tsp. pepper

2 (1 lb.) cans lima beans
Light cream or dairy half-
  and-half
½ c. bread crumbs
2 tblsp. butter

Brown dried beef slightly in butter in skillet. Blend in flour, mustard and pepper.

Drain liquid from limas and add enough cream to make 2½ c. liquid. Stir into flour mixture and cook until thickened, stirring constantly.

Remove from heat. Add limas. Spoon into greased 2-qt. casserole. Toss bread crumbs with butter until well coated. Sprinkle over lima mixture. Bake in moderate oven (350°) until bubbly, 25 to 30 minutes. Makes 6 servings.

Broccoli Luncheon Special

For an informal neighborhood women's gathering at noon, green and red Broccoli Luncheon Special is an ideal choice. Make the toast cups ahead; fixing the filling for them is quick. The toast cups resemble flowers and they take the place of bread or rolls.

Since the toast holds the warm filling in place, you can serve a chilled salad on the plates with it. You'll not go wrong if you select a molded fruit salad. Among the fruits that are especially good with this dish are pineapple, grapefruit, cranberries or apricots.

BROCCOLI LUNCHEON SPECIAL

Simple, easy, colorful and tasty

1 (10 oz.) pkg. frozen
  chopped broccoli
1 (4 oz.) pkg. dried beef,
  shredded
2 tblsp. butter or margarine

2 tblsp. flour
1 c. milk
2 hard-cooked eggs, diced
Toast Cups

Cook broccoli by package directions; drain.
Cook dried beef with butter until frizzled; blend in

flour. Gradually stir in milk to make sauce. Then add broccoli and eggs. Spoon into Toast Cups. Makes 2⅔ cups.

Toast Cups: Cut crusts from bread slices, brush with melted butter and press slices into 3″ muffin-pan cups. Toast in moderate oven (350°) about 12 minutes, or until golden brown. Each cup will hold about 3 tblsp. broccoli.

Corned Beef with Vegetables

Corned beef is seldom made by farm homemakers today, but they buy it, sometimes canned, for its characteristic taste, especially in New England Boiled Dinner. This dish continues to hold its long-time place on the list of great American country dishes. It's a satisfying way to salvage some of your late garden vegetables.

Slices of this fork-tender meat on a big platter, wreathed with vegetables, tempt almost everyone. Be sure to have hot corn bread, a jar of prepared mustard and the ketchup bottle handy. Then give your family plenty of time to eat!

NEW ENGLAND BOILED DINNER

An old-fashioned dinner cooked in one kettle—
a modern favorite

1 (3 to 4 lb.) corned brisket of beef	4 parsnips, peeled and cut in halves crosswise
3 qts. water	3 onions, peeled and cut in halves crosswise
2 bay leaves	
¼ tsp. peppercorns	1 turnip, peeled and quartered
6 whole cloves	
6 whole medium potatoes, peeled	1 head cabbage, cut in 6 wedges
6 whole carrots, peeled	

Place meat in deep kettle. Cover with water. Add bay leaves, peppercorns and cloves. Cover, bring to a boil; reduce heat and simmer until tender, about 3 hours.

Add potatoes, carrots, parsnips, onions and turnip. Simmer 30 minutes. Add cabbage and continue cooking until all vegetables are tender, about 20 minutes.

Place meat in center of platter, and surround with vegetables. (Reserve the broth for soups.) Makes 6 servings.

NOTE: Many women prefer to cook a 5-lb. corned brisket of beef to have leftovers for sandwich making.

TOMATOES STUFFED
WITH CORNED BEEF HASH

Serve this for a supper main dish . . . pass biscuits hot from the oven

6 tomatoes	2 tblsp. chopped parsley
½ c. chopped onion	1 (1 lb.) can corned beef
2 tblsp. butter	hash
¼ tsp. salt	6 process cheese slices
⅛ tsp. pepper	

Cut slices from tops of tomatoes. Scoop out centers and save.

Cook onion in butter until soft. Add tomato pulp and cook, stirring occasionally, until thick. Add salt, pepper, parsley and corned beef hash. Stir well. Spoon into tomato cups.

Bake in moderate oven (350°) 30 minutes. Top each tomato with a cheese slice. Continue baking until cheese has melted. Makes 6 servings.

Vegetables with Lamb

Never underestimate the goodness of lamb teamed with vegetables. Lamb Pie Supreme and Rich Brown Lamb and Potato Dinner prove how rewarding the combination can be (especially if someone at your table thinks he doesn't like lamb). The men who taste-tested these two main dishes agreed with the home economists that they were superior.

LAMB PIE SUPREME

The batter makes a golden crust on this excellent stew— a praise-winner

2 lbs. lamb shoulder, cubed
½ c. flour
2 tblsp. salad oil
2 c. water
1 tblsp. salt
¼ tsp. pepper
1 tsp. Worcestershire sauce
1 clove garlic, minced
½ c. barley
1 c. sliced carrots

1 c. chopped onion
1½ c. sliced potatoes
½ c. diced celery
1 (1 lb.) can peas
2 c. sifted flour
½ tsp. salt
2 tsp. baking powder
3 tblsp. salad oil
1 c. milk
1 egg, beaten

Toss lamb in bag with ½ c. flour to coat lightly. Brown in 2 tblsp. hot oil. Add water, 1 tblsp. salt, pepper, Worcestershire sauce and garlic. Cook until meat is tender, about 1½ hours.

Add barley, carrots, onion, potatoes and celery. Drain peas, reserving liquid. Add peas to mixture and ½ c. liquid from peas. Simmer until vegetables are tender, about 30 minutes.

Meanwhile, prepare batter topping. Sift together 2 c. sifted flour, ½ tsp. salt and baking powder. Combine 3 tblsp. oil, milk and egg. Stir into flour mixture.

Spoon hot lamb mixture into 3-qt. casserole. Drop batter by spoonfuls over lamb, lightly spread to cover.

Bake in hot oven (400°) until topping is browned, about 30 minutes. Makes 6 servings.

RICH BROWN LAMB AND POTATO DINNER

You'll like this new taste for lamb and the vegetables that support it

¼ c. salad oil
6 meaty lamb shanks,
   cracked, or 6 thick
   shoulder lamb chops
2 tblsp. bottled browning
   sauce
1 c. hot water
⅓ c. mint jelly or mint-
   flavored apple jelly
2 tsp. garlic salt

¼ tsp. pepper
10 to 12 small whole
   potatoes, peeled, fresh
   or frozen
2 tblsp. flour
½ c. cold water
½ c. evaporated milk
2 (1 lb.) cans small whole
   boiled onions, drained
Salt and pepper to taste

Heat salad oil in large, deep skillet. Brush lamb shanks

with bottled sauce; stir remaining sauce into oil. Brown lamb well on all sides.

Combine hot water, jelly, garlic salt and pepper; add to browned shanks. Cover and simmer 1 hour, or until meat is tender.

Add potatoes and cook until tender, about 25 minutes for fresh, 15 for frozen potatoes.

Remove shanks and potatoes to a heated platter; keep warm.

Blend flour and ½ c. cold water together to make a smooth paste. Stir into drippings along with the milk; cook over medium heat, stirring until thick and smooth. Add drained onions; heat through. Season with salt and pepper. Pour some gravy over meat and potatoes; serve remainder separately. Makes 6 servings.

Vegetable-Pork Main Dishes

Pork of all kinds, including ham, bacon and sausage, appears in many much-praised country main dishes. Mexican Squash-Corn Casserole is one recipe from South of the Border that deserves a place in your repertoire of ways to team zucchini with pork steaks.

MEXICAN SQUASH-CORN CASSEROLE

*Serve this zucchini-corn treat with hot corn bread
and a tossed salad*

6 pork steaks, cut in ½"
  cubes
½ c. chopped onion
½ c. chopped green pepper
1 clove garlic, cut in half
  (optional)
Salt and pepper to taste

3 lbs. zucchini, cut in ¼"
  slices
1 (10 oz.) pkg. frozen
  whole kernel corn
1 (8 oz.) can tomato sauce,
  or 1 (1 lb.) can stewed
  tomatoes

Brown pork in skillet; remove with slotted spoon and reserve.

Cook onion, green pepper and garlic in pork fat in skillet about 10 minutes; remove from skillet and reserve, discarding garlic.

Return pork to skillet with salt, pepper and a small amount of water; cover and steam until tender.

Pour off all but 2 tblsp. fat from pork. Add cooked onion and green pepper, zucchini, corn and tomato sauce to pork. Simmer until zucchini is just done, about 15 minutes. Check for seasoning, adding more salt and pepper if necessary. Serve immediately. Makes 6 servings.

SCALLOPED POTATOES WITH PORK CHOPS

Cheese and celery soup give extra-good flavor
to this farm favorite

6 rib pork chops (½ to ¾" thick)
1 tblsp. salad oil
3 qts. sliced peeled potatoes (about 6 large)
½ c. chopped onion
1 tsp. salt

½ tsp. pepper
6 slices process cheese
1 can condensed cream of celery soup
1¾ c. milk
½ tsp. salt

Brown pork chops in salad oil in skillet.

Place half of potatoes in greased 13 × 9 × 2" casserole. Top with onion, ½ tsp. salt and ¼ tsp. pepper. Top with cheese slices, then remaining potatoes, ½ tsp. salt and ¼ tsp. pepper.

Blend together soup and milk in saucepan. Heat to boiling. Pour over potatoes. Top with pork chops. Sprinkle with ½ tsp. salt. Cover pan with foil.

Bake in moderate oven (350°) 30 minutes. Remove foil and continue baking until potatoes are tender, about 1 hour. Makes 6 servings.

PORK CHOP MAIN DISH

This meat dish is complete with vegetables—
and can be made in a hurry

8 loin pork chops
2 tblsp. salad oil
2 (5.8 oz.) pkgs. au gratin potato mix
2 tblsp. butter or margarine
4½ c. boiling water
1⅓ c. milk

Few drops Tabasco sauce
2 (10 oz.) pkgs. frozen green beans, partially thawed
¾ tsp. salt
¼ tsp. pepper
⅛ tsp. ground thyme

271

Brown pork chops on both sides in salad oil.

Meanwhile, place potato slices in 13 × 9 × 2″ pan. Sprinkle with the 2 packets of cheese sauce mix that come with potatoes.

Combine butter, boiling water, milk and Tabasco sauce. Pour over potatoes, stirring to mix in cheese.

Separate green beans and stir into potato mixture. Top with pork chops, overlapping if necessary. Sprinkle with salt, pepper and thyme.

Cover with foil and bake in moderate oven (375°) 35 minutes. Remove foil and continue baking until potatoes are tender and liquid is absorbed, 20 to 30 minutes. Makes 8 servings.

DEVILED BAKED BEANS

Spicy ham blends tastily with beans

1 c. sliced onions
2 tblsp. fat
1 (3 oz.) can deviled ham
1 tblsp. prepared mustard
2 tblsp. molasses
¼ tsp. salt

2 (1 lb. 5 oz.) cans pork and beans
2 fresh tomatoes, peeled and sliced, or 1 c. well-drained canned tomatoes

Cook onions in hot fat until transparent and golden in color.

Combine remaining ingredients, except tomatoes. Alternate layers of bean mixture, onion and tomato slices in greased 1½-qt. casserole.

Bake in moderate oven (350°) 30 minutes. Makes 6 to 8 servings.

All-American Ham 'n' Hominy

Our Indians get credit for teaching Europeans, the new settlers in America, how to turn corn into hominy. It was a tedious process but pioneers believed the results justified their efforts. Homemade hominy today is practically extinct, but there's plenty of it in cans on supermarket shelves ready to use.

Ham 'n' Hominy features a famous food team, for the

spicy, smoked meat and mild hominy complement each other. (Look in the Index for other hominy recipes.)

The corn meal in the Southwest that people use for making tortillas and other corn breads is actually ground hominy. In making hominy for this purpose, Southwesterners use lime water. It's the trace of lime left in the kernels, according to nutritionists, that helps account for the sound teeth many Spanish-Americans have.

HAM 'N' HOMINY

Ham tastily seasons hominy and adds protein
to this country fare

2 c. diced cooked ham	½ c. light cream or dairy
2 tblsp. butter	half-and-half
2 (1 lb.) cans hominy	¼ tsp. salt
	¼ tsp. pepper

Brown ham in melted butter slightly. Add remaining ingredients. Heat. Makes 6 servings.

Rancher Potato Special

Ranchers and farmers sometimes complete their day's business in town sooner than anticipated and head home early in the afternoon without eating dinner. When they come into the house, the usual question is: "What's to eat?" A second comment follows: "I'm hungry as a bear."

Most wives have a few favorite quick-to-get, satisfying dishes to make for these meals at off-beat hours. Rancher Potato Special is a good one to add to the collection. Made with potatoes, onion and ham and served hot from the skillet, it pleases.

RANCHER POTATO SPECIAL

Most ranchers know good spuds when they taste them—
here's an example

273

4 to 5 tblsp. lard
1 c. diced cooked ham
1 large baking potato,
  peeled and thinly sliced

1 large sweet onion, sliced,
  or 2 medium
Salt and pepper to taste
1 c. water

Put a large skillet over high heat and add lard. When sizzling, add ham and brown slightly. Add potatoes, onion, salt and pepper; mix thoroughly. Cook until potatoes are lightly browned, turning occasionally to avoid scorching. Add water and cover; lower heat and allow to simmer until water is absorbed (check occasionally so that potatoes do not scorch). Makes 1 big serving.

ACORN SQUASH WITH HAM AND APPLES

*Perfect main dish for supper and a good way
to use leftover ham*

3 acorn squash
½ tsp. salt
2 c. diced cooked ham
1 c. diced unpeeled tart
  apples

¼ c. brown sugar
½ tsp. dry mustard
⅛ tsp. pepper
2 tblsp. butter

Wash and cut squash in halves lengthwise. Remove seeds. Place, cut side down, in 15½ × 10½ × 1" jelly roll pan. Pour in ¼" boiling water; bake in hot oven (400°) 30 minutes.

Remove from oven and turn squash halves cut side up. Sprinkle with salt.

Combine ham, apples, brown sugar, mustard and pepper. Spoon into squash cavities. Top each with 1 tsp. butter.

Return to oven and bake until apples are tender, 20 to 25 minutes. Makes 6 servings.

SCALLOPED POTATOES AND HAM

A favorite way to serve potatoes

¾ lb. ham, cut in ½"
  cubes
1 tblsp. ham drippings or
  shortening
2 tblsp. flour

2 c. milk
6 to 8 medium potatoes,
  peeled and sliced
1 tsp. salt
⅛ tsp. pepper

Lightly brown ham in hot drippings in skillet. Blend in flour.

Heat milk to boiling; add ham and potatoes, and again heat to boiling. Add salt and pepper.

Place in greased 2-qt. casserole. Bake in slow oven (325°) 30 to 45 minutes, until potatoes are tender. Makes 6 servings.

HAM WITH VEGETABLES

Ham, apple juice and vegetables make this
a fine-flavored dish

1 (2 to 3 lb.) smoked pork
  shoulder butt
1 (1 lb.) can sauerkraut
  (2 c.)

2 c. apple juice
6 medium potatoes, peeled
3 onions, halved
6 carrots, peeled

Place pork butt in large Dutch oven or kettle. Add sauerkraut and apple juice. Cover and bring to a boil. Reduce heat and simmer 45 minutes.

Add potatoes, onions and carrots. Continue simmering until tender, 45 minutes to 1 hour. Makes 6 servings.

BAKED BEAN STACK-UPS

Try these quick and easy hot sandwiches—
they rate with all ages

3 hot dog buns, halved
Butter or margarine
1 (1 lb.) can baked beans,
  or 2 c. leftover baked
  beans

3 to 4 tblsp. ketchup
⅓ lb. American cheese,
  grated
6 slices bacon

Toast cut sides of bun halves under broiler until lightly browned. Spread with butter.

Top buns with beans, ketchup and cheese; lay a bacon slice over each. Broil about 3″ from heat until cheese is melted and bacon is crisp. Serve very hot. Makes 6 servings.

NOTE: You can use round hamburger buns instead of long

hot dog buns. Just cut each bacon slice in half and arrange over top of each sandwich.

Vegetables and Sausage

The recipe for Lentils and Sausage comes from the West, where lentils grow. With lentils, carrots, onions, frozen Swiss chard and smoked pork sausage cooked together, you produce a substantial dish that's a real treat in cold weather.

If you have teen-agers at your house, you'll want to make Potato-Franks. Our taste-testers include a family of three boys and all gave the dish a perfect score.

LENTILS AND SAUSAGE

Substantial and mighty good eating

1½ c. lentils	1 tsp. salt
1 large onion, sliced	Few grains coarse grind
2 carrots, sliced	pepper
1 (12 oz.) pkg. frozen	2 c. boiling water
Swiss chard	1 (1 to 1½ lb.) smoked
1 bay leaf	pork sausage ring

Rinse lentils thoroughly. Combine with remaining ingredients, except sausage. Bring to a boil; lower heat and simmer gently 30 minutes.

Add sausage; continue to cook 20 to 30 minutes longer. Remove to serving platter; slice sausage and place in overlapping rows on top. Makes 6 to 8 servings.

POTATO-FRANKS

Youngsters call these groovy

¾ c. flour	1 tsp. prepared mustard
½ tsp. salt	6 frankfurters
1 tsp. baking powder	2 c. cold mashed potatoes
1 egg	1 c. cracker crumbs
½ c. milk	Fat or oil for deep-fat
2 tblsp. salad oil	frying

Make batter by sifting together flour, salt and baking powder.

Beat egg; stir in milk, salad oil and mustard. Stir into flour mixture and beat until smooth.

Parboil frankfurters 5 minutes in simmering water; drain. Pat mashed potatoes (made with butter and milk added) around frankfurters to coat completely.

Pour batter into shallow pan, such as a pie pan. Dip potato-coated frankfurters in batter, then roll them in cracker crumbs.

Fry in deep fat heated to 350° about 12 minutes, or until golden brown. Drain on paper towels; serve hot. Makes 6 servings.

LIMA BEAN-SAUSAGE BAKE

Well-seasoned, and kind-to-the-budget main dish hearty enough to satisfy

1 lb. dried lima beans (2 c.)	¼ c. liquid from cooked
6 c. water	beans
2 tsp. salt	1 tsp. horse-radish
2 lbs. pork sausage links	2 tsp. Worcestershire sauce
½ c. chopped onion	2 tblsp. brown sugar
1 c. ketchup	

Wash beans, cover with water. Bring to a boil and boil 2 minutes. Remove from heat and let stand, covered, 1 hour. Add salt and simmer until tender, about 1 hour. Drain, reserving liquid.

Brown sausage links in skillet. Remove from skillet. Add onion and cook until soft. Remove onion from skillet and add to beans. Combine with ketchup, ¼ c. liquid from beans, horse-radish, Worcestershire sauce and brown sugar.

Place half of beans in greased 2½-qt. casserole. Top with half of sausage. Repeat layers. Bake in moderate oven (350°) 35 to 40 minutes. Makes 8 servings.

BROCCOLI WITH SAUSAGE

An extra-good, different way to fix broccoli—spinach, too

½ lb. bulk pork sausage   ½ tsp. salt
2 (10 to 12 oz.) pkgs.
  frozen chopped broccoli

Brown sausage in heavy saucepan; break into small pieces. Add frozen broccoli; cover and steam until tender, about 20 to 25 minutes. Season with salt, or, if desired, with a little soy sauce. Makes 6 servings.

POPPYKRAUT VIENNESE

Exciting new way to fix sauerkraut

1 small onion, chopped
1 tblsp. butter or margarine
1 (4 oz.) can Vienna sausage
1 (15 oz.) can sauerkraut

1 tsp. poppy seeds
¼ c. herb-seasoned bread
  stuffing
1 tblsp. butter, melted

Cook onion in 1 tblsp. butter until tender. Add drained Vienna sausages, cut in bite-size pieces; cook until browned. Combine with sauerkraut and poppy seeds. Put in 1-qt. casserole.

Combine bread stuffing with melted butter; sprinkle over sauerkraut. Bake in moderate oven (375°) about 30 minutes. Makes 4 servings.

NOTE: You can double this recipe and bake in 1½-qt. casserole for 8 servings.

Vegetable-Chicken Main Dishes

Chicken cooked with vegetables tastes so different from chicken with mashed potatoes and gravy that many women depend on the combination to provide a change of pace in their chicken dinners. Mushrooms, a vegetable with many friends, take the spotlight in Mushroom-Cheese Strata, which contains chicken. This is a fine dish to tote to potluck suppers, but fix it for the family, too . . . really delicious.

BROCCOLI-CHICKEN

Luncheon main dish—serve with a molded cranberry or other fruit salad

2 c. diced cooked chicken
1 (10 oz.) pkg. frozen
  broccoli stalks, cooked
  by package directions
½ tsp. salt

1 can condensed cream of
  chicken soup
½ c. mayonnaise
2 tsp. lemon juice
¼ tsp. curry powder

Place chicken and broccoli in bottom of 1½-qt. casserole. Sprinkle with salt. Combine remaining ingredients and spread over top of chicken-broccoli mixture.

Bake, uncovered, in moderate oven (350°) until bubbling hot, about 30 minutes. Serve hot. Makes 4 servings.

NOTE: To make 8 servings, bake 2 casseroles of Broccoli-Chicken.

MUSHROOM-CHEESE STRATA

Perfect for a women's luncheon

1 lb. fresh mushrooms,
  sliced, or 1 (8 oz.) can
  sliced mushrooms,
  drained
½ c. finely chopped onion
¼ c. butter or margarine,
  melted
10 slices white bread

2 c. shredded process
  American cheese
2 c. diced cooked chicken
  or turkey
5 eggs, slightly beaten
2¾ c. milk
1 tsp. salt
⅛ tsp. pepper

Cook mushrooms and onion in butter until onion is soft.

Trim off bread crusts. With a 3″ cutter, cut a round from each slice of bread and set aside. Tear remaining pieces of bread into greased 3-qt. casserole. Top with mushroom mixture, then cheese and chicken. Arrange circles of bread, overlapping a little, around edge of casserole.

Combine the remaining ingredients. Pour over casserole, being sure to moisten bread thoroughly. Bake in moderate oven (350°) 1 hour and 15 minutes, or until top is lightly browned and mixture is set. Makes 8 servings.

NOTE: You can fix dish a couple of hours ahead, refrigerate and bake when getting remainder of meal.

VEGETABLES 'N' CHICKEN IN PAPRIKA SAUCE

A new way to fix chicken and fresh vegetables. Sauce is good on cooked noodles, rice or baked potatoes

4 lbs. frying chicken pieces
¼ c. butter or margarine
2 green peppers, seeded and cut in large pieces
10 small white onions, peeled
4 large tomatoes, cut in wedges, or 12 whole cherry tomatoes
4 branches celery, cut in pieces

¾ c. dairy sour cream
½ can condensed cream of mushroom soup
1 tblsp. paprika
⅛ tsp. ground red pepper (cayenne)
2 tsp. salt
¼ tsp. Worcestershire sauce
1 to 2 tblsp. cornstarch
2 tblsp. cold water (about)

Brown pieces of chicken in butter in large skillet or Dutch oven. Add vegetables; simmer, covered, 15 minutes.

Combine sour cream, soup, paprika, red pepper, salt and Worcestershire sauce in a small saucepan. Heat just to boiling point over moderate heat, stirring constantly.

Pour sauce over chicken and vegetables. Cover and continue cooking over low heat about 1 hour, or until chicken is fork-tender. If sauce is thin, thicken with cornstarch dissolved in cold water. Makes 6 to 8 servings.

Nobody splits "split peas." They have a natural break which splits them apart when they're dried.

VEGETABLE-CHICKEN BAKE

Try this country-style company dish

Thighs, drumsticks and
breasts of 2 (3 lb.) frying
chickens
½ c. flour
1 tsp. salt
¼ tsp. pepper
½ c. butter
1 c. rice
3 medium onions, peeled
and cut in halves

1 medium eggplant, peeled
and cubed
½ lb. fresh mushrooms,
sliced
1 (4 oz.) can pimientos,
drained and chopped
1 clove garlic, minced
1¾ c. chicken broth
1½ tsp. salt
¼ tsp. pepper

Shake chicken pieces in bag with mixture of flour, 1 tsp.
salt and ¼ tsp. pepper. Fry in melted butter in Dutch
oven until brown on all sides.

Add remaining ingredients. Cover and bake in moderate
oven (375°) until vegetables and chicken are tender, 50
to 55 minutes. Makes 6 servings.

VEGETABLE-CHICKEN SKILLET SUPPER

*Sure to please a hungry family—the water chestnuts
add crunch*

3½ lbs. chicken pieces
(thighs, legs, breasts)
2 tsp. garlic salt
½ tsp. pepper
¼ c. salad oil
1 c. sliced onions
1 (8 oz.) can tomato sauce
2 c. canned or homemade
chicken broth (skim off
fat)
1 c. tomato juice

1 c. diagonally sliced celery
1 c. sliced carrots
¾ c. parboiled rice, or 1 c.
raw rice (not instant)
1 tblsp. parsley flakes
¼ c. chopped pimiento
(optional)
1 (8½ oz.) can water
chestnuts, drained and
sliced

Sprinkle chicken pieces with garlic salt and pepper.
Heat oil in large chicken fryer or Dutch oven; brown
chicken quickly in oil. Reduce heat and push chicken to
one side.

Cook onion slices in oil until clear and tender. Stir in
tomato sauce, chicken broth, tomato juice, celery, carrots
and rice. Cover and cook over medium heat 25 minutes.

Add parsley flakes, pimiento and water chestnuts. Simmer, uncovered, 5 minutes. Let stand a few minutes to thicken. Skim off any excess oil. Makes 6 to 7 servings.

VEGETABLE CHICKEN-HAM CURRY

Another tasty supper recipe you'll want to double
for company

4 to 5 green onions with tops, sliced	2 tblsp. shredded coconut
1 clove garlic, minced	3 to 4 canned green chili peppers, sliced
1 tsp. curry powder	½ c. water
⅓ c. butter or margarine	½ tsp. salt
1 (10 oz.) pkg. frozen mixed vegetables	1 c. diced cooked chicken
	1 c. diced cooked ham

Cook onions, garlic and curry powder in butter until light golden yellow. Add vegetables, coconut, chili peppers, water and salt. Stir lightly to blend.

Cover and simmer until vegetables are tender-crisp, about 10 minutes. Add chicken and ham and continue cooking just enough to heat thoroughly. Serve over hot rice. Makes 4 to 5 servings.

NOTE: You can use 2 c. diced cooked chicken and omit the ham, if desired.

Vegetables with Tuna and Salmon

Some of the best main dishes made with tuna and canned salmon owe their success to their combination with vegetables. Corn and Tuna Bake, Baked Stuffed Tomatoes and Salmon-Stuffed Tomatoes are welcome lunch or supper dishes.

CORN AND TUNA BAKE

A supper main dish they'll like

¼ c. chopped onion
2 tblsp. butter
2 tblsp. flour
2 (12 oz.) cans whole kernel
  corn
Light cream or dairy half-
  and-half

½ tsp. salt
¼ tsp. pepper
2 (7 oz.) cans tuna
½ c. dry bread crumbs
2 tblsp. melted butter

Cook onion in 2 tblsp. butter until tender. Blend in flour. Drain liquid from corn and add enough cream to make 2 c. liquid. Add to flour mixture and cook until thickened, stirring constantly.

Add seasonings, corn, tuna, broken into chunks, and oil from tuna. Put in greased 2-qt. casserole; top with bread crumbs tossed with 2 tblsp. melted butter. Bake in moderate oven (350°) until bubbly, about 30 minutes. Makes 6 servings.

VARIATION

Mexican Corn-Tuna Bake: Substitute 2 (12 oz.) cans Mexicorn for the whole kernel corn.

TUNA-BROCCOLI SUPREME

*An easy dish in which lemon juice points up
the best flavors*

2 (10 oz.) pkgs. frozen
  chopped broccoli
2 cans condensed cream of
  mushroom soup

⅔ c. milk
⅓ c. lemon juice
2 (7 oz.) cans tuna, drained
1 c. crushed potato chips

Cook broccoli in boiling salted water until all pieces are separated. Drain.

Blend together soup and milk. Stir in lemon juice and tuna. Add broccoli. Spoon into greased 2½-qt. casserole. Top with crushed potato chips.

Bake in moderate oven (350°) until bubbling, about 30 minutes. Makes 8 servings.

BAKED STUFFED TOMATOES

*Just the right vegetable to serve with your next
fish supper*

6 large tomatoes
2 slices bread, crusts
  removed and crumbled
1 (7 oz.) can tuna, drained
  and flaked
6 anchovies, chopped
1 tblsp. grated onion
½ tsp. garlic salt

⅛ tsp. pepper
½ tsp. basil leaves
Salt
¼ c. dry bread crumbs
2 tblsp. butter
2 tblsp. grated Parmesan
  cheese

Cut tops from tomatoes and discard. Scoop out pulp
and chop it. Combine 1½ c. tomato pulp with bread, tuna,
anchovies, onion, garlic salt, pepper and basil.

Salt tomato cups lightly and fill with tuna mixture. Toss
¼ c. bread crumbs with melted butter and Parmesan
cheese. Sprinkle over tuna mixture.

Place in oiled muffin-pan cups and bake in moderate
oven (375°) about 25 minutes. Makes 6 servings.

TUNA-STUFFED PEPPERS

*Stuff green peppers to brighten your meals—
tuna stuffing is different*

6 green peppers
1 (6 to 7 oz.) can tuna,
  drained
1 c. dry bread crumbs
1 (15 oz.) can tomato
  sauce with tomato bits
1 tsp. salt

⅛ tsp. pepper
1 tsp. minced onion
½ c. bread crumbs
2 tblsp. butter or margarine
3 slices process cheese, cut
  in halves

Cut tops from green peppers; remove seeds and membrane. Parboil 5 minutes in boiling salted water. Drain
and place in muffin-pan cups.

Combine tuna, 1 c. crumbs, 1 c. tomato sauce, salt,
pepper and onion; mix well.

Fill peppers with tuna mixture; sprinkle tops with ½ c.

bread crumbs; dot with butter. Bake in moderate oven (350°) 25 minutes. Remove from oven.

Lay cheese slices on top of peppers and run under broiler just long enough to melt cheese.

Meanwhile, heat remainder of tomato sauce. Serve peppers with hot tomato sauce spooned over. Makes 6 servings.

SALMON-STUFFED TOMATOES

Serve these with hot corn muffins and bowls of
Lima Bean Chowder (see Index) at a women's luncheon

6 medium tomatoes, chilled	1 tblsp. chopped green
1 (1 lb.) can salmon (2 c.),	pepper
drained	¼ tsp. salt
½ c. diced cucumber	⅛ tsp. pepper
½ c. diced celery	1 tblsp. lemon juice
1 tblsp. chopped green	¾ c. mayonnaise
onion	Chopped parsley (optional)

Place tomatoes in boiling water 20 seconds. Slip off skin. Cut slices off tops; scoop out centers. Carefully turn upside down to drain on paper toweling while you make salmon mixture.

Break salmon into small pieces. Remove bones and skin. Combine with cucumber, celery, onion, green pepper, salt, pepper, lemon juice and mayonnaise.

Lightly salt inside of tomatoes. Fill with salmon mixture. Garnish with chopped parsley, if desired. Makes 6 servings.

BAKED SALMON AND PEAS

Salmon, cottage cheese and vegetables share honors
in this supper main dish

⅓ c. chopped onion	1 can condensed cream of
⅓ c. chopped celery	mushroom soup
¼ c. chopped green pepper	1 c. small curd creamed
¼ c. butter	cottage cheese
3 tblsp. flour	1 (1 lb.) can peas, drained
1 tsp. salt	(2 c.)
¼ tsp. pepper	1 (1 lb.) can pink salmon
1 c. milk	2 c. crushed potato chips

Cook onion, celery and green pepper in butter in saucepan until soft. Blend in flour, salt and pepper. Combine milk and mushroom soup; add to saucepan and cook, stirring constantly, until mixture comes to a boil. Remove from heat and add cottage cheese.

In bottom of greased 2-qt. casserole, add half of peas and salmon; top with half of soup mixture and potato chips. Repeat layers.

Bake in moderate oven (350°) until bubbling, 25 to 30 minutes. Makes 6 to 8 servings.

CHAPTER SEVEN

Vegetable Salads

MORE AND more, in America, salads are becoming the big vegetable success story. Tossed green salads with leaves so crisp they crackle under a fork; shimmering, delicate molded salads that quiver slightly; shredded cabbage with sweet-sour cream dressing in true country style—these and many other vegetable salads tempt the appetite and please the palate.

Men who once called salad greens "fodder" or "woman-food" now take second helpings when they have a chance. Just watch them at outdoor barbecue meals, or at buffets in the church basement. For additional proof of salad popularity, look at the makings for them in supermarkets. Decorative as these vegetables are, they are on display because you and other customers want them.

A plus for salads is that they contain many healthful vitamins and food mineral substances the human body needs. Mothers and wives take comfort in knowing vegetable salads help them feed their families well.

One added reason for salad success is that we know more about how to select, store and prepare salad vegetables. This chapter gives the latest approved methods. Our kitchen wisdom about teaming vegetables with various dressings increases every year (sse Salad Dressings in Index). This chapter tells how to fix ahead all or parts of salads to relieve the last-minute rush at mealtime.

We include vegetable salad recipes for all seasons. Pink and green Pea-Shrimp Salad is perfect for the guest supper or lunch when new peas are ready in the garden. Salads with zucchini show how to use the squash when abundant. Tomato Perfection and Hearty Beet Salads provide cheerful splashes of color in winter meals, and cool-looking Cucumber Green Salad perks up jaded hot weather appetites.

This chapter starts with tossed salads. We'll tempt you by suggesting that you be sure to make the classic, special-occasion Caesar Salad, a California original. Then take your choice of the marvelous salad recipes in this chapter. They'll bring you compliments aplenty.

The Remarkable Lettuce Family

Beautiful, tender, fresh green lettuce makes beautiful, fresh-tasting salads. Don't settle for one leaf lettuce and familiar head lettuce—get acquainted with the *many* kinds available today. Your rewards in good eating will be great and your reputation as a champion salad maker will rise. Here are some of the favorite lettuces:

Bunching or Looseleaf Lettuce: Many kinds of bunching lettuce come to our tables and most of them have leaves with ruffled edges. One exception is delicate oak leaf lettuce; its leaves are the shape of those on oak trees. Red bunching lettuce has reddish-bronze leaves; it grows in California but is shipped to all parts of the country.

All bunching lettuce, including that which grows in your garden, is exceptionally tender in its prime. It is therefore ideal for wilting, for combining with country-style cream dressings and for combining with other kinds of greens in salad bowls. You'll find garden leaf lettuce in markets most of the year now. Commercial gardeners grow it in greenhouses during the cold months, in truck gardens during the other seasons.

Select bunching or looseleaf lettuce with fresh, tender, soft leaves. Avoid wilted bunches.

Allow 1 large bunch for 4 servings.

Once this lettuce is in the kitchen, rinse it under running cold water and shake off the excess water. Put it in a plastic bag or wrap it in plastic film. Store in the refrigerator crisper. It will hold in good condition up to 3 days.

When ready to use, cut off base stem. Separate leaves and wash them in cool water. Drain in colander or wire salad basket. Remove all the water before adding salad dressing by twirling it in salad basket or patting dry with paper towels. (Do you know the wire salad basket? Many housewares sections in department stores now carry this European utensil—a good way to shake excess water off greens.) Add the dressing just before serving and hurry to the table.

288

Butterhead Lettuce: Members of this branch of the lettuce family have rather small, soft heads; the tops are somewhat flat with a rosette pattern in the center. The inner leaves feel a little buttery when you touch them, which explains how they got their name. Three varieties are available throughout the year in markets and in some home gardens during spring—Big Boston, White Boston and Bibb. The cup-shaped leaves are a medium green on the outside shading to a lighter green or yellowish green in the center. Big Boston lettuce leaves have a brownish tint at the edge. Bibb lettuce heads are small and tulip-shaped; like other butterhead varieties, their flavor is delicate and sweet.

Select heads that appear fresh without signs of wilting.

Allow 1 medium head of Boston lettuce for 4 servings of tossed salad, 1 head Bibb lettuce for 1 serving.

When butterhead lettuce reaches the kitchen, wrap it in plastic film or put in plastic bag and store in refrigerator crisper. It will hold in top condition 2 to 3 days.

When ready to use, trim stem and remove any discolored or wilted leaves. Run cool water into the center of the head. If you find grit at the base of the leaves, break them off, one at a time, and swish them in cool water. You will find the leaves separate easily. Drain them in a colander or wire salad basket and twirl them gently in basket or in a clean dish towel to dry them; or pat them dry with paper towels. Place in bowl, cover with plastic film and store in refrigerator until the latest minute possible before serving.

For tossed salads, tear Boston lettuce in bite-size pieces and cut Bibb lettuce heads in quarters. Toss with salad dressing at the last moment before mealtime, or at the table, and serve on chilled plates.

Crisphead Lettuce: Iceberg lettuce is the most widely used member of this branch of the lettuce family, but there are other kinds, such as the Great Lakes varieties. Iceberg lettuce grows extensively in California and Arizona and also in Texas, New Mexico, Colorado and other states. It is sometimes called Western Iceberg Lettuce, although it also grows in the East. This is the lettuce most women mean when they speak of "head lettuce." The heads are fairly large and firm with medium green, crisp leaves. It's available 12 months of the year.

Select heads of medium weight for their size. Gently

squeeze the head; if it gives a little, it's an indication that the lettuce is of top quality. Look for fresh-appearing leaves and avoid heavy, hard heads which may be over-mature and bitter. The reddish discoloration at the stem base is not a sign of age, but rather that nature healed the cut made in harvesting.

Allow 1 head for 4 to 6 servings of tossed salad.

If you will not serve the salad for several days, rinse the head in cool water, shake off excess water and put in plastic bag. (Some women like to tuck a few paper towels in bag to absorb any water not removed by shaking.) Store in the refrigerator crisper. The lettuce will hold at least a week.

If you are going to use the lettuce within a day or two, or are ready to fix salad with the chilled head, remove the core with a little knife. Hold the head upside-down under running cool water so that it runs into the center of the head. Then turn upright in colander or wire salad basket to drain. Twirl lettuce in basket or a clean dish towel or pat leaves dry with paper towels. Put in bowl, cover with plastic film and store in refrigerator until the last minute before mealtime.

You may cut iceberg lettuce in quarters for wedges; slice or shred lettuce to make a base for other vegetables, fruits, sea food, chicken, et cetera; pull off leaves to make lettuce cups; or tear leaves in bite-size pieces for tossed salad.

When ready to serve, arrange or combine salad at last moment possible. Either add dressing in the kitchen just before serving or add at the table. Chill and drain foods before adding them to tossed salads.

Romaine or Cos Lettuce: This lettuce looks different from other members of the family. Its head is elongated and the deep green leaves also are long and rather coarse; their midribs are heavy. Romaine is tender and it has a slightly sharp taste. It is available throughout the year.

Select heads with fresh-appearing leaves and with as few blemishes as possible.

Allow 1 head for 4 servings unless combined with other greens; then allow 1 head for 6 or 8 servings.

Rinse head in running cool water, shake off excess water and wrap in plastic film or put in plastic bag. Store in refrigerator crisper. It will hold a week.

When ready to use, cut off base, break off leaves and

wash them, one by one, in cool water; drain in colander or wire salad basket. Pat each leaf dry with paper towels. If you want to cut out heavy midribs, do it this way: Lay leaf on cutting board and, with a sharp knife, make two quick cuts, one on each side of the midrib. Out it comes. Tear leaf in bite-size pieces for tossed salads, place in bowl, cover with plastic film and store in refrigerator until the last minute before serving.

Add the salad dressing and toss in kitchen or at the table. If you wish to garnish salad bowl with romaine leaves, add them in the kitchen after tossing salad. Using attractive whole leaves, cut points on leaf tips with kitchen shears or lay them on cutting board and cut the points with a sharp knife. Tuck the whole leaves, pointed ends up, under salad around the edge of the bowl to give the salad an attractive green frame.

Variety Salad Greens

There are many salad greens, cousins of lettuce, that add variety in taste, color and texture to tossed salads. You can combine them with lettuce. Among the dependable favorites are these:

Endive, Curly (Chicory): This vegetable has floppy heads with feathery, narrow, crisp leaves with edges that curl tightly. Leaves are deep green on the outside, fading to a bleached yellowish center; midribs are heavy. Curly endive or chicory has a slightly bitter taste in comparison with lettuce. Although it is available throughout the year, like escarole, it is most plentiful in winter and spring.

Select fresh-appearing, crisp, tender leaves with good green coloring on the outer edges.

Since curly endive is almost always combined with other salad greens in tossed salads, buy 1 head at a time.

Hold the head under running cool water; shake to remove surplus water. Wrap in plastic film or place in plastic bag and store in refrigerator crisper. It will hold a week or longer.

When ready to use, hold head under running cool water and break off leaves. Drain in colander or wire salad basket and pat dry with paper towels. Tear in bite-size pieces, put in a bowl, cover with plastic film and chill until the last minute before serving.

Add salad dressing, toss and serve.

Endive, Belgian: Witloof or Belgian endive is quite different from curly endive. It is a compact, cigar-shaped plant that is creamy white due to bleaching. Commercial vegetable farmers grow it in complete darkness. While it is available from September to May, it usually appears only in metropolitan markets and its price is comparatively high. It is considered a delicacy.

Select fresh-appearing, well-bleached stalks 4 to 6" long.

There are 4 to 6 stalks, depending on size, in 1 lb. Belgian endive. Allow 1 stalk for 1 serving.

Keep endive wrapped when storing it, to prevent leaves from turning green. Wrap in plastic film or put in plastic bag and place in refrigerator crisper. Use within a day or two.

When ready to use, quickly wash in cool water, dry gently with paper towels, cut thin slice from stem base of each stalk and then cut each stalk in half lengthwise or separate each stalk as recipe suggests.

Serve on chilled salad plates with French or other salad dressing.

To cook Belgian endive, place in saucepan containing 1" boiling chicken broth or salted water. Cover and simmer 20 to 25 minutes or until tender, adding more broth or water if needed. Drain and add butter, salt and pepper. Serve hot. (Some cooks add lemon juice to the cooking broth or water to keep the endive white.)

Escarole: Escarole is a cross between lettuce and curly endive or chicory. It resembles curly endive, but its leaves are much broader and they are less curled or wrinkled. Select escarole by the same guidelines as for curly endive; store and use it in the same way.

Water Cress: The shiny, small leaves of water cress are round and deep green; they grow on narrow stalks. While this spicy vegetable is highly esteemed for a garnish, it also is excellent in tossed green salads. It is available throughout the year. (If you have the right kind of water supply on your farm, try growing water cress. You need a clear, cool running stream or spring of fresh, pure water.)

Select bright, deep green water cress with crisp leaves.

Pour a little cool water into a jar and place water cress stems, not leaves, in the water; cover with plastic bag or jar cap and store in refrigerator. Use within 3 or 4 days.

When ready to use, remove heavy stem ends and add leaves to tossed salads. (Do not remove stems when you use sprays of water cress for garnishing salads, meat platters, et cetera.) Some women chop water cress leaves and sprinkle them over salads.

Parsley: You can use parsley to garnish salads and you can add it to green salads, like cress, after removing heavy stem ends. (See chapter on Garden-Fresh Vegetables.)

More Good Salad Makings

Radishes: Although radishes contribute color and crisp texture to more relish trays and plates than to salads, they are delicious when sliced in tossed salads. They are available the year round, but are more plentiful from May to July. Radishes come in red and white.

Select well-formed, medium-size (¾ to 1½″ in diameter) radishes that are plump, firm and of good color. Fresh-appearing green tops indicate quality.

Allow 2 bunches for 6 servings on the relish tray, 1 bunch to slice for a salad that makes 6 servings.

Put in a plastic bag and store in refrigerator. Radishes will hold about a week.

When ready to serve in salads, wash, cut off tops and rootlets and slice. Refrigerate on ice until time to toss into the salad.

Ever cook radishes? Simmer them, whole, in ½″ boiling salted water 5 to 10 minutes. Drain, season with salt, pepper, butter and a dash of lemon juice. Serve hot. They taste something like mild turnips.

Chinese Cabbage: This vegetable has a pleasing texture and a fascinating half-and-half flavor—half celery and half cabbage. It is an elongated plant about the size of a small bunch of celery. The white-green leaves are compact, crisp and firm.

Select fresh-appearing plants that are free from blemishes.

Allow 1 medium head for 4 servings.

Rinse in cool water and shake to remove excess water. Wrap in plastic film or put in plastic bag and store in refrigerator crisper. Chinese cabbage will hold a week or longer.

When ready to use, cut off root and shred fine with knife or tear in bite-size pieces, depending on the kind of salad you are making. If you have a large head of Chinese cabbage, you can cut slices 1″ thick, starting at base. Serve the slices (they'll stay in circles) on salad plates with Thousand Island dressing.

You can cook shredded Chinese cabbage in ½″ boiling salted water for 5 to 10 minutes, drain and season with butter, salt and pepper.

Other Good Salad Makings

Many uncooked vegetables, described in the chapter on Garden-Fresh Vegetables, are delightful additions to green salads. Among them are tender broccoli heads or buds, young spinach and mustard leaves, tomatoes, cucumbers, cabbage, green onions, celery, zucchini cut in strips or slices, cauliflower flowerets, green and red sweet peppers, carrots and others.

Some tender-crisp cooked vegetables, such as green or wax beans, also are fine to toss in salads.

Last-Minute Salads

Some of the most fabulous salads take little fixing, but you toss or combine the ingredients at the last minute, or just before mealtime or at the table. Certainly, most green salads are in this class. Among them is Caesar Salad. This star salad was originated by a Southern California chef, more than a quarter century ago. His idea skyrocketed— thousands of hosts and hostesses across country started making it. When the newness of such an astonishingly successful dish wears off, it usually fades away. Not so with Caesar Salad. Many hostesses still consider it tops in green salads. Here is the authentic recipe:

CAESAR SALAD

*This is our most famous tossed salad—it makes
its own tangy dressing*

1 clove garlic	Freshly ground pepper
¾ c. olive or salad oil	1 egg
2 c. croutons from French bread	¼ c. lemon juice
2 large heads romaine	¼ tsp. Worcestershire sauce
½ tsp. salt	½ c. grated Parmesan cheese

Crush garlic in small bowl. Add oil and let stand several hours.

Cut croutons in ½″ cubes; brown in ¼ c. of the garlic oil in skillet. (Or, if you prefer, toss bread in oil and toast in slow oven.)

Tear romaine in bite-size pieces and put in large salad bowl. Sprinkle with salt and pepper.

Place egg in small pan of cold water. Bring to a boil and simmer 1 minute. Break over salad. Add oil, lemon juice, Worcestershire sauce and cheese. Toss until every leaf is coated. Add croutons and toss. Serve immediately. Makes 10 to 12 servings.

NOTE: This salad is traditionally made at the table, but you can add egg to lemon juice and Worcestershire sauce and beat with rotary beater before adding to salad (in case children or a guest might object to seeing the almost raw egg)—really tastes marvelous.

SALAD BOWL

He-man tossed salad

2 tblsp. sesame seeds, toasted	3 tblsp. grated Parmesan cheese
1 head lettuce or endive	1 green pepper, cut in strips
6 tblsp. grated Romano cheese	1 bunch radishes, sliced
	Italian-style dressing

Toast sesame seeds in heavy skillet until medium brown, or spread in pan and toast in moderate oven (350°) about 20 minutes, stirring two or three times.

Break or tear lettuce or endive in small pieces. Place in salad bowl and add cheese, green pepper and radishes. Sprinkle sesame seeds over salad in bowl and toss with Italian-style or French dressing. Serve at once after tossing. Makes 4 to 5 servings.

ARTICHOKE SALAD BOWL

This recipe comes from Hawaii—it makes an elegant tossed salad

½ c. salad oil
½ c. vinegar
2 tblsp. water
4 thin slices onion
1 clove garlic, minced
¼ tsp. celery seeds
½ tsp. salt
⅛ tsp. pepper

1 (9 oz.) pkg. frozen
   artichoke hearts
2 qts. torn salad greens
1 tomato, chopped
½ tsp. salt
Freshly ground pepper to
   taste
2 to 3 tblsp. vinegar

Combine oil, ½ c. vinegar, water, onion, garlic, celery seeds, ½ tsp. salt and ⅛ tsp. pepper in saucepan. Bring mixture to a boil. Add artichoke hearts and cook until tender, about 5 minutes. Cool in cooking liquid, then chill until serving time.

When ready to serve, put salad greens (lettuce, endive, spinach, etc.) and chilled mixture in salad bowl. Add tomato, ½ tsp. salt, pepper and 2 to 3 tblsp. vinegar. Toss gently. Makes 8 to 10 servings.

Butter Bowl Salad

If you've never eaten salad with delicately browned butter and lemon juice taking the place of oil and vinegar dressing, you've missed one of the good things of life. Most people taste this first in California, land of marvelous salads, where hostesses have served it for several years. In fact, our recipe comes from there, contributed by a home economist-homemaker.

Butter is more of a stranger on lettuce than cream. Certainly country dwellers know how extraordinarily good garden lettuce is with cream, a little salt, sugar and vinegar. Butter tastes different, but is equally delicious. It's an important ingredient in Butter Bowl Salad, which is superior in every way. Use care not to scorch the butter. Watch it the few seconds of heating (in a small skillet) until it turns a light golden color, not a dark brown. And don't let the salad stand; serve it immediately after adding the butter.

BUTTER BOWL SALAD

Browned butter contributes extra-good flavor
to this superb salad

½ head lettuce, shredded
1 avocado, peeled and
  cubed
1 grapefruit, peeled and
  separated in sections

2 tomatoes, peeled and
  quartered
3 tblsp. chopped chives
2 tblsp. lemon juice
Salt and pepper to taste
⅓ c. butter

Combine in salad bowl, lettuce, avocado, grapefruit sections, tomatoes and chives. Season with lemon juice, salt and pepper.

Heat butter until foamy and golden brown. Pour immediately over salad. Toss ingredients lightly to blend. *Serve at once.* Makes 4 servings.

FARMHOUSE GREEN SALAD WITH CHEESE-GARLIC DRESSING

This dressing adds a distinctive note to all kinds
of green salads

¼ lb. bacon
1 head lettuce, broken into
  bite-size pieces
1 c. chopped celery

2 hard-cooked eggs,
  chopped
Cheese-Garlic Dressing

Fry bacon until crisp; drain and crumble into bits.
Combine all ingredients in bowl; toss with Cheese-Garlic Dressing. Makes 6 servings.

Cheese-Garlic Dressing: Stir together 1 tblsp. cheese garlic salad dressing mix, 1 c. dairy sour cream and 2 tblsp. lemon juice.

DILLED BEANS AND CARROTS

Whole beans and carrot sticks are picture-pretty and taste wonderful

2 c. fresh green beans (½ lb.)	4 small to medium carrots, peeled and cut in 3" strips
¾ c. boiling water	Low calorie Italian salad dressing
1 tsp. sugar	
½ tsp. salt	
½ tsp. dill seeds	

Wash and trim beans; leave whole. In a saucepan combine ¾ c. boiling water, sugar, salt and dill seeds; bring to a boil and add beans. Cook 5 to 10 minutes, until tender-crisp.

Add carrots and cook about 10 minutes longer, until vegetables are tender but not soft. With pan still over heat, remove cover and allow liquid to evaporate. Add salad dressing and toss to mix well. Serve hot or cold. Makes 5 to 6 servings.

FRUITED CABBAGE SALAD

You'll give this salad top score for its harmoniously blended flavors

2 c. shredded cabbage	½ c. chopped nuts (optional)
1 c. chopped celery	½ c. mayonnaise
1 medium banana, peeled and sliced	1 tblsp. sugar
½ c. green grapes	2 tsp. vinegar
1 (8 oz.) pineapple tidbits	¼ tsp. salt

Combine cabbage, celery, banana and grapes in salad bowl. Drain pineapple, reserving juice. Add pineapple and nuts to cabbage mixture.

Blend together 2 tblsp. reserved pineapple juice and remaining ingredients. Add to salad and toss. Makes 6 servings.

CAULIFLOWER SALAD

Unusual, color-bright and tasty salad—
it's on the sweet side

3 c. shredded lettuce
1 c. grated raw cauliflower
½ c. grated carrot
3 tblsp. sweet pickle relish
¼ c. vinegar

¼ c. salad oil
3 tblsp. sugar
½ tsp. onion salt
⅛ tsp. pepper
⅛ tsp. paprika

Combine lettuce, cauliflower, carrot and pickle relish in salad bowl.

Shake together the remaining ingredients. Pour over salad and toss. Makes 6 servings.

CARROT PLUS THREE SALAD

Apples, raisins and almonds complement carrots,
as does sour cream dressing

3 c. grated carrots
2 unpeeled red apples, chopped
½ c. white or dark raisins
¼ c. toasted slivered almonds

1 c. dairy sour cream
¼ c. mayonnaise
1 tblsp. lemon juice
¼ tsp. salt

Combine carrots, apples, raisins and almonds in salad bowl. Blend together remaining ingredients and stir into salad. Makes 6 servings.

YAM FRUIT SALAD

Honey and lemon juice in the dressing spark
this unusual salad

1 c. mayonnaise or salad dressing
1 tblsp. honey
1 tblsp. lemon juice

3 medium yams, cooked
2 firm bananas
2 red apples
2 c. seedless grapes

299

Combine mayonnaise, honey and lemon juice for dressing.

Peel and cube the yams. Slice the bananas. Dice unpeeled apples.

Combine yams and fruit; toss together lightly. Serve on crisp cabbage leaves or lettuce with the honey dressing. Makes 4 to 6 servings.

VEGETABLES ROQUEFORT

The meal's vegetables and salad are in a bowl—
have cold cuts and rolls

Crisp salad greens
1 small onion
1 c. sliced raw cauliflower
1 (1 lb.) can cut green beans

1 (13 to 14 oz.) can or jar
   green asparagus spears
Roquefort Cheese Dressing

Line 6 individual salad bowls with salad greens and fill about half full with greens.

Slice onion and separate into rings.

Arrange onion, cauliflower, drained chilled green beans and asparagus on greens. Serve with Roquefort Cheese Dressing. Makes 6 servings.

Roquefort Cheese Dressing: Combine 1 (3 oz.) pkg. cream cheese, 3 oz. crumbled Roquefort cheese, ¼ tsp. salt, ¼ tsp. garlic powder, ¼ tsp. dry mustard and ½ tsp. Worcestershire sauce; beat well. Gradually add ½ c. light cream, beating until smooth. Stir in ½ c. mayonnaise. Chill. Makes about 1¼ cups.

WINTER FARMHOUSE SALAD

Children like the vegetable-peanut get-together
in this hearty salad

1½ c. chopped celery
2 c. grated carrots
⅓ c. finely chopped sweet
   pickle
4 hard-cooked eggs, diced

½ c. coarsely chopped
   peanuts
½ tsp. salt
1 c. mayonnaise or salad
   dressing
2 tblsp. sweet pickle juice

Combine celery, carrots, pickle, eggs, peanuts and salt in salad bowl.

Blend together mayonnaise and pickle juice. Add to salad mixture and toss. Makes 6 servings.

Chill Salads to Perfection

When you read the recipes in this chapter, you'll observe that the directions for making some salads suggest that you chill them before serving. The chilling time extends from 30 minutes to an hour or longer. In a few recipes you chill only part of the ingredients before combining them with the others. Good salad makers heed these temperature tips, for the seasonings blend and mellow during the chilling. Arizona Green Salad, for instance, tastes best if you toss it and put it in the refrigerator for half an hour before dinner.

ARIZONA GREEN SALAD

This gay-with-color salad is perfect to serve
with roast beef or steak

1 medium head romaine
2 tblsp. lemon juice
1 ripe avocado, peeled and
   sliced

1 (16 oz.) can grapefruit
   sections, drained and
   chilled
1 red onion, thinly sliced
   and separated in rings
Oil-Vinegar Dressing

Tear romaine in bite-size pieces. Sprinkle lemon juice on avocado slices to prevent discoloration.

Add avocado, grapefruit and onion rings to romaine. Toss with Oil-Vinegar Dressing. Chill 30 minutes before serving. Makes 6 to 8 servings.

Oil-Vinegar Dressing: Put ½ c. salad oil, ¼ c. wine vinegar, 1 tblsp. lemon juice, 2¼ tsp. seasoned salt and ¼ tsp. seasoned pepper in pint jar with screw-type lid. Shake well. Makes ¾ cup.

HOLIDAY ARTICHOKE SALAD

Serve this pretty, refreshing salad for special-occasion dinners

½ c. salad oil
⅓ c. vinegar
2 tblsp. water
¼ c. coarsely chopped
  onion
2 tsp. sugar
1 clove garlic, minced
¼ tsp. celery seeds
½ tsp. salt

Dash freshly ground pepper
1 (9 oz.) pkg. frozen
  artichoke hearts
1 (4 oz.) jar pimientos,
  drained and chopped
1 (2 oz.) can anchovy filets,
  rinsed, drained and diced
6 c. torn salad greens

Combine salad oil, vinegar, water, onion, sugar, garlic, celery seeds, salt and pepper; heat to boiling.

Add frozen artichoke hearts; cook until tender, 4 to 5 minutes. Cool.

Stir in pimientos and anchovies; chill mixture thoroughly.

At serving time, drain off dressing and reserve. Combine artichoke mixture with greens (iceberg lettuce, romaine, endive, spinach—as desired); toss with enough reserved dressing to coat greens well. Makes 8 to 10 servings.

BEAN-BEEF BOWL

Men voted this substantial make-ahead salad tops— this carries well

2 c. green beans, cut in
  1½″ pieces
2 c. wax beans, cut in 1½″
  pieces
1 (10 oz.) pkg. frozen
  Fordhook lima beans,
  cooked and drained
1 (1 lb.) can kidney beans,
  drained
1 (1 lb.) can garbanzos
  (chick-peas), drained

1 (12 oz.) can corned beef,
  cut in small pieces
1 medium onion, thinly
  sliced
⅓ c. green pepper strips
1 tsp. salt
¼ tsp. pepper
1 c. bottled Italian salad
  dressing

Cook green and wax beans in boiling salted water until tender-crisp; drain. Combine with remaining ingredients. Chill several hours. Makes 12 servings.

VARIATION

Bean-Ham Bowl: Substitute 2 c. cooked ham, cut in slender strips, for the corned beef in Bean-Beef Bowl.

GARBANZO-SALAMI SALAD

Serve this hearty main dish salad for lunch on a hot summer day

½ tsp. dry mustard
½ tsp. salt
½ tsp. garlic salt
⅓ c. olive or salad oil
3 tblsp. white wine vinegar
1 (15 or 15½ oz.) can garbanzos (chick-peas) drained

1 (4 oz.) pkg. thinly sliced salami
1 head butter lettuce
1 head romaine lettuce
2 c. firmly packed snipped raw spinach
⅛ tsp. coarse grind pepper

Combine dry mustard, salt and garlic salt in salad bowl. Add oil and vinegar; mix well. Add garbanzos; cover and chill at least 30 minutes before serving time.

Wrap salami in foil; heat in moderate oven (350°) 15 minutes, or until hot.

Tear lettuce and cut spinach in bite-size pieces (you should have about 6 c.). Add to garbanzos along with pepper; toss lightly to mix. Just before serving add salami slices. Makes 6 servings.

HEARTY BEET SALAD

Brighten winter meals with this salad made with foods usually on hand

2 c. diced pickled beets
4 hard-cooked eggs, diced
4 slices bacon, cooked, drained and crumbled

2 tblsp. mayonnaise or salad dressing

Combine all ingredients. Chill. Makes 6 servings.

COUNTRY-STYLE BEET SALAD

This salad takes the spotlight in a meal—
rich in color and flavor

¼ c. vinegar
1 small onion, chopped
1 (1 lb.) can or jar sliced
   beets

Crisp salad greens
½ c. grated Cheddar
   cheese
Bottled French dressing

Combine vinegar, onion and ¼ c. liquid drained from beets; pour over drained beets. Chill at least 1 hour.

Put mounds of drained beets on salad greens and sprinkle with cheese. Pass French dressing. Makes 6 servings.

Old-Fashioned Kidney Bean Salad

If you've been fortunate enough to picnic a few times in Indiana, you need no introduction to kidney bean salads. Not that they are only for outdoor meals. They're often the main dish for lunch or supper in seasons when it's too chilly to eat outdoors. Nor do Indiana women have a corner on all exceptionally good red bean salads, for they appear on salad plates across country. Hoosier women, though, are experts in filling bowls with them.

The ingredients change with the season. Cucumber is a part of the salad in summer, but after frost and throughout the winter, cucumber pickles, often those flavored with dill, take its place. Spring brings tiny, red radishes; thinly sliced, they show red and white alongside the pickles and add pleasing crispiness.

Have Old-Fashioned Kidney Bean Salad for lunch some Saturday with corn bread hot from the oven, honey and a fruit dessert.

OLD-FASHIONED KIDNEY BEAN SALAD

Mix salad a few hours ahead, chill
so flavors will ripen and blend

1/3 c. mayonnaise
1 tblsp. prepared mustard
1 medium onion, finely
    chopped
1 c. thinly sliced celery
1 small cucumber, diced

2 (1 lb.) cans red kidney
    beans, drained
4 hard-cooked eggs, cut in
    eighths
Seasoned salt to taste
Lettuce

Mix mayonnaise, mustard, onion, celery and cucumber. Fold in kidney beans and eggs. Sprinkle with seasoned salt. Chill 2 to 3 hours, until flavors are blended.

Serve on lettuce; garnish with tomato or cucumber slices, if desired. Makes 6 servings.

CABBAGE-KIDNEY BEAN SALAD

Mustard gives this zip and color

1 (8 oz.) pkg. shell macaroni,
    cooked and drained
6 c. chopped cabbage
1/2 c. chopped celery
1/2 c. green pepper strips
1/4 c. minced onion
2 (1 lb.) cans red kidney
    beans, drained

3 eggs, slightly beaten
1/2 c. sugar
1 (9 oz.) jar prepared
    mustard
3 tblsp. butter
1/2 tsp. salt
1/4 tsp. pepper

Toss together macaroni, cabbage, celery, green pepper, onion and kidney beans.

Blend together remaining ingredients in top part of double boiler. Cook over simmering water for about 5 minutes or until mixture thickens slightly. Cool. Pour over vegetables; toss. Makes 10 to 12 servings.

CABBAGE-ORANGE SLAW

Orange cups make gala containers for this delicious party cabbage salad

3 oranges
2 c. finely shredded cabbage
2 tblsp. finely chopped
    onion
1/3 c. chopped water cress
1/3 c. mayonnaise

1/4 tsp. salt
1/8 tsp. sugar
Dash celery salt
1 1/2 tsp. vinegar
Pepper to taste

305

Cut oranges in halves; remove pulp, leaving good firm shells. Remove membrane from the orange sections and cut up enough to make 1 c. Drain orange sections of all free juice.

Mix 2 c. cabbage, onion and water cress with orange sections.

Combine mayonnaise with remaining ingredients; toss with cabbage mixture. Fill orange shells and refrigerate. Serve cold and crisp, garnished with water cress. Makes 6 servings.

FESTIVE COLESLAW

Peanuts and cheese step up the good
unusual taste in this colorful salad

4 c. shredded green cabbage	⅛ tsp. pepper
2 c. shredded red cabbage	1 tblsp. vinegar
½ c. chopped celery	2 tblsp. chopped onion
½ c. thinly sliced cauliflower	2 tblsp. chopped green pepper
½ c. chopped cucumber	2 tblsp. grated Parmesan cheese
½ c. dairy sour cream	¼ c. chopped salted peanuts
½ c. mayonnaise	1½ tsp. butter
1 tblsp. sugar	
1 tsp. salt	

Combine cabbage, celery, cauliflower and cucumber in salad bowl.

Combine sour cream, mayonnaise, sugar, salt, pepper, vinegar, onion and green pepper. Toss with cabbage mixture about 1 hour before serving. Chill to blend flavors.

Just before serving, add Parmesan cheese and peanuts, heated in butter, and toss. Makes 8 servings.

FARMHOUSE CABBAGE SLAW

Splendid salad to serve with pork chops,
roast pork or baked ham

4 c. shredded cabbage
¾ c. seedless raisins
1 apple, unpeeled and chopped
½ c. chopped celery
¼ c. chopped onion
¼ c. mayonnaise
2 tblsp. lemon juice
1 tblsp. salad oil
1 tblsp. sugar
½ tsp. salt
⅛ tsp. pepper

Combine cabbage, raisins, apple, celery and onion in salad bowl.

Blend together remaining ingredients. Add to cabbage mixture and toss. Chill 30 minutes. Makes 6 servings.

CAULIFLOWER SALAD BOWL

*Flashes of red tomatoes garnish this
different, interesting salad*

1 medium head cauliflower
10 ripe olives, sliced
1 tblsp. minced onion
½ c. diced sharp Cheddar cheese
7 anchovy filets, cut in small pieces (optional)
1 tsp. salt
¼ tsp. pepper
3 tblsp. olive or salad oil
1 tblsp. vinegar
Lettuce
Cherry tomatoes or tomato wedges

Wash and trim cauliflower. Break into small flowerets. Cook in boiling salted water until tender-crisp, 8 to 10 minutes. Drain and chill.

Combine cauliflower with remaining ingredients, except tomatoes. Chill at least 30 minutes. Serve in lettuce-lined bowl garnished with cherry tomatoes or tomato wedges. Makes 6 servings.

CAULIFLOWER-OLIVE SALAD

*Perfect salad to accompany roast beef
and steaks—a men's favorite*

½ c. olive oil
¼ c. lemon juice or white wine vinegar
½ tsp. salt
Dash freshly ground pepper
2 Bermuda onions, thinly sliced and separated in rings
½ small head cauliflower, sliced (about 3 c.)
½ c. sliced stuffed olives
½ c. crumbled blue cheese
1 medium head iceberg lettuce, torn in bite-size pieces

307

Combine oil, lemon juice, salt and pepper. Add onions, cauliflower and olives to mixture; marinate at least 30 minutes.

Sprinkle cheese over lettuce in salad bowl. Add marinated mixture and toss gently. Makes 6 servings.

CELERY COLESLAW

Crunchiness plus pleasing blend of flavors
makes this salad a winner

3 c. thinly sliced celery	½ c. mayonnaise
½ c. grated carrots	2 tblsp. sugar
1 apple, unpeeled, cored	½ tsp. salt
and chopped	2 tblsp. vinegar

Combine celery, carrots and apple in bowl.

Blend together remaining ingredients. Fold into celery mixture. Chill at least 30 minutes. Makes 6 servings.

CELERIAC (CELERY ROOT) SALAD

Want to try something different? Tastes like
celery-flavored potato salad

2 medium firm celeriacs	4 to 5 tblsp. mayonnaise
2 tblsp. lemon juice	or salad dressing
4 hard-cooked eggs	Salt to taste
¼ c. chopped onion	Pimiento-stuffed olives
1 tblsp. minced parsley	Paprika
⅛ tsp. pepper	

Peel celery roots, cutting away fibrous roots at bottom and any adhering top growth. Cut in halves; cook in boiling salted wated to cover, with 1 tsp. lemon juice added, until tender, 20 to 30 minutes for halves, about 40 to 60 minutes for whole roots.

Drain; cut in cubes, place in bowl and add remaining lemon juice (or French salad dressing) to help keep it white instead of turning gray.

When celery roots are cool, add 3 diced hard-cooked eggs, onion, parsley, pepper and mayonnaise. Add more salt, if needed. Mix well; turn into serving bowl. Garnish with slices of hard-cooked egg and olives and sprinkle with paprika. Chill 1 hour, or several hours, before serving. Makes 6 to 8 servings.

Garden Fresh Cucumbers

The Ohio reader who sent us directions for fixing Garden Fresh Cucumbers said: "If you're up to your ears in cucumbers you'll love this recipe. It transforms the common cuke into a gourmet salad." She's 100% right if your family and friends enjoy cucumbers. And most people do on sultry days.

GARDEN FRESH CUCUMBERS

Surprising what a spoonful of little seeds
does for this country favorite

¼ c. vinegar
1 tblsp. lemon juice
1 tsp. celery seeds
2 tblsp. sugar
¾ tsp. salt

⅛ tsp. pepper
2 tblsp. chopped onion
3 c. sliced peeled
   cucumbers (2 medium)
Chopped parsley (optional)

Combine vinegar, lemon juice, celery seeds, sugar, salt, pepper and onion. Pour over cucumbers. Chill thoroughly. Serve topped with chopped parsley, if desired. Makes 3 cups.

"Cole slaw" means "cabbage salad." Cole is the generic word for any plant of the Brassica genus, which includes cabbage. Slaw comes from the Danish word for salad. If you see it written, sometimes, as "Cold slaw," this is not correct, because the "cole" has nothing to do with temperature.

CUCUMBER-SOUR CREAM SALAD

An inviting choice for a meal that features
fried chicken or fish

1 tblsp. sugar	2 tblsp. white vinegar or
1½ tsp. salt	lemon juice
1 c. dairy sour cream	4½ c. thinly sliced peeled
3 tblsp. grated onion	cucumbers (6 medium)

Blend together sugar, salt, sour cream, onion and vinegar. Stir in cucumbers. Chill at least 2 hours.

Serve in lettuce cups for salad or on the tray with other relishes. Makes about 6 cups, the exact amount depending on size of cucumbers.

VARIATION

Cucumber Salad with Dill: Stir 1 tsp. dill seeds into Cucumber-Sour Cream Salad. Omit sugar if you like a tart salad.

In America, lettuce is used primarily for salads, but European cooks fix this vegetable in a variety of ways: braised, baked, stewed, stuffed and in soups.

Pea-Shrimp Salad

Hurry peas in their prime from the garden, shell and cook them promptly. Then chill them until time to make this scrumptious salad. You'll find no better way to feature peas from your garden at a women's luncheon. Your guests will exclaim: "What a wonderful salad!"

This country salad capitalizes on the marvelous flavor of garden-fresh peas. That's why we used a high proportion of peas to shrimp.

While the salad is a perfect main dish for guest luncheons, it's bound to please for supper, too. Serve it with hot rolls or biscuits. If there are men around the table, add a hearty dessert, such as strawberry-rhubarb pie, strawberry shortcake or a favorite chocolate pie or cake.

PEA-SHRIMP SALAD

Picture-pretty green and pink salad

1 lb. cooked shrimp, shelled
  and deveined
4 c. shelled peas
1 c. dairy sour cream
½ c. mayonnaise
1 tblsp. lemon juice
½ tsp. salt
½ tsp. dill weed

4 hard-cooked eggs,
  chopped
¼ c. chopped sweet pickle
  or pickle relish
2 tblsp. chopped green
  onion
1 c. sliced celery
Lettuce

Chill shrimp.

Cook peas until barely tender. Pour into colander; cool under cold running water. Chill.

Combine sour cream, mayonnaise, lemon juice, salt and dill weed. Refrigerate.

Just before serving, combine all ingredients. Serve in lettuce cups. Makes 6 servings.

Add a grated potato to your meat loaf in place of bread or cracker crumbs. The potato makes a more moist meat loaf.

Pantry-Shelf Pea Salad

Everyone who ate this salad gave it a top rating. Our recipe testers believe it tastes so exceptionally good because the vegetables are combined with tarragon vinegar and chilled, which permits the flavors to blend.

You can keep this salad in the refrigerator a couple of days; it's handy to have ready to serve.

PANTRY-SHELF PEA SALAD

*The surprise is that this simple do-ahead
salad tastes so wonderful*

½ c. salad oil
¼ c. tarragon vinegar
2 tsp. salt
2 tsp. sugar
¼ tsp. pepper
2 (1 lb.) cans peas, drained
  (4 c.)

2 c. diced celery
2 c. diced cucumbers
½ c. minced green onions
⅓ c. chopped pimiento
½ c. grated carrot
Salad greens

Combine salad oil, vinegar, salt, sugar and pepper in bottom of medium salad bowl. Add remaining ingredients and chill at least 1 hour to blend flavors. Serve on salad greens. Makes 10 servings.

VEGETABLE-POTATO SALAD

This five-vegetable salad is tart, highly seasoned and flavorful

4 large potatoes
2 tblsp. vinegar
1 tsp. salt
⅛ tsp. pepper
1 to 2 tblsp. finely chopped onion
2 tblsp. chopped green pepper

½ c. chopped celery
¼ c. diced cucumber
2 hard-cooked eggs, chopped
¼ c. chopped sweet pickle (optional)
½ c. mayonnaise
½ tsp. prepared mustard

Cook potatoes in packets in boiling water. Peel and cube. Sprinkle with vinegar, salt and pepper while hot. Cool and chill.

Several hours before serving add onion, green pepper, celery, cucumber, eggs and pickle.

Blend together mayonnaise and mustard. Gently fold into potato mixture. Chill. Makes 6 servings (about 6 cups).

OLD-FASHIONED POTATO SALAD

Do heat potatoes in salad dressing and chill—then make the salad. Flavor dividends will be big

3 (15 to 16 oz.) cans whole potatoes
½ c. bottled Italian dressing
5 hard-cooked eggs, chopped
¼ c. diced celery
1 small onion, chopped
¾ c. mayonnaise

¼ c. light cream or dairy half-and-half
1 tblsp. vinegar
2 tsp. mustard
1 tblsp. sugar
1 tsp. salt
¼ tsp. pepper
Lettuce

Drain and dice potatoes; combine with dressing in saucepan and simmer gently about 10 minutes. Chill.

Add eggs, celery and onion to potatoes.

In a small bowl combine remaining ingredients; mix well. Chill to blend flavors. Serve in lettuce cups, sprinkled with paprika or chopped parsley. Makes 6 to 8 servings.

SPINACH SALAD PAR EXCELLENCE

Decidedly different, decidedly good

1 lb. spinach, washed and
  torn in pieces
1 (1 lb.) can bean sprouts,
  chilled and drained
8 slices bacon, diced, fried
  and drained
3 hard-cooked eggs,
  chopped
½ tsp. salt

1 c. salad oil
½ c. sugar
⅓ c. ketchup
¼ c. vinegar
1 tsp. salt
1 tsp. instant minced
  onion
1 tsp. Worcestershire
  sauce

Combine spinach, bean sprouts, bacon and eggs in salad bowl. Sprinkle with ½ tsp. salt.

Combine remaining ingredients to make dressing. Shake to blend. (Good made in advance and chilled to blend flavors.)

At serving time, sprinkle about half the dressing on spinach mixture and toss well. Chill remaining dressing to use on a repeat of this salad or any green salad. Makes 8 to 10 servings.

MARINATED TOMATOES

Family and friends will praise these

5 large, ripe tomatoes
¼ c. salad oil
1½ tblsp. lemon juice
½ clove garlic, minced

½ tsp. salt
½ tsp. orégano leaves
⅛ tsp. pepper

Peel tomatoes; cut in thick slices.

Combine remaining ingredients. Pour over tomatoes. Chill thoroughly, stirring once or twice. Makes 6 servings.

313

HERB TOMATO RELISH

Fascinating flavors transform this relish salad
into a gourmet's choice

6 to 8 tomatoes, peeled and
    cut in ½″ slices
⅔ c. salad oil
⅓ c. vinegar
¼ chopped parsley
¼ c. sliced green onions

1 clove garlic, minced
¼ tsp. thyme leaves
¼ tsp. marjoram leaves
¼ tsp. basil leaves
1 tsp. salt
¼ tsp. pepper

Place tomato slices in a flat-bottomed dish such as a
10 × 6 × 1½″ glass baking dish.

Combine remaining ingredients; pour over tomatoes.
Chill several hours, occasionally spooning dressing over
tomatoes. Makes 8 servings.

NOTE: Use leftover marinade for salad dressing or for
meat marinade.

EGG SALAD IN TOMATO CUPS

Serves this salad plus ham sandwiches—
they'll leave the supper table happy

6 medium tomatoes
6 hard-cooked eggs,
    chopped
½ c. minced green pepper
½ c. chopped celery
½ c. chopped cucumber

1 tblsp. chopped green
    onion
1 tsp. salt
¼ c. mayonnaise
1 (3 oz.) pkg. cream cheese
    with chives
Lettuce

Scald and peel tomatoes; hollow out centers. Turn upside down on paper toweling and drain.

Mix eggs, green pepper, celery, cucumber, green onion
and salt.

Blend together mayonnaise and softened cream cheese.
Stir into egg mixture. Spoon into tomato cups. Chill several hours. Serve in lettuce cups. Makes 6 servings.

Summer's Zucchini-Tomato Salad

An Iowa farm couple accepted generous praise when they carried this salad to a supper meeting of their Gourmet Club. The salad is a medley of the season's bright garden colors and fresh flavors.

Uncooked zucchini slices provide the distinctive though subtle taste, while the other ingredients add exactly the right amount of zip. To dress up this country-kitchen salad, spoon individual servings on lettuce or other greens. For buffet service, edge the inside of the salad bowl with a ruffle of crisp greens.

ZUCCHINI-TOMATO SALAD

Gala summer make-ahead

6 small zucchini	**½ tsp. salt**
4 tomatoes, cut in wedges	**½ tsp. garlic salt**
1 green pepper, cut in strips	**½ tsp. pepper**
¼ c. chopped green onion	**¾ c. salad oil**
¼ c. chopped parsley	**Lettuce or greens**
¼ c. vinegar	

Wash zucchini; cut in very thin slices. Combine with tomatoes, green pepper, onion and parsley in a large bowl.

Stir together remaining ingredients, except lettuce. Pour over zucchini mixture. Chill several hours, stirring occasionally. Serve on lettuce or other greens. Makes 8 servings.

PEANUT VEGETABLE SALAD

Perfect for church or club suppers

2 (1 lb.) cans kidney beans	**1 (1 lb.) can sliced carrots**
1 (1 lb.) can cut wax beans	**1 (12 oz.) can whole kernel**
1 (1 lb.) can cut green	**corn**
beans	**1 (8 oz.) bottle Italian**
1 (16 or 17 oz.) can green	**dressing**
lima beans	**2 heads lettuce**
1 (1 lb.) can small whole	**1 (13½ oz.) can salted**
white onions	**peanuts (about 2 c.)**

Drain kidney beans in colander; rinse thoroughly. Drain other canned vegetables. Combine in large bowl. Pour salad dressing over, and toss to coat vegetables. Cover and chill several hours.

To serve, line large salad bowl with lettuce; save about 1 qt. lettuce, torn in bite-size pieces. Toss torn lettuce and peanuts with chilled vegetables; turn into lettuce-lined bowl. Makes about 4½ quarts, about 20 to 24 servings.

SALMON-VEGETABLE SALAD

This salad is on the tart side—delicious for
supper or lunch in summer

1 (1 lb.) can red salmon, drained, boned and flaked	½ c. chopped celery
1 tblsp. lemon juice	1 tblsp. chopped onion
2 c. shredded cabbage	½ tsp. salt
½ c. grated carrots	¼ tsp. pepper
½ c. chopped green pepper	½ c. salad dressing or mayonnaise
	2 tblsp. vinegar

Place salmon in bowl. Sprinkle with lemon juice and toss. Add remaining ingredients and mix lightly. Chill at least 1 hour. Makes 6 servings.

Make carrot curls by shaving thin strips, lengthwise, from long straight carrots. Curl each strip around your finger tightly, fasten with half a toothpick if necessary, and place on ice or in ice water. You can remove the toothpick after the curl has set.

VEGETABLE MEDLEY SALAD

Spring this bright-with-color and flavorful salad
at your next potluck

2 c. cooked green beans, cut small	¼ c. minced onion
	1 c. dairy sour cream
2 c. cooked diced carrots	¾ c. mayonnaise or salad dressing
2 c. cooked peas	
2 c. cooked diced potatoes	2 tblsp. vinegar
1½ c. chopped celery	2 tsp. salt
¾ c. chopped parsley	¼ tsp. pepper

Combine vegetables in large bowl.

Blend together sour cream, mayonnaise, vinegar, salt and pepper. Add to vegetables and toss. Chill thoroughly. Makes about 16 servings (12 cups).

When you serve tender young dandelion leaves to your family, tell them they're eating "lion's tooth." That's the translation from the French dent de lion—*and a good description of the teeth on the dandelion leaves.*

QUINTET VEGETABLE SALAD

Crunchiness of toasted bread cubes
contrasts deliciously with vegetables

2 c. drained cooked fresh
  green beans, chilled
1 tblsp. minced onion
½ c. chopped cucumber
1 tomato, diced
2 tblsp. vinegar
6 tblsp. salad oil

½ tsp. salt
½ tsp. garlic salt
¼ tsp. pepper
1 c. toasted bread cubes
1 tblsp. grated Parmesan
  cheese (optional)
Lettuce

Combine all ingredients, except toasted bread cubes, cheese and lettuce. Cover and chill thoroughly.

At serving time toss in bread cubes and cheese; spoon into lettuce cups on individual salad plates. (You can sprinkle each salad with a dash of grated or shredded cheese, if desired.) Makes 6 servings.

VARIATION

Herb Quintet Vegetable Salad: Use package herb-seasoned croutons instead of the toasted bread cubes.

FLOATING VEGETABLE SALAD

Use garden-fresh vegetables and chill salad
long enough to blend flavors—you'll have
a great country treat

3 large tomatoes, peeled and sliced rather thick	1½ tsp. salt
1 medium onion, thinly sliced	¼ tsp. pepper
	3 tblsp. vinegar
1 green pepper, seeded and sliced in rings	3 tblsp. salad oil
	1 tsp. paprika
1 cucumber, thinly sliced	½ tsp. dry mustard
	½ tsp. celery seeds

Arrange layers of vegetables in bowl. Sprinkle each with salt and pepper.

Combine remaining ingredients and pour over vegetables; cover and chill several hours, gently lifting vegetables occasionally to distribute dressing. Makes 6 servings.

Overnight Vegetable Salads

Country homemakers believe in kitchen preparedness because friends or business callers often stop in unexpectedly and stay for dinner. A ready-to-go salad in the refrigerator perks up the menu. Our Midwinter Bean Salad actually requires refrigeration for a day before use, but you can keep it two or three days longer. Have a jar of it on hand for what one farm woman calls her "insurance against frustration."

MIDWINTER BEAN SALAD

Handy salad to have ready to serve—
it's a great favorite with men

1 (12 oz.) pkg. frozen French-style green beans, cooked	¼ c. pimiento, cut in strips
	¼ c. chopped green pepper
	2 tblsp. sugar
1 (16 oz.) can wax beans	2 tblsp. vinegar or lemon juice
2 tblsp. chopped onion	
½ c. thinly sliced celery	2 tblsp. salad oil

Drain beans. Combine all ingredients and chill overnight. Makes 8 servings.

318

CITRUS-MARINATED SALAD

*Just the salad to make ahead and tote to your
club supper or potluck*

1 (1 lb.) can cut green
  beans, drained
1 (1 lb.) can green peas,
  drained
2 medium carrots, cut in
  1″ strips
2 c. sliced celery
1 (2 oz.) jar pimientos,
  drained and diced
2 medium sweet onions, cut
  in rings

½ c. sliced, pimiento-stuffed
  green olives
¾ c. orange juice
¼ c. lemon juice
¼ c. vinegar
½ tsp. paprika
½ c. salad oil
⅓ c. sugar
2 tsp. salt

Place beans, peas, carrots, celery, pimientos, onions and
olives in a large glass or ceramic bowl.

Mix remaining ingredients to make marinade. Pour over
vegetables and toss lightly.

Cover and marinate overnight in refrigerator (will keep
several days in the refrigerator). Makes 12 servings.

Frozen Relish Slaw

The route of this zesty relish slaw extends from cabbage
patch through kitchen to picnic or camping grounds. Tuck
a jar of Frozen Relish Slaw in a basket with other cold
food. It will thaw and be ready to eat by the time you
want to serve it.

You can make the relish and freeze it a week or two
before you'll need it. This relieves the pressures that arise
at the last minute before taking off on an outing.

FROZEN RELISH SLAW

*One of its remarkable talents
is the way it sparks up meals*

9 c. grated cabbage	1 tsp. celery seeds
(1 medium head)	1 tsp. mustard seeds
1 tsp. salt	1 carrot, grated
1 c. vinegar	1 green pepper, finely
¼ c. water	chopped
2 c. sugar	

Combine cabbage and salt and let stand 1 hour.

Meanwhile combine vinegar, water and sugar. Tie celery seeds and mustard seeds in cloth bag and drop into vinegar mixture. Bring to a boil and boil 1 minute. Let stand until lukewarm.

Press juice out of cabbage. Stir in carrot and green pepper. Discard cloth bag and pour vinegar mixture over cabbage. Place in containers, seal and freeze. Thaw before serving. Makes about 2 quarts.

SAUERKRAUT SALAD

Perfect meat dish or sandwich go-with
to tote to the men in the field

1 (1 lb. 11 oz.) can	3 tblsp. vinegar
sauerkraut	½ tsp. salt
¾ c. sugar	⅛ tsp. pepper
1 c. diced celery	1 tsp. celery seeds
1 c. diced green pepper	3 tblsp. diced pimientos
¼ c. diced onion	

Drain sauerkraut in colander for 15 minutes. Cut in 1″ pieces with kitchen scissors; place in large mixing bowl.

Add remaining ingredients; mix well. Store, covered, in refrigerator at least 24 hours. Keeps indefinitely. Makes 10 servings.

Old-Fashioned Turnip Salad/Relish

The turnip is a strong-flavored vegetable; that's the main reason why people either heartily like or dislike it. If you enjoy its robust taste, you'll like this old-fashioned country salad/relish our grandmothers made to serve with fork-tender, brown beef pot roast, mashed potatoes, gravy and hot biscuits.

These women knew their turnips well; for salads, they selected the young ones with a milder, sweeter taste than the mature vegetable. Often they planted turnips in August to get a crop for early autumn eating.

Try fresh onion rings in a tossed salad. To crisp them, put them in ice water for an hour; then drain and dry with paper towels before adding to salad.

OLD-FASHIONED TURNIP SALAD/RELISH

You can refrigerate this for a few days; spoon it out quickly to serve

5 c. grated peeled turnips (4 medium)	**½ c. vinegar**
	¼ c. salad oil
¾ c. grated onion (1 large)	**1 tblsp. water**
2 red apples, unpeeled, cored and chopped	**1 tsp. salt**
	⅛ tsp. pepper
½ c. sugar	

Combine all ingredients. Let stand overnight. Serve in lettuce cups, if you wish. Makes 1½ quarts.

Zucchini Salad Italienne

Home gardeners never cease to marvel about how prolific the squash vines are. One of our readers spoke for many when she confessed: "I collect and develop zucchini recipes in a desperate effort to keep up with my garden."

She offers a prized recipe for Zucchini Salad Italienne, hoping it will be as well received at your house as hers.

Taste-testers admitted that they surprised themselves in liking the salad as much as they did. It's so unusual. One of them called it a new exciting food adventure. The recipe for the dressing is generous—on purpose. You'll use only half of it in this salad. Store the other half in your

321

refrigerator for a second appearance of Zucchini Salad Italienne. Also good on any green salad or as a marinade for meats you're going to grill. Red wine vinegar darkens the zucchini somewhat, but it adds flavor.

ZUCCHINI SALAD ITALIENNE

If you enjoy early-bird cooking and Italian
seasonings, you'll like this

2 lbs. zucchini
½ c. water
2 tsp. seasoned salt
12 large ripe olives
⅔ c. olive oil
½ c. wine vinegar
1 tsp. salt
½ tsp. paprika

½ tsp. pepper
½ tsp. sugar
¼ tsp. basil leaves
1 clove garlic
1 avocado
Pimiento or red pepper
   strips

Wash zucchini. Cut off ends and cut into 1½" slices. Combine water and seasoned salt and pour over zucchini in saucepan. Cook until barely tender, but still crisp. Drain.

Cut ripe olives in quarters, removing pits (or use pitted olives).

Combine oil, vinegar, salt, paprika, pepper, sugar and basil. Put garlic clove on toothpick and add to dressing.

Pour over zucchini and olives in bowl. Chill at least overnight. Remove garlic after several hours. Stir occasionally.

Several hours before serving, peel avocado and cut into slices. Add to squash. Serve in salad bowl or on plates garnished with strips of pimiento or red pepper. Makes 12 servings.

NOTE: The dressing for this salad can be made several days in advance.

MEDLEY VEGETABLE MARINADE

Make-ahead hostess salad—you add
only the lettuce at serving time

322

2 c. cauliflower, cut in bite-
  size pieces
2 c. (2 × ¼″) carrot sticks
1 (1 lb.) can cut green beans,
  drained or 1 (9 oz.) pkg.
  frozen cut green beans,
  cooked and drained
1 (4 oz.) can mushrooms,
  drained and sliced
1 medium onion, sliced
  (optional)

½ c. sweet pickle slices, cut
  in halves
¼ c. salad oil
¾ c. vinegar
2 tblsp. sugar
1 tsp. salt
⅛ tsp. freshly ground
  pepper
1 tsp. dill weed
2 c. shredded lettuce

Cook cauliflower and carrot pieces just until tender;
drain. Combine in bowl with green beans, mushrooms,
onion and sweet pickle.

Mix together salad oil, vinegar, sugar, salt, pepper and
dill weed; pour over vegetables. Refrigerate 24 hours; toss
carefully a few times.

Just before serving, add lettuce. Drain off excess dressing. Makes 10 to 12 servings.

MARINATED VEGETABLE SALAD

*You can make this salad and refrigerate it
a day or more before serving*

1 (1 lb.) can peas, drained
  (2 c.)
1 (1 lb.) can French-style
  green beans, drained (2 c.)
1½ c. chopped celery
¾ c. chopped green pepper
1 c. chopped onion
3 tblsp. chopped canned
  pimiento

¾ c. sugar
½ c. vinegar
½ c. salad oil
2 tblsp. water
1 tsp. salt
½ tsp. pepper
½ tsp. paprika

Combine vegetables in large bowl.

Shake together remaining ingredients in covered jar until
sugar is dissolved. Pour over vegetables. Chill in refrigerator 24 hours, stirring several times. Makes 8 servings,
about 7½ cups (without dressing).

Salad for All Seasons

For a tempting color-bright spot on your buffet or dinner table, Red Potato-Vegetable Salad is your dish. You make it ahead and chill it at least 4 hours or overnight to let the flavors and colors blend.

When we taste-tested the recipe, shared by an Indiana farm woman, one of the home economists who made it took the leftover salad home, made more of it and put it in her refrigerator. She heaped the salad in a big lettuce-lined bowl the next evening and set it on the buffet table to get the reactions of members of the Couples Club meeting at her house for supper.

She was amazed at the attention guests paid to it and how many of them took second helpings. They commented on the pretty pink potatoes in it, proving that people do part of their eating with their eyes.

RED POTATO-VEGETABLE SALAD

Pink potato cubes in red mixture

2 c. cubed cooked cold
   potatoes
1 c. chopped pickled beets
2 c. shredded red cabbage
2 tblsp. chopped onion

6 tblsp. salad oil
1 tsp. salt
¼ tsp. pepper
Lettuce

Combine all ingredients, including ⅔ c. pickled beet liquid reserved from chopped pickled beets. Chill at least 4 hours, or overnight. Serve on lettuce, or in lettuce-lined salad bowl. Makes 6 servings.

Hot Salads

Some country salads owe their superior flavors to time in the oven or skillet. Others get their warmth from a piping hot dressing poured over the salad ingredients. Serve these salads before they cool off, for the right temperature influences the reception they get.

Hot Kidney Bean Salad is hearty enough to take the spotlight in supper or lunch. Team it with crusty rolls or garlic bread, sliced tomatoes when they're in season and dessert. You'll have a fast-fix meal that pleases.

HOT KIDNEY BEAN SALAD

Keep cans of kidney beans in your cupboard
to make this supper main dish.
Easy to double the recipe

1 (1 lb.) can red kidney
  beans (2 c.)
1 c. thinly sliced celery
⅓ c. chopped sweet pickle
¼ c. finely chopped onion
1 c. diced sharp process
  Cheddar cheese (¼ lb.)
½ tsp. salt

½ tsp. chili powder
½ tsp. Worcestershire sauce
Few drops hot pepper sauce
½ c. mayonnaise or salad
  dressing
1 c. coarsely crushed corn
  chips
Green pepper rings

Drain beans; combine with celery, pickle, onion and cheese.

Blend seasonings into mayonnaise; add to bean mixture, and toss lightly. Spoon into 1-qt. shallow baking dish; sprinkle with corn chips. Bake in very hot oven (450°) about 10 minutes. Garnish with green pepper rings. Makes 4 servings.

SKILLET POTATO SALAD

Serve this potato salad piping hot

8 to 10 thin slices bacon
¼ c. bacon drippings
½ c. chopped celery
½ c. chopped onion
3 tblsp. sugar
3 tblsp. flour
1½ tsp. salt

½ tsp. celery seeds
¼ tsp. coarse grind pepper
½ c. water
⅓ c. vinegar
4 to 5 c. cubed cooked
  potatoes

Broil or fry bacon until crisp; drain on paper towels and crumble. Reserve ¼ c. drippings.

Add celery to reserved bacon drippings in skillet; cook

and stir until tender-crisp. Add onion and cook 1 to 2 minutes longer.

Combine sugar, flour, salt, celery seeds and pepper; stir into celery-onion mixture. Add water and vinegar, stirring until smooth. Bring to a bubbling boil; add potatoes and bacon. Mix thoroughly over heat. Serve as soon as hot. Makes 6 servings.

DEVILED HOT POTATO SALAD

Yes, there is something new in good
potato salads and here's an example

4 c. hot cooked cubed potatoes	1 c. dairy sour cream
	2 tblsp. prepared mustard
¼ c. chopped green onion with tops	1 tsp. salt
	1 tsp. sugar

Combine potatoes and onion.

Heat sour cream, being careful not to boil. Blend in seasonings. Pour over potatoes and onion; toss lightly to coat potatoes well. Serve topped with smoked sausage links, frankfurters or ham slices. Makes 6 servings.

NOTE: This salad is delicious, too, made with hot mashed potatoes—either fresh or instant.

HOT ZUCCHINI SALAD

Prolific vines encourage gardeners to collect zucchini
recipes. Here's a new one that makes good eating

6 small zucchini, thinly sliced (about ½ lb. each)	¼ tsp. coarse grind pepper
	¼ c. French or Italian salad dressing
¼ c. olive oil or butter	
1 tsp. salt	

Cook zucchini in oil in skillet 1 minute; cover, lower heat and cook 3 minutes more. Add salt, pepper and salad dressing; shake pan to coat slices well (be careful not to overcook). Serve at once. Makes 6 servings.

PENNSYLVANIA DUTCH SPINACH

They'll scrape the bowl clean—takes the
place of salad in your meal

2 qts. spinach, washed and
torn
3 green onions, chopped
6 slices bacon, chopped
3 tblsp. flour
3 tblsp. sugar

1 tsp. salt
¼ tsp. pepper
1½ c. hot water
3 tblsp. vinegar
2 hard-cooked eggs,
chopped

Place spinach and onions in bowl.

Cook bacon until crisp; remove from skillet and drain on paper towels.

Blend flour into bacon drippings. Add sugar, salt, pepper and hot water. Cook, stirring constantly, until mixture comes to a boil. Stir in vinegar.

Add eggs to spinach. Pour vinegar mixture over spinach and toss. Serve immediately, topped with bacon bits. Makes 6 servings. May be garnished with extra hard-cooked egg slices.

OLD-TIME SPINACH SALAD

Young spinach leaves makes a salad
with that good old-fashioned taste

2 lbs. fresh spinach
8 slices bacon
¼ c. chopped onion
3 tblsp. vinegar

½ tsp. salt
⅛ tsp. pepper
1 hard-cooked egg, sliced
(optional)

Wash spinach; cook in large kettle with water that clings to leaves until tender, 8 to 10 minutes. Drain.

Meanwhile, cook bacon until crisp. Drain and crumble. Reserve 2 tblsp. bacon fat.

Cook onion in reserved bacon fat until soft. Add to spinach with bacon, vinegar, salt and pepper. Toss. Serve garnished with egg slices. Makes 6 servings.

SPINACH-BACON SALAD

Gather your spinach young and tender
for this spring salad

3 cloves garlic
¾ c. bottled French
   dressing
2 qts. crisp young spinach,
   washed well

3 hard-cooked eggs,
   chopped
8 bacon slices, cooked,
   drained and crumbled
1 tblsp. chopped green
   onion

Cut garlic cloves in halves; place in small bowl and crush with back of spoon. Add French dressing; cover and refrigerate 2 hours.

Combine remaining ingredients just before serving. Remove garlic from French dressing. Pour over salad and toss to coat every leaf. Makes 6 servings.

Prize-Winning Molded Vegetable Salads

If you've ever looked at or tasted Garden Salad Loaf and Three-Row Garden Salad, you'll know why these two recipes are among the most praised molded mixed-vegetable salads that FARM JOURNAL ever printed. Both are beauties, sparkling with color. And they taste as delicious as they look.

Since these two star performers yield a good number of servings—10 to 12—they fit perfectly into buffet suppers and other company meals. And like other molded salads, you make them hours, or better still, a day ahead and put them in the refrigerator. This eliminates some of the rush from the day you entertain.

We repeat these recipes as an encore to the written and spoken approval from readers following their appearance in print.

GARDEN SALAD LOAF

Cool and beautiful—shimmering gelatin
holds fresh garden vegetables

2 green peppers, cut in
small strips
4 chopped green onions
with tops
20 radishes, thinly sliced
2 medium carrots, thinly
sliced
4 small tomatoes, cut in
thin wedges
¾ c. French dressing
2 envelopes unflavored
gelatin

¼ c. sugar
1 tsp. salt
2⅔ c. very hot water
½ c. vinegar
2 tblsp. lemon juice
2 c. shredded chicory or
lettuce
1 c. coarsely torn spinach
or shredded cabbage
¼ c. minced parsley

Combine first 5 vegetables and marinate in French dressing (15 minutes or more).

Combine gelatin, sugar and salt; add hot water and stir to dissolve ingredients. Add vinegar and lemon juice. Chill until gelatin thickens.

Drain vegetables well. Fold marinated vegetables and crisp greens into gelatin mixture. (Chicory, spinach and parsley do not wilt easily, but you may use lettuce or shredded cabbage, too.) Pour into 8½ × 4½ × 2½" oiled loaf pan; chill until firm.

Unmold on platter. Makes 10 to 12 servings.

Fancy Touches: For a design of vegetables on top of mold when you turn it out, pour about ½ c. dissolved gelatin mixture into loaf pan and let set. On this arrange an interesting pattern with radish slices, green pepper and tomato strips. Spoon a little of gelatin mixture over vegetables to "anchor" them; let set before adding vegetable-gelatin mixture. A border of tomato wedges may be arranged around outer edge of mold for color.

NOTE: You can omit unflavored gelatin and sugar; substitute 2 (3 oz.) pkgs. lemon flavor gelatin and 3½ c. very hot water. Follow same procedure as for Garden Salad Loaf.

THREE-ROW GARDEN SALAD

*Color-bright, refreshing salad resembles
striped ribbon when served*

Orange Layer:

1 (3 oz.) pkg. orange flavor
  gelatin
1 c. boiling water
¾ c. pineapple juice

2 tblsp. lemon juice
1½ c. finely shredded
  carrots

Green Layer:

1 (3 oz.) pkg. lime flavor
  gelatin
1 c. boiling water

¾ c. pineapple juice
2 tblsp. lemon juice
1½ c. grated cabbage

Red Layer:

2 tsp. unflavored gelatin
½ c. cold water
1 (3 oz.) pkg. lemon flavor
  gelatin
½ tsp. salt
1 c. boiling water
2 tblsp. beet juice

2 tblsp. vinegar
1 c. well-drained finely
  diced cooked beets
1 tblsp. horseradish
Cheese-Horseradish
  Dressing

Prepare layers separately, allowing about 15 minutes between each so that gelatins set at intervals.

To make orange layer, dissolve orange flavor gelatin in boiling water. Add pineapple and lemon juices; chill until syrupy. Fold in carrots.

To prepare green layer, dissolve lime flavor gelatin in boiling water. Add pineapple and lemon juices; chill until syrupy. Fold in cabbage.

To make red layer, soften unflavored gelatin in cold water. Dissolve lemon flavor gelatin and salt in boiling water; immediately stir in unflavored gelatin mixture. Add beet juice and vinegar; chill until syrupy. Fold in beets and horse-radish.

Layer gelatins—orange, green, then red—in 9 × 5 × 3" loaf pan. Allow each layer to set before adding second or third layer. Chill until firm.

To unmold set pan in warm (not hot) water about 5 seconds; loosen around beet layer and turn out on platter. Garnish with green fresh carrot tops, young beet leaves or lettuce. Slice, then serve each person individual salad. Pass Cheese-Horseradish Dressing. Makes 10 servings.

Cheese-Horseradish Dressing: Soften 1 (3 oz.) pkg. cream cheese; beat until creamy. Blend in ¼ c. mayonnaise, 2 tblsp. light cream or milk, ½ tsp. celery salt and 2 tsp.

horseradish. Fold in 2 tsp. chopped fresh or dried chives (optional). Makes ¾ cup.

PICKLED BEET SALAD

Piquant flavors and ruby-red beauty
win approval for this beet salad

½ tsp. onion salt	2 tblsp. vinegar
1 (3 oz.) pkg. lemon flavor gelatin	½ c. (about) cold water
1 c. hot water	1 c. chopped pickled beets
⅓ c. pickled beet liquid	1 c. shredded cabbage
	½ c. chopped celery

Combine onion salt and gelatin. Dissolve in hot water. Put pickled beet liquid and vinegar in measuring cup. Add enough cold water to make 1 c. Add to gelatin mixture. Chill until partially set.

Fold in vegetables. Pour into 1-qt. mold or 8 × 8 × 2″ pan. Chill until firm. Makes 6 servings.

LEMON BEET SALAD

Dress salad with ½ c. dairy sour cream
mixed with 2 tblsp. mayonnaise

1 (3 oz.) pkg. lemon flavor gelatin	½ tsp. salt
1 c. boiling water	¼ tsp. celery salt
¾ c. cold water	1 (8 oz.) can chopped beets, drained
2 tblsp. lemon juice	¾ c. finely shredded cabbage
2 tblsp. beet liquid	
1½ tblsp. horseradish	1 c. finely diced celery

Dissolve gelatin in boiling water. Stir in cold water, lemon juice, beet liquid, horseradish, salt and celery salt. Chill until partially thickened.

Stir in remaining ingredients. Chill until firm. Makes 6 servings.

Cool Cucumber Salads

Cucumbers and onions belong together as surely as do strawberries and cream. Capture them in lovely, green lime flavor gelatin and you produce a salad that seems to make sizzling summer heat vanish at mealtime. We have two such salads for you.

Cucumber Green Salad also contains celery and carrots, and herbs and sour cream boost its flavors. Cucumber and onions, spiked with a touch of vinegar, do the trick in Lime-Cucumber Circle. Fill the center of the emerald ring with pink shrimp salad and dismiss all worries about the success of your supper or luncheon party. It's assured.

LIME-CUCUMBER CIRCLE

Fill emerald ring with shrimp
or crab salad for your guest luncheon

2 (3 oz.) pkgs. lime flavor gelatin	**2 tblsp. grated onion**
2 c. hot water	**2 c. grated or finely chopped peeled cucumbers**
¼ c. vinegar	
½ tsp. salt	**1 c. mayonnaise**

Dissolve gelatin in hot water; add vinegar and cool until slightly thickened.

Meanwhile, add salt to grated onion and cucumbers. Mix well and drain off excess juice.

Beat thickened gelatin with rotary beater until fluffy. Fold in cucumber-onion mixture and mayonnaise. Blend thoroughly.

Pour into lightly oiled 2-qt. ring mold. Chill several hours or overnight. Makes 12 servings.

CUCUMBER GREEN SALAD

Mold cucumbers and salad dressing in lime flavor gelatin
for a refreshing, cooling and different green salad

2 (3 oz.) pkgs. lime flavor
  gelatin
2 c. hot water
¾ c. cold water
¼ c. vinegar
¼ tsp. dried chopped
  chives
⅛ tsp. dried chevril
  (optional)

½ c. sour cream
½ c. mayonnaise
1½ c. chopped cucumber
¾ c. diced celery
¾ c. shredded carrots
1 tsp. grated onion
Lettuce

Dissolve gelatin in hot water. Add cold water, vinegar, chives and chervil. Chill until partially thickened.

Blend together sour cream and mayonnaise. Blend in a little gelatin mixture. Return to remaining gelatin mixture and blend. Fold in vegetables. Chill. Serve on lettuce. Makes 10 to 12 servings.

Merry Christmas Salad

Some recipes please women so much that they circulate from kitchen to kitchen in neighborhoods and then jump state boundaries. Molded Holiday Salad is one of these travelers. Serve it to friends and be ready to get out paper and pencils; they'll want to copy the recipe.

The unusual ingredient combination of canned stewed tomatoes with raspberry flavor gelatin provides delightful flavor and gay red color. You can mold chopped green pepper in the salad, or use it as a garnish on salad servings. Sour Cream Dressing is just right for the final touch. While it's a great salad for the Yuletide season, it's equally tasty the year around.

MOLDED HOLIDAY SALAD

Give this red and green, make-ahead salad
a place in Yuletide meals

1 (3 oz.) pkg. lemon flavor
  gelatin
1 (3 oz.) pkg. raspberry
  flavor gelatin
1 c. hot water

2 (16 oz.) cans stewed
  tomatoes (4 c.)
Few drops hot pepper sauce
½ c. chopped green pepper
  or green pepper strips
Sour Cream Dressing

Dissolve gelatin in hot water; add stewed tomatoes and hot pepper sauce. Cool thoroughly.

When cooled, add chopped green pepper, if desired. Pour into 12 × 7½ × 2" glass dish or individual molds. Chill until set.

If you omit chopped green pepper, at serving time garnish salad with strips of green pepper. Serve with Sour Cream Dressing. Makes 12 to 15 servings.

Sour Cream Dressing: Mix together 1 c. dairy sour cream, 1 tsp. horse-radish, ½ tsp. sugar and ¼ tsp. salt. Serve with Molded Holiday Salad. Makes about 1 cup.

TOMATO PERFECTION SALAD

A tasty, colorful carry-out salad
for church and other group suppers

1½ c. tomato juice	¼ tsp. salt
1 bay leaf	½ c. chopped celery
1 (3 oz.) pkg. lemon flavor	½ c. shredded carrots
gelatin	½ c. shredded cabbage
⅓ c. water	¼ c. chopped green onion
2 tblsp. vinegar	¼ c. chopped green pepper

Combine tomato juice and bay leaf in saucepan. Bring to a boil and simmer a few minutes. Remove bay leaf.

Dissolve gelatin in hot tomato juice. Stir in water, vinegar and salt. Chill until partially thickened. Fold vegetables into gelatin. Pour into 8" square pan. Chill until firm. Makes 6 servings.

Beautiful Two-Tone Molded Salad

Two-Tone Molded Salad is a gorgeous country treat. The recipe is really a two-in-one special. You can fix only the tomato aspic or the cottage cheese layer, but do put them together for a more showy and larger salad. It's worth the extra work.

TWO-TONE MOLDED SALAD

Red and white beauty contains many flavors
blended perfectly

Tomato Aspic Layer:

1 tblsp. unflavored gelatin	1 tsp. sugar
¾ c. canned tomato juice	¼ tsp. seasoned salt
⅔ c. canned tomato sauce	1 tblsp. grated onion
2 tsp. canned lemon juice	

Cottage Cheese Layer:

1 tblsp. unflavored gelatin	½ c. diced cucumber
¼ c. cold water	¾ c. light cream
¾ tsp. salt	2 c. small curd creamed
¼ tsp. paprika	cottage cheese

To make tomato aspic, sprinkle gelatin over tomato juice in saucepan to soften. Heat slowly until gelatin is dissolved, stirring. Add remaining ingredients, mixing well. Pour into mold and chill until firm.

To make cottage cheese layer, soften gelatin in cold water 5 minutes; dissolve over hot water. Add to remaining ingredients; mix well. Pour over tomato aspic layer. Chill until firm.

To serve, unmold on plate; garnish with salad greens and lemon wedges. Pass mayonnaise. Makes 6 to 8 servings.

JELLIED VEGETABLES IN TOMATO CASES

The filled tomatoes look like flowers

8 medium firm tomatoes	2 c. mixed cooked
1 (3 oz.) pkg. lemon flavor	vegetables (carrots, green
gelatin	beans, peas and celery)
½ tsp. salt	Lettuce greens

Wash tomatoes; remove a thin slice from top of each. Scoop out centers and reserve. Place tomato cases upside down on plate to drain until ready to fill. Chill.

Add enough water to scooped out tomato centers to make 1½ c. Bring to a boil. Dissolve gelatin in boiling tomato juice; add salt. Chill until mixture is slightly thickened.

Fold in vegetables and fill tomatoes with gelatin mixture. Chill several hours.

To serve, cut each tomato almost through, into sixths, using sharp knife that has been dipped in hot water. Arrange on crisp lettuce greens; garnish with mayonnaise. Makes 8 servings.

NOTE: You can use frozen mixed vegetables, cooked and drained, in this salad. Take care not to overcook.

COLORFUL VEGETABLE SALAD

This make-ahead vegetable-fruit mold
adds brightness and texture to meals

1 (3 oz.) pkg. lime flavor gelatin	½ c. chopped celery
	½ c. grated carrots
1 c. boiling water	½ c. finely shredded
1 (8 oz.) can crushed pineapple	cabbage
	½ c. finely chopped red or
2 tblsp. vinegar	green pepper
¼ tsp. salt	Lettuce

Dissolve gelatin in boiling water. Drain pineapple. Add pineapple juice to vinegar in measuring cup; add enough cold water to make 1 c. Stir into gelatin mixture. Chill until partially thickened.

Fold in remaining ingredients. Pour into 1-qt. mold, or 8 × 8 × 2″ pan. Chill until firm. Serve unmolded on lettuce. Makes 6 servings.

SPINACH-CHEESE SALAD

A zippy salad that's not too sweet. Creamy lemon
flavor gelatin base tenderly holds crisp raw vegetables

2 (3 oz.) pkgs. lemon flavor gelatin	½ tsp. pepper
	½ c. diced celery
2 c. boiling water	½ c. diced green pepper
1 c. cold water	2 tblsp. finely chopped
2 c. small curd creamed cottage cheese	onion
	2 c. coarsely chopped fresh,
½ c. salad dressing	or 2 (10 oz.) pkgs. frozen
3 tblsp. vinegar	spinach
½ tsp. salt	Lettuce

336

Dissolve gelatin in boiling water. Stir in cold water; refrigerate until gelatin is syrupy.

Meanwhile, beat cheese, salad dressing, vinegar, salt and pepper together until smooth. Beat in partially set gelatin. Fold in vegetables; pour into 12 × 7½ × 2″ glass dish. Refrigerate. When firm, cut into 12 servings and serve on crisp lettuce.

NOTE: If you use frozen spinach, thaw, drain well and gently squeeze out excess liquid before adding to gelatin mixture.

STAG LINE SALAD

Church Supper Salad is the nickname for this colorful, inexpensive and unusually flavorful molded salad

1 (3 oz.) pkg. lemon flavor
   gelatin
½ tsp. salt
1 c. boiling water
¾ c. cold water
2 tblsp. vinegar

½ c. shredded cabbage
½ c. shredded carrots
½ c. finely diced celery
¼ c. minced green pepper
2 tblsp. bottled French
   dressing

Dissolve gelatin and salt in boiling water. Add cold water and vinegar; chill until partially thickened.

Combine vegetables and French dressing. Chill until gelatin is ready. Fold into gelatin. Chill until firm in 10 × 6 × 1½″ glass dish. Makes 6 servings.

MIXED VEGETABLE SALAD

A fine fix-ahead salad for company— with a dressing just right for it

1⅓ c. chopped cucumber (1
   medium)
2½ c. chopped onions
¾ c. chopped green pepper
2 c. chopped celery
¾ c. sugar
1 tsp. salt
⅛ tsp. pepper
⅓ c. vinegar

2 (3 oz.) pkgs. lemon flavor
   gelatin
2 c. boiling water
2 c. cold water
1 c. mayonnaise or salad
   dressing
1 tblsp. sugar
2 tblsp. chili sauce or
   ketchup
⅛ tsp. garlic salt

Combine vegetables with sugar, salt, pepper and vinegar. Let stand several hours or overnight. Drain dry.

Dissolve gelatin in boiling water. Add cold water. Chill until partially set. Fold in vegetables. Pour into 13 × 9 × 2″ pan. Chill until firm.

Serve topped with salad dressing made by combining mayonnaise, sugar, chili sauce and garlic salt. Makes 12 servings.

VEGETABLE RIBBON SALAD

Brilliant and colorful for a crowd

9 (3 oz.) pkgs. lemon flavor
    gelatin
2 qts. boiling water
1¾ qts. cold water
⅔ c. vinegar
2 tblsp. salt
1½ qts. finely chopped
    cabbage

1½ qts. grated carrots
1½ qts. raw spinach, finely
    chopped
3 tblsp. finely cut green
    onions
Crisp lettuce

Dissolve gelatin in boiling water; add cold water, vinegar and salt. Divide into three parts. Chill until slightly thickened.

Add cabbage to first part of gelatin. Turn into six 8½ × 4½ × 2½″ loaf pans, to depth of 1″. Chill until firm.

Add carrots to second part of thickened gelatin; pour over firm cabbage layers. Chill until firm.

Add spinach and onion to remaining gelatin; pour over carrot layers. Chill until firm.

Unmold; cut each loaf into 8 slices. Serve on crisp lettuce. Makes 48 servings.

CHAPTER EIGHT

Vegetable Soups

EVERY DAY is a good day to serve soup. Warm weather or cold, summer or winter, we have soup specialties that really satisfy. Our winter favorites are hot and hearty. While many of the summer soups are frosty cold, there also are wonderful piping hot soups made from fresh garden vegetables. They furnish the appetizing hot dish in an otherwise cold supper. You'll find recipes for both kinds in this chapter.

On a sultry evening, try Cucumber Cool Soup. Made with chopped cucumbers combined with canned condensed frozen cream of potato soup, thoroughly chilled and topped with a sprinkling of chopped chives, it's a dream come true. Or fix hot Cream of Squash-Corn Soup, delightful with tiny summer squash and corn cut from the cob, accented with bacon flavor. Since this soup has a milk base, you can understand why the Texas mother who invented it calls it a meal-in-a-bowl. Our taste-testers insisted on a vote of honor for Creamy Cauliflower Soup. Undertones of Cheddar cheese make it special.

While summer soups, both hot and cold, continuously gain prestige in country meals, they do not subtract from the popularity of winter soups. A Nebraska farm woman told one of our food editors that there's no more cheerful sight on a cold day than a kettle of soup simmering and sputtering on the kitchen range. Her husband quickly retorted: "Not unless it's a bowl of steaming soup already at your place on the table!"

Men praise Potato Soup with Dumplings, a recipe from an Iowa farmer's wife, who says her mother-in-law taught her how to make it. This chapter also contains many new versions of old-time classic soups, such as Chicken Gumbo from Mississippi, color-gay with chopped tomatoes and okra, and Two-Bean Soup, which starts out with pea beans, to which green beans are added later. Ham butt reinforces this soup's flavors. Recipes for split pea and lentil soups also enhance this chapter. And, for good measure, we list soup garnishes that provide texture, flavor and often color as well.

Garnishes for Country Soups

When the soup is in bowls ready to take to the table, add a garnish to each serving. Here are a few trims our readers have suggested. Let your imagination furnish you with others.

Crunchy slivered almonds, toasted (especially on potato soups)
Popped corn on tomato and other soups
Bits of crisp-cooked bacon
Chopped or snipped parsley
Chopped chives
Dollops of dairy sour cream on hot as well as cold soups
Pats of butter on hot soups
Puffs of whipped cream (a touch of horseradish added)
Topping of salted whipped cream
Thin frankfurter slices (especially on bean and split pea soups)
Grated cheese
Thin lemon slices
Thin slices of pimiento-stuffed olives
Paper-thin carrot or radish slices
Crumbled potato chips
Crumbled corn chips
Chopped or scissors-snipped water cress
Finely diced red tomatoes
Crisp ready-to-eat cereals
Tiny dumplings
Tiny meat balls
Croutons

NOTE: To make croutons, spread bread slices with butter, adding a touch of garlic if desired. Toast in a slow oven (300°) or in a little hot fat in a skillet. Trim off crusts and cut bread in ½″ squares. Or cut trimmed bread slices in ½″ squares and toss in melted butter. Toast in broiler.

Potato Soup with Dumplings

This soup ranks first with a young Iowa dairyman, whose mother taught his wife, a trained home economist, how to make it. The hearty dish with crisp crackers or rolls and a tray of relishes, such as carrot sticks, celery and pickles, frequently takes the spotlight in company suppers.

POTATO SOUP WITH DUMPLINGS

The dumplings are light and tasty

Soup:

1 c. diced celery	1 medium onion, chopped
½ c. water	2 tsp. salt
6 medium potatoes	¼ tsp. pepper
2 c. water	3 c. milk

Dumplings:

1 c. sifted flour	1 tsp. parsley flakes
1½ tsp. baking powder	1 egg
½ tsp. salt	½ c. milk
½ tsp. sugar	

Cook celery in ½ c. water just until tender. Do not drain.

Peel and cube potatoes. Place in 4-qt. saucepan with 2 c. water. Add cooked celery, onion, salt and pepper. Cook until potatoes are tender. Mash slightly to eliminate definite cubes. Add milk; set aside until dumplings are mixed.

To make dumplings, sift together flour, baking powder, salt and sugar. Stir in parsley flakes.

Beat egg; add milk; add to dry ingredients and mix just until moistened.

Bring soup to a boil. Drop dumplings by tablespoonfuls into liquid so they don't touch. Turn heat to simmer, cover tightly; simmer gently 20 minutes. *Don't lift lid.* Makes 6 servings.

LIMA BEAN CHOWDER

*A good soup for any season. Took high honors
in our taste tests*

2 c. chopped onions (2
   medium)
½ c. chopped green pepper
   (1 small)
2 tblsp. butter or margarine
1 (10 oz.) pkg. frozen lima
   beans
1 c. cubed potatoes (1
   medium)
3 c. water

2 tsp. salt
¼ tsp. pepper
1 c. shredded cabbage
1 (1 lb.) can whole kernel
   corn (2 c.)
1 (14½ oz.) can evaporated
   milk
1 (4 oz.) pkg. process
   American cheese, grated

Cook onions and green pepper in butter until soft. Add
lima beans, potatoes, water and seasonings; bring to a boil
and simmer 5 minutes. Add cabbage and corn and continue simmering until vegetables are tender, about 10
minutes.

Add remaining ingredients; cook, stirring frequently,
until heated thoroughly and cheese is melted. Makes 6
servings.

POTATO CHOWDER

*It's nice to come home to on a cool evening.
Try it on your family*

3 tblsp. butter
1 c. chopped onion
3 c. diced peeled potatoes
¾ c. chopped celery
¾ c. grated carrot

2 tsp. salt
⅛ tsp. pepper
3 c. water
3 c. milk
½ tsp. parsley flakes

Melt butter in large saucepan. Add onion and cook
until soft. Add potatoes, celery, carrot, salt, pepper and
water. Simmer until all vegetables are tender, about 15
minutes. Add milk and parsley. Heat just to boiling. Makes
6 big servings.

WATER CRESS SOUP

A spring song in the soup bowl

2 cans condensed cream of chicken soup	**½ c. chopped water cress (about ¼ bunch)**
2 soup cans milk	**2 hard-cooked eggs, sliced**

Empty soup into saucepan. Add milk; heat as directed on can.

Wash water cress. Save sprigs for garnish. Chop very fine. Add to hot soup just before serving.

Pour into soup bowls. Top each serving with egg slice and sprig of water cress. Makes 6 servings.

Vegetable-Beef Soup

You can't make the traditional vegetable-beef soup on the run; it must simmer lazily for a few hours. But if you're going to be at home, you need to do almost no pot watching while the beef cooks to tenderness. It takes about the same time to prepare and cook the vegetables in the soup as it does to get most dinners—about 1 hour. And if you make a large quantity and freeze what you do not use at the first serving, you're meals ahead.

Reheating frozen soup is something the men can do at noon when you're away. With a molded salad or plenty of relishes in the refrigerator and a pie on the kitchen counter, no one will complain of starving while you are gone. Frozen soup also is great for you to heat when you return home late in the afternoon and want to get supper fast. Remember to set the container of frozen soup on the kitchen counter or in the refrigerator before you leave home so it will start to thaw.

VEGETABLE-BEEF SOUP

Recipe for this "like mother used to make" soup provides 6 quarts. Freeze some for days you're away at noon

3 lbs. shin beef with bone	1 c. sliced carrots
3 qts. water	1 c. sliced potatoes
2 tblsp. salt	1 c. shredded cabbage
2 tsp. Worcestershire sauce	1 turnip, peeled and cubed
¼ tsp. pepper	1 (1 lb. 12 oz.) can
1 medium onion, chopped	tomatoes (3½ c.)
1 c. chopped celery	2 tsp. parsley flakes

Combine beef, water, salt, Worcestershire sauce and pepper in large kettle. Cover and simmer until meat is tender, 2½ to 3 hours. Remove meat from soup; cut from bone in small pieces and return meat to soup.

Add remaining ingredients. Simmer until vegetables are tender, about 45 minutes. Makes about 6 quarts.

NOTE: If desired, you may add one or two of the following loose-pack frozen vegetables: peas, corn, green beans. Add 1 c. of each vegetable that you use just long enough before serving for the vegetables to cook tender. Or you can add ⅓ c. barley, regular rice or broken-up spaghetti.

Minestrone—the Hearty Soup

There are as many versions of this substantial soup as there are women of Italian descent or chefs in Italian restaurants, both of whom make it superlatively. All versions feature many vegetables, simmered low until tender. Some of the soups contain meat and others only beef stock.

All the good cooks we consulted, when we tested recipes for minestrone, agreed on one point. Here's the way one woman put it: "Be sure to sprinkle a wee touch of dried basil leaves (crushed fresh ones if you have them) and grated Parmesan cheese on the soup after you ladle it into serving bowls."

We heeded the advice and were glad we did. Our own Test Kitchen variation was to add the basil to the Parmesan cheese, passing a bowl of the mixture and letting everyone help himself. This is one recipe where the bit of basil actually seems essential.

MINESTRONE

This is a big recipe for the great Italian soup
—freeze the surplus

1½ lbs. shin beef with bone
1 c. dried navy beans
5 qts. water
2 tblsp. salt
½ tsp. pepper
2 c. chopped onion
1 clove garlic, minced
1½ c. diced celery
2 c. finely shredded
  cabbage
1½ c. diced carrots
1 medium potato, peeled
  and cubed

1 tblsp. parsley flakes
½ lb. ground chuck
1½ c. thinly sliced fresh or
  frozen zucchini or small
  yellow squash
1 c. frozen loose-pack green
  beans
1½ c. broken-up uncooked
  spaghetti
Grated Parmesan or
  Romano cheese
Basil leaves

Place shin beef, beans, water, salt and pepper in large kettle. Cover and simmer 3 hours. (This may be done a day ahead.)

Remove meat from mixture and cut meat from bones. Add meat to soup. Add onion, garlic, celery, cabbage, carrots, potato and parsley.

Brown ground chuck and add to mixture. Cover and simmer until vegetables are tender, about 30 minutes. Add squash, green beans and spaghetti. Simmer until spaghetti is cooked, about 10 to 15 minutes. Taste for seasonings; you may wish to add an additional tablespoon salt. Serve in bowls and sprinkle with cheese and a pinch of dried basil leaves. Makes about 7 quarts.

VEGETABLE-HAMBURGER SOUP

Broth bolsters beef flavor and helps soup earn a top rating

1 lb. ground beef
½ c. chopped onion
1 (1 lb.) can tomatoes (2 c.)
2 c. diced carrots
2 c. cubed potatoes
½ c. diced celery

2 tsp. salt
¼ tsp. pepper
¼ c. rice
1 (14 oz.) can beef broth
1 qt. water

Brown ground beef in large kettle or Dutch oven. Add remaining ingredients; cover, and simmer 1 hour. Makes 8 servings.

NOTE: If you cannot buy canned beef broth, use a scant cup of water and a packaged beef flavor, following label directions.

DEVILED GREEN PEA SOUP

Ham and pea flavors combine so well—promise goodness in serving bowls

3 cans condensed green pea
  soup
1 (4½ oz.) can deviled
  ham, or 2 (2¼ to 3 oz.)
  cans

3 soup cans water
Snipped parsley

Combine soup and deviled ham. Add water gradually, blending until smooth; heat. Serve garnished with snipped parsley. Makes 8 servings.

SPEEDY VEGETABLE SOUP

A quick, tasty soup for lunch or supper; make it with foods on hand

1 (12 oz.) can roast beef,
  broken in bite-size pieces
  with fork
2 qts. water
2 to 3 c. canned tomatoes
  or tomato juice
1 tsp. salt
1 tsp. onion flakes, or 1
  medium onion, chopped

½ tsp. garlic salt, or ⅛ tsp.
  garlic powder
⅛ tsp. coarse grind pepper
2 tsp. beef-seasoned stock
  base, or 2 beef bouillon
  cubes
1 (10 oz.) pkg. frozen mixed
  vegetables

Place beef in large (3- to 4-qt.) kettle. Add water, tomatoes (break up whole ones in bite-size pieces), salt and onion flakes. Bring to a boil; add remaining ingredients. Heat to simmering; continue simmering until vegetables are tender, about 15 minutes. Serve piping hot in preheated soup bowls. Makes 6 to 8 servings.

NOTE: You can substitute 1½ c. leftover roast beef or pot roast for the canned roast beef.

Split Pea-Vegetable Soup

When the cold north wind whirls noisily around the house, it challenges farm women to fix a big kettle of Split Pea-Vegetable Soup. They know it will warm the hearts as well as the stomachs of family members doing outdoor chores. This is one of the thick, hot country soups that carries the aroma and flavor of smoked ham.

Soup is the ideal place for split peas, which tend to lose their shape and become mushy during cooking. This gives split pea soup that "full body." Apple or pear salad is a pleasing accompaniment.

SPLIT PEA-VEGETABLE SOUP

You can float frankfurter or Polish sausage slices on piping hot soup

1 lb. dried split peas (2 c.)	½ tsp. pepper
3 qts. water	¼ tsp. marjoram leaves
1 meaty ham bone, or 1½ lbs. ham hocks	1½ c. chopped onions
	¾ c. chopped carrots
2 tsp. salt	¾ c. chopped celery

Combine peas and water in large kettle. Bring to a boil; simmer 2 minutes. Remove from heat, cover and let stand 1 hour.

Add ham bone, salt, pepper, marjoram and onions. Cover and simmer 1½ hours.

Add carrots and celery. Continue simmering until tender, 30 to 40 minutes. Add more salt if necessary. Serve piping hot. Makes about 3½ quarts.

VALENCIA SOUP

A vegetable soup so Spanish that you almost hear guitar music

2 c. diced peeled potatoes
2 c. shredded cabbage
1 tblsp. minced onion, or 1
   tsp. instant minced onion
1 tblsp. minced parsley, or 1
   tsp. dried parsley flakes
3 tblsp. olive or salad oil
1 c. canned tomatoes

1 c. chopped cooked ham or
   other leftover meat
1 tsp. salt
⅛ tsp. coarse pepper
1½ qts. soup stock
3 tblsp. uncooked rice
1 c. fresh or frozen peas,
   cooked

Put potatoes and cabbage in large heavy saucepan or stew pot; add onion, parsley and oil. Stir and cook until onion is soft, cabbage wilted and limp and potatoes barely cooked and retaining shape. Add tomatoes, meat, salt, pepper and soup stock.

Simmer 20 minutes; add rice and cook 20 minutes longer, or until rice is done. Add peas; heat and serve. Makes 8 servings.

NOTE: If you do not have soup stock, you can make your own by dissolving 3 tblsp. beef- or chicken-seasoned stock base in 1½ qts. water.

Bacon Seasons Wax Bean Chowder

Just as bacon so marvelously seasons many of the best vegetable dishes, it makes soups enticing. Added discreetly, which means in small amounts, it does something good to the delicate warm soups of summer. Wax Bean Chowder is a perfect example. Taste-testers excitedly exclaimed: "Wonderful!"

Select it for your soup of the evening when the garden furnishes tender, slender yellow beans. It supplies the right warm touch to an otherwise cold supper or lunch. Do try it (also Cream of Squash-Corn Soup) on a day sultry enough to make chilled melon or ice cream the dessert that most appeals.

WAX BEAN CHOWDER

Serve this soup piping hot with cold cuts or sandwiches, for supper

2½ c. wax beans, cut in
¼" pieces
3 c. water
2 tsp. salt
¼ tsp. pepper
1 c. diced potatoes (1
medium)

¼ c. chopped onion
2 slices bacon, diced
3 c. milk
2 tblsp. flour
1 tblsp. butter

In large saucepan, cook wax beans with water, salt, and pepper until almost tender. Add potatoes, onion and bacon, and cook until potatoes are tender.

Blend a little milk into flour until mixture is smooth. Add flour mixture and milk to beans. Heat just to boiling, stirring occasionally. Add butter. Makes 8 servings.

TWO-BEAN SOUP

Freeze part of soup to reheat later. For a sure-to-please supper serve with garlic bread and apple dessert

1 lb. dried white beans
(navy or Great Northern)
2 qts. water
2 c. chopped onions (2
medium)
2 c. chopped celery
2 lean smoked ham hocks
(about 2 lbs.)
2 tblsp. salt

1 tsp. pepper
⅛ tsp. thyme leaves
⅛ tsp. orégano leaves
2 bay leaves
2 qts. water
1 c. sliced carrots
4 c. green beans, cut in 1"
strips (1 lb.)

Wash white beans. Place in 8-qt. kettle with 2 qts. water. Bring to a boil and boil 2 minutes. Remove from heat and let beans soak, covered, 1 hour.

Add onions, celery, ham hocks, salt, pepper, thyme, orégano, bay leaves, and 2 qts. water to beans. Cover and simmer until beans are tender, about 1½ hours.

Add carrots and green beans; simmer until beans are tender, about 45 minutes. Check seasonings—the amount of salt required varies with saltiness of the ham hocks. Makes about 5 quarts.

Cream of Squash-Corn Soup

A Texas farm woman explains the origin of her favorite summer soup this way: "Corn, squash, onions and green peppers mature at the same time in our garden. Finding enough ways to use these vegetables to break the monotony is a problem. When I invented Cream of Squash-Corn Soup," she reports, "it made a great hit.

"To complete the supper menu," she says, "I often have grilled cheese sandwiches and juicy-ripe peaches, sliced."

All our taste-testers agreed that they'd be happy to sit down to this kind of supper on a summer evening. Chances are good that your family will have the same reactions.

CREAM OF SQUASH-CORN SOUP

Perfect go-with for supper sandwiches—you can easily double recipe

2 c. grated white or yellow squash
2 c. fresh corn, cut from cob
2 c. boiling water
1 c. chopped onion
½ c. chopped green pepper
6 tblsp. butter or margarine

6 tblsp. flour
5 c. milk
1 tblsp. salt
¼ tsp. pepper
8 slices bacon, diced, cooked and drained (optional)

Combine squash, corn, and water. Cover and simmer until tender.

Meanwhile, cook onion and green pepper in melted butter until soft. Stir in flour. Add milk, and cook, stirring constantly, until thickened. Add to squash-corn mixture along with salt and pepper. Heat thoroughly.

Serve in bowls. Garnish with bacon, if you like. Makes 9 cups.

BEAN AND BACON SOUP

Six vegetables get together in this hearty soup— no wonder it's so good

1 lb. dried navy beans (2½ c.)	2 c. diced celery
3 qts. water	1 c. sliced carrots
8 slices bacon, diced	1 (1 lb. 14 oz.) can tomato juice (5½ c.)
3 c. chopped onions (2 large)	4 tsp. salt
2 c. diced potatoes	1 tsp. pepper
	1 bay leaf

Combine beans and water in large kettle. Bring to a boil and boil 2 minutes. Remove from heat. Cover and let stand 1 hour.

Fry bacon until crisp. Remove from skillet and add to soup. Cook onions in bacon drippings until soft. Add to soup along with bacon drippings.

Bring soup to a boil and simmer, covered, 1 hour. Add remaining ingredients. Simmer until vegetables are tender, about 30 minutes. Remove bay leaf. Makes about 4 quarts.

PASTA AND BEAN SOUP

Superb for a cold weather supper

1 lb. dried Great Northern beans	1 (1 lb.) can stewed tomatoes
2 qts. water	½ bay leaf
2½ tsp. salt	½ tsp. orégano
1 large whole carrot	½ tsp. salt
6 strips bacon	¼ tsp. pepper
½ c. chopped onion	¼ c. water
½ c. chopped celery	1 c. ditalini or small elbow macaroni
1 small clove garlic, minced	

Soak beans 8 hours or overnight. Or bring them to a boil and boil 2 minutes; remove from heat and let them stand, covered, 1 hour. Rinse and drain.

Combine beans, 2 qts. water, salt and carrot in a 6-qt. pot; simmer 2 hours or until beans are tender.

Meanwhile, fry bacon until crisp. Remove bacon, reserving ¼ c. bacon drippings. Cook onion, celery and garlic in bacon drippings. Stir in tomatoes, bay leaf, orégano, salt, pepper and ¼ c. water. Bring to boil; simmer 30 minutes. Remove bay leaf.

Cook macaroni according to package directions. Drain.

Purée half of the beans. Cube the carrot. Crumble bacon. Combine all ingredients and heat through before serving. Makes 3½ quarts.

NOTE: With crusty bread, salad and dessert, this soup makes a meal.

SEPTEMBER VEGETABLE SOUP

This soup is the best way to salvage
the end-of-the-garden vegetables

2 qts. boiling water
3½ tsp. salt
2 c. sliced carrots
2 c. cubed peeled potatoes
2 c. diced peeled tomatoes
2 c. snipped green onions
   with tops
1½ c. small fresh limas, or
   1 (10 oz.) pkg. frozen
   lima beans

1 lb. green beans, cut in 1"
   pieces
1 c. uncooked corn, scraped
   from cob
¼ tsp. coarse-grind pepper
3 c. cooked rice
½ c. crisp-cooked bacon
   bits or chopped cooked
   ham

Bring water and salt to a boil in large kettle. Add carrots, potatoes, tomatoes, onions, limas and green beans. Simmer 30 minutes; add corn and pepper and cook 15 minutes more.

To serve, spoon heaping tablespoonfuls hot cooked rice in soup bowls or soup plates. Ladle soup over rice and sprinkle with bacon bits. Makes 8 servings.

CREAM OF VEGETABLE CHOWDER

This hearty, rich, thick soup, plus a sandwich, make a
pleasing Sunday or Saturday night supper menu

4 slices bacon, diced
½ c. chopped onion
1 branch celery, sliced
½ c. canned mushrooms,
   stems and pieces
3 tblsp. flour
1 qt. milk

1 (10 oz.) pkg. frozen
   mixed vegetables
1½ c. coarsely crushed
   potato chips
1 to 1½ tsp. salt
⅛ tsp. pepper

Fry bacon in large saucepan until crisp. Add onion, celery and mushrooms. Cook 5 minutes.

Stir in flour, then remaining ingredients. Bring to boil, stirring constantly. Simmer until vegetables are tender, about 15 minutes; stir occasionally. Makes 6 to 8 servings.

NOTE: If you like a thinner soup, add a little more milk. Or reduce amount of flour, if you prefer.

French Peasant Soup

When you eat the many delicious vegetable soups made by recipes in this cookbook, you'll conclude, as our testers did, that soup bowls are neglected in too many American homes. Some of the most famous dishes of foreign countries are substantial soups that hold many succulent vegetables. With salad and a fruit dessert, they make a meal.

French Peasant Soup is a splendid example. If you travel in France, you discover that there are many variations in different areas. We give you one of them, a soup enriched and flavored by seven vegetables, all of which are commonly available in our markets, with the exception of leeks.

FRENCH PEASANT SOUP

*Freeze or refrigerate leftover soup to reheat later—
seems to improve in flavor the next time around*

¾ c. dried white navy
  beans
1 qt. water
8 slices bacon, chopped
3 onions, sliced
12 c. shredded cabbage (3
  lb. head)
4 medium turnips, peeled
  and cubed
2 carrots, peeled and sliced
2 leeks, thickly sliced
  (optional)

2 cloves garlic, minced
6 boiling potatoes, peeled
  and cubed
2½ qts. water
2 tblsp. salt
½ tsp. pepper
½ tsp. thyme leaves
1 lb. uncooked garlic pork
  sausage, fresh or smoked
  (French, Italian or Polish)

Wash beans. Combine with 1 qt. water in an 8-qt. kettle. Bring to a boil and boil 2 minutes. Remove from heat, cover and let stand 1 hour. Simmer beans until tender, 1 to 1½ hours.

Cook bacon. Add to beans. Cook onion slices in bacon fat until slightly browned on both sides. Add to beans along with bacon fat.

Add remaining ingredients, except sausage. Bring to a boil and simmer, covered, 30 minutes. Add sausage and continue cooking until all vegetables are tender, 15 to 20 minutes.

Remove sausage. The French slice this and serve it separately, but most American women prefer to return slices to soup. Serve in large soup plates. You can ladle the soup over slices of toasted and buttered hard rolls or crusty bread. Makes about 6 quarts.

CORN CHOWDER

Cool chowder before serving if there's time—
reheating improves it

¼ lb. salt pork, diced
3 medium onions, chopped
3 or 4 potatoes, peeled and diced
½ c. water

4 c. corn, cut from cob
1 qt. milk
2 tsp. salt
⅛ tsp. pepper

Fry pork until almost crisp; add onions and cook until golden brown—this gives a definite tang to the chowder.

Add potatoes and water; simmer 5 minutes. Add corn and cook 5 minutes more, or until tender.

Stir in milk, salt and pepper. Heat slowly until chowder is piping hot. Makes 6 to 8 servings.

Idaho Lentil Soup Supreme

"Most people who taste lentils for the first time are pleasantly surprised at their delicious, nutty flavor," says the wife of an Idaho lentil grower. And she points out that a major advantage of the vegetable is the splendid way it teams with other vegetables and takes to a variety of seasonings.

Like other dried peas and beans, lentils are inexpensive and nutritious. They supply a big share of the daily requirements for protein, vitamin and mineral needs. And unlike dried peas and beans, lentils cook quickly, in 30 minutes, without presoaking.

You don't have to live in Idaho or Washington, where most of this country's lentils grow, to locate the vegetable. Look for it alongside the dried beans and split peas in supermarkets.

Hundreds of people at Idaho's Latah County Fair enjoy bowls of steaming lentil soup—that's how the growers show pride in their crop and promote it. The recipes for this Idaho Lentil Soup and for Vegetable-Lentil Chowder follow (see Index for recipe for Ranch-Style Lentil Casserole).

The recipe for Idaho Lentil Soup is a big one, but you'll find it comforting to have a supply in the freezer to fall back on for a hurry-up meal.

Once your family and friends get acquainted with the taste of lentil soup or chowder, they'll rejoice when they see you ladling it into soup bowls for supper on a chilly evening.

VEGETABLE-LENTIL CHOWDER

You'll like this hearty soup. It has color and fine flavor

1½ c. lentils, washed	⅓ c. butter or margarine
1 qt. water	½ c. chopped pimientos
2½ tsp. salt	1 (1 lb. 14 oz.) can
¾ c. chopped onion	tomatoes
⅔ c. chopped green pepper	¼ tsp. pepper

Combine lentils, water and salt in large saucepan. Cook, covered, over medium heat 30 minutes.

Cook onion and green pepper in butter until tender. Combine all ingredients; simmer, covered, 30 minutes. Makes 6 large servings.

IDAHO LENTIL SOUP

This 4-gallon recipe freezes well

½ c. bacon drippings
½ lb. onions, thinly sliced
3 large carrots, chopped
8 branches celery, finely
  chopped
⅓ c. flour
3¼ lbs. lentils, washed
2 meaty ham bones
3¼ gals. beef broth or
  bouillon

1 tblsp. sugar
2 tsp. pepper
½ tsp. garlic powder
  (optional)
2 bay leaves (optional)
6 frankfurters, diagonally
  sliced
Salt

Combine bacon drippings, onions, carrots and celery in 4-gal. kettle. Cook, covered, 20 minutes.

Stir in flour, then other ingredients, except the sliced frankfurters. Simmer, uncovered, 3 hours. After 1 hour, cut meat from bones; chop. Return meat and bones to kettle.

Just before serving, remove the bones, add sliced frankfurters to heat, and salt to taste. Makes 50 servings.

When preparing soup stock for your freezer, pour it into loaf pans. After the soup is frozen, it can be removed from the pans and wrapped in plastic bags. Return it to the freezer for storage.

Broth Enriches Soups

Chicken broth, as well as beef broth, is the magic seasoning in many meatless vegetable soups. Keep home-made broth in the freezer and bring some out when you're in a soup-making mood. Or buy cans from your super-market. Once you get the habit of substituting broth for part of water or milk in vegetable soups, you'll stick to it. And you'll get out the soup ketttle more frequently.

Creamy Cauliflower Soup made with 2 c. chicken broth is an example. Enriched also with cheese and sprinkled with chopped chives or parsley, it will tempt everyone around your dining table. Equally tasty and appealing are the other broth- or stock-flavored vegetable soups in this chapter.

CHICKEN BROTH OR STOCK

Keep this on hand in the freezer

1 large stewing chicken, or
    4 lbs. chicken necks and
    backs
1 medium onion, peeled
2 whole cloves
1 branch celery (with
    leaves)

1 peeled carrot (optional)
2 sprigs parsley
1 tsp. salt
⅛ tsp. pepper
Water

Wash chicken and put into a kettle with vegetables and seasonings (stick cloves into onion).

Add boiling water to cover the chicken completely. Cover and simmer gently for about 2 hours, or until chicken is tender.

Remove chicken, strip meat from bones and refrigerate for other use. Return bones to broth and simmer for another 45 minutes.

Strain broth; remove fat as directed in recipe that follows for Beef Broth. Makes about 1 qt.

BEEF BROTH OR STOCK

The foundation for superior soup

4 lbs. beef soup bones
    (pieces)
2½ qts. cold water
1 tsp. salt
1 bay leaf
1 medium onion, peeled

2 whole cloves
5 whole peppercorns
1 carrot, scraped
1 branch celery (with
    leaves)
2 sprigs parsley

Remove meat from bones; cut it in small pieces. Put meat, bones, water, seasonings and vegetables in a kettle (stick cloves into onion). Do not cover. Simmer (do not boil) 3 hours. Strain. (You can use the meat in hash or sandwiches.)

To remove fat from broth: Skim off with spoon. Or lay a paper towel on surface of fat; when it's saturated, repeat with more towels until fat is removed. Or wrap an ice cube in a paper towel and draw across the top of the broth, changing paper as needed. Or refrigerate the broth overnight; you can then lift off the congealed fat with a spoon.

To clarify broth: Crush an eggshell; mix with 1 egg and ¼ c. cold water. Stir into lukewarm defatted broth. Heat to boiling; let stand about 5 minutes and strain through two thicknesses of cheesecloth or a fine wire sieve. Makes 2 quarts.

NOTE: You can omit vegetables and seasonings in the above recipe if you are making beef broth to use in Garden Row Soup (recipe follows).

GARDEN ROW SOUP

*Get out soup bowls and invite guests to share
this end-of-the-garden treat*

2 qts. Beef Broth (made
    without vegetables),
    clarified
2 tsp. salt
½ tsp. orégano leaves
½ tsp. marjoram leaves
½ tsp. celery seeds
⅛ tsp. ground cumin
6 peppercorns
1 clove garlic, crushed
1 large onion, chopped
¼ c. chopped parsley

4 carrots, scraped and sliced
1 large green pepper,
    scalded, skinned, seeded
    and cut in strips
1 c. green beans, cut in
    pieces
1 zucchini, cut in ¾″ slices
3 ears sweet corn, cut in 3″
    lengths
2 large pink tomatoes,
    peeled and quartered

Simmer broth with salt, spices and garlic for 30 minutes.

Add onion, parsley, carrots, green pepper and beans; simmer 20 minutes.

Add zucchini and corn; simmer 15 minutes. Add tomatoes; simmer 15 minutes. Makes 8 servings.

NOTE: If you like, cut the corn in thin slices—they will look like rosettes in the soup.

CREAMY CAULIFLOWER SOUP

*Chicken broth plays an important seasoning role
in this superior soup*

1 medium head cauliflower,
  cut in tiny flowerets
¼ c. butter
⅔ c. chopped onion (1
  small)
2 tblsp. flour

2 c. chicken broth
2 c. light cream or rich milk
½ tsp. Worcestershire sauce
¾ tsp. salt
1 c. grated Cheddar cheese
Chopped chives or parsley

Cook cauliflower in boiling salted water; drain, reserving liquid.

Melt butter. Add onion and cook until soft. Blend in flour; add broth, and cook, stirring constantly, until mixture comes to a boil. Stir in 1 c. liquid drained from cauliflower (adding water if necessary to make 1 c.), milk, Worcestershire sauce and salt. Add cauliflower. Heat to boiling. Stir in cheese. Serve sprinkled with chopped chives or parsley. Makes about 2 quarts.

To point up the flavor of cream soups, add a tiny bit of fresh vegetable, finely chopped, just before serving. For example, add chopped tomatoes to cream of tomato; or chopped celery to cream of celery. In summer months, it's helpful to remember that most cream soups are good cold —but they have to be really cold! They'll look appetizingly frosty served in clear glass bowls.

SALSIFY SOUP

*Mock oyster stew is the Pennsylvania Dutch name
for oyster-plant soups*

1⅔ c. sliced peeled salsify
  (about ¾ lb.)
1 qt. water
1 tblsp. vinegar
2 tblsp. butter
1 tblsp. onion

2 tblsp. flour
1 c. chicken broth
1 c. milk
½ tsp. salt
½ tsp. parsley flakes
⅛ tsp. pepper

Plunge salsify slices immediately into 1 qt. water with

1 tblsp. vinegar added to prevent discoloration. Drain, and cook in 1" boiling salted water until tender, 15 to 20 minutes.

Meanwhile, melt butter. Add onion and cook until soft. Blend in flour, then chicken broth and milk. Cook, stirring constantly, until mixture comes to a boil. Add remaining ingredients and salsify with water in which it was cooked. Makes about 1 quart.

Continental Borsch

American travelers in Europe and the Near East almost always like the native Borsch, a hot beet soup. Most women return home hoping they can duplicate the pink soup.

Our recipe for Continental Borsch is simple; it gives tasty results. If your family and friends like the taste of beets, they'll enjoy this colorful soup.

CONTINENTAL BORSCH

An all-vegetable soup spiked with beef broth—
sour cream decorates it

2½ c. shredded fresh beets	2 c. beef broth
1 c. chopped carrots	1 c. shredded cabbage
1 medium onion, chopped	1 tblsp. butter
3 c. water	1 tblsp. lemon juice
2 tsp. salt	½ c. dairy sour cream
⅛ tsp. pepper	

In a kettle, cook beets, carrots, onion, water, salt and pepper until vegetables are tender, about 20 minutes.

Add beef broth and cabbage. Cook, uncovered, 15 minutes. Stir in butter and lemon juice. Spoon into bowls. Top with a spoonful of sour cream. Makes 6 servings.

PUMPKIN SOUP

Taste this soup and you'll know why swanky restaurants serve it

2 tblsp. butter
¼ c. chopped green pepper
2 tblsp. chopped onion
1 large sprig parsley
⅛ tsp. thyme leaves
1 bay leaf
1 (8 oz.) can tomatoes (1 c.)

1 (1 lb.) can pumpkin
2 c. chicken broth or stock
1 tblsp. flour
1 c. milk
1 tsp. salt
⅛ tsp. pepper

Melt butter in large saucepan. Add green pepper, onion, parsley, thyme and bay leaf. Cook 5 minutes. Add tomatoes, pumpkin and chicken broth. Cover and simmer 30 minutes, stirring occasionally. Press mixture through food mill or wire strainer.

Blend together flour and milk and stir into soup. Add salt and pepper and cook, stirring frequently, until mixture comes to a boil. Serve immediately. Makes 6 servings.

GREEN SOUP

If you're in an experimental mood fix this distinctive Mexican soup

1 (10 oz.) pkg. frozen
  chopped spinach, cooked
1 (1 lb.) can small peas
½ c. water
1 tblsp. butter, margarine or
  salad oil
¼ c. chopped onion
2 qts. chicken stock
1 tsp. salt

⅛ tsp. coarse grind black
  pepper
1 thin slice fresh ginger
  root, or ¼ tsp. powdered
  ginger
8 medium cooked prunes,
  seeded
1 c. chopped cooked ham

Put spinach, peas with their liquid and ½ c. water in blender container; blend 3 or 4 seconds. Or put through sieve or food mill.

Melt butter, add onion and cook until soft. Combine with blended vegetables and chicken stock in 3- to 4-qt. saucepan. Add salt, pepper and ginger root; bring to boil and let simmer over medium heat 15 minutes.

Remove ginger root. Add prunes and ham. Heat through and serve. Makes 8 servings.

NOTE: If you do not have chicken stock, dissolve 4 tblsp. chicken-seasoned stock base in 2 qts. water.

PURÉE OF CARROT SOUP

*Absolutely delicious—surprising that carrots can taste
so wonderful*

2 tblsp. butter
⅔ c. chopped onions
3 c. finely chopped carrots
1 qt. chicken broth
2 tblsp. uncooked rice

½ tsp. salt
⅛ tsp. pepper
½ c. light cream
Chopped parsley (optional)

Melt butter in large saucepan. Add onions and cook
until soft. Add carrots, chicken broth, rice and seasonings.
Simmer, uncovered, 30 minutes. Purée soup through a
food mill.

Return to saucepan and add cream. Heat just to boiling.
Garnish with chopped parsley. Makes 5 cups.

NOTE: You can double this recipe.

COUNTRY-STYLE SOUP-STEW

*Let the children fix this for lunch on Saturday—
it's almost a meal*

1 lb. frankfurters, cut in ½"
slices
2 tblsp. bacon fat or salad
oil
1 can condensed tomato
soup
1 can condensed bean with
bacon soup

½ soup can water
1 tsp. onion flakes
¼ tsp. pepper
1 (1 lb.) can mixed
vegetables
½ c. evaporated milk

Brown franks in bacon fat in kettle. Add soups, water
and seasonings, mixing until smooth.

Add mixed vegetables with their liquid; heat. Just before serving, stir in evaporated milk; heat briefly. Makes
4 to 6 servings.

*Piping hot corn bread—sticks or squares—is an excellent
go-with when you plan a soup supper.*

ZUCCHINI SOUP BASE (TO FREEZE)

*Keep handy in your freezer to make an unusual soup
that's really good*

3 lbs. zucchini (about 5
  medium)
1½ c. canned beef broth
2 c. boiling water
1½ tsp. salt

½ c. chopped onion, or 1
  tblsp. instant minced
  onion
⅛ tsp. garlic powder

Wash zucchini, remove stem and blossom ends and cut
in quarters lengthwise.

Combine zucchini and remaining ingredients. Cook until
zucchini is tender, then strain, reserving liquid.

Put strained mixture into blender to purée, or put it
through a food mill. Return to saucepan with reserved
liquid. Heat to simmering, stirring to prevent scorching.

Ladle into three 1-pt. jars, leaving ¾" head space for
expansion in freezing. Adjust lids and cool, then label and
freeze. Makes 3 pints.

NOTE: Instead of canned beef broth, you can substitute
1½ c. water and 2 tsp. beef-seasoned stock base or 2 beef
bouillon cubes.

ZUCCHINI SOUP

A nice surprise for luncheon guests

1 pt. frozen Zucchini Soup
  Base, thawed
1 c. milk or dairy half-and-
  half

Grated Parmesan cheese
Crisp-cooked bacon bits

Combine soup base and milk. Heat in double boiler or
in heavy pan over water to avoid scorching. Serve garnished with Parmesan cheese and cooked bacon bits.
Makes 4 to 5 servings.

Farmer's Welcome Chicken Soup

A big pot of soup bubbling contentedly on the stove welcomes the farm family coming in to supper after doing the chores. And especially when the evening is chilly, rainy and dark. But no matter where you live, it's heartening to return home to when the weather is nippy.

One of our food editors, visiting in Mexico City, met a chicken-vegetable soup so color-bright and tasty that it was unforgettable. When she returned to our Test Kitchens, she worked out the following recipe for it.

An unusual feature of the soup is that you eat it with knife and fork as well as a spoon.

A Missouri country woman made this soup and promptly christened it Farewell-to-Summer Soup. That's because it contains the last of summer's vegetables. She recommends that you serve hot corn bread with it for a really cheerful and filling meal.

FARMER'S WELCOME CHICKEN SOUP

Use your biggest soup plates for this hearty meal in a bowl

6 small whole chicken
  breasts or 2 frying
  chickens, cut up
3 qts. water
1 tblsp. salt
6 whole peppercorns, or
  ¼ tsp. ground pepper
⅛ tsp. ground red pepper
  (cayenne)

½ tsp. ground cumin
  (optional)
6 small onions
3 small carrots, cut in sticks
½ lb. fresh whole green
  beans—trim ends
2 small zucchini, cut in
  sticks

Place chicken pieces, water, salt, peppercorns, red pepper, cumin and onions in a large kettle. Bring to a boil and simmer, loosely covered, 1 hour, or until chicken is tender. Strain and cool broth. Save small onions. Skim off fat.

Remove and discard skin from chicken pieces (broth and chicken can be refrigerated overnight, if you wish). Trim small rib bones from chicken breasts to improve appearance.

About 30 minutes before serving, return broth to large kettle. Add carrots to one side of kettle. Bring to boil and cook 10 minutes. Add green beans to other side of kettle and continue cooking 10 minutes.

Add chicken pieces, small cooked onions and zucchini. Cook 10 minutes, until all vegetables are just tender.

To serve: Place 1 chicken breast or several pieces of chicken in bottom of each bowl. Add 1 c. broth and portions of each vegetable. Makes 6 servings.

NOTE: Vegetables can be cooked separately from soup.

CHICKEN GUMBO

Bring out the soup bowls and get ready for compliments

1 (3 to 3½ lb.) chicken, cut in pieces
½ lb. ham, cut in ½" cubes
¼ c. salad oil
1 c. chopped onion (1 medium)
⅓ c. chopped green pepper
2 tblsp. chopped hot pepper

6 large tomatoes, peeled and chopped
2 c. sliced okra
1 qt. boiling water
1 bay leaf
2 tsp. salt
½ tsp. pepper
Cooked rice (see Note)

Cook chicken pieces and ham in salad oil in large Dutch oven until browned.

Add remaining ingredients, except rice. Simmer until tender, about 45 minutes.

To serve, place spoonfuls of cooked rice in soup bowls or plates. Ladle gumbo over rice. Makes 8 servings.

NOTE: Cook rice according to package directions. To cook regular rice, combine 1 c. uncooked rice, 1 tsp. salt and 2 c. boiling water in saucepan with tightly fitting lid. Bring to a boil; stir two or three times, lower heat, cover tightly and simmer about 14 minutes without removing lid or stirring, or until all the liquid is absorbed and rice is tender. If there is leftover rice, package and freeze it. To thaw, unwrap and let stand at room temperature 3 to 3½ hours. To reheat, cover bottom of saucepan with water, add thawed rice, cover and simmer until rice is hot and fluffy. It will be ready in 8 to 10 minutes.

ZUPPA VERDE

*You'll have chicken and broth left over to freeze
or use in casserole*

1 (4 lb.) chicken	**½ tsp. pepper**
4 qts. water	**1 whole carrot, scraped**
1 large onion	**1 medium head endive**
2 branches celery with	**Grated Parmesan or**
leaves	**Romano cheese**
1 tblsp. salt	

Place all ingredients, except endive and cheese, in large
kettle. Bring to a boil and simmer, loosely covered, until
chicken is tender, about 2 hours. Strain and cool broth;
skim off fat. Save carrot.

Remove and discard skin from chicken breasts. Cut
breast meat into slivers to make 2 c.

Cook endive in boiling salted water 10 minutes. When
tender, drain and squeeze dry. Chop.

Add carrot, diced, and slivered chicken to 2 qts. chicken
broth. Heat; add endive, garnish with cheese and serve.
Makes 8 servings.

Corn-Oyster Soup

Oyster prices have soared in recent years, but the tradition of oyster stew for Christmas Eve supper lingers.
We're glad to share with you the favorite recipe of a Wisconsin farmer's wife for Corn-Oyster Soup. It tastes wonderful on a holly-decorated evening or on any winter day.

Corn stretches the oysters beautifully; the blend of
flavors is excitingly good. So before the children hang up
their Christmas stockings, why not serve them Corn-Oyster
Soup, crackers, a fruit cup or salad, Christmas cookies and
chocolate milk? They'll go to bed happy and well fed.

CORN-OYSTER SOUP

*Call this Christmas Eve soup—
it's a real special-occasion treat*

1 tblsp. butter	1 lb. oysters (about 2 c.)
1 tblsp. flour	1½ tsp. salt
1 qt. milk	¼ tsp. pepper
1 (1 lb. 1 oz.) can whole	Paprika (optional)
kernel corn	Chopped parsley (optional)

Melt butter in large saucepan. Blend in flour, then milk. Cook, stirring constantly, until mixture comes to a boil. Add corn, oysters (with their liquid), salt and pepper. Simmer 10 minutes. Serve sprinkled with paprika and parsley, if desired. Makes 6 servings.

OYSTER CHOWDER

You can keep ingredients on hand to make
this chowder on short notice

1 small onion, chopped	1 (8 oz.) can white potatoes,
2 tblsp. butter or margarine	drained and cubed
2 cans condensed oyster	2 tsp. Worcestershire sauce
stew	1 pimiento, chopped
1½ soup cans milk	(optional)

Cook onion in butter until tender. Add remaining ingredients and heat. Makes 5 cups.

Hostess trick: *Try serving soup in mugs, in the living room. That permits you to set the dining table for the main course before guests arrive. You can ladle the soup from a tureen before your guests, or fill the mugs in the kitchen.*

SPINACH-OF-THE-SEA SOUP

Pass crisp bacon bits to spoon into bowls
of this inviting hot soup

1 (10 oz.) pkg. frozen	2⅔ c. milk
chopped spinach	4 slices bacon, chopped,
1 can frozen condensed	fried and drained
oyster stew	(optional)
1 can frozen condensed	
cream of shrimp soup	

Cook spinach in boiling salted water. Drain.

Combine oyster stew, shrimp soup and milk. Add spinach. Simmer until thoroughly heated. Serve in soup bowls garnished with bacon, if desired. Makes 6 servings.

Bayou Sea Food Gumbo

It's a myth that you have to live near a bayou in Louisiana or in a coastal city to enjoy a dish like Bayou Sea Food Gumbo. Ranchers' and farmers' wives across country, with homes surrounded by wheat, corn and soybean fields, also like to serve such treats for the main dish in their guest luncheons. They frequently complete the menu with a molded cranberry, fresh grapefruit or other fruit salad, and cookies with tea or coffee for dessert.

Gumbo, by the way, is the name for cooked okra or soup containing this vegetable. You can omit the sherry in this recipe, but you'll lose some of the distinctive flavor just as you would if you left vanilla out of the cakes you bake.

BAYOU SEA FOOD GUMBO

*On cold days hot soup is a splendid main dish—
here's one for guests*

⅓ c. chopped onion	1½ c. canned clam juice or
2 tblsp. butter or margarine	chicken broth
2 (4½ to 5 oz.) cans shrimp	1 (5 to 7 oz.) can crab meat
1 can condensed tomato	1 (1 lb.) can cut okra
soup	2 tblsp. dry sherry
2 cans condensed	3 to 4 c. hot cooked rice
Manhattan clam chowder	

In a kettle, cook onion in butter until tender.

Drain and rinse shrimp in cold water.

Add soups, clam juice, shrimp and crab meat to onion. Heat almost to boiling. Add okra with the liquid from it; bring to boiling. Reduce heat and simmer gently 10 minutes. Add sherry just before serving.

To serve, mound ½ c. rice in center of each flat soup plate. Pour gumbo around rice. Makes about 8½ cups, or 6 to 8 servings.

Frosty Summer Soups

Your family and friends may think cold soups are not for them, but wait until they taste Cucumber Cool Soup. Our recipe taste-testers praised the refreshing flavor extravagantly.

Given a place on the table on an uncomfortable, sultry day, this soup is a sure winner. It both pleases and satisfies. And for a summer luncheon party, it is admirably appropriate.

Another cold soup gaining a widening circle of friends is our FARM JOURNAL Frosty Spanish Vegetable Soup. Here are recipes for it and Cucumber Cool Soup. Try them the next hot day.

CUCUMBER COOL SOUP

This refreshing soup wins compliments
of everyone who tastes it on a hot day

1 c. milk	½ tsp. salt
1 medium cucumber, peeled, seeded and diced	⅛ tsp. pepper
	1 c. heavy cream
2 cans frozen condensed cream of potato soup, thawed	Chopped chives

Pour milk and cucumber in blender container. Blend until cucumber is finely minced. Add 1 can soup; blend. Pour out half of mixture into bowl. Blend other can of soup with remaining mixture in blender. Combine in bowl with remaining ingredients, except chives. Chill thoroughly.

If desired, pour into a 13 × 9 × 2″ pan and place in freezer 30 minutes before serving, chilling until mixture just begins to freeze. Stir smooth. Or chill thoroughly in refrigerator. To serve, spoon into cups; sprinkle with chopped chives. Makes 6 servings, or 5 cups.

VICHYSSOISE

Dip in your spoon and taste—you'll want to give
thanks to the French chef in New York
who invented this cold soup

¼ c. unsalted butter	Few grains ground nutmeg
4 leeks, chopped	Few drops Worcestershire
1 onion, minced	sauce
1 qt. chicken broth	2 potatoes, peeled and thinly
1 sprig parsley	sliced
1 branch celery	1 c. heavy cream
Salt and pepper to taste	Chives to garnish

Melt butter over low heat. Add leeks and onion; cook slowly until tender, but not brown.

Add chicken broth, parsley, celery, salt, pepper, nutmeg, Worcestershire sauce and potatoes. Cook until potatoes are tender.

Put through fine sieve into china or glass bowl. Stir in heavy cream; chill.

Serve cold, sprinkled lightly with chopped chives. Makes 6 to 8 servings.

FROSTY SPANISH VEGETABLE SOUP

Make in morning to serve as evening meal
on particularly sultry days

1 c. finely chopped peeled	2 tsp. chopped or snipped
tomatoes	chives
½ c. finely chopped green	1 small clove garlic, minced
pepper	2½ tblsp. wine vinegar
½ c. finely chopped celery	2 tblsp. olive oil
½ c. finely chopped peeled	1 tsp. salt
cucumber	¼ tsp. pepper
¼ c. finely chopped onion	½ tsp. Worcestershire sauce
2 tsp. finely chopped or	2 c. tomato juice
snipped fresh parsley	

Combine all ingredients in a glass bowl; stir to mix. Cover and chill thoroughly several hours. Serve in chilled cups. Makes 6 servings.

NOTE: Double the recipe if you need more servings. You can save time by chopping the vegetables in a blender, if you like.

CHAPTER NINE

Seasonings, Sauces and Salad Dressings

No MATTER how busy you are, you can become the best vegetable cook in the neighborhood. The how-to is in this chapter, where we share kitchen secrets on seasoning and saucing vegetables. The flavor boosters we recommend are simple and quick to add, for the most part: a dash of lemon juice, a shake of seasoned salt, a pinch of dill. . . . In seasoning, you really accomplish a lot with a little. Try pouring a few spoonfuls of cream into hot, buttered garden peas; or crushing a whiff of basil over thick tomato slices ready for broiling; or cooking carrots in chicken broth instead of water.

Take a tip from the French and whip up smooth, satiny sauces to enhance the taste of vegetables. This chapter gives you new sauce recipes but also new uses for familiar well-established ones, such as Harvard Sauce. No doubt you've teamed it with beets, but you can glorify other vegetables with it.

You know, as do all country women, what pats of butter stirred into hot vegetables contribute to flavor. But have you tried seasoned butters (described in this chapter)? Keep them in the refrigerator ready to go. Our Herb Butter quickly elevates humble vegetable dishes to the gourmet class. And do try brown and black butters for their fascinating flavors.

Take chicken broth from your freezer or buy it in cans and substitute the broth for water in cooking vegetables. Your family will like the delicious change of pace. Survey the amazing number of convenient seasonings and packaged salad dressing, soup and seasoning mixes on supermarket shelves. We list some of our Test Kitchens' favorites. While many of the salad recipes in this cookbook include the dressings designed especially for them, this chapter also contains a few country specialties.

371

The pages that follow may start you on a cooking adventure that will lead to more interesting and tasty vegetable dishes—and to compliments for you.

Quick Mayonnaise Sauces

For quick, tasty sauces that elevate common vegetables to elegant dishes, combine equal parts of mayonnaise and heavy cream, whipped. Fold this cool sauce into hot peas, spinach or asparagus for a taste treat. You can substitute dairy sour cream for the whipped cream and with a little imagination, you can add seasonings that bring out the superlative flavors of the hot vegetables you wish to dress with it. Here is the recipe for the sauce base with suggestions of how to make it just right for several vegetables:

QUICK MAYONNAISE BASE

A fast start for many fine sauces

½ c. mayonnaise   ½ c. heavy cream, whipped,
                          or ½ c. dairy sour cream

Put mayonnaise in a small bowl; fold in whipped cream or dairy sour cream, mixing well. Add the desired seasonings and spoon over hot cooked vegetables. Makes about 1½ c. with whipped cream, about 1 c. with dairy sour cream.

To Quick Mayonnaise Base add the seasonings to make the following sauces:

Chili Sauce: Add ¼ c. chili sauce; mix well. Serve over corn, lima beans or baked beans.

Mustard-Dill: Add 2 tblsp. prepared mustard and ¼ tsp. dill weed. Serve on carrots, cauliflower, broccoli or Brussels sprouts.

Pickle-Horse-radish: Add 3 to 4 tblsp. well-drained pickle relish and ¼ tsp. grated horse-radish. Serve on beets, spinach and beet or mustard greens.

Place ingredients for Quick Mayonnaise Base in blender, add the following seasonings and blend:

Easy Cheese: Add ½ c. shredded sharp Cheddar cheese. It's good on most vegetables.

Velvety Sauce: Use whipped cream instead of dairy sour cream to make Quick Mayonnaise Base. Add 2 tsp. chicken-seasoned stock base and 1 tblsp. lemon juice. Marvelous on asparagus.

Creamy Coleslaw: Use whipped cream instead of sour cream to make Quick Mayonnaise Base. Add 1 tblsp. lemon juice, 1 tblsp. sugar, 1 tsp. celery seeds, ¼ tsp. salt and a few grains pepper. Toss with shredded cabbage.

Chinese Sauce: Add 1 tblsp. soy sauce, 1 slice fresh ginger root, about ⅛″ thick and the size of a 50-cent piece (or use ¼ to ½ tsp. ground ginger), and 4 green onions, cut in 1″ lengths. Blend until fresh ginger is finely chopped. Serve hot or cold over hot, tender-crisp green beans. To serve hot, warm over low heat 2 to 3 minutes, stirring constantly.

CHICKEN-MAYONNAISE SAUCE

Serve this chicken-flavored sauce on hot
vegetables for a happy change

1 can condensed cream of chicken soup	**1½ tblsp. lemon juice**
¼ c. mayonnaise	**Paprika**

Blend together soup, mayonnaise and lemon juice in saucepan. Cook over low heat, stirring occasionally, until sauce is hot. Sprinkle with paprika and serve at once. Good over asparagus, broccoli, carrots and green beans. Makes 1½ cups.

Smooth-as-Satin White Sauces

The test of a good sauce cook used to be the smoothness of her white sauces. While this still is important, now it's also how imaginative the seasonings are in the satiny sauce she makes. Creamed vegetables may be old-fashioned, but with calcium one of the deficiencies in our diets, and milk a rich source of it, perhaps it will be smart to revive them.

You can add the sauce to the hot, cooked vegetable and reheat, or you can top the vegetable, after it is in the serving dish, with the hot sauce and sprinkle on a dash of paprika. When you want to cream canned vegetables, such as peas, drain them and cook down the liquid about one third; then use it for part of the milk in making the white sauce. Allow about ½ c. sauce for 1 c. cooked vegetable.

If you want a cream sauce, substitute light cream or dairy half-and-half for the milk in the sauce. Once you have the sauce made, the fun of seasoning begins. There's nothing wrong in using only salt, but you can stir in your own touches that will give the sauce individuality and interesting flavors. Here is the recipe for Medium White Sauce, the kind generally used for creaming vegetables, with variations and tips on seasonings (use Thin White Sauce if you prefer it):

MEDIUM WHITE SAUCE

Consider it the start for many good,
intriguing and exciting sauces

¼ c. butter or margarine	2 c. milk
¼ c. flour	1 tsp. salt

Melt butter over low heat in saucepan; do not let brown. Stir in flour to make a smooth paste. Add milk all at once and cook quickly, stirring constantly. When sauce bubbles and starts to thicken, remove it from the heat at once.

Add salt and any other desired seasonings. (If cooked too long, white sauce gets too thick and the butter separates out. When this happens, add a little more milk and cook quickly only until sauce bubbles.) Makes about 2 cups.

VARIATIONS

Thin White Sauce: Use 2 tblsp. butter or margarine and 2 tblsp. flour.

Thick White Sauce: Use 6 tblsp. butter or margarine and 6 tblsp. flour.

Bacon: Pan-fry 3 slices bacon and use drippings for part of butter. Add drained crumbled bacon to sauce.

Ham: Pan-fry ¼ c. minced ham with some fat and use drippings for part of butter. Add ham to sauce.

Mustard: Add ½ tsp. dry mustard, first dissolved in 2 tsp. water to make a smooth paste.

Horseradish: Add 1½ to 2 tsp. grated horseradish.

Curry: Add ½ to 1 tsp. curry powder, first mixed with 2 tsp. water to make a paste.

Parsley: Add 2 tsp. parsley flakes or 2 tblsp. chopped fresh parsley.

Chives: Add 2 tsp. freeze-dried chives or 2 tblsp. chopped fresh chives.

Dill: Add 1 to 2 tsp. dill weed.

Saffron: Add a pinch (too little to measure) saffron for an attractive yellow color.

Egg: Add 2 diced hard-cooked eggs (wonderful on spinach, asparagus and broccoli).

Cheese: Add 2 c. grated or shredded process cheese and stir until it melts, heating if necessary. Some women like to make white sauce with 3 tblsp. flour instead of 4 tblsp. (¼ c.) when making Medium White Sauce to which cheese will be added. The cheese thickens the sauce a little.

Hollandaise Sauces

True Hollandaise Sauce glorifies any plain vegetable and especially tender-crisp asparagus, broccoli or artichokes. Unfortunately, this sauce is not the easiest one to handle in the kitchen, but you can turn out a perfect sauce if you follow recipe directions carefully. And it will reach the dining table in splendid condition if you serve it immediately. That's not always easy to do in these days of busy country living. Reheating this sauce causes the ingredients to separate, or breaks the emulsion, as the scientists say. There's no way to repair the damage.

Many Americans do follow the French recipe with excellent results. Making it challenges women who have an interest in gourmet cooking and many of them get great satisfaction out of serving perfect True Hollandaise Sauce. Here's the recipe to use:

TRUE HOLLANDAISE SAUCE

This is the aristocrat of sauces

½ c. butter   1½ tblsp. lemon juice
4 egg yolks, beaten   ¼ tsp. salt
½ c. boiling water   Paprika

Melt butter in top of double boiler; gradually add beaten egg yolks, stirring thoroughly. Gradually add boiling water, stirring, and lower heat so that water in lower part of double boiler simmers gently; it is important that it does not touch top of double boiler and that it does not boil. Continue stirring until sauce thickens.

Remove double boiler from heat; slowly stir in lemon juice. Add salt and serve immediately; or hold over hot water for as brief a time as possible before serving. Add a dash of paprika for color. Makes about 1 cup.

Standard Hollandaise: This is delicious and has a virtue that women making it appreciate. If it curdles, by acting fast, you can redeem it. The trick is to add boiling water. This recipe tells how to do it:

STANDARD HOLLANDAISE SAUCE

It turns eating asparagus and other green
vegetables into an adventure

4 egg yolks   3 tsp. lemon juice
½ c. butter (divide 1 stick   Salt and white pepper to
   in thirds)   taste

Place egg yolks in top of double boiler; beat slightly. Add a third of the butter; place over hot, not boiling, water, being careful to have top of double boiler just above surface of water. Cook, stirring rapidly, until butter disappears. Add another third of butter; continue stirring; as mixture thickens and butter melts, add remaining butter, still stirring constantly.

When butter is melted, remove top of double boiler and stir rapidly about 2 minutes more. Stir in lemon juice, 1 tsp. at a time; add salt and pepper. Place pan over hot water and stir 2 or 3 minutes. If sauce curdles, immediately beat in 1 to 2 tblsp. boiling water. Makes 1 cup, or enough for 6 to 8 generous vegetable servings.

Easy Blender Hollandaise: Just what its name implies—fast to fix. Spoon it over broccoli for a picture-pretty dish.

EASY BLENDER HOLLANDAISE SAUCE

Takes only a few seconds to make

3 egg yolks	⅛ tsp. ground red pepper
2 tblsp. lemon juice	(cayenne)
	½ c. butter

Place egg yolks, lemon juice and red pepper in blender. Cover and blend, using the quick on-and-off technique for 3 to 4 seconds.

Heat butter almost to boiling (bubbling) but do not allow to brown. Turn blender to either mix or blend speed (on blender with low, medium and high speeds, use high); remove top or small cap in top and add hot butter slowly, blending until thick and fluffy, about 30 seconds. Turn into small saucepan or top of double boiler and hold over warm, not hot, water until ready to serve. Makes 1 cup.

Quick Hollandaise: If you don't have a blender, you can make Quick Hollandaise Sauce with little effort. The taste pleases.

QUICK HOLLANDAISE SAUCE

A little stirring and presto! you have
a most acceptable sauce

2 large egg yolks (or 3	1½ to 2 tblsp. lemon juice
medium)	½ c. butter (divide 1 stick
⅛ tsp. salt	in thirds)
⅛ tsp. white pepper	

Place egg yolks, salt, pepper and lemon juice in saucepan; beat together. Add a third of the butter; place over very low heat and stir until butter is melted. Add another

377

third butter, continue stirring until melted. Add last third butter, stirring until it is melted.

Remove from heat, stir for 1 or 2 minutes, then serve. If necessary to hold sauce briefly, place over warm water. Makes 1 cup.

Mock Hollandaise: This isn't temperamental. It's really hot Medium White Sauce (the recipe is in this chapter) with egg yolks, extra butter and lemon juice added.

MOCK HOLLANDAISE SAUCE

Does something special to Brussels sprouts, asparagus and broccoli

1 c. hot Medium White Sauce (see Index)	**3 tblsp. butter**
3 egg yolks, slightly beaten	**5 tblsp. lemon juice**

Stir hot white sauce slowly into beaten egg yolks; place over low heat and stir constantly until thickened, 4 to 5 minutes. Remove from heat; add butter and lemon juice and stir to blend well. Serve at once, or hold over warm water until ready. Makes 1⅓ to 1½ cups, depending on size of eggs.

Keep Instant Sauce Cubes on Hand

Here's a new, double-quick way to sauce vegetables. Just add a handful of frozen sauce cubes when the vegetable is almost cooked and stir them into the juices. And you have an expertly seasoned dish!

Home economists in our Test Kitchens developed these sauce cubes to make ahead, freeze, place in plastic bags and store in the freezer. They're really handy.

Recipes for the sauce cubes and some vegetables with which to use them follow. This is just the beginning. Let your imagination help you discover other exciting uses for them—not only for saucing vegetables, but also other foods, such as cooked chicken, or serving the cheese sauce on toast. The more our home economists worked with this new seasoning idea, the more ways they found to use the cubes. Here are recipes that make 32 sauce cubes at a time and some good ways to use them.

TOMATO SAUCE CUBES

Four of these frozen cubes add the
tomato-basil flavor—and fast

¼ c. butter or margarine	2 tsp. salt
½ c. flour	½ tsp. basil leaves
1 (6 oz.) can tomato paste	¼ tsp. pepper
1 tsp. prepared mustard	¼ tsp. garlic powder
2 tsp. sugar	1 tblsp. olive oil
2 tsp. onion powder	¾ c. water

Melt butter in saucepan; remove from heat. Add flour and stir until moistened. Add remaining ingredients, except water; stir until smooth. Gradually stir in water.

Pour sauce into an 8½ × 4½ × 2½″ loaf dish. Freeze until consistency of ice cream. Cut into 32 cubes; remove to chilled tray. Freeze until solid. Package; store in freezer. Makes 32.

Tomato Sauced Green Beans: Cook 1 (1 pt.) pkg. frozen green beans in ½ c. lightly salted water until tender. Add 4 Tomato Sauce Cubes. Stir and continue cooking until sauce is smooth and thick.

VARIATIONS

Tomato Sauced Italian Beans: Use 1 (1 pt.) pkg. frozen Italian beans for green beans.

Tomato Sauced Zucchini: Use 1 pt. sliced zucchini, cooked, with ¼ c. cooking liquid, for the green beans.

Tomato Sauced Celery: Use 1 pt. celery slices, cooked, with ¼ c. cooking liquid, for the green beans.

Tomato Sauced Onions: Use 1 pt. small onions, cooked, with ¼ c. cooking liquid, for the green beans.

NOTE: You can make a bowl of tomato soup by heating 5 Tomato Sauce Cubes in ¾ c. milk.

CHEESE SAUCE CUBES

Make delicious sauce with these cubes
to dress up many dishes in a jiffy

1 (8 oz.) pkg. sharp process cheese	1½ tsp. salt
¾ c. water	1 tsp. dry mustard
⅓ c. butter or margarine	2 tsp. Worcestershire sauce
½ c. flour	½ c. nonfat dry milk
	2 tblsp. water

Grate cheese; add to ¾ c. water in saucepan. Heat over low heat, stirring occasionally, until melted and smooth.

Melt butter in another saucepan; remove from heat. Add flour; stir until smooth. Stir in salt, mustard and Worcestershire sauce. Add melted cheese; stir until smooth. Add milk and 2 tblsp. water; stir until smooth.

Pour sauce into 8½ × 4½ × 2½" loaf dish. Freeze until consistency of ice cream. Cut into 32 cubes; remove to chilled tray. Freeze until solid. Package; store in freezer. Makes 32.

Cheese Sauce: Stir 6 frozen Cheese Sauce Cubes into ¾ c. milk. Cook over medium heat until thick and smooth. Makes ¾ cup. This sauce is wonderful with cooked green beans, cauliflower flowerets, chopped broccoli or broccoli spears, small onions and boiled potatoes.

Cheese Sauced Lima Beans: If you prefer to sauce lima beans in the saucepan in which you cook them, cook 1 (1 pt.) pkg. frozen lima beans in ¾ c. boiling lightly salted water until tender. Add 8 Cheese Sauce Cubes. Stir and cook until sauce is smooth and thick.

LEMON-BUTTER SAUCE CUBES

You makes sauce with these cubes to spoon
quickly on cooked vegetables

½ c. butter or margarine	½ tsp. grated lemon peel
¼ c. flour	3 tblsp. lemon juice
1 tblsp. sugar	¾ c. water
2 tsp. salt	Few drops yellow food color
1 tsp. ground nutmeg	

Melt butter; add flour; stir until moistened. Stir in remaining ingredients. Cook, stirring constantly, until mixture begins to bubble and thicken.

Pour sauce into 8½ × 4½ × 2½" loaf dish. Freeze until consistency of ice cream. Cut into 32 cubes; remove to chilled tray. Freeze until solid. Package; store in freezer. Makes 32.

Lemon-Butter Sauce: At serving time, combine 8 Lemon-Butter Sauce Cubes and ¼ c. water in saucepan. Heat and stir until smooth and thick. Keep hot over low heat, but *do not allow to boil.*

Lemon Sauced Asparagus: Just before serving 1 (10 oz.) pkg. frozen asparagus, cooked by package directions, spoon Lemon-Butter Sauce over the hot vegetable.

VARIATIONS

Lemon Sauced Artichoke Hearts: Substitute frozen artichoke hearts for the frozen asparagus.

Lemon Sauced Carrots: Spoon Lemon-Butter Sauce over hot cooked diced or sliced carrots just before serving, instead of the asparagus.

Lemon Sauced Beets: Just before serving, spoon Lemon-Butter Sauce over hot cooked diced beets, instead of the asparagus.

CURRY SAUCE CUBES

*Delicate flavored peas are special with
sauce made from these cubes*

½ c. butter or margarine	¼ c. nonfat dry milk
2 tsp. salt	¾ c. warm water
¾ tsp. curry powder	2 tblsp. grated Parmesan
½ tsp. onion powder	cheese
⅔ c. flour	

Melt butter; remove from heat. Add salt, curry and onion powders; stir to dissolve. Add flour; stir until moistened. Gradually stir in milk and water. Stir in cheese.

Pour into 8½ × 4½ × 2½" loaf dish. Freeze until consistency of ice cream. Cut into 32 cubes; remove to chilled tray. Freeze until solid. Package; store in freezer. Makes 32.

Curry Sauced Peas: Cook 1 (1 pt.) pkg. frozen peas in ⅔ c. lightly salted water until tender. Add 8 Curry Sauce Cubes. Stir and continue cooking until sauce is smooth and thick. Do not overcook delicate peas. (For less sauce, use ⅓ c. water and 4 cubes.)

VARIATIONS

Curry Sauced Mixed Vegetables: Substitute 1 (1 pt.) pkg. frozen mixed vegetables for the frozen peas.

Curry Sauced Green Beans: Substitute 1 (1 pt.) pkg. frozen green beans for the frozen peas.

Tomato Cocktail and Spaghetti Sauce

When you have a bigger crop of tomatoes than you know how to use, get out your big canning kettle to make Basic Tomato Mixture. That's the beginning of two home-canned products, Tangy Tomato Cocktail and Spicy Spaghetti Sauce, to use in spaghetti suppers all winter. An upstate New York farm woman contributed these recipes to FARM JOURNAL, saying they were her answer to salvaging a bumper tomato supply. When we printed them one enthusiastic homemaker wrote: "I make a point of serving some of the Tangy Tomato Cocktail in sparkling glasses during the holiday season when it really refreshes and provides Christmas red."

BASIC TOMATO MIXTURE

Both the tangy cocktail and spaghetti
sauces start with this

20 lbs. firm ripe tomatoes (about 60 medium)	3 tblsp. Worcestershire sauce
2 tblsp. salt	2 tsp. onion powder
1 tsp. celery salt	¼ tsp. Tabasco sauce

Wash tomatoes, cut in halves and remove stem ends; do not peel. Remove any spoiled or green spots.

Place tomatoes in large canning kettle over high heat. Add remaining ingredients; bring to a full boil, stirring frequently to prevent sticking. Cook 5 minutes.

382

Remove from heat and ladle mixture into a food mill, colander or large sieve. Strain off any liquid that pours through easily. Stir just enough to let the juice pour through. Use it to make the cocktail.

Tangy Tomato Cocktail: Taste the juice to make sure it is well seasoned. If you wish, add another 1 tsp. celery salt. If juice is too tart, add 1 to 2 tblsp. sugar. Heat mixture just until boiling. Pour into quart canning jars, adjust lids and process boiling water bath 10 minutes. Makes about 4 quarts.

Spicy Spaghetti Sauce: Transfer the juice tomato pulp into another container without passing through a food mill, colander or sieve. Add 1 tblsp. orégano leaves, 2 cloves garlic, peeled and quartered, and 2 tblsp. Worcestershire sauce. Place in electric blender, about 2 c. at a time; blend until smooth. Make sure tomato skins are blended. (If you want to remove all the small bits of tomato skin and seeds, run this mixture through a colander, food mill or sieve after blending.) Heat mixture until boiling. Pour into pint canning jars, adjust lids and process 10 minutes in boiling water bath. Makes about 7 pints.

Hot Sour Cream Sauces

Sour cream is the flavorful ingredient in these warm sauces that do something good to hot vegetables. Our Sour Cream-Dill Sauce carries the taste of dill seeds and a faint garlic aroma. You can make it in a jiffy to glamorize vegetables. For a decidedly different sauce, sour cream shares honors with cream cheese in Tangy Cream Sauce. The home economists who tested these recipes and tasted the sauces gave them high scores. Try them and see if your family won't also rate them highly.

SOUR CREAM-DILL SAUCE

Looking for a new way to dress up
carrot strips? If so, try this

1 tblsp. butter or margarine	¼ tsp. garlic salt
½ c. water	½ tsp. sugar
1 tblsp. flour	1 c. dairy sour cream
½ tsp. salt	2 tsp. dill seeds

383

Melt butter in saucepan. Mix together water, flour, salt, garlic salt and sugar; add to butter and cook until thickened. Add sour cream and dill seeds; heat, stirring, but do not let boil. Good over hot cooked carrots, zucchini or other summer squash. Makes 1½ cups.

TANGY CREAM SAUCE

Seasoned cream cheese and sour cream
boost vegetables' finest flavors

1 (3 oz.) pkg. cream cheese, softened
⅛ tsp. salt
⅛ tsp. dry mustard

Dash ground red pepper (cayenne)
1 egg
1 tblsp. lemon juice
¼ c. dairy sour cream

Cream together cheese and seasonings in top of double boiler. Beat in egg; stir in lemon juice and sour cream.

Place over simmering water and cook, stirring, until heated through. Serve on green vegetables or broiled tomato halves. Makes ¾ cup.

SOUR CREAM SAUCE

A superior sauce for many vegetables
including baked potatoes and beets

½ c. dairy sour cream
2 tblsp. salad dressing
1 tblsp. finely chopped green onion

1½ tsp. lemon juice
½ tsp. sugar
⅛ tsp. salt

Combine all ingredients in small saucepan. Place over low heat until warm, stirring constantly; do not let come to a boil. Makes about ½ cup.

Sour Cream Toppings for Baked Potatoes

Sour cream topping ladled over baked potatoes has many loyal boosters—especially among men. A California friend shares two of her favorites—Blue Cheese and Dilled Sour

Cream Toppings—with the suggestion that you offer a choice. This thoughtfulness pleases guests who may prefer the taste of blue cheese to dill, or vice versa.

BLUE CHEESE TOPPING

The cheese flavor is fairly mild

½ c. dairy sour cream
2 tblsp. vinegar

1½ tsp. blue cheese salad
dressing mix

Combine all ingredients. Serve with baked potatoes. Makes about ⅔ cup.

DILLED SOUR CREAM TOPPING

Dill and potatoes are a famous team

½ c. dairy sour cream

1 tsp. dill weed

Combine ingredients. Serve with baked potato. Makes ½ cup.

CHEESE-ONION TOPPER

*Please your guests by doubling this recipe
to provide second helpings*

½ c. dairy sour cream
¼ c. butter or margarine,
softened

1 c. shredded sharp process
American cheese
2 tblsp. chopped green onion
with tops

Have all ingredients at room temperature. Place in small deep mixer bowl and beat with electric mixer until light and fluffy. Serve at room temperature—good on baked potatoes, cauliflower, broccoli and asparagus. Makes enough for 5 to 6 vegetable servings.

French Velvet Sauce

If there's anything in country kitchens that quickly and easily transforms humble garden vegetables into gourmet dishes, it's chicken broth. If you don't have your own stored in the freezer, you can buy it in cans to keep in the cupboard. One of the splendid ways to use the broth is in French Velvet Sauce, good on many vegetables—asparagus, green and wax beans, peas, carrots and potatoes.

FRENCH VELVET SAUCE

No better way to use chicken broth

2 tblsp. butter or margarine   1 c. chicken broth
3 tblsp. flour   ⅓ c. dairy half-and-half

Melt butter in saucepan; blend in flour, but do not brown. Stir in broth and half-and-half. Cook quickly until sauce bubbles and thickens. Makes about 1½ cups.

VARIATION

Almond French Velvet Sauce: Add ¼ c. toasted slivered almonds just before serving sauce on vegetables.

SAVORY SAUCE FOR BOILED POTATOES

*Old-hat boiled potatoes go glamorous
when you ladle on this savory sauce*

¼ c. butter   ¼ tsp. ground nutmeg
2 tblsp. olive or salad oil   ½ tsp. salt
Grated peel 1 lemon   Few grains coarse grind
⅓ c. lemon juice   pepper
2 tblsp. snipped fresh   1 tsp. flour
  parsley, or 1 tsp. parsley
  flakes

Melt butter in saucepan (do not brown). Add olive oil, lemon peel and juice; then add remaining ingredients.

Heat slowly but do not boil. At serving time ladle a spoonful over each serving of potatoes, or place in a gravy boat and pass at table. Makes enough for 6 servings.

Sweet-Sour Broccoli Sauce

When a mother discovers a dress-up for vegetables that her children praise, she knows it's worth remembering. The Vermont reader who shares this recipe for Broccoli Sauce says that's what her three sons call it because they especially like the sauce on hot broccoli. She suggests that you can regulate the tartness by slightly altering the amount of vinegar. "The sauce is one of the best encouragements to eating vegetables that I've found," she says.

BROCCOLI SAUCE

Try this also on hot cauliflower

1 egg, beaten	½ tsp. dry mustard
½ c. sugar	⅓ c. vinegar
½ tsp. salt	2 tblsp. butter
⅛ tsp. pepper	

Blend together egg, sugar, salt, pepper, mustard and vinegar in saucepan. Cook over low heat, stirring constantly, until thickened. Remove from heat and add butter. Stir until melted.

Serve over hot cooked broccoli. Makes enough sauce for 6 vegetable servings.

SWEET-SOUR SAUCE

*A perfect team—tender-crisp green beans
and this oriental-type sauce*

½ c. sugar	⅛ tsp. pepper
1 tsp. salt	¼ c. water
1 tblsp. cornstarch	¼ c. vinegar

Mix together dry ingredients in saucepan. Combine

water and vinegar; mix into dry ingredients, stirring to prevent lumps. Cook and stir over low heat until mixture is clear and thick. Makes 1 cup.

NOTE: This sauce is good in vegetable and meat combinations, such as Chinese and Japanese dishes featuring spareribs or chicken with bean sprouts, water chestnuts, celery, Swiss chard and green pepper.

Soy Sauce Seasoning: Add 2 or 3 tblsp. soy sauce to each 2 lbs. leafy vegetables (such as spinach, Swiss chard, Chinese chard and Chinese cabbage) during cooking for a pleasant flavor addition. Thicken any pot juices remaining at end with 1 tsp. cornstarch mixed to paste with 3 tblsp. water, adding a little more water if needed for a thin sauce. (This is the way the Chinese do it.) Soy sauce contains salt, so use less salt when soy sauce is added.

New Roles for Harvard Sauce

Discovering new recipes adds interest to cooking and keeps meals from getting in a rut. It's also exciting to try an old favorite in a new role. Harvard Sauce is usually associated with beets, but why not try it on other vegetables? Once you start looking for ways to broaden a recipe's usefulness, you're bound to come up with some distinctive dishes. Start with our recipe for Harvard Sauce and combine it with the vegetables we suggest. You'll be amazed how much good eating comes from your saucepans.

HARVARD SAUCE

This is traditional on diced beets but it's equally good on carrots, whole green beans and lima beans

2 to 4 tblsp. sugar	¼ c. water
1 tblsp. cornstarch	¼ c. vinegar
½ tsp. salt	2 tblsp. butter or margarine

In a saucepan, mix sugar, cornstarch and salt.
Combine water and vinegar and stir into dry ingredients. Cook over medium, then low heat, stirring until thickened,

5 to 7 minutes. Blend in butter and serve on cooked vegetables. Makes 1 cup.

Use the last bit of ketchup that clings to the bottle for flavor in French dressing. Pour oil, vinegar and seasonings into bottle and shake the ingredients together.

SIMPLE CHEESE SAUCE

Delicious over cooked hot onions, potatoes, carrots, cauliflower or broccoli. Just try it and see

1 can condensed cream of celery soup	**⅓ c. milk**
½ c. shredded sharp Cheddar cheese	**⅛ tsp. paprika**

In a saucepan mix together soup, cheese, milk and paprika. Cook over low heat, stirring until cheese is melted and sauce is thoroughly heated. Makes 1⅔ cups.

VARIATION

Cream Cheese-Chive Sauce: Substitute 1 (3 oz.) pkg. softened cream cheese for the Cheddar cheese, and add 1 tblsp. minced chives, or 1 tsp. freeze-dried chives; blend together before adding to soup.

Marvelous Butter Seasonings

Country women are experts in seasoning hot cooked and drained vegetables with butter. It imparts an unsurpassable rich flavor. While experienced cooks rarely measure the butter they add, a good rule to remember is to use 1 to 3 tblsp. for every 2 c. of vegetable. To bring delightful change into meals, add seasonings to butter. It's surprising how they glorify vegetable dishes. Take Lemon Butter or Maître d'Hôtel Butter, as the French call it, for instance. It transforms plain boiled potatoes, especially young, new ones, into regal fare. And it's good on hot broccoli, cauliflower and spinach. Here are a few favorite butters from the FARM JOURNAL Test Kitchens:

Lemon: Let ¼ lb. butter (1 stick) soften at room temperature. Cream with spoon and slowly add 1 tblsp. lemon juice. Add 1 tsp. salt. Whip until fluffy. (A blender with a small or 1-cup mini container is excellent to use.) This sauce, covered, keeps several days in the refrigerator. Add a dollop of it to hot vegetables and toss gently to mix. Makes about 1 cup.

VARIATIONS

Parsley-Lemon: Add 2 tblsp. finely chopped parsley to Lemon Butter.

Hot Lemon: Melt butter and add remaining ingredients for Lemon Butter. Use immediately.

Hot Lemon Butter Supreme: Make Hot Lemon Butter, cool and stir in ½ c. heavy cream, whipped. Use immediately.

Chinese Lemon Butter: Omit salt in Lemon Butter and stir in 2 tblsp. soy sauce. Try this on cooked, tender-crisp cabbage and green beans.

BROWN BUTTER

Browning butter in a tiny skillet or saucepan makes the Beurre Noisette of the French or our Brown Butter. The trick is to brown the butter to a light delicate brown without scorching. Make whatever amount you need and pass it in a small pitcher so everyone can pour the butter over the hot vegetable. You can vary ¼ c. browned butter in these ways:

Celery: Stir in 1 tsp. celery seeds. Good on potatoes and carrots.

Cheese: Stir in 2 tblsp. grated Parmesan cheese.

Garlic: Stir in 1 small clove garlic, cut in half. Let stand for several minutes. It's a good idea to make this garlic butter when you start to cook the vegetable. Especially tasty on cabbage, cauliflower, parsnips or peas.

Horseradish: Stir in 1 tblsp. prepared horseradish. Excellent on beets.

BLACK BUTTER

This is like Brown Butter, but you brown the butter

more—the French say *beurre noir*, black butter. Heat the butter until it froths and turns golden brown. Here's how to do it:

Black Butter: Let ⅓ c. butter bubble in a tiny saucepan and turn golden brown. Add 1 tblsp. lemon juice or vinegar and ⅛ tsp. salt; serve at once on hot cooked carrots, green beans or cabbage.

HERB BUTTER

Be stingy and add just a touch
of this for a subtle herb flavor

2 tblsp. boiling water	½ c. butter or margarine
1 tsp. dried basil leaves	(room temperature)

Pour boiling water over dried basil leaves. Cover and let stand until lukewarm.

Blend into butter. Cover and refrigerate. It will keep several days. Add sparingly to cooked vegetables, not more than 1 or 2 tsp. to 2 c. vegetables. Heat together a few minutes. Makes ½ cup.

NOTE: Use any dried herb you wish instead of basil. Among the favorites are thyme, rosemary, parsley and tarragon.

DILL BUTTER

It enhances the taste of many garden offerings—
keep on hand ready to go

1 tsp. dill seeds	½ c. butter or margarine
½ tsp. dill weed	¼ tsp. dill weed
2 tblsp. boiling water	

Add dill seeds and ½ tsp. dill weed to 2 tblsp. boiling water. Cover and let stand 5 minutes; strain out dill seeds and discard.

Whip into butter, adding remaining ¼ tsp. dill weed. Let stand at least 2 hours or longer before adding to hot cooked vegetables. Makes ½ cup, or enough to dress 4 c. cooked vegetables.

NOTE: Dill Butter is good on potatoes, beets, cabbage, carrots, peas, spinach, tomatoes and turnips.

SESAME SEED BUTTER

*Toss lightly with cooked vegetables and serve
potato—tastes wonderful*

¼ c. butter or margarine
2 tsp. sesame seeds
2 tsp. lemon juice

2 drops onion juice or 1
drop garlic juice

Melt butter in small saucepan; add sesame seeds and cook to a golden brown over low heat. Add lemon juice and onion juice. Add to hot vegetables. Makes about ¼ cup, or enough to season 2 c. cooked vegetables.

SAVORY BUTTER

Spread on corn for exciting flavor

Combine ¾ c. soft butter or margarine with 2½ tsp. salt. Season with one of the following:

Orégano: Add 1½ tsp. orégano leaves and ½ tsp. garlic salt.

Chives: Add 2 tsp. dried chopped chives.

Onion: Add 2 tsp. minced green onion.

Barbecue: Add 1½ tsp. barbecue spice.

MINT BUTTER

Toss with hot carrots and/or peas

2 sprigs fresh mint

3 tblsp. butter (room
temperature)

Snip mint fine with scissors. Mix with butter. Let stand while vegetables cook. Makes enough to season 3 c. cooked vegetables.

HERB BUTTER FOR CORN

Marjoram and thyme leaves seem to
bring out corn's best taste

½ c. butter	⅛ tsp. pepper
1 tblsp. chopped parsley	¼ tsp. marjoram leaves
1 tsp. salt	¼ tsp. thyme leaves
1 tsp. paprika	

Melt butter; blend in remaining ingredients. Pour or brush over freshly cooked sweet corn, or toss lightly with cooked whole kernel corn. Makes ½ cup.

Bread and Butter Topping

It's surprising how quickly and easily you can glorify hot, cooked vegetables with Crumb Sauce (bread crumbs and butter, seasoned simply with salt, pepper and a little lemon juice). Don't use the packaged dry bread crumbs for this. Here's how to make your own.

Fresh Bread Crumbs: Use firm or day-old bread; crumble or grate on a grater. Or use a blender if you have one: tear bread in pieces and whirl on low speed, 1 slice at a time. Use the crusts of the slices or not, as you like.

CRUMB SAUCE

Delicious on asparagus, cauliflower, broccoli
and Brussels sprouts

1 c. Fresh Bread Crumbs	Pepper
¼ c. butter or margarine	Paprika
Salt	1 tblsp. lemon juice

Cook and stir bread crumbs and butter in small skillet until crumbs are light brown. Add a speck (too little to measure in spoon) each of salt, pepper and paprika. Stir in lemon juice.

Sprinkle over hot, cooked vegetables and serve at once. Makes 1 cup.

Cheese Crumb Sauce: Omit lemon juice from Crumb Sauce and stir in ½ c. grated cheese when crumbs are a light brown. Season and sprinkle over hot, cooked green beans, cauliflower or broccoli.

Seasoning Guide for Vegetables

An excellent way to win compliments on your vegetable dishes is to season them with imagination. Among the favorite seasonings in country kitchens are salt, pepper, a touch of sugar (especially for tomatoes and root vegetables), parsley, onion and garlic. This is just the beginning. Herbs and spices, if used sparingly, improve the taste of vegetables.

How to Use Herbs: If you've been timid about trying a wide variety of herbs, here's a way to get acquainted with them, using our taste-tested recipes. Look through this book for recipes listing herbs among the ingredients— especially herbs you haven't tried before. When you find a recipe that intrigues you, add the herb to your grocery list; then you'll be ready to try it. Your family may or may not approve, but that's how you'll learn what appeals to them. More than likely, you'll discover that your family likes more vegetables in more ways than you ever thought possible!

We predict that your recipe trials with herbs will arouse your interest and you may then want to take off on your own. Here are some guidelines on how to cook with herbs.

How Much Is Enough? Use a light hand when you experiment with herbs. It's better to add too little of any herb than too much. Taste as you go.

Dried herbs are more potent than fresh. Allow ¼ tsp. dried herb to 2 c. vegetable. Rub it in the palm of your hand before measuring. If you're using a fresh herb, use three or four times as much as dried; that is, from ¾ to 1 tsp. fresh herb to 2 c. vegetable. To measure, remove stems and snip the leaves very fine with scissors.

Start your herb cookery by using a single herb in a dish, and only one herb-seasoned dish in a meal. Later in your experiments, if you want to add several herbs to a dish, just be sure that the flavor of one predominates to avoid a clash of flavors. Remember that herbs should heighten the natural flavors of food.

When to Add Herbs: To vegetables and sauces that cook only a short time, add herbs at the start of cooking. To soups and stews, which cook longer, add herbs and spices about 30 to 35 minutes before end of cooking time—this will avoid losing some of the flavor and aroma. To uncooked foods (salad dressings, dips, cottage cheese and spreads), add herbs and allow time for them to stand a while before serving—the waiting distributes the flavors evenly.

How to Store Herbs: Buy dried herbs (also spices) in small containers. Write the date of the purchase on the label with a marking pen. Herbs, like spices, tend to lose some of their flavors in time—try to use them within a year or replace them. Store them away from light and heat (over the range is *not* a good place). Keep the containers tightly closed to conserve flavor and aroma.

How to Freeze and Use Frozen Herbs: Select sprays of young herbs. Dip them in and out of cold water to wash them. Then scald them in boiling water 10 seconds—no longer. Plunge immediately into iced water to chill quickly. Then gently pat dry with paper towels.

Seal enough of each herb to use in special dishes, in little foil packages. Label, place in a plastic bag and freeze.

When ready to use, snip unthawed herbs with scissors into the dish they are to season.

VEGETABLE-HERB GUIDE

Here are suggestions of herbs to try with different vegetables:

Artichokes, Globe, French or Italian: Basil, orégano, bay leaves, fennel—add to cooking liquid. Curry powder, chervil—add to sauce.

Asparagus: Any herbs you like, especially basil, tarragon, thyme or rosemary—add to cooking liquid. Sesame or poppy seeds—sauté in butter and pour over. Curry powder —add to sauce. Nutmeg—sprinkle over.

Beans, Baked (dried): Cloves, ginger, mustard, orégano, savory—add to bean pot or casserole before baking. Try cumin in bean soup.

Beans, Green and Wax: Savory, thyme, marjoram, orégano, rosemary—add to cooking liquid. Basil, dill weed or seeds —add to cooking liquid or sauce. Poppy seeds, sesame seeds, nutmeg—sprinkle over.

Beans, Lima: Orégano, savory, thyme, dill weed, celery seeds, marjoram—add to cooking liquid. Sage, chili powder, curry powder—add to sauce. Nutmeg—sprinkle over.

Beets: Allspice, orégano, savory, tarragon, caraway and celery seeds—add to cooking liquid. Cloves, ginger—add to butter or sauce.

Broccoli: Caraway and celery seeds, dill weed or seeds, fennel, rosemary, savory, basil, thyme—add to cooking liquid. Marjoram, tarragon—add to cooking liquid or to sauce or butter. Nutmeg—sprinkle over.

Brussels Sprouts: Same as broccoli.

Cabbage: Savory, cayenne or red pepper, fennel—add to cooking liquid. Allspice, dill weed, marjoram, tarragon —add to melted butter. Add caraway seeds to butter for red cabbage. Add dill, caraway or celery seeds, or marjoram, to coleslaw and sauerkraut.

Carrots: Basil, marjoram, rosemary, savory—add to cooking liquid. Allspice, cloves, curry powder—add to sauce. Chives, cinnamon, ginger, chervil—add to butter or sprinkle on. Mint, nutmeg, poppy seeds—sprinkle on.

Cauliflower: Same as for broccoli.

Celery: Almost all herbs, especially basil, thyme, rosemary —add to cooking liquid or to butter.

Collard Greens: Marjoram—add to cooking liquid. Cayenne or red pepper—sprinkle on.

Corn: Orégano, celery seeds—add to cooking liquid. Curry and chili powders—add to sauce or cream-style corn.

Cucumbers: Dill, fennel, basil, chervil, savory—add to sauce or vinegar.

Eggplant: Almost all herbs, especially basil, sage, and chili or curry powders—add to sauce or butter, or use in coating for fried eggplant.

Kale: Marjoram, orégano, tarragon—add to cooking liquid. Mustard—add to sauce. Nutmeg, cayenne or red pepper —sprinkle on.

Lentils: Orégano—add to cooking liquid. Cumin—add to soup.

Lettuce: Practically all herbs, including chervil and tarragon—add to dressing.

Mushrooms: Practically all herbs, with orégano, rosemary and thyme the favorites—add to cooking liquid or to butter when sautéeing. Nutmeg—sprinkle on. Curry powder—add to sauce.

Mustard Greens: Same as for kale.

Onions: All herbs, including rosemary, sage, celery seeds —add to cooking liquid. Mustard, curry and chili powders —add to sauce.

Parsnips: Cumin, rosemary, thyme—add to cooking liquid. Curry and chili powders—add to sauce or butter. Allspice, cinnamon, ginger, nutmeg—sprinkle on or mix with mashed parsnips.

Peas, Green: Basil, thyme, marjoram, tarragon, rosemary, savory—add to cooking liquid. Mint, nutmeg—sprinkle on.

Peppers, Green: Orégano—add to cooking liquid. Chili powder, mustard, celery seeds—add to sauce or dressing.

Potatoes, Sweet: Allspice, cardamom, ground cloves, cinnamon, nutmeg, ginger—mix with mashed.

Potatoes, White: Practically all herbs; with dill weed and basil the favorites—add to cooking liquid. Orégano—add to butter for baked potatoes. Cumin, marjoram—add to potato soup. Caraway and celery seeds—add to sauce or dressing. Dill seeds, chervil—add to potato salad.

Spinach: Almost all herbs, with basil, marjoram and cardamom the favorites—add to butter or sauce. Orégano, tarragon—add to cooking liquid. Nutmeg, curry powder —sprinkle on.

Squash, Summer: Practically all herbs, especially basil, marjoram and chili and curry powders—add to stuffing, sauce or butter.

Squash, Winter: Same as for sweet potatoes. Also toasted sesame seeds—sprinkle on or add to butter.

Tomatoes: Bay leaves, caraway and celery seeds, rosemary marjoram, dill weed, sesame seeds, thyme, orégano—add to cooking liquid. Basil—sprinkle on or add to cooking liquid. Cumin—add to stew or rice/tomato dishes. Curry powder, cinnamon (in very small amounts)—add to sauce or stew.

Turnips, White and Yellow: Bay leaves, celery and caraway seeds, orégano—add to cooking liquid. Allspice, curry powder—mix with mashed. Basil—add to butter or sauce. Poppy seeds—sprinkle on.

Turnip Greens: Marjoram, cayenne or red pepper—add to cooking liquid.

TIPS FROM COUNTRY WOMEN
ON USING SEASONINGS

Part of getting acquainted with herbs and spices is learning how to use them and how much to use—some herbs are more powerful than others. Here are a few suggestions:

Bay Leaf: Add it to the water in which you cook vegetables. Allow 1 bay leaf for 6 vegetable servings.

Cloves: A pinch (too small to measure) of ground cloves does something good to sweet yellow vegetables—sweet potatoes and winter squash. It's also good in beets. Add with the salt.

Cumin: Try it in vegetable-beef or chicken stews and in cooked tomatoes. Allow ½ tsp. cumin to 6 servings.

Dill Weed: A moderately mild herb; add it with salt, allowing ¼ to ½ tsp. dill weed for 6 vegetable servings. Allow the same amount for potato salad.

Marjoram: Allow ¼ to ½ tsp. for 6 vegetable servings.

Mustard: Add ¼ to ½ tsp. dry mustard to 1 tsp. water and let stand 10 minutes before using. It is good in white sauces and in salad dressings, such as mayonnaise.

Nutmeg: This sweet spice is delicious when used sparingly in creamed spinach, green beans, cauliflower, cabbage and onions, also succotash and summer squash. Add a tiny pinch to the sauce or sprinkle on lightly with the salt.

Orégano: A potent herb with a special affinity for tomatoes and for clear vegetable soups. Add about ½ tsp. orégano for 6 servings of tomatoes, other vegetables and soups.

Poppy Seeds: Heat seeds in butter until butter is golden; then add to cooked, drained vegetable and toss to mix.

Rosemary: Use this pleasant herb more sparingly than other herbs—it's potent! Try adding it to melted butter to pour over cooked vegetables such as asparagus, green beans, tomatoes and zucchini.

Savory: Some people call this the "bean herb" because it is delicious in bean dishes—all beans, dried as well as green, wax or lima beans.

Tarragon: The wise cook will do less experimenting with tarragon than with other herbs because it has a pronounced aroma; the flavor is something like licorice. One of the best ways to use it is in salad: scatter a few fresh tarragon leaves, or a touch of dried tarragon, over greens when you're ready to toss the salad.

Thyme: This herb is potent; allow no more than ¼ tsp. for 6 vegetable servings. If using it in long-cooking dishes, such as soup, don't add it until the last 10 minutes of cooking.

Ready-to-Go Seasonings from Your Supermarket Shelves

Ready-to-use seasonings add interest to cooking and exciting flavors to foods. Use them sparingly for best results. Here are favorites of the home economists in our Test Kitchens. Look for these and other seasoners when you shop for food.

Liquid Smoke: Stir a few drops into vegetable-meat stews and casseroles to give an appealing camp-out flavor. Good in bean and pea soups, too.

Spaghetti and Chili Mixes: Use these (in either dry or liquid form) to add zest to pinto, navy or pea, kidney and Great Northern beans, chick-peas (garbanzos), black-eyed peas and lentils. Add sparingly, tasting to determine the right amount.

Dry Soup Mixes: Try them with root vegetables and vegetable-meat stews and casseroles.

Stock and Flavor Bases: Look for bottles of beef and chicken seasoning stock bases, and foil packets of chicken, beef or vegetable broth flavor bases in your supermarket. Add them to sauces, or to the water in which you cook vegetables. Or use bouillon cubes or instant bouillon, dissolved in hot water; or try canned chicken and beef broths. With stock and flavor bases in your cupboard, you'll find it easy to give any vegetable dish flavor assistance.

Bacon Bits: Sprinkle these bits, made from soy protein, over corn, green beans, green salads or any vegetable dish in which you like the taste of bacon. Add bits the last minute before serving to keep them from absorbing liquid and changing texture.

Dry Salad Dressing Mixes: Use them to season white sauce when you sauce cooked vegetables—gives a different flavor accent.

Bottled Salad Dressings: Stir a little French or Italian dressing into hot vegetable dishes. Marinate vegetables in them for salads.

Flavored Vinegars: Basil, herb and spice, tarragon and mixed herb vinegars are the kinds most widely available. Use them lightly on all cooked greens, cabbage and beets.

SPEEDY SHAKER SEASONINGS

Monosodium Glutamate: A white crystalline salt (sometimes abbreviated MSG) which brings out the natural flavors of vegetables and other foods, although it has no distinctive flavor of its own. Use only a small amount, approximately ¾ to 1 tsp. for 6 servings. Add it with other seasonings before or after cooking.

Seasoned Salt: A blend of salt with spices, herbs and, usually, monosodium glutamate. Sometimes labeled "savory" or "spiced" salt. Use it with salt in seasoning, or as a substitute for salt.

Smoked Salt: Add a dash to buttered peas and to sauces for green beans that contain a small amount of mustard. Good also in baked beans.

Seasoned Pepper: This is a blend of imported and domestic peppers with spices. Its flavor is mellow and fairly mild. You'll also find flavored peppers on the spice shelves of supermarkets—lemon and garlic, for example.

Celery Salt: It is made with ground celery seeds and table salt, mixed thoroughly. Use with or for part of the salt.

Onion Salt: This is made with dehydrated onions and table salt. It imparts a mild onion flavor.

Garlic Salt: It consists of garlic powder mixed with table salt. Sprinkle over vegetables for a mild garlic taste. Don't mistake garlic powder for garlic salt. Garlic powder is very potent; if you use it instead of garlic salt, don't shake it. Measure no more than $\frac{1}{16}$ tsp. (a tiny pinch) for 6 servings of vegetables.

Paprika: Gives color to vegetable dishes, but the paprika in our markets is mild in flavor compared to the kind used in European countries, especially Hungary. Hungarian paprika with more zip is obtainable in some urban food stores.

Chili Powder: Add a few shakes to corn, lima beans, cooked onions, eggplant and tomatoes.

Curry Powder: Use it on root vegetables such as beets, carrots, parsnips and turnips; also sweet potatoes and winter squash.

INSTANT SAUCES FROM THE SUPERMARKET

Sauce Mixes: White sauce and cheese sauce mixes are basics to keep on hand for speedy sauce making. You'll find other flavors, too, such as sour cream sauce mix— with new ones coming on the market all the time.

Canned Condensed Soups: These are favorites for saucing vegetables. Heat condensed cream of asparagus, celery and mushroom soups as they come from the can (without adding liquid) and spoon over cooked vegetables. Because they are condensed they are salty, so watch the amount of salt you use in your vegetables. Soups also add flavor and substance to vegetable casserole dishes.

Dairy Sour Cream: It makes an excellent topping for hot or cold vegetable dishes—salads, soups and, of course, baked potatoes. Fold in a little chopped chives or parsley for superior flavor.

Salad Dressing Specialties

Much of the success of any salad depends on its dressing. The next four salad dressing recipes are favorite specialties of a home economist who entertains beautifully. Her friends consider her salads unsurpassable. When FARM JOURNAL asked for her salad secrets, she said that different, distinctive salad dressings were the quick, sure road to superior salads.

She graciously shares her recipes for Decidedly Dill, "Great for Greens," Zippy Garlic and East Indies Salad Dressings. If your family and friends are not accustomed to some of the seasonings, use a little less of them the first few times you make each of these dressings. You then can use the full amounts of the ones that please you.

ZIPPY GARLIC DRESSING

What a salad dressing! Piquant French dressing at its best

⅔ c. salad oil	¾ tsp. dry mustard
¼ c. wine vinegar	Dash freshly ground pepper
1 tsp. sugar	1 clove garlic, minced
¾ tsp. salt	

In a screw-top jar, combine all ingredients; shake well. Chill thoroughly before serving. Makes about 1 cup.

"GREAT FOR GREENS" SALAD DRESSING

The name is correct—it is great

½ c. mild white vinegar	½ tsp. dry mustard
¼ c. olive oil	½ tsp. seasoned salt
½ c. salad oil	½ tsp. monosodium
¼ tsp. salt	glutamate
¼ tsp. freshly ground pepper	Dash garlic salt

402

Combine all ingredients in a screw-top jar; shake well to blend. Refrigerate, and shake well again before using. Makes 1¼ cups.

DECIDEDLY DILL SALAD DRESSING

*Dill balances with other seasonings to produce
an excellent flavor blend*

½ c. salad oil
¼ c. lemon juice
⅛ tsp. garlic powder
½ tsp. salt

¼ tsp. freshly ground
   pepper
½ tsp. sugar
¾ tsp. dill weed

Combine all ingredients in screw-top jar; shake well. Chill thoroughly. Use on tossed green salads, coleslaw or lettuce wedges. Makes about ¾ cup.

EAST INDIES SALAD DRESSING

*Also serve this dressing on chilled asparagus. You can use
less curry powder or a milder seasoning if you don't like
curry. But try it before you decide to change the recipe*

1 beef bouillon cube
¼ c. boiling water
1 tsp. instant minced green
   onion

1 c. mayonnaise or salad
   dressing
½ tsp. curry powder

Dissolve bouillon cube in boiling water. Add onion and blend into mayonnaise. Blend in curry powder.

Chill dressing thoroughly. Serve on tossed greens, lettuce wedges or Bibb lettuce. Makes about 1¼ cups.

FRENCH SALAD DRESSING MIX

*An easy, make-ahead mix to keep handy as the base
for excellent French dressing*

½ c. onion powder, or 2 (2
   oz.) jars
¼ c. garlic powder, or
   1 (2 oz.) jar

¼ c. black pepper (2 oz.)
1 tblsp. paprika
½ c. salt

403

Combine ingredients in a quart jar and shake to blend well. Pour into a smaller jar with tight lid and store to use in making French Salad Dressing. Makes about 1½ cups.

FRENCH SALAD DRESSING

A mixture of dried seasonings is what makes this a superior dressing

¼ c. French Salad Dressing Mix
1 pt. salad dressing or mayonnaise
½ c. sugar

¼ c. salad oil
¼ c. cider or wine vinegar
1 c. buttermilk
1 c. ketchup

Stir French Salad Dressing Mix to blend thoroughly. Add to remaining ingredients and mix in blender or electric mixer. Makes about 5 cups.

Cucumber Salad Dressing

Here's an imaginative salad dressing with faint overtones of blue cheese, onion and lemon juice blending with grated cucumber. You'll like what it does to juicy, ripe tomato slices and combination vegetable salads. For garnishing fish, it's unsurpassed. And it does flavor wonders when spread on lettuce or sliced tomatoes in sandwiches. You'll find a jar of the pale green Cucumber Salad Dressing in your refrigerator a mealtime inspiration throughout the summer.

CUCUMBER SALAD DRESSING

Make potato salad with this dressing and you'll have a gourmet treat

1 (8 oz.) bottle blue cheese dressing
2 c. mayonnaise or salad dressing (1 pt.)

1 c. grated peeled cucumber (1 medium)
2 tblsp. grated onion
¼ c. lemon juice
4 drops green food color

Combine all ingredients. Chill thoroughly. Serve with tossed salad. Makes about 1 quart.

COUNTRY CREAM DRESSING

Adds zest to green salads; try it on sliced cucumbers for a special treat

2 c. dairy sour cream	1 tblsp. salt
6 tblsp. vinegar	¾ tsp. dry mustard
¼ c. sugar	Pepper (optional)

Mix all ingredients together, adding pepper to taste, if desired. Makes about 2¼ cups dressing, or enough for 2 quarts tender leaf lettuce or finely shredded cabbage.

Cut a thin slice from the stem end of a large green or sweet red pepper. Clean out the inside and fill with salad dressing; place in center of ring mold or bowl of salad.

COTTAGE-BLUE CHEESE DRESSING

This creamy, milk cheese-flavored dressing is great for salad greens

2 tblsp. vinegar	⅔ c. mayonnaise
⅛ tsp. salt	½ c. crumbled blue cheese
3 drops Tabasco sauce	⅓ c. cottage cheese

In a small bowl, blend vinegar, salt and Tabasco sauce; blend in mayonnaise and beat until smooth.
Stir in blue cheese and cottage cheese. Makes 1⅓ cups.

Make-Ahead Salad Dressings

If your family likes salads, treat them to a choice of dressings—an easy way to add variety to your menus. The four recipes that follow each make a pint of dressing which will stay fresh in the refrigerator for a month.

You'll find the herby blend of Italian Tomato Dressing

delectable on cucumbers and tomato slices. Sweet/Sour Bacon Dressing will be the perfect mixer in your favorite potato, macaroni or egg salad. Try adding Creamy Thousand Island to sandwich fillings, cabbage slaw or crisp lettuce wedges. Gelatin salads will taste even better when you glaze them with Orange-Honey Dressing. Any one of the four will give its own special touch to your favorite tossed greens.

Prepare these dressings at least one day in advance to allow their flavors to blend and mellow. Store the dressings, tightly capped, in the refrigerator.

ITALIAN TOMATO DRESSING

A superb blend of tangy seasonings

½ c. oil
⅓ c. cider vinegar
1 (8 oz.) can tomato sauce
½ tsp. sugar
1 tsp. dry mustard
1 tsp. paprika
½ tsp. orégano

2 tsp. Worcestershire sauce
½ clove garlic, finely chopped
2 tsp. finely chopped onion
1 tblsp. finely chopped celery
2 tblsp. salad dressing

Combine all ingredients in 1-qt. mixing bowl. Beat at medium speed 2 minutes. (Or blend ingredients in blender for 15 seconds on high speed.) Chill. Store in refrigerator; storage time, 1 month. Makes 1 pint.

CREAMY THOUSAND ISLAND

Sour cream is the secret

½ c. salad dressing
½ c. chili sauce
1 tsp. Worcestershire sauce
Dash of Tabasco sauce
½ tsp. salt
¼ tsp. paprika
2 tblsp. chopped celery

2 tblsp. pickle relish
2 tblsp. chopped stuffed olives
1 tsp. minced onion
1 hard-cooked egg, chopped
½ c. sour cream

Combine salad dressing, chili sauce, Worcestershire,

Tabasco, salt and paprika in 1-qt. bowl. Stir in celery, relish, olives, onion and egg; mix well. Fold in sour cream. Chill. Store in refrigerator; storage time, 1 month. Makes 1 pint.

SWEET/SOUR BACON DRESSING

*Creamy smooth dressing studded with crispy crumbles
of bacon*

4 slices bacon	3 tblsp. white vinegar
2 tblsp. chopped onion	½ c. water
3 tblsp. sugar	1⅓ c. salad dressing

Fry bacon until crisp and brown. Drain bacon and crumble into small pieces. Set aside.

Sauté onion in bacon drippings until tender. Add sugar, vinegar and water; bring to boiling point. Cool. Combine mixture with salad dressing; beat until smooth. Stir in bacon chips. Chill. Store in refrigerator; storage time, 1 month. Makes 1 pint.

ORANGE-HONEY DRESSING

*A hint of tartness balances its delicate,
honey-tinged sweetness*

¼ tsp. paprika	3 tblsp. lemon juice
½ tsp. dry mustard	2 tblsp. cider vinegar
1 tsp. salt	3 tblsp. orange concentrate
½ tsp. celery salt	1 c. salad oil
½ c. honey	

Combine dry ingredients in 1-qt. mixer bowl. Add honey, lemon juice, vinegar and orange concentrate; blend well. Beating constantly, slowly add oil; beat 5 minutes longer at medium speed. (Or blend all ingredients in blender for 20 seconds at high speed.) Chill. Shake before serving. Store in refrigerator; storage time, 1 month. Makes 1 pint.

HONEYED DRESSING

Use this to make Spinach Toss—
a special occasion salad

1 c. garlic wine vinegar   ⅓ c. honey
1 c. salad oil

Measure vinegar, oil and honey into a shaker or jar with tight-fitting lid. Shake to blend thoroughly. Refrigerate. Makes about 2⅓ cups, enough to dress 3 to 4 family-size bowls of salad.

Spinach Toss: Carefully wash and remove any coarse stems from the amount of spinach you plan to serve. Drain and refrigerate. At serving time, tear spinach in bite-size pieces; place in salad bowl. Pour just enough Honeyed Dressing over greens to coat them lightly. Toss and garnish with chopped hard-cooked eggs and drained, crumbled, crisp-cooked bacon. Serve immediately.

CHAPTER TEN

Appetizers and Relishes

APPETIZERS AND relishes brighten meals, taste good—and make other foods taste better. Appetizers appear before or at the beginning of supper or dinner, not to satisfy hunger, but to stimulate it. Relishes show up in the main course and point up the best flavors of foods they accompany.

Uncooked vegetable appetizers delight weight-watchers, who nibble on them without worrying about what the scales will register as a result. They are as simple as midget carrot, turnip, zucchini, green pepper and cucumber sticks, sections of celery hearts, cherry tomatoes, cauliflower broken in flowerets, small radishes and tiny bouquets of broccoli heads. You can serve them with or without dips for dunking, but do set a salt shaker nearby.

Be sure to fix Antipasto Platters, a recipe from a New York farm woman, who likes to serve them instead of salad at picnics because, as she says, "They taste and look so good." You do most of the fixing a day ahead so assembling the vegetables on the platters is simple. Serve this handsome appetizer in buffet suppers too, or take it proudly to potlucks.

Some fresh vegetables make excellent dips for dunking potato and corn chips. Our Eggplant Appetizer, colorful with chopped tomatoes and parsley, is an example. Encourage your guests to spread it on crisp crackers. Once they try it, you'll wonder if you made enough.

Most women appreciate the zest and flavor which relishes contribute to a meal. You'll find interesting relish recipes in this chapter. We culled some of them from our Test Kitchen favorites, collected during the last few years. You don't have to be an expert pickle maker to turn out brilliant-colored Red Pepper Relish or Winter Salad Relish, which so deliciously salvages the late green tomatoes. And your guests don't have to be Texans to endorse the tastiness of Pickled Black-eyed Peas, which you make from the canned vegetable a day before the party.

Try the recipes that follow so your family and friends can experience some taste-pleasing surprises.

Vegetable Appetizers from Faraway Places

People in faraway kitchens excel in making delightful appetizers with vegetables. Two splendid examples are Garbanzo Dip and Eggplant Appetizer. You use canned garbanzos (chick-peas) to make the dip in which this vegetable stars. Serve with crackers or crisp raw vegetable appetizers. These dips, like many appetizers in this cookbook, can do double duty—as appetizers and as snacks.

GARBANZO DIP

Our taste-testers all voted this a topnotch dip—it is an adaptation of a favorite Middle Eastern dish

1 (15 oz.) can garbanzos (chick-peas)	3 cloves garlic, chopped
1½ tsp. salt	½ c. salad oil
⅛ tsp. pepper	¼ c. lemon juice
	2 tblsp. chopped parsley

Drain chick-peas through sieve and wash under cold running water until water runs clear. Place in blender with salt, pepper, garlic, salad oil and lemon juice. Blend until smooth. You may need to add 1 extra tblsp. oil to make mixture liquid enough.

Remove from blender container and combine with parsley. Chill thoroughly. Garnish with extra parsley sprigs, and serve as a dip for crisp fresh vegetables or with sesame seed crackers. Makes about 2 cups.

EGGPLANT APPETIZER

A zesty relish borrowed from Balkan countries where people call it poor man's caviar. It's really good

1 large eggplant (1¼ lbs.)	2 tblsp. lemon juice
½ c. chopped onion	1 tsp. garlic salt
¼ c. olive or salad oil	½ tsp. salt (about)
½ c. chopped peeled	⅛ tsp. pepper
tomato	2 tblsp. chopped parsley

Place eggplant in large kettle; add water and cook until tender, about 25 minutes. Cool, peel and chop.

Cook onion in olive oil in skillet until tender. Add chopped tomato and eggplant. Cover; simmer 5 minutes, or until tomato is tender. Mash. Stir in lemon juice, garlic salt, salt, if needed (amount depends on size of eggplant), and pepper. Chill.

To serve as an appetizer, garnish with chopped parsley and have crackers and ripe olives alongside. Or serve as a relish on the dinner table. Makes about 2½ cups.

Pick-up Vegetable Appetizers

Bring in an assortment of crisp, icy-cold raw vegetables, arranged attractively on a tray, platter or big plate. Or put them in big bowls of crushed ice. Then carry in tempting, go-with dips, chilled thoroughly. You'll not need to coax people to gather round and eat.

Bright vegetable nibblers appeal to almost everyone, but especially to calorie counters. You'll even encounter a few braves who eat the dippers and resist the dips. Pamper them by providing a shaker of salt or a small bowl of seasoned salt.

Hostesses like to serve raw vegetable appetizers for several reasons. They have eye and taste appeal and require no cooking. And they don't dull appetites for the meal to follow. (Incidentally, many of the appetizers make pretty salad garnishes.)

We've mentioned several raw vegetable appetizers in the introduction to this chapter, but here, for your convenience, is a longer list. Select any of them that you like, but do remember to consider color and shape contrasts.

Cut all vegetable strips about 3" long and ½" wide. Soak all the vegetables in ice water 1 hour and dry. If you aren't ready to serve them, put each vegetable in a jar, cover tightly and refrigerate for a few hours.

411

Asparagus stalks, 2 to 3" tip ends
Broccoli buds, bite-size
Carrots, scraped and cut in sticks
Cauliflower flowerets, bite-size
Celery, cut in 3" lengths, or celery fans
Cucumbers, peeled and cut in sticks
Green onions or scallions, small
Peppers, sweet green and red, cut in strips
Radishes, small red (if fresh from garden, leave tufts of leaves on top end, or make radish roses or accordions)
Sweet onions, large (slice crosswise, remove outer skin and separate in rings)
Turnips, young, peeled and cut in slender strips
Zucchini and other summer squash, young, cut in strips without peeling

Celery Fans: Cut each celery branch or rib in 3" lengths. Make 3 to 6 parallel cuts close together almost to the other end. Or cut from both ends almost to the center. Put in ice water about 1 hour so strips will curl.

Radish Roses: Use a small sharp knife with a thin blade. Cut off root, then cut 4 or 5 petals from root end almost to stem end, leaving a thin uncut strip between petals. Put in ice water for at least an hour.

Radish Accordions: Cut long, red radishes crosswise in 10 to 12 thin strips, but not quite through to the opposite side. Chill in ice water so slices will spread.

Add some of these chilled raw vegetables to your arrangement:
Cherry tomatoes, tiny
Yellow tomatoes, small
Firm, ripe tomatoes, peeled and cut in quarters
Whole mushrooms, small
Water cress, small sprigs

Miniature Vegetable Sandwiches

Men like onion and cucumber sandwiches. To make them, butter the bread slices and sprinkle with chopped parsley and a bit of salt. Put them together in pairs with very thin onion or cucumber slices between. Then slice to make finger sandwiches. Keep them small so they'll not take away appetites for the main meal.

Vegetables on Picks

Impale bite-size pieces of crisp, raw vegetables on one end of toothpicks or cocktail picks; stick toothpicks into a big satiny, purple eggplant. Use vegetables of contrasting colors and set the eggplant holding appetizers on small pine branches or a leaf-covered plate. You can substitute a well-shaped, firm, green cabbage head for the eggplant. Here are some vegetables appropriate to serve this way:

Cherry tomatoes

Yellow tomatoes, small

Celery fans

Red radishes or radish roses

Green peppers cut in squares

Chinese cabbage, cut in bite-size chunks

Canned whole mushrooms, drained

Fresh mushroom caps, filled with blue or other cheese spread

Small green pepper squares centered on carrot slices, one end of pick holding pepper in place (pepper looks like center of carrot "flower")

Artichoke hearts, frozen, cooked by package directions, drained and chilled

Luscious Dips for Vegetable Appetizers

You can serve one dip, two, or three or more. Most hostesses prefer to offer their guests a choice. Dips containing cheese are special favorites. We give you a couple of FARM JOURNAL favorites, Cheese-Dried Beef Dip and Smoky Cottage Cheese Dip.

CHEESE-DRIED BEEF DIP

Also good for stuffing celery

413

1 (8 oz.) pkg. cream cheese
(room temperature)
1½ c. small curd creamed
cottage cheese
½ c. finely cut dried beef

1½ tsp. onion flakes
¼ tsp. salt
1 beef bouillon cube
¼ c. boiling water

Put cream cheese and cottage cheese in large mixer bowl. Beat until blended. Add beef, onion flakes and salt.

Dissolve bouillon cube in boiling water. Add to cheese mixture. Beat well. Refrigerate to blend flavors. Serve with carrot sticks. Makes 2½ cups.

SMOKY COTTAGE CHEESE DIP

Serve this with carrot, celery and cucumber sticks and cauliflowerets

1 c. cottage cheese
1 (3 oz.) pkg. cream cheese
2 tblsp. light cream or milk
1 tsp. minced onion

½ tsp. liquid smoke
¼ tsp. garlic salt
½ c. minced ripe olives

Beat together cottage cheese, cream cheese and cream. Blend in remaining ingredients. Makes 1⅔ cups.

CURRIED EGG DIP FOR VEGETABLES

Good with almost every vegetable—especially chilled crisp cucumber strips

¼ tsp. Tabasco
½ tsp. curry powder
¼ tsp. dry mustard
½ tsp. salt
½ c. mayonnaise

1½ tblsp. finely chopped
onion
½ c. finely chopped celery
1 tsp. minced parsley
4 hard-cooked eggs, finely
chopped

Combine Tabasco, curry powder, dry mustard and salt. Stir into mayonnaise.

Combine onion, celery and parsley; stir into mayonnaise mixture. Fold in eggs. Chill until ready to serve. Makes about 2 cups.

NOTE: This dip is pretty served in a clear glass bowl, surrounded with colorful vegetables. A black or dark-colored platter or tray sets off the bright vegetable colors.

Sour Cream/Onion Dips

If you have dairy sour cream in the refrigerator and instant minced onion or dry onion soup mix in the cupboard, you can whip up tasty dips in a jiffy. While they taste wonderful with most raw vegetables, they have a special affinity for cucumber and carrot sticks and for frozen artichoke hearts, cooked, drained and chilled.

SOUR CREAM/ONION DIP

Simple to make, delicious to eat

1 c. dairy sour cream	2 tsp. instant minced onion
¼ tsp. lemon juice	Few grains pepper

Combine all ingredients and blend. Serve in a bowl on a tray surrounded by carrot, cucumber and other vegetable sticks. Makes about 1 cup.

SOUR CREAM/MAYONNAISE DIP

For a few guests, cut recipe in half and serve dip
in a big green pepper

⅔ c. dairy sour cream	2 tblsp. dry onion soup mix
⅔ c. mayonnaise	

Combine ingredients, cover and chill so flavors will blend. Makes about 1⅓ cups.

Appetizers or Relishes?

Sometimes the line between appetizers and relishes is exceedingly thin. Marinated Green Beans and Marinated Mushrooms are an example. Hungry guests nibble happily on them just before a meal and they equally enjoy them served in a relish dish with the meat course.

Antipasto Platters are another of these double-duty vegetable ideas. The member of the FARM JOURNAL Family Test Group who contributed the recipe recommends the antipasto for a salad substitute at picnics as well as for an appetizer. Serve the antipasto on small individual plates; the brief cooking of the vegetables tenderizes them enough so that you can eat them easily with a fork. Marinated Mushrooms or Antipasto Platters served as appetizers alongside dips are eaten with picks. No matter where in a meal you serve them, they're make-ahead treats.

MARINATED MUSHROOMS

Different, distinctive, easy to fix

⅓ c. red wine vinegar
⅓ c. salad oil
1 tsp. prepared mustard
1 tblsp. brown sugar
2 tsp. parsley flakes
1 tsp. salt

⅛ tsp. pepper
1 small onion, sliced and
   separated in rings
2 (8 oz.) cans button
   mushrooms, drained

Combine vinegar, oil, mustard, sugar, parsley, salt, pepper and onion rings in saucepan. Heat to boiling. Add mushrooms; simmer 5 minutes, stirring occasionally.

Pour into bowl. Cover; cool and chill several hours, or overnight. Drain and serve with toothpicks or cocktail picks. Makes about 3 cups.

MARINATED GREEN BEANS

Tarragon makes these beans special

½ c. salad oil
¼ c. tarragon vinegar
1 tblsp. chopped onion
1 tsp. parsley flakes
½ tsp. salt

⅛ tsp. pepper
1 (1 lb.) can cut green
   beans, drained
Pimiento strips

Combine salad oil, vinegar, onion, parsley, salt and pepper in bowl. Add beans. Cover and chill several hours or overnight, stirring once or twice.

To serve, pour off marinade and reserve to use as salad dressing. Drain beans on paper toweling. Serve garnished with pimiento strips. May be eaten with fingers. To use as a relish, skip the draining on paper towels. Makes 2 cups.

Antipasto Platters for Picnics

A New York dairy farmer and his family, members of the FARM JOURNAL Family Test Group, entertain with a picnic on the Fourth of July, at the end of the busy haying season. Their guests are neighbors, other friends and businessmen who helped to make their haying time run smoothly.

Their dairy farm is a wonderful spot for the picnic. A heart-shaped, spring-fed pond gives the children a splashy afternoon of fun. Grandparents and parents relax under the trees. Some of the men play softball. But the highlight of the occasion is the picnic food.

Colorful antipasto platters of fresh and canned vegetables are the popular picnic special. They're different from the usual salads. But you don't have to wait for a picnic to share these Antipasto Platters with family and friends. Take them to a church or other community supper. The reception they get will please you. Here's the recipe for the treat. You'll notice that much of the fixing takes place the day before the picnic.

ANTIPASTO PLATTERS

The way picknickers help themselves to this is proof of its popularity

1 head cauliflower, broken into flowerets
1 lb. fresh green beans
1 c. salad oil
⅓ c. wine or cider vinegar
1¼ tsp. salt
¼ tsp. pepper
1 clove garlic, cut in 3 pieces
2 tsp. orégano leaves

1 (14½ oz.) can asparagus spears, drained
3 large tomatoes
1 large cucumber
1 (5 oz.) jar green olives, drained
2 bunches green onions, cleaned
12 deviled egg halves
2 tblsp. chopped parsley

417

The day before serving, cook separately, cauliflowerets, green beans just until tender-crisp. Drain.

Mix salad oil, vinegar, salt, pepper, garlic and orégano.

Toss separately in marinade the cauliflowerets, green beans and asparagus spears. Place each vegetable in a separate small bowl.

Divide marinade and pour over the three vegetables. Cover bowls; refrigerate overnight.

On day of picnic, drain marinated vegetables, reserving marinade. Arrange on large platters along with sliced tomatoes, peeled and sliced cucumbers, olives, green onions and deviled egg halves.

Sprinkle all vegetables lightly with marinade and chopped parsley. Makes enough to fill 2 large platters.

ITALIAN APPETIZER

Overnight chilling explains why this party appetizer tastes so good

1 (7 oz.) can solid-pack tuna, drained

1 (6 to 7 oz.) can pitted ripe olives, drained

1 (4 oz.) can mushroom stems and pieces, drained

1 (15 oz.) can artichokes, drained and cut in halves

1 (3½ oz.) jar cocktail onions, drained

1 c. drained sweet mixed pickles

1 (8 oz.) can tomato sauce

1 c. sliced celery

3 tblsp. salad or olive oil

¼ c. wine vinegar

1 tsp. salt

Combine all ingredients in bowl. Toss lightly. Cover and chill overnight. Stir occasionally. Serve with crisp crackers. Makes 8 servings.

Refrigerator Relishes

The right vegetable relishes make foods they accompany taste better. It's a traditional country kitchen custom to can them during summer months when vegetables are plentiful—traditional long before refrigerators were universal home equipment.

What's exciting news to many of today's busy home-makers, who find less time for summer canning than their mothers did, is that you can make relishes throughout the year.

Most of these relishes require a few hours of refrigeration, although others need to chill overnight or longer. You don't have to pay attention to them while they refrigerate. Farmhouse Garden Relish, a tomato-cucumber specialty, gives a lift to fried chicken dinners and picnic or other outdoor meals.

Blue Devil Onions do something remarkable in bringing out superior flavors, especially in broiled steak, hamburgers and pork chops.

FARMHOUSE GARDEN RELISH

Tarragon vinegar gives a new taste to this—
a rather sweet relish

3 medium tomatoes, peeled
  and sliced
1 c. thinly sliced unpeeled
  cucumber
1 medium onion, thinly
  sliced
½ c. thinly sliced celery
½ c. thinly sliced carrot
  rounds

6 green pepper rings
½ c. tarragon vinegar
⅓ c. water
¼ c. sugar
1 tsp. paprika
1 tsp. basil leaves
½ tsp. salt
¼ tsp. pepper

Arrange tomatoes, cucumber, onion, celery and carrots in a 10 × 6 × 1½″ glass baking pan or deep platter. Garnish top with green pepper rings.

Combine remaining ingredients and pour over vegetables. Cover; chill at least 4 hours or overnight. Makes 6 servings.

BLUE DEVIL ONIONS

Watch these onion rings disappear from the relish tray—
they go fast

419

4 medium onions, thinly
  sliced and separated in
  rings
1 (3 oz.) pkg. blue cheese,
  crumbled (about ¾ c.)
½ c. salad oil

2 tblsp. lemon juice
1 tsp. salt
½ tsp. sugar
Dash pepper
Dash paprika

Place onion rings in shallow dish. Combine remaining ingredients thoroughly; pour over onions and stir to coat onions well. Refrigerate at least 3 to 4 hours. Makes about 1 quart.

UNCOOKED TOMATO RELISH

Fresh tasting with lots of zip!

18 medium-size ripe
  tomatoes
2 branches celery
2 green peppers
2 sweet red peppers
4 medium onions
½ c. finely ground horse-
  radish

⅓ c. salt
2½ c. sugar
½ tsp. pepper
½ tsp. ground cloves
2 tsp. ground cinnamon
3 tblsp. whole mustard seed
3 c. cider vinegar

Scald tomatoes; remove skins and as many seeds as possible. Chop into small pieces. Should make about 3 quarts of chopped tomatoes.

Put celery, peppers, onions through food chopper; use coarse grind. Use finest grind for horseradish.

Combine vegetables and salt; let stand overnight in refrigerator. Drain thoroughly in a strainer. Add sugar, spices, mustard seed and vinegar. Mix well.

Pack in sterile jars, seal and store in the refrigerator. Should keep for several months. (Do not store at room temperature.) Makes about 4 quarts.

PICKLED BLACK-EYED PEAS

*You can substitute red kidney beans or garbanzos
for the black-eyed peas in this appetizing relish*

2 (15 oz.) cans cooked
   black-eyed peas, drained
½ c. salad oil
⅓ c. wine vinegar
1 clove garlic, mashed

½ c. thinly sliced onion
½ tsp. salt
1½ to 2 tsp. sugar
⅛ tsp. freshly ground
   pepper

Mix all ingredients together. Place in 1-qt. jar and refrigerate from 2 days to 2 weeks before eating. Remove garlic after 1 day. Makes 1 quart.

SAUERKRAUT RELISH

*Wine gives this a milder flavor but you can use
apple juice instead*

1 (15 oz.) can sauerkraut,
   drained
½ c. dry white wine
1 medium apple, finely
   chopped

1 small onion, finely
   chopped
1 tsp. celery seeds

Put sauerkraut and wine in skillet. Simmer 15 minutes; cool.

Add apple, onion and celery seeds to sauerkraut; mix well. Chill overnight in covered container to blend flavors. Makes 2 cups.

CARROT PICKLES

Perfect accompaniment for roasts

1 qt. cut peeled carrots
   (¾" slices or 2" sticks)
1 c. cider vinegar
¾ c. water
¾ c. sugar

10 whole cloves
2 (2½") sticks cinnamon,
   broken into small pieces
1½ tsp. salt

Cook carrots in small amount of boiling salted water until tender-crisp, about 5 minutes (do not overcook). Drain.

Combine remaining ingredients in a small saucepan; bring to a boil and boil gently 3 minutes.

Pack carrots into a 1-qt. sterilized jar; pour in hot syrup. Cover; cool and refrigerate at least 1 or 2 days. Pickles keep well in refrigerator for a week or two. Serve cold with meats. Makes 1 quart, or 6 to 8 servings.

VARIATION

Cauliflower Pickles: Substitute 1 small head cauliflower, broken into flowerets, for the carrots in Carrot Pickles.

CHILLY-DILLY BRUSSELS SPROUTS

These chilled sprouts, sliced, also are fine tossed in a green salad

1 (10 oz.) pkg. frozen Brussels sprouts	½ tsp. dill weed
½ c. Italian salad dressing	1 tblsp. sliced green onion

Cook Brussels sprouts according to package directions, until just tender but still slightly firm.

Combine salad dressing with dill weed and onion; pour over drained hot Brussels sprouts. Chill thoroughly. Serve as appetizer or relish. Makes 1½ cups.

PICKLED BEETS

Make this lively relish frequently to brighten and flavor your meals

2 c. whole cooked or canned small beets, drained	1 (1") stick cinnamon
¾ c. vinegar	1 slice lemon
¼ c. water	1 slice onion
3 whole cloves	6 tblsp. sugar
	¼ tsp. salt

Combine all ingredients in saucepan. Bring to boil and boil 1 minute. Remove from heat; cool and chill. Makes 1 pint.

BEET RELISH

Taste will remind you of Grandma's marvelous piccalilli, but it's red

1 qt. small beets	1 c. sugar
3 large onions, peeled	1 tsp. salt
3 green peppers, seeded	1 tsp. mixed pickling spices
¾ c. vinegar	6 whole cloves
½ c. water	

Wash beets. Cook 20 minutes; peel. Run through food chopper along with onions and green peppers.

Combine remaining ingredients in small saucepan. Simmer 10 minutes.

Strain vinegar and add to vegetable mixture. Bring to a boil and simmer until vegetables are tender. Cool and keep in refrigerator, or process in boiling water bath (212°) 30 minutes (directions for water bath in chapter 11—see Index). Makes about 4 pints.

TOMATO-OLIVE RELISH

This special-occasion red, black and white relish adds zest and eye appeal

1 (6 oz.) can pitted ripe olives, drained	1 pt. cherry tomatoes
2 cloves garlic, crushed	2 medium onions, sliced and separated into rings
Olive or salad oil, or a mixture of both	½ c. chopped parsley
	1 tblsp. wine vinegar

Place olives and garlic in jar. Cover with oil. Cover jar and chill at least 24 hours.

Drain olives, reserving oil. Add washed and stemmed tomatoes, onion rings and parsley. Add 1 tblsp. of the marinating oil (use remainder in salad dressings) and vinegar. Toss.

Serve as garnish on a platter of steak or grilled hamburgers, or in a bowl on the buffet. Makes 8 small servings.

QUICK CORN RELISH

Men say this makes meals taste better—
wives say it fixes fast

1 (12 or 16 oz.) can whole
    kernel corn
2 tblsp. onion flakes
2 tsp. celery seeds

⅓ c. sugar
⅓ c. vinegar
⅓ c. sweet pickle relish
⅓ c. diced pimientos

Combine ¼ c. liquid drained from corn and drained corn with remaining ingredients; simmer 10 minutes. Serve hot or cold. Makes about 2½ cups.

PICKLED WAX BEANS

Fill the relish dish with these—provide the zest
many meals need

1 (1 lb.) can cut wax beans
¼ c. pickle relish

1 tblsp. butter or margarine

Heat beans; drain. Toss with relish and butter. Serve hot. Makes 4 servings.

Vegetable Relishes to Can

Relish recipes in this cookbook are selected from those FARM JOURNAL readers praised most lavishly. We include here Red Pepper Relish and Winter Salad Relish, mentioned in the introduction to this chapter. You'll be proud of your productions.

RED PEPPER RELISH

Lemon slices add fruit flavor

12 medium red peppers
2 c. chopped onions
2 c. white vinegar
3 c. sugar

4 tsp. pickling salt
1 lemon, sliced
4 tsp. whole allspice
½ tsp. ground ginger

Remove stem and seeds from peppers. Cover peppers with boiling water; let stand 5 minutes; drain. Repeat; drain well. Then put through coarse blade of food chopper. Should measure about 4 c.

Combine all ingredients (tie allspice in cloth bag). Boil 30 minutes. Let stand overnight in glass bowl.

Bring to boil; simmer 10 minutes. Remove allspice. Pour at once into hot, sterilized pint jars; seal. Process 10 minutes in boiling water bath (see Index). Makes about 3 pints.

WINTER SALAD RELISH

Has a mild flavor, crunchy texture

2 qts. sliced green tomatoes	2 tsp. mustard seed
¼ c. pickling salt	2 qts. shredded cabbage
2 c. sugar	1 qt. chopped onion
1 qt. white vinegar	2 qts. peeled and seeded
2 tblsp. pickling salt	sliced cucumbers
2 tsp. ground tumeric	1 c. chopped green pepper
1 tsp. whole allspice	1⅓ c. chopped red pepper

Mix tomatoes and ¼ c. pickling salt; let stand overnight. Rinse in fresh unsalted water; drain well.

Mix sugar, vinegar, 2 tblsp. salt and spices (tie spices in cloth bag). Boil 10 minutes. Add tomatoes and other vegetables; heat to full boil. Remove cloth bag.

Pour into hot, sterilized pint jars; seal. Process 10 minutes in boiling water bath (see Index). Makes about 10 pints.

Aristocratic Pickles

The most fragrant cooking this side of the moon—that's the way one home economist in our Test Kitchens described pickle-making. Farm homemakers agree. They also know how these relishes pep up meals. That's why they adhere to the country custom of keeping jars of pickles and other relishes in their cupboards.

Aristocratic Pickles are a favorite of a Nebraska farmer's wife, who makes them when the cucumber crop is good.

When you treat guests to this relish, have the recipe ready—
they'll want to copy it.

ARISTOCRATIC PICKLES

*Very crisp; sweet, sliced pickle has excellent flavor
and appearance*

2 c. pickling salt	2 c. white vinegar
4 qts. water	2 c. water
4 qts. thinly sliced	6 c. sugar
cucumbers (4 to 5″ in	1 stick cinnamon
length)	1 tsp. whole cloves
1 tblsp. powdered alum	1 tsp. celery seeds
1 tblsp. ground ginger	½ tsp. whole allspice

Dissolve salt in 4 qts. of water; add cucumbers. Let
stand 8 days in stone crock, glass, pottery or enamel-lined
(should not be chipped) pan.

On the ninth day, drain well. Add fresh unsalted water
to cover; add alum. Simmer 30 minutes.

Drain well. Add fresh unsalted water to cover; add
ginger. Simmer again 30 minutes. Drain well.

Mix vinegar, 2 c. water, sugar and spices (tie spices
in cloth bag). Add cucumbers and simmer again until
pickles are clear. Pack in hot, sterilized pint jars; seal.
Process 10 minutes in boiling water bath (see Index).
Makes about 6 pints.

DILLY BEANS

Make these pickles with tender beans

2 lbs. small tender green	4 large heads dill
beans	2 c. water
1 tsp. ground red pepper	¼ c. pickling salt
(cayenne)	1 pt. vinegar
4 cloves garlic	

Stem green beans and pack uniformly in hot, sterilized
pint jars.

To each pint, add ¼ tsp. red pepper, 1 clove garlic and
1 head dill.

Heat together water, salt and vinegar. Bring to boil; pour over beans. Seal; process 10 minutes in boiling water bath (see Index). Makes 4 pints.

SWEET GREEN PICKLES

Good with hamburgers or roast meat

3 c. pickling salt	5 c. white vinegar
6 qts. water	10 c. sugar
30 whole pickling	2½ tblsp. powdered alum
cucumbers (3 to 4″ in	1¼ tsp. whole cloves
length)	2½ sticks cinnamon

Add salt to water; bring to boil. Pour over cucumbers in stone crock. Weight down with plate. Let stand 8 to 10 days. Rinse well in fresh unsalted water. Slice pickles; rinse again. Let stand in fresh unsalted water 1 hour. Drain.

Combine remaining ingredients (tie spices in cloth bag); bring to boil. Pour over cucumbers; cover and let stand 24 hours.

Drain syrup; bring syrup to boil, pour over cucumbers. Let stand 24 hours. Repeat this process for a total of 3 mornings.

On fourth morning, drain pickles, reserving syrup. Pack pickles in hot, sterilized pint jars. Bring syrup to boil. Add green food color, if you wish. Pour hot syrup over pickles in jars; seal. Process 10 minutes in boiling water bath (see Index). Makes about 6 pints.

DILLED OKRA PICKLES

Let stand 3–4 weeks before opening

3 lbs. young okra, uncut	1 qt. water
Celery leaves	1 pt. vinegar
Cloves garlic	½ c. pickling salt
Large heads and stems dill	

Pack scrubbed okra into hot, sterilized pint jars with a few celery leaves, 1 clove garlic and 1 head and stem dill for each jar.

Make brine of water, vinegar and salt; heat to boiling. Pour over okra; seal; process 10 minutes in boiling water bath (see Index). Makes about 6 pints.

Tomato Juice—A Prime Favorite

When it comes to vegetable appetizers that you sip, tomato juice leads all the rest. This is a perennial favorite of people in all age groups—especially of men. It has almost everything desirable in an appetizer, such as lovely color, stimulating flavor, wide availability and congeniality with most of the dips and vegetable nibbles. Stuffed celery and crisp crackers are ideal accompaniments.

TOMATO JUICE COMBINATIONS

Tomato-Clam: Combine 2 parts tomato juice with 1 part clam juice. Serve heated or cold with lemon wedges, carrot sticks or celery. You can give it a gourmet touch by adding 1 or 2 tblsp. sherry to 1 qt. of this mixture.

Tomato-Sauerkraut: Combine 2 parts tomato juice with 1 part sauerkraut juice; chill thoroughly.

Hot Buttered: Serve hot tomato juice in cups or mugs, stirring in 1 tsp. butter for each cup.

Tomato-Lemon: Combine 1 qt. tomato juice and ⅓ c. lemon juice; add 1½ tsp. Worcestershire sauce, ¼ tsp. celery salt and ¼ tsp. dill weed.

Tomato-Cream: Float 1 tblsp. whipped cream on top each serving of tomato juice.

Tomato-Pineapple: Fill a glass half full with chilled pineapple juice; tip glass and slowly pour tomato juice down the side of glass until nearly full. Serve at once.

SEASONINGS AND GARNISHES
FOR TOMATO JUICE

Herb Seasonings: To 1 qt. tomato juice add ¼ tsp. of one of the following dried herbs: basil leaves, thyme leaves, dill weed, parsley flakes, or ½ bay leaf. Heat juice slowly 15 minutes. Serve either hot or cold with a thin slice of lemon or lime sprinkled with paprika. (Remove bay leaf at end of heating period.)

Spicy Seasonings: To 1 qt. tomato juice add ¼ tsp. of one of the following: chili powder, celery salt, onion salt or seasoned salt. Or, add ½ tsp. cloves or 6 whole cloves. Heat slowly 15 minutes and serve hot or cold. (Remove whole cloves.)

Hot Seasonings: To 1 qt. tomato juice add 1 to 3 tsp. red or green taco sauce, 4 drops Tabasco sauce or ½ tsp. prepared horseradish. Any of these hot-flavored seasonings may be added to ½ c. heavy cream, whipped; float a dollop on each serving of cold or hot tomato juice.

Garnishes: Decorate your servings of tomato juice with any of the following: thin lemon slices—add a sprinkle of paprika for red or a dash of dill weed for green; thin slices of small frankfurters or precooked sausages in hot tomato juice; or sprigs of fresh herbs such as basil, thyme, marjoram or parsley. For something different, use leaves or either lemon verbena or rose geranium, or any of the minty geraniums in the Pelargonium line.

STUFFED CELERY

Everyone will enjoy crisp celery to snack on,
or for a party appetizer

1 c. small curd creamed cottage cheese	Crisp celery branches
2 tblsp. chopped pimiento-stuffed olives	⅛ tsp. seasoned salt

Place cottage cheese in blender and beat until smooth. Or press through a sieve. Fold in olives. Spread in crisp celery sticks or branches and sprinkle with seasoned salt. Chill thoroughly. Serve on relish tray. You can cut stuffed celery in 2 to 3″ lengths, or in bite-size pieces with a sharp knife if you like. Makes enough to stuff about 1 cup (2 to 3″) celery sticks.

CHAPTER ELEVEN

Freezing and Canning Vegetables

COUNTRY WOMEN with gardens frequently produce more vegetables than their families and friends, with whom they share their crops, can eat. The season's growing conditions and the gardener's enthusiasm at planting time have much to do with the yield. An Iowa mother of three preschool children says: "Last fall, from early September until well into October, I prayed every night for frost. Because every morning, when I looked out the kitchen door, I saw a bushel basket heaped with beautiful ripe tomatoes my father-in-law had picked to 'help out.' I couldn't let them waste so I canned tomatoes day after day even though our fruit closet was overflowing. This year we're going to plan our garden with discretion, starting on those wintry days when we look at new seed catalogues. Of course, it *was* wonderful to have all the tomatoes and tomato juice I could use."

For those of you who freeze and can some vegetables and for city brides of young farmers, we include the latest approved freezing and canning directions in this chapter. They are from the FARM JOURNAL *Freezing & Canning Cookbook,* with a few revisions; we have added directions for freezing potatoes, for instance.

The rules for freezing and canning come from long and painstaking scientific research. It is important to follow them to the letter. Pay no attention to the woman who says you don't need to blanch or scald corn and other vegetables when freezing them. Sometimes you can "get by" for years, but many times spoilage takes the entire batch. And for safety's sake process vegetables, when canning them, in a pressure cooker at the pressure specified and for the exact number of minutes. Tomatoes are the only vegetable you can safely process in a boiling water bath. We start this chapter with directions for canning them and for canning and freezing tomato juice.

HOW TO CAN TOMATOES

Tomatoes: Select sound, ripe tomatoes. Wash. Dip into boiling water ½ minute or until skins crack; dip quickly into cold water. Cut out stem ends, remove cores and slip off skins.

Raw Pack: Leave tomatoes whole or cut in halves or quarters. Pack in jars, pressing down gently after each 2 tomatoes are added, to release juice and fill spaces. Add no water or liquid to cut tomatoes; tomato juice made of imperfect, ripe fruit may be added to whole tomatoes, rotating jars to remove air bubbles. Leave ½″ head space. Add ½ tsp. salt to pints, 1 tsp. to quarts. Adjust lids. Process in boiling water bath (212°).

Pint jars   35 minutes
Quart jars   45 minutes

Remove jars from canner and complete seals unless closures are self-sealing type.

Hot Pack: Prepare as directed for raw pack. Cut tomatoes in quarters or halves. Put in kettle and bring to a boil. Stir gently to prevent sticking, but use care not to make tomatoes mushy. Fill jars with boiling hot tomatoes to within ½″ of jar top. Add ½ tsp. salt to pints, 1 tsp. to quarts. Adjust lids. Process in boiling water bath (212°).

Pint jars   10 minutes
Quart jars   10 minutes

Remove jars from canner and complete seals unless closures are self-sealing type.

Tomato Purée, Seasoned: Choose firm ripe tomatoes. Prepare about 4 qts. at a time.

Hot Pack Only: Wash, chop and simmer tomatoes until soft. Prepare seasoning mixture as follows: Chop 3 onions, 3 branches celery and 3 sweet red or green peppers. Simmer in boiling water until soft. Add to tomatoes and put through a sieve. Add ½ tsp. each of salt and sugar for each pint of pulp. Reheat to the boiling point. Mixture should be thick. Ladle into hot jars, leaving ½″ head space. Adjust lids. Process in boiling water bath (212°).

Pint jars   35 minutes

Remove jars from canner and complete seals unless closures are self-sealing type.

HOW TO CAN AND FREEZE TOMATO JUICE

Tomato juice may be canned or frozen. Here are the steps to follow:

(1) Use only sound, red-ripe tomatoes. Wash, peel and core and cut them into small pieces.

(2) Cook at once and quickly until soft to inactivate the enzymes that may change the color and consistency and destroy vitamin C.

(3) Put them through a fine sieve or food mill to remove seeds.

(4) Heat the extracted, strained juice at once to the simmering point (204° F.). Salt the juice to taste; most people like 1 tsp. salt to 1 qt. tomatoes.

(5) To freeze, quickly pour the heated juice into freezer containers, leaving 1″ head space for quart containers with wide tops, 1½″ for those with narrow tops. Cool and freeze.

(6) To can or bottle, pour the simmering hot juice into clean hot jars to within ¼″ from top, bottles to within ½″ from top; adjust the lids and process in a boiling water bath 10 minutes. (For the best-tasting tomato juice, follow directions given below for cooling.)

Water Bath: Use a deep kettle with rack and lid. The rack should have openings and allow jars or bottles to stand without danger of tilting. It should be raised ½″ from bottom of kettle. The kettle should be deep enough to hold water to cover the jars or bottles 1″ to 2″ above tops.

The jars or bottles should not touch one another or the sides of the kettle. Heat the water before putting in the jars or bottles of hot juice. If necessary, add more hot water to keep the water 1″ to 2″ above tops of jars or bottles.

When you have put in the jars or bottles, bring the water quickly to the boiling point. Start counting the processing time when the water boils again.

Remove the jars or bottles from boiling water and tighten jar seals if lids are not the self-sealing type. Cool, leaving space between jars or bottles for air circulation. Do not set on a cold surface or in a draft.

Cooling: Lower the filled jars into a large kettle of water just hot enough so you cannot put your hand in it with comfort. In 5 minutes, remove one third of the water and refill it with cold tap water. Repeat after another 5-minute interval. Then place container of bottles or jars under the cold water tap and let the cold water run into the container, but *not directly on the jar or bottle,* for another 5 minutes. The juice will cool to temperature of the water in 30 minutes if in bottles, 30 to 40 minutes if in jars.

TOMATO JUICE COCKTAIL

You can freeze or can it

3 tsp. salt
2 tsp. grated celery
1 tsp. prepared horse-radish
3 tblsp. lemon juice

⅛ tsp. Worcestershire sauce
1 tsp. onion juice
2 qts. tomato juice, freshly extracted

Add seasonings to tomato juice.
Freeze or can like Tomato Juice. Makes about 2 quarts.

MAKE ALTITUDE ADJUSTMENTS

Tomatoes in Water Bath: If you live at an altitude less than 1000 feet above sea level, use the processing times given in this chapter. When processing time is 20 minutes or less, add 1 minute if you live at 1000 feet above sea level; add 1 minute for each additional 1000 feet altitude. If processing time is more than 20 minutes, add 2 minutes if at 1000 feet and 2 minutes for each additional 1000 feet altitude.

HEAT-AND-EAT POTATO TREATS
FROM YOUR FREEZER

Many FARM JOURNAL readers have asked our food editors how to freeze potatoes when they're at their peak quality so they will store successfully in their freezers. This was the incentive that initiated work in our Test Kitchens to determine the best way to do it. We discovered

how to handle potatoes so you can freeze them successfully for up to two months.

The trick is to cook the potatoes and freeze them in
ready-to-use shapes so they go directly from freezer to
range or oven. It's important not to let the potatoes thaw
before heating; thawing softens them and makes them
mushy.

Many homemakers now use our recipes to stock their
freezers with several meals of hashed browns and fluffy
mashed potatoes. Frequently they cook double amounts,
use one portion and freeze the other. Here are the directions:

FROZEN HASHED BROWN POTATOES

Cook two skilletfuls of these golden,
crisp-crusted potatoes for 8 or 9

To Freeze:
Boil baking-type potatoes in their jackets until just tender but still firm (10 to 15 minutes). Drain, cool and
peel. Grate potatoes on a coarse grater.

Line a 10″ skillet with aluminum foil, bringing foil up
to cover sides. Mix 1½ tsp. salt with 4 c. grated potatoes.
Pack in foil-lined skillet, pressing down firmly. Remove
from skillet with foil. Seal, label and freeze. Repeat to
stock your freezer.

To Cook:
Heat ½ c. shortening over medium heat (350° in
electric skillet) in same skillet in which potatoes were
shaped for freezing. Remove foil and add the disk of frozen potatoes (shortening will spatter, so quickly cover the
skillet). Cook 5 minutes over medium heat. Uncover and
continue cooking 10 to 12 minutes, or until potatoes are
browned on the bottom. Cut into 4 wedges; turn each piece
separately with spatula or pancake turner. Continue cooking 5 minutes, or until attractively browned. Makes 4 generous servings.

BASIC MASHED POTATOES

Freeze these plain or make into one
of our five interesting variations

| 4 lbs. boiling potatoes | ¼ c. butter |
| 1 c. milk (amount varies with moisture in potatoes) | 1½ tsp. salt |

Peel potatoes. Boil until soft; drain. Press potatoes through a ricer or mash.

Heat milk, butter and salt together. Gradually whip in until the potatoes are smooth and fluffy.

Form into shapes that are ready to use with no thawing. Freeze by directions in variations that follow.

VARIATIONS

Potato Puffs: Add ½ c. grated Cheddar cheese or 2 egg yolks to Basic Mashed Potatoes. Chill. Form into balls; roll into a mixture of ¾ c. corn flake crumbs and 3 tblsp. toasted sesame seeds. Freeze on tray until firm. Package, label and return to freezer. Makes 48 small or 24 medium balls.

To Serve: Place frozen puffs on baking sheet. Brush lightly with melted butter. Bake in hot oven (400°) 20 minutes for small puffs and 30 minutes for medium puffs. To serve without freezing, omit brushing with butter and bake puffs only until they brown, 5 to 10 minutes.

Snowcaps: Add 2 egg yolks to Basic Mashed Potatoes. Spoon hot potatoes in mounds on baking sheet. Cool; freeze until firm. Remove from baking sheet; place in plastic bags. Seal, label and return to freezer. Use to top meat and vegetable casseroles. Makes 24 snowcaps.

Pimiento Nests: Add ½ c. chopped, drained pimiento to Basic Mashed Potatoes. Line a 1½-qt. casserole with aluminum foil. Spoon half the potato mixture into casserole. Shape into a nest, building up the sides to top of casserole. Remove from casserole with foil to hold shape of the nest. Reline casserole with foil and shape remaining potato mixture. Cool; freeze nests until firm. Remove from freezer; package, seal and label. Return to freezer. Serve with chicken filling (see recipe for Chicken in Potato Nest).

Cheese Nests: Add ½ c. grated Cheddar cheese to hot Basic Mashed Potatoes; omit the pimiento and proceed as for Pimiento Nests. Serve with onion filling (see recipe for Cheese-Onion Pie).

Potato Nests: Omit the pimiento and shape like Pimiento Nests.

CHICKEN IN POTATO NEST

*You can use two Pimiento Nests and double
the other ingredients for 12 servings*

1 frozen Pimiento Nest
4 tblsp. melted butter or
  margarine
2 tblsp. flour
1 c. chicken broth
Salt

Pepper
1 (4 oz.) can sliced
  mushrooms, drained
½ c. diced celery
1 c. diced cooked chicken

Remove wrapper from frozen Pimiento Nest. Place in casserole in which it was shaped originally. Drizzle with 2 tblsp. melted butter. Cover and bake in hot oven (400°) 30 minutes. Uncover and bake 30 minutes.

In the meantime, combine remaining 2 tblsp. butter and flour in heavy saucepan. Slowly add broth; stir constantly until sauce is smooth and thick. Season with salt and pepper. Add remaining ingredients; heat. Spoon hot mixture into baked Pimiento Nest. Makes 6 servings.

CHEESE-ONION PIE

*Potatoes make the crust for this pie—
serve with fish, ham or fried chicken*

1 frozen Cheese Nest
2 tblsp. melted butter
1 beef bouillon cube
½ c. boiling water
2 c. chopped onions

¼ c. butter or margarine
3 tblsp. flour
1 c. milk
Salt
Pepper

Remove wrapper from frozen Cheese Nest. Place in casserole in which it was shaped originally. Drizzle with 2 tblsp. melted butter. Cover and bake in hot oven (400°) 30 minutes. Uncover and bake 30 minutes.

In the meantime, dissolve bouillon cube in boiling water. Add onions, cover and simmer until tender; drain.

Melt ¼ c. butter in heavy saucepan. Add flour to make a smooth paste. Add milk slowly; stir constantly until white sauce is smooth and thick.

Season with salt and pepper. Add drained onions. Spoon

onion mixture into baked Cheese Nest for serving. Makes 6 servings.

Flavor-Fresh Frozen Vegetables

For top quality, hurry vegetables from garden to freezer —this *does* make a difference in flavor and texture. If the weather is hot, gather vegetables early in the morning before they have absorbed much heat from the sun. When you must keep them a short time before preparing for freezing, spread in a cool, ventilated place or pack loosely and put in the refrigerator. Cooling unshelled peas and asparagus immediately after picking protects flavors and vitamins. Place these vegetables in ice water until cold, drain and refrigerate. Or pack them in crushed ice. Do not hold shelled or cut vegetables before freezing or they may sour. Other causes of souring are inadequate scalding, or stacking packages in the freezer before they are thoroughly frozen. First, spread packages out in freezer; stack later if space is scarce.

Plant Varieties for Freezing: Many varieties of all vegetables freeze successfully, but some are not good freezers. Ask your County Home Agent or write to your State Agricultural Experiment Station to find out which ones in your area freeze well.

Scald Vegetables: Scalding is extremely important. It prevents loss of flavor, toughening, retains vitamins, increases potential storage time in freezer and results in products of superior quality. Use rapidly boiling water. Properly scalded, vegetables may be stored in the freezer from 9 to 12 months. Green vegetables will have a brighter color when scalded, and the heat will shrink vegetables slightly so they handle more easily and conserve freezer space. Scalding also removes objectionable odors and bitter flavors from some vegetables. Here are up-to-date detailed directions:

SCALD VEGETABLES THIS WAY

1. Place water in a large aluminum, stainless steel or enamelware kettle with cover. Use at least 1 gal. water to

1 pt. vegetable, except for the leafy greens. For them, use 2 gal. water. Bring the water to a full rolling boil.

2. Put the prepared vegetable in a wire basket (a covered one is excellent) or loosely in a cheesecloth bag and *submerge in boiling water*. Start counting time immediately. The time is so important in scalding that we recommend use of a timer. Keep the heat high, kettle covered and the water boiling. A practical test for sufficient scalding is to cut a few pieces of the product to see if it has been heated to the center. Beans with green and yellow pods will bend without breaking if scalded long enough. But avoid overscalding; it results in soft textures, destroys vitamins and nutrients and produces inferior flavors. Use the same water several times if you wish, but add more from time to time to keep it at the proper level throughout the scalding process.

3. *Increase scalding time if you live in high elevations.* At 2000 to 4000 feet, add ½ minute; 4000 to 6000 feet, add 1 minute; over 6000 feet, add 2½ minutes to time given.

Chill Quickly: Plunge basket or cloth bag of scalded vegetables into cold running water or ice water *immediately* (1 lb. ice per 1 lb. vegetable). Rapid chilling checks the cooking, saves nutrients and helps make for top quality. A practical test for sufficient chilling is to bite into a few pieces. If they feel cold to the tongue, drain the vegetable in a colander or wire basket and pack. It takes about as long to chill as to scald vegetables.

Use Steam Scalding for Broccoli: Some people believe they get a better product if they scald broccoli with steam rather than in hot water. However, steaming is not recommended for most vegetables and fruits because it is difficult to scald thoroughly with the equipment available in most home kitchens. Pumpkin, winter squash and sweet potatoes sometimes are scalded in steam, but most homemakers prefer to bake them before freezing.

To scald with steam, place from 1 to 3″ water in the bottom of a large kettle. Bring to a full rolling boil. Place a single layer of the prepared vegetable in a wire basket or in a cheesecloth bag. Suspend over the rapidly boiling water, preferably on a rack. Keep the cover on the kettle during the steaming and start counting the time when the lid is placed on the kettle. Steaming takes longer than scalding in water.

Leave Head Space: Allow ½" for pints and quarts. Vegetables that pack loosely, like broccoli and asparagus, require no head space.

DIRECTIONS FOR FREEZING VEGETABLES, IN ALPHABETICAL ORDER

Artichokes, Globe: Select small artichokes; pull leaves from them and cut top from buds. Trim stem to within 1" of base. Wash thoroughly.

Scald artichokes in boiling solution of 1 tblsp. citric acid crystals (or 1 tblsp. lemon juice) and 1 qt. water for 8 to 10 minutes, counting time when solution returns to boiling again. Cool 15 minutes under cold running water or in ice water. Drain and package.

Artichoke hearts may be frozen separately. Scald them in the boiling solution 2 to 3 minutes. Cool like whole artichokes. Package, label, date and freeze.

Asparagus: Select young, bright-colored, brittle stalks that snap when broken and have compact tips. Harvest early in the morning if weather is warm. Discard woody, blemished stalks. Wash in cold running or ice water. Remove bracts (scales). Sort into medium and large stalks. Pack in lengths to fit package or cut in 2" lengths, discarding woody ends. For top quality, process as soon as possible after harvesting. Asparagus becomes tough or woody and loses vitamins after picking. The tips are rich in vitamin C and full of flavor.

Scald medium stalks 3 minutes, large stalks (½" to ¾" in diameter) 4 minutes. Chill in cold running or ice water. Drain, package, label, date and freeze.

Beans, Green: Home economists in our Test Kitchens experimented with various ways to freeze green beans, and their results prove the following two methods are best. It is especially important to choose varieties recommended for freezing in your area—check with the Horticulture Department of your state agricultural college. Pick young, tender beans that snap when broken and that have small, tender seeds. Wash in cold running water and process them right after picking. (If you can't process them immediately, keep beans in ice cold water until processing time.) Snip off tips and sort for size. Cut or break beans in 1½" pieces, or leave them whole, if you wish.

Standard 3-Minute Blanch: Have ready a kettle with at least 1 gal. rapidly boiling water. Place 1 pt. beans in wire basket and immerse in boiling water. Cover and count time for 3 minutes. Remove basket from boiling water and immerse it in ice water to chill beans. Test coolness by biting into the vegetables. When it is cool to the tongue, it is ready to pack. Drain beans right away and package them. Label, date and freeze immediately.

Cooked, Frozen in Seasoned Bouillon: Combine 2 qts. water, 8 beef bouillon cubes, 1 tsp. onion powder and 1 tsp. salt in 8-qt. kettle; heat to boiling. Add 4 qts. cut green beans; cover and bring to a boil again. Boil 12 minutes. Remove cover and place kettle in ice water bath. Cool quickly, stirring occasionally. Fill containers with beans and liquid; *be sure liquid covers beans.* Seal and freeze. Makes 8 pints. To serve, dip freezer container in hot water to loosen beans. Slip block of beans and liquid into heavy saucepan. Cover; heat slowly until defrosted and liquid begins to boil (about 20 minutes).

Beans, Italian: Select any good garden variety. Wash in cold water and cut or break in 1 to 1½" pieces. Scald in water 3½ minutes. Chill in cold running or ice water. Drain, package, label, date and freeze.

Beans, Lima: Harvest well-filled pods containing green, tender young beans. Do not freeze white beans; they are overmature. Wash and remove beans from pods, using scissors to snip tough pods. Do not wash after shelling. Discard blemished beans. Process them at once because shelled beans lose flavor quickly if allowed to stand.

Scald small and medium bean 3 minutes, larger beans 4 minutes. Chill in cold running or ice water. Drain, package, label, date, freeze.

Beans, Soy: Harvest well-developed pods containing green beans. Wash in cold running water.

Scald in pods 5 minutes. Chill in cold running or ice water; shell, discarding blemished beans; package, label, date and freeze. You need not scald them after shelling.

Beans, Yellow: Follow directions for green beans.

Beets: Select smooth, tender beets of small to medium size. Discard blemished beets, remove green tops and wash thoroughly.

Scald by cooking in water until tender. Chill in cold

440

running or ice water, slip off the skins, slice or dice larger beets; package, label, date and freeze.

Broccoli: Use tender, firm stalks with compact heads. Discard off-color heads and those that have started to blossom. Remove tough leaves and woody stalks. Cut through stalks lengthwise. When cut, heads should be about 1″ in diameter. (The cutting makes uniform scalding possible and gives attractive servings when cooked.) Soak stalks, heads down, for ½ hour in salt water (¼ c. salt to 1 qt. cold water). This drives out the small insects. Rinse in cold water.

Scald 4 minutes or steam 5 minutes. (For steaming see directions that precede.) Steaming usually is preferred. Chill in cold running or ice water; drain. Place heads and stalks alternately in the container to make compact package. Label, date and freeze.

Brussels Sprouts: Select firm, compact heads of good color. Wash, trim and discard discolored heads. Soak in salt water (¼ c. salt to 1 qt. water) ½ hour to drive out small insects. Rinse in cold water and drain.

Scald medium heads 4 minutes; larger heads, 5 minutes. Chill in cold running or ice water, drain, package, label, date and freeze.

Carrots: Harvest smooth, tender carrots before roots are woody. Plan plantings so you can harvest them in cool weather. The small, immature roots often harvested in hot weather contains less carotene and they rarely are of good quality when frozen. Remove tops, wash and scrape. Dice or slice ¼″ thick.

Scald 3½ minutes. Chill in cold running or ice water; drain, package, label, date and freeze.

Cauliflower: Pick well-formed, compact white heads with fresh leaves. Trim, discard leaves and wash. Slit heads into pieces about 1″ in diameter. Soak about ½ hour in salt water (¼ c. salt to 1 qt. water) to drive out small insects. Rinse in cold water and drain. Work fast to prevent discoloration. Scald 4 minutes. Chill in cold running or ice water; drain, package, label, date and freeze.

Celery: If freezer space is limited, it is questionable whether it is wise to freeze celery. But the green varieties may be frozen for use in cooked dishes. Trim, discarding tough and blemished stalks. Wash and cut in 1″ pieces or finely dice.

Scald 4 minutes. Chill in cold running or ice water; drain, package, label, date and freeze.

Corn, Sweet: Harvest early in morning if weather is warm. Freeze corn when at its "eating best." It remains at this stage of optimum maturity a short time, usually only about 48 hours. A practical test for maturity: press the thumbnail into a kernel. If the milk spurts out freely, the corn is at or near the stage of desired maturity. Immature corn kernels will be watery; when overmature, doughy.

Process as quickly as possible after harvesting. A delay of more than a few hours often results in loss of quality unless ears are refrigerated.

Husk ears, remove the silk and trim ends. Scald, using a large kettle that holds 12 to 15 qts. boiling water. Keep kettle covered during scalding. For whole kernel corn, scald the ears 4½ minutes. Cool in cold running water or ice water, drain and cut kernels from cobs at about ¾ depth of kernels. Package, label, date and freeze.

For corn on the cob, scald small ears (up to 1½″ in diameter) 8 minutes, and large ears (diameter more than 1½″) 11 minutes. (Measure diameter of corn at large end, after trimming.) Chill quickly in cold running or ice water; drain and freeze on a tray or baking sheet. Then wrap in moisture-proof packaging material or place in popcorn or potato chip cans, cover, seal, label, date and freeze.

Eggplant: Harvest eggplant before it is too mature and when the seeds are tender. For top quality, select firm, heavy eggplant of uniform dark color. Peel and slice in ¼ to ⅓ slices, or dice. Drop pieces into cold water containing ¼ c.salt to 1 gal. water to prevent color loss.

Scald eggplant in boiling salted water (¼ c. to 1 gal. water) 4½ minutes. Chill in cold running or ice water. Drain and package in layers separated by sheets of freezer paper. Label, date and freeze.

Many homemakers prefer to freeze cooked eggplant.

Greens: (spinach, beet, chard, collard, kale, mustard, turnip): Pick young; tender leaves early in morning if weather is warm. Remove large, tough stems and discard blemished leaves. Wash in cold running water.

Scald 2 minutes, except collards and stem portions of Swiss chard. Steam these 3 to 4 minutes. Very tender young spinach is best scalded 1½ minutes. Chill in cold running or ice water; drain and package with the water that clings to leaves. Label, date and freeze.

A good way to chill greens after scalding is to swish them in ice water or to spread them on ice, turning often.

Herbs, Garden: Wrap a few sprigs of leaves in foil or seal in film bags and place in a glass jar or carton. Freeze.

Do not scald leaves—just wash them thoroughly and drain.

Kohlrabi: Pick when young and tender. Cut off tops, wash, peel and cut in ½" cubes.

Scald 2½ minutes. Chill in cold running or ice water; package, label, date and freeze.

Mixed Vegetables: Prepare each vegetable and scald separately according to directions. Freeze the vegetables separately if desired, thaw just enough to separate the pieces, combine as desired, package, label, date and refreeze.

Mushrooms: Process young, firm mushrooms as soon as possible after picking. They bruise and deteriorate rapidly. Wash and remove base of stem. Freeze small mushrooms whole. Cut large ones in four or more pieces. To prevent browning, add 1 tsp. citric acid, 3 tsp. lemon juice or ½ tsp. ascorbic acid to every quart of water used in scalding.

Scald medium or small whole mushrooms 4 minutes; cut pieces, 3 minutes. Chill, drain and package. If the mushrooms are very mild in flavor, steam them instead of scalding. Before steaming, put them in water containing 1½ tsp. citric acid or 1 tsp. lemon juice to 1 pt. water for 5 minutes. Steam whole mushrooms not larger than 1" across for 5 minutes, small or quartered, 3½ minutes and sliced, 3 minutes. (See general directions for steaming earlier in this chapter.) Chill at once in cold running or ice water; drain, package, label, date and freeze.

Or cut washed mushrooms in slices ¼" thick and sauté in butter for 2 minutes. Cool quickly and pack. Pour excess butter over packed mushrooms. Package in meal-sized amounts. Label, date and freeze.

Okra: Select young, tender pods 2 to 4" long. Remove stems and wash.

Scald under water, 3 to 4 minutes. The large-podded varieties grown in the West need to be scalded 5 minutes. Chill in cold running or ice water; drain, package, label, date and freeze.

Onions: Onions keep well in a cool, dry place. Usually, they are not home frozen, but you can freeze chopped onions successfully. They will hold from 3 to 6 months, but after that they tend to lose flavor. Select mature sweet Spanish or any good garden onion. Peel, wash and cut in quarters. Chop and scald in water 1½ minutes. Chill in cold running or ice water. Drain, package, label, date and freeze.

Parsnips: Select smooth, firm roots of top quality that are not woody. In northern areas, parsnips may be harvested in spring or late fall. Remove tops, wash and peel. Slice, dice or cut in lengthwise strips.

Scald 3 minutes. Chill in cold running or ice water; drain, package, label, date and freeze.

Peas, Chinese or Edible Pod: Select any good variety with bright green, flat tender pods. Wash well and remove stems, blossom ends and strings; leave whole. Scald in water 2½ to 3 minutes. Chill in cold running or ice water. Drain, package, label, date and freeze.

Peas, English or Green: Pick bright green, crisp pods containing tender peas that are sweet, but not overmature. Peas are at their best for a short time, about 24 hours. If peas are hard to shell, scald pods in boiling water for 1 minute. Scald and shell a few at a time; you need not wash them after shelling. Discard small, undeveloped peas. Or before scalding, you may separate overmature peas from tender ones by floating the peas in cold salt water—½ c. salt to 1 gal. water with 55° temperature. After 10 seconds, remove the floaters, which are the tender peas; the overmature will sink. *Avoid delay between shelling and freezing to prevent toughening of skins.* Some homemakers like to mix 2 to 3 tsp. sugar in 3 to 3¼ c. peas (1 lb.) after scalding and chilling.

Scald shelled peas 1½ to 2 minutes. Chill in cold running water; drain, package, label, date and freeze.

Peas, Field (like Black-eyed): Follow directions for green peas, except scald them 2 minutes.

Peppers, Green and Pimientos: Pick crisp, well-developed peppers of good color, green or red. Wash, cut out stem; remove seeds from green peppers. Cut in halves, dice or slice. Pimiento peppers may be peeled by roasting them in a hot oven (400°) 3 to 4 minutes or until peel is charred.

Cool peeled pimientos and pack dry. Label, date and freeze.

Scald green pepper halves 3 minutes; sliced and diced, 2 minutes. Chill in cold running or ice water; package; label, date and freeze.

Peppers lose crispness in freezing but are satisfactory for cooked dishes. They are one vegetable that may also be packed and frozen without scalding.

Peppers, Hot: Wash; package without scalding, label, date and freeze.

Potatoes, French Fries: Peel and cut potatoes in thin strips, about ⅜″ wide and ⅜″ thick. Fry in hot fat (370° on deep-fat frying thermometer) until potatoes are a *light* brown. Drain on paper towels spread in a baking pan. Cool and package. Label, date and freeze immediately. (To serve, spread potatoes on a baking sheet and place in medium oven (350°) 8 to 10 minutes or until brown. Or spread in broiler pan and broil 8 to 10 minutes. Salt to taste.)

Potatoes, Sweet: Pick firm, smooth roots of bright color. Wash and bake in moderate oven (350°) until soft. Cool, peel and slice into ½″ slices. To keep the bright color, dip slices in solution made by dissolving ¼ c. lemon juice in 1 pt. cold water. For candied sweet potatoes, drain slices and roll in granulated or brown sugar. The color is less bright when they are rolled in brown sugar.

Or freeze sweet potatoes in purée form. Steam or bake them, cool, remove pulp from skins and mash or put through food mill. Add 2 tblsp. lemon juice for every 10 c. purée to help preserve color. You can add 1 c. sugar if you wish. You can freeze this sweetened purée mixed with milk, eggs and spices (except cloves) for pie filling. Package, label, date and freeze.

Potatoes, White or Irish: Select any good potato. Wash, peel, cut out deep eyes and any green spots (sun or light burn). Cut in ¼ to ½″ cubes. Scald 5 minutes. Chill in cold running or ice water. Drain; package, label, date and freeze.

Pumpkin: Select good pie pumpkins. Pick at maximum maturity, indicated by good color and a stem that breaks easily from vine. Wash, cut or break into uniform pieces, remove seeds and bake in moderate oven (350°) or steam

445

until tender. Cool, scoop pulp from skins and mash or put through food mill. Package, label, date and freeze.

Or make pie filling by your favorite recipe and freeze.

Rutabagas: Freeze tender, young rutabagas. Wash, remove tops, peel and slice, or dice in ¼″ cubes.

Scald 3 minutes, chill in cold running or ice water; drain, package, label, date and freeze.

Spinach: See Greens.

Squash, Summer (Crookneck, Zucchini and Straightneck): Pick when small, 5 to 7″ long, and while rind is tender and seeds are small. Wash, but do not peel. Cut in pieces not more than 1½″ thick.

Scald 3 minutes for ¼″ slices, 6 minutes for 1½″ slices. Chill in cold running or ice water; drain, package, label, date and freeze.

Squash, Winter: Pick fully ripe or mature squash, with shells hard enough so that you cannot push your thumbnail through them. "Dry" types are recommended. Wash and cut or break into fairly uniform pieces and remove seeds. Bake in moderate oven (350°) or steam until tender. Cool, scoop out pulp and mash or put through food mill. Package, label, date and freeze.

You can fix your favorite pie filling with sugar, milk, eggs and spices (except cloves) and freeze.

Some homemakers like to mix one or two varieties or to blend squash and pumpkin purées.

Tomatoes: Whole tomatoes may be wrapped and frozen. Use them for cooking within 2 months. For best results, stew the tomatoes before freezing, but do not add bread or crackers until you heat the frozen tomatoes for serving. Stew the tomatoes and cool them by placing saucepan in larger pan containing ice water. Package, label, date and freeze.

You can freeze uncooked tomato pulp and store it for a few months without great flavor loss.

Tomatoes, Husk (Ground Cherries): Husk, scald 2 minutes, chill and pack in sugar syrup. Use 3 c. sugar to 1 qt. water. Package, label, date and freeze.

Turnips: Harvest young tender turnips. Remove tops, wash, peel, slice, or dice in ½″ cubes. Scald 2½ minutes; chill

446

in cold running or ice water; drain, package, label, date and freeze.

Vegetable Purées: Scald the prepared vegetables as directed, cool, drain and put through food chopper or food mill. Package, label, date and freeze.

Freezing Vegetables in Boilable Bags

You've probably tried the commercially frozen vegetables that are sauced and seasoned and packed in boilable plastic bags. To cook, you drop the bag into a pan of boiling water to heat; then slit the bag and serve.

Now you can put up your own vegetables in boilable bags. With the help of a small heat-sealing appliance, you pack food in a special heavy plastic bag, then heat-seal the opening.

You can use this method for packaging fresh vegetables that go into the freezer (follow directions in this chapter for blanching vegetables before packing them into the bags), or for packaging precooked foods or leftovers to be frozen or stored in the refrigerator. You can pack food in individual or family-size servings (largest bag holds 2 quarts).

We've found this method especially good for foods with sauces and seasonings that would be lost or changed if you heated the foods in a pan or in water. Note that the manufacturer suggests you pack foods only 1″ thick to ensure even cooking when food is to be heated.

Peak-of-the-Season Canned Vegetables

If you have a pressure canner and a bountiful garden, you have the first two requirements of a good vegetable canner. Add the knowledge of up-to-date methods and the will to follow them—then you have what it takes to put up prize-winners. Your family will have better meals at a lower cost.

This chapter contains the latest approved canning methods for vegetables, arranged alphabetically. Read directions before you pick the succulent peas or tender asparagus to can. You'll be well informed for the job at hand and pleased with the results you get. And do hurry vegetables from garden into cans. They lose their finest flavors fast if allowed to wait after you bring them to the house.

TO CAN VEGETABLES

Artichokes, Globe: Wash and trim small artichokes from 1¼ to 2″ in length. Prepare a vinegar-water solution (¾ c. vinegar to 1 gal. water).
Hot Pack Only: Precook artichokes 5 minutes in vinegar solution. Drain and pack hot in hot jars, being careful not to overfill. Prepare a brine by adding ¾ c. vinegar (or lemon juice) and 3 tblsp. salt to 1 gal. water. Pour boiling hot over artichokes to within ½″ of top of either pint or quart jars. Adjust lids. Process in pressure canner at 10 pounds pressure (240°).

Pint Jars	25 minutes
Quart Jars	25 minutes

Remove jars from canner and complete seals unless closures are self-sealing type.

Asparagus: Choose young, fresh asparagus. Wash, trim bracts (scales) and tough ends and wash once again. Cut into 1″ pieces, or cut in lengths ¾″ shorter than jar and pack in bundles.
Raw Pack: Pack asparagus very tightly to within ½″ of jar top. Add salt (½ tsp. to pints; 1 tsp. to quarts). Cover to within ½″ of top with boiling water. Adjust lids. Process in pressure canner at 10 pounds pressure (240°).

Pint jars	25 minutes
Quart jars	30 minutes

Remove jars from canner and complete seals unless closures are self-sealing type.
Hot Pack: Precook in boiling water from 1 to 3 minutes to wilt asparagus. Plunge quickly into cold water. Pack hot and very loosely to within ½″ of jar top. Add salt (½ tsp. to pints; 1 tsp. to quarts) and cover with boiling hot cooking liquid (or plain boiling water), leaving ½″ head space. Adjust lids. Process in pressure canner at 10 pounds pressure (240°).

Pint jars	25 minutes
Quart jars	30 minutes

Remove jars from canner and complete seals unless closures are self-sealing type.

Beans, Green: Wash beans, trim and string. Cut into 1″ pieces or leave whole. (If whole, pack standing on end in jars.)

Raw Pack: Pack tightly to within ½″ of jar top. Add salt (½ tsp. to pints; 1 tsp. to quarts). Fill with boiling water to cover to within ½″ of jar top. Adjust lids. Process in pressure canner at 10 pounds pressure (240°).

Pint jars	20 minutes
Quart jars	25 minutes

Remove jars from canner and complete seals unless closures are self-sealing type.

Hot Pack: Prepare as directed for raw pack. Cover with boiling water and boil for 5 minutes. Pack hot beans loosely to within ½″ of jar top. Add salt (½ tsp. to pints; 1 tsp. to quarts). Cover with fresh boiling water or use the liquid in which beans were precooked, leaving ½″ head space. Adjust lids. Process in pressure canner at 10 pounds pressure (240°).

Pint jars	20 minutes
Quart jars	25 minutes

Remove jars from canner and complete seals unless closures are self-sealing type.

Beans, Lima: Choose only young, tender beans for canning.

Raw Pack: Shell and wash. Pack small raw beans into clean jars. Fill to within 1″ of jar top for pints; 1½″ for quarts. If beans are large, fill to within ¾″ for pints; 1¼″ for quarts. Do not shake or press down. Add salt (½ tsp. to pints; 1 tsp. to quarts) and fill jars to within ½″ of top with boiling water. Adjust lids. Process in pressure canner at 10 pounds pressure (240°).

Pint jars	40 minutes
Quart jars	50 minutes

Remove jars from canner and complete seals unless closures are self-sealing type.

Hot Pack: Shell beans and cover with boiling water; bring to boil. Pack loosely to within 1″ of jar top. Add salt (½ tsp. to pints; 1 tsp. to quarts). Fill jars with boiling water, leaving 1″ head space. Adjust lids. Process in pressure canner at 10 pounds pressure (240°).

Pint jars	40 minutes
Quart jars	50 minutes

Remove jars from canner and complete seals unless closures are self-sealing type.

Beets: Remove beet tops except for 1 to 2″ of stem; leave roots on. Wash and sort to uniform size to ensure even cooking. Cover beets with boiling water; boil 15 to 25 minutes; dip in cold water and slip skins, roots and stems. Baby beets (diameter under 2″) may be left whole, but larger ones should be cubed in ½″ pieces or sliced. Large slices should be quartered or halved.

Raw Pack: Not recommended.

Hot Pack: Pack hot beets to within ½″ of jar top. Add salt (½ tsp. to pints; 1 tsp. to quarts). Cover with boiling water to which 1 to 2 tblsp. vinegar, depending on jar size, has been added to retain color. Leave ½″ head space. Adjust lids. Process in pressure canner at 10 pounds pressure (240°).

Pint jars	30 minutes
Quart jars	35 minutes

Remove jars from canner and complete seals unless closures are self-sealing type.

Carrots: Use only young, tender carrots. Wash, scrape or peel. Slice, dice or, in the case of very small carrots, leave whole.

Raw Pack: Pack tightly to within 1″ of jar top. Add salt (½ tsp. to pints; 1 tsp. to quarts). Cover with boiling water to within ½″ of jar top. Adjust lids. Process in pressure canner at 10 pounds pressure (240°).

Pint jars	25 minutes
Quart jars	30 minutes

Remove jars from canner and complete seals unless closures are self-sealing type.

Hot Pack: Prepare as directed for raw pack. Cover with boiling water and bring to boil. Pack hot carrots to within ½″ of jar top. Add salt (½ tsp. to pints; 1 tsp. to quarts). Cover with boiling hot cooking water, leaving ½″ head space. Adjust lids. Process in pressure canner at 10 pounds pressure (240°).

Pint jars	25 minutes
Quart jars	30 minutes

Remove jars from canner and complete seals unless closures are self-sealing type.

Celery: Wash and slice or cut into asparagus-style lengths.

Raw Pack: Pack loosely to within ½″ of jar top. Add salt

(½ tsp. to pints; 1 tsp. to quarts). Cover with boiling water, leaving ½" head space. Adjust lids. Process in pressure canner at 10 pounds pressure (240°).

| Pint jars | 30 minutes |
| Quart jars | 30 minutes |

Remove jars from canner and complete seals unless closures are self-sealing type.

Hot Pack: Prepare as directed for raw pack. Precook 1 to 3 minutes. Pack hot into hot jars and add salt (½ tsp. to pints; 1 tsp. to quarts). Cover with boiling liquid retained from precooking, adding boiling water, if needed, to fill jars to within ½" of top of either pint or quart jars. Adjust lids. Process in pressure canner at 10 pounds pressure (240°).

| Pint jars | 35 minutes |
| Quart jars | 35 minutes |

Remove jars from canner and complete seals unless closures are self-sealing type.

Celery and Tomatoes: Prepare celery as directed for raw pack, but chop it. Wash, core, peel and chop tomatoes.
Hot Pack Only: Use equal parts of the two vegetables and boil, without water added, for 5 minutes. Fill jars to within ½" of jar top. Adjust lids. Process in pressure canner at 10 pounds pressure (240°).

| Pint jars | 35 minutes |
| Quart jars | 35 minutes |

Remove jars from canner and complete seals unless closures are self-sealing type.

Corn, Cream-Style: Harvest in small quantities (2 to 3 doz. ears at a time), if convenient. *Immediately prepare for processing.* Cut ends from ears, peel off husks and silk. Trim blemishes from ears. Cut kernels from cob about ⅔ the depth of the kernels. Scrape cob to remove the remaining corn, but not any of the cob. Use pint jars only.
Raw Pack: Fill to within 1" of jar top, being careful not to shake or pack down. Add ½ tsp. salt to each pint and fill to top with boiling water. Adjust lids. Process in pressure canner at 10 pounds pressure (240°).

| Pint jars | 95 minutes |

Remove jars from canner and complete seals unless closures are self-sealing type.

Hot Pack: Prepare as directed for raw pack. Add 1 pt. boiling water to each quart of prepared corn and heat to boiling. Pack hot corn into pint jars to within 1" of jar top.

Add ½ tsp. salt to each pint jar. Adjust lids. Process in pressure canner at 10 pounds pressure (240°).

Pint jars   85 minutes

Remove jars from canner and complete seals unless closures are self-sealing type.

Corn, Whole Kernel: Prepare as directed for raw pack cream-style corn, but do not scrape the cob. Use only the whole kernels.

Raw Pack: Pack corn in either pint or quart jars to within 1″ of jar top. Add salt (½ tsp. to pints; 1 tsp. to quarts). Fill jar with boiling water, leaving ½″ head space. Adjust lids. Process in pressure canner at 10 pounds pressure (240°).

Pint jars   55 minutes
Quart jars   85 minutes

Remove jars from canner and complete seals unless closures are self-sealing type.

Hot Pack: Prepare as directed for hot pack cream-style corn, but do not scrape the cob. Use only whole kernels. Add 1 pt. boiling water to each quart of prepared corn and heat to boiling. Pack corn in jars to within 1″ of jar top and cover with hot cooking liquid. Leave 1″ head space. Add salt (½ tsp. to pints; 1 tsp. to quarts). Adjust lids. Process in pressure canner at 10 pounds pressure (240°).

Pint jars   55 minutes
Quart jars   85 minutes

Remove jars from canner and complete seals unless closures are self-sealing type.

Hominy: Shell 2 qts. dry white or yellow field corn. Make a solution of 8 qts. water and 2 oz. lye in an enameled pan or iron kettle. Add the dry corn to this brine and boil hard for 30 minutes, or until hulls come loose. Let stand for about 20 minutes, then rinse corn thoroughly with several hot water rinses, followed by cold water rinses to cool the corn sufficiently for handling and to remove all of the lye. Work hominy, using your hands, to remove dark kernel tips. The corn and the tips are more easily separated if placed in a coarse sieve and floated off by water.

Next, add about 1″ of water to cover hominy and boil for 5 minutes; change water. Repeat four times. Then cook the corn kernels about 30 to 45 minutes (or until soft) and drain. Makes about 6 quarts.

Hot Pack: Fill jars with hot hominy to within ½″ of jar

top. Add salt (½ tsp. to pints; 1 tsp. to quarts). Fill with boiling water, leaving ½" head space. Adjust lids. Process in pressure canner at 10 pounds pressure (240°).

| Pint jars | 60 minutes |
| Quart jars | 70 minutes |

Remove jars from canner and complete seals unless closures are self-sealing type.

Mushrooms: Soak fresh mushrooms in cold water for 10 minutes before washing, to remove all the soil. Trim stem ends and remove discolored portions. Rinse well through several changes of cold water. Leave small mushrooms whole; cut larger ones in halves or quarters. Proceed with any of the three following methods: (1) steam for 4 minutes, (2) heat gently for 15 minutes in a covered saucepan with no liquid added, or (3) cover with boiling water and boil for 2 to 3 minutes.

Hot Pack Only: Pack hot mushrooms to within ½" of jar top in half-pint or pint jars only. Add ¼ tsp. salt and $\frac{1}{16}$ tsp. crystalline ascorbic acid to each half pint; ½ tsp. salt and ⅛ tsp. ascorbic acid to pints. Add boiling water or boiling hot cooking liquid to mushrooms, leaving ½" head space. Adjust lids. Process in pressure canner at 10 pounds pressure (240°).

| Half-pint jars | 30 minutes |
| Pint jars | 30 minutes |

Remove jars from canner and complete seals unless closures are self-sealing type.

Okra: Wash and trim only tender pods, being careful not to remove the "cap" unless okra will be used for soup. For soup, slice across pods in ½ to 1" lengths. Cook in boiling water for 1 minute. If canning whole, do not cut into the pod.

Hot Pack Only: Pack hot okra in jar, leaving ½" at top. Add salt (½ tsp. to pints; 1 tsp. to quarts). Cover with boiling water, leaving ½" head space. Adjust lids. Process in pressure canner at 10 pounds pressure (240°).

| Pint jars | 25 minutes |
| Quart jars | 40 minutes |

Remove jars from canner and complete seals unless closures are self-sealing type.

Okra and Tomatoes: Prepare okra as directed for that vegetable. Leave small pods whole, or cut in 1" lengths. Combine with peeled, quartered tomatoes. Add salt (½ tsp. to pints; 1 tsp. to quarts). Heat to boiling.

Hot Pack Only: Pack hot seasoned vegetables in either pint or quart jars, leaving ½″ head space. Adjust lids. Process in pressure canner at 10 pounds pressure (240°).

Pint jars	25 minutes
Quart jars	35 minutes

Remove jars from canner and complete seals unless closures are self-sealing type.

Peas, Fresh Black-eyed (Cowpeas, Black-eyed Beans): Shell and wash, discarding the too-mature peas.

Raw Pack: Pack raw peas loosely in jars to within 1½″ of top of pints; 2″ for quarts. Add salt (½ tsp. to pints; 1 tsp. to quarts). Cover peas with boiling water, leaving ½″ head space. Adjust lids. Process in pressure canner at 10 pounds pressure (240°).

Pint jars	35 minutes
Quart jars	40 minutes

Remove jars from canner and complete seals unless closures are self-sealing type.

Hot Pack: Prepare as directed for raw pack; cover with boiling water. Bring to a rolling boil; drain. Pack hot vegetable, being careful not to shake down, to within 1¼″ from top of pint jars; 1½″ for quarts. Add salt (½ tsp. to pints; 1 tsp. to quarts). Cover with boiling water, leaving ½ to 1″ head space. Adjust lids. Process in pressure canner at 10 pounds pressure (240°).

Pint jars	35 minutes
Quart jars	40 minutes

Remove jars from canner and complete seals unless closures are self-sealing type.

Peas, Fresh Green: Harvest at the best stage for eating. Can immediately after picking to assure sweet-flavored freshness.

Raw Pack: Fill jars with fresh peas, shelled and washed, being careful not to press down, to within 1″ of jar top. Add salt (½ tsp. to pints; 1 tsp. to quarts). Pour boiling water over to cover, leaving 1″ head space. Adjust lids. Process in pressure canner at 10 pounds pressure (240°).

Pint jars	40 minutes
Quart jars	40 minutes

Remove jars from canner and complete seals unless closures are self-sealing type.

Hot Pack: Prepare as directed for raw pack. Cover with

454

boiling water and bring to a boil. Pack hot peas gently and loosely to within 1″ of jar top. Add salt (½ tsp. to pints; 1 tsp. to quarts). Cover with boiling water or liquid in which peas were precooked, leaving 1″ head space. Adjust lids. Process in pressure canner at 10 pounds pressure (240°).

Pint jars 40 minutes
Quart jars 40 minutes

Remove jars from canner and complete seals unless closures are self-sealing type.

Peppers—Bell, Green and Red: Wash, remove stem, core inside partitions, remove seeds.

To peel: cook in hot water 3 minutes or until skins will slip easily. Or heat in a hot oven (450°) 8 to 10 minutes until skins blister and crack. Do not let burn. Remove skins with slender knife blade. Chill peppers immediately in cold water.

Raw Pack: Not recommended.

Hot Pack: Flatten peppers and pack carefully in horizontal layers. Fill hot jars to within ½″ from top; cover with boiling water to within ½″ of jar top. Add ½ tsp. salt and ½ tblsp. lemon juice (or 1 tblsp. vinegar instead of lemon juice)to pints; 1 tsp. salt and 1 tblsp. lemon juice to quarts (2 tblsp. vinegar if substituted for lemon juice). Vinegar and lemon juice improve flavor. Adjust lids. Process in pressure canner at *only 5 pounds pressure.* High pressure injures both the texture and the flavor.

Pint jars 50 minutes
Quart jars 60 minutes

Remove jars from canner and complete seals unless closures are self-sealing type.

Potatoes, New: Wash, scrape and rinse small freshly dug new potatoes. Boil 10 minutes in water; drain.

Hot Pack Only: Pack hot to within ½″ of jar top. Add salt (½ tsp. to pints; 1 tsp. to quarts). Cover with fresh boiling water. Leave ½″ head space. Adjust lids. Process in pressure canner at 10 pounds pressure (240°).

Pint jars 30 minutes
Quart jars 40 minutes

Remove jars from canner and complete seals unless closures are self-sealing type.

Potatoes, Sweet: Wash and sort for size. Boil or steam 20 to 30 minutes to facilitate slipping the skins. Cut in uniform pieces if large or leave smaller ones whole.

Dry Pack: Pack hot sweet potatoes tightly, pressing gently to fill air spaces to within 1″ of jar top. Do not add salt or liquid. Adjust lids. Process in pressure canner at 10 pounds pressure (240°).

| Pint jars | 65 minutes |
| Quart jars | 95 minutes |

Remove jars from canner and complete seals unless closures are self-sealing type.

Wet Pack: Prepare as directed for dry pack. Pack hot sweet potatoes to within 1″ of jar top. Add salt (½ tsp. to pints; 1 tsp. to quarts). Cover with either boiling water or medium syrup, as you prefer. Leave 1″ head space. Adjust lids. Process in pressure canner at 10 pounds pressure (240°).

| Pint jars | 55 minutes |
| Quart jars | 90 minutes |

Remove jars from canner and complete seals unless closures are self-sealing type.

Pumpkin, or Mature Winter Squash: Wash, remove seeds, scrape out fibrous material and peel. Cut into 1″ cubes or strips. Steam in a tightly covered kettle with a small amount of water until flesh is soft.

Raw Pack: Not recommended.

Hot Pack: Pack hot pumpkin or squash, in strips or cubed, in hot jars to within ½″ of jar top. Add salt (½ tsp. to pints; 1 tsp. to quarts). Cover with hot cooking liquid, leaving ½″ head space. Adjust lids. Process in pressure canner at 10 pounds pressure (240°).

| Pint jars | 55 minutes |
| Quart jars | 90 minutes |

Remove jars from canner and complete seals unless closures are self-sealing type.

Pumpkin, Strained: Wash, remove seeds and scrape fibrous material from flesh. Cut in cubes or strips. Steam (as directed for regular pumpkin) 25 minutes or until tender Scrape flesh from rind and put through colander or food mill. Simmer pulp until heated through, stirring to prevent sticking.

Hot Pack Only: Pack hot pulp in hot jars to within ½″ of jar top. Add no liquid or salt to strained pumpkin. Adjust lids. Process in pressure canner at 10 pounds pressure (240°).

| Pint jars | 65 minutes |
| Quart jars | 80 minutes |

Remove jars from canner and complete seals unless closures are self-sealing type.

Spinach and Other Greens: Pick fresh, tender spinach and wash thoroughly. Cut out tough stems and midribs. Put about 2½ lbs. spinach in a cheesecloth bag and steam until well wilted (about 10 minutes).

Hot Pack Only: Pack loosely, while hot, to within ½″ of jar top. Add salt (¼ tsp. to pints; ½ tsp. to quarts). Cover with boiling water. Leave ½″ head space. Adjust lids. Process in pressure canner at 10 pounds pressure (240°).

Pint jars	70 minutes
Quart jars	90 minutes

Remove jars from canner and complete seals unless closures are self-sealing type.

Squash, Banana: Prepare as directed for Strained Pumpkin.

Squash, Summer: Wash, trim ends, remove any imperfect portions, but do not peel. Cut uniform pieces, quarters, halves or ½″ slices.

Raw Pack: Pack tightly to within 1″ of jar top. Add salt (½ tsp. to pints; 1 tsp. to quarts.) Fill jar with boiling water to the top. Adjust lids. Process in pressure canner at 10 pounds pressure (240°).

Pint jars	25 minutes
Quart jars	30 minutes

Remove jars from canner and complete seals unless closures are self-sealing type.

Hot Pack: Prepare as directed for raw pack. Add water to cover squash and bring to a boil. Pack hot squash loosely to within ½″ of jar top. Add salt (½ tsp. to pints; 1 tsp. to quarts). Pour boiling hot cooking liquid over squash, leaving ½″ head space. Adjust lids. Process in pressure canner at 10 pounds pressure (240°).

Pint jars	30 minutes
Quart jars	40 minutes

Remove jars from canner and complete seals unless closures are self-sealing type.

Squash, Winter: (see Pumpkin)

Turnips: Prepare as directed for carrots. Process in pressure canner at 10 pounds pressure (240°). The time for *pint* jars is 5 minutes longer than for carrots.

Pint jars	30 minutes
Quart jars	30 minutes

Remove jars from canner and complete seals unless closures are self-sealing type.

Vegetable Soup Mixture: Any mixture of vegetables may be used. Prepare them as directed in previous instructions for canning each individually. Combine vegetables and boil 5 minutes with water to cover. Peeled, cut-up tomatoes may be used for part of the liquid.

Hot Pack Only: Pour hot vegetable mixture into jars. Cover with boiling liquid. If enough tomatoes are used, no additional water will be necessary. Add salt (½ tsp. to pints; 1 tsp. to quarts). Leave ½" head space. Adjust lids. Process in pressure canner at 10 pounds pressure (240°).

Pint jars	60 minutes
Quart jars	70 minutes

Remove jars from canner and complete seals unless closures are self-sealing type.

Vegetable-Beef Stew: Cube and combine the following ingredients:

2 qts. stewing beef (1½" cubes)	3 c. celery (¼" pieces)
2 qts. potatoes (½" cubes)	1¾ qts. small whole onions (1" or less in diameter)
2 qts. carrots (½" cubes)	

Raw Pack Only: Fill jars with meat-vegetable mixture. Add salt (½ tsp. to pints; 1 tsp. to quarts). Do not add liquid. Adjust lids. Process in pressure canner at 10 pounds pressure (240°).

Pint jars	60 minutes
Quart jars	75 minutes

Remove jars from canner and complete seals unless closures are self-sealing type.

Vitamins in Vegetables

Vegetables don't supply all the nutrients your body needs, but they are rich in some important ones—especially the vitamins that keep you feeling well and looking good. If you don't get all the vitamins you need, you feel "below par"—tired and nervous, with a poor appetite and lowered resistance to infection. And you won't look as bright and healthy as you should—your skin, hair and eyes need vitamins, too.

Here is a chart, easy to refer to, which tells you which vegetables supply *important amounts* of the vitamins, iron and calcium you need every day:

Vitamin A: In dark green and deep yellow vegetables—all the leafy greens (chard, collards, kale, spinach, turnip greens, other dark leaves), broccoli, carrots, pumpkin, sweet potatoes, winter squash. Heat (cooking) does not harm vitamin A.

You need vitamin A for normal vision (to prevent night blindness), and to help keep the skin healthy—especially the linings of nose, mouth, throat and inner organs. Children cannot grow normally without vitamin A.

Ascorbic Acid (Vitamin C): In leafy greens, broccoli, Brussels sprouts, spinach, raw cabbage, cauliflower, red and green peppers, tomatoes, sweet potatoes and white potatoes (especially new potatoes) cooked in their jackets.

Vitamin C dissolves in water and too much heat destroys it. That's why it is a good idea to include some raw vegetables in daily meals. It also helps to cook vegetables *quickly* and in a *small* amount of water.

You need vitamin C to help you resist infections, and to help heal wounds and broken bones. This vitamin makes a cementing substance (collagen) to hold body cells together and strengthen the walls of blood vessels.

Thiamine (Vitamin B$_1$): In lima beans and peas, including black-eyed peas (but you'll depend mainly on other foods for this important vitamin).

You need thiamine to keep your appetite and your digestion normal, and your nervous system healthy. It also helps your body to convert the food you eat into energy and heat.

Riboflavin (Vitamin B$_2$): In asparagus, broccoli, leafy greens, spinach and mushrooms.

You need riboflavin to keep your skin smooth, to help your body cells use oxygen, and for good vision.

Niacin: In mushrooms, peas, lima beans, leafy greens, dried peas and beans.

You need niacin to maintain the normal functions of

your nervous system, digestive tract and skin; it's the anti-pellagra vitamin. It forms enzymes which are important to energy metabolism.

Iron: In leafy greens, peas, lima beans, spinach.

You need iron to combine with proteins to make hemo-globin; this is the red substance in blood that carries oxygen to the cells.

Calcium: In broccoli and the leafy greens (collards, kale, turnip and mustard greens). Milk and cheese (especially Cheddar-type cheeses) are primary sources of calcium and they are ingredients in many of our recipes because they taste so good with vegetables. Thus, many of the vegetable *recipes* in this book will rate high in calcium.

You need calcium to help build bones and teeth, to help blood to clot and to help muscles and nerves react normally.

Index

464

466

467

470

472

The Best Recipes from America's Favorite Farm Magazine...